PERGAMON GENERAL PSYCHOLOGY SERIES
EDITORS
Arnold P. Goldstein, Syracuse University
Leonard Krasner, Stanford University & SUNY at Stony Brook

THE PRACTICE OF
BEHAVIOR THERAPY
(PGPS-1)

Pergamon Titles of Related Interest

Barlow/Hayes/Nelson THE SCIENTIST PRACTITIONER: Research and Accountability in Clinical and Educational Settings

Barlow/Hersen SINGLE CASE EXPERIMENTAL DESIGNS: Strategies for Studying Behavior Change, Second Edition

Bellack/Hersen BEHAVIORAL ASSESSMENT: A Practical Handbook, Third Edition

Hersen/Bellack DICTIONARY OF BEHAVIORAL ASSESSMENT TECHNIQUES

Kanfer/Goldstein HELPING PEOPLE CHANGE: A Textbook of Methods, Fourth Edition

Martin HANDBOOK OF BEHAVIOR THERAPY AND PSYCHOLOGICAL SCIENCE: An Integrative Approach

White THE TROUBLED ADOLESCENT

Related Journals
(Free sample copies available on request.)

ADVANCES IN BEHAVIOUR RESEARCH AND THERAPY

BEHAVIOUR CHANGE

BEHAVIORAL ASSESSMENT

BEHAVIOUR RESEARCH AND THERAPY

JOURNAL OF BEHAVIOR THERAPY AND EXPERIMENTAL
   PSYCHIATRY

CLINICAL PSYCHOLOGY REVIEW

THE PRACTICE OF BEHAVIOR THERAPY
Fourth Edition

JOSEPH WOLPE, M.D.
Pepperdine University and
University of California, Los Angeles

PERGAMON PRESS
Member of Maxwell Macmillan Pergamon Publishing Corporation
New York • Oxford • Beijing • Frankfurt
São Paulo • Sydney • Tokyo • Toronto

Pergamon Press Offices:

U.S.A.	Pergamon Press, Inc., Maxwell House, Fairview Park, Elmsford, New York 10523, U.S.A.
U.K.	Pergamon Press plc, Headington Hill Hall, Oxford OX3 0BW, England
PEOPLE'S REPUBLIC OF CHINA	Pergamon Press, 0909 China World Tower No. 1 Jian Guo Men Wei Avenue, Beijing, 100004, People's Republic of China
FEDERAL REPUBLIC OF GERMANY	Pergamon Press GmbH, Hammerweg 6, D-6242 Kronberg, Federal Republic of Germany
BRAZIL	Pergamon Editora Ltda, Rua Eça de Queiros, 346, CEP 04011, Paraiso, São Paulo, Brazil
AUSTRALIA	Pergamon Press Australia Pty Ltd., P.O. Box 544, Potts Point, NSW 2011, Australia
JAPAN	Pergamon Press, 8th Floor, Matsuoka Central Building, 1-7-1 Nishishinjuku, Shinjuku-ku, Tokyo 160, Japan
CANADA	Pergamon Press Canada Ltd., Suite 271, 253 College Street, Toronto, Ontario M5T 1R5, Canada

---

Copyright © 1990 Pergamon Press, Inc.

Library of Congress Cataloging in Publication Data

Wolpe, Joseph.
    The practice of behavior therapy / Joseph Wolpe. -- 4th ed.
       p.   cm. -- (Pergamon general psychology series : 1)
    Includes bibliographical references.
    ISBN 0-08-036455-1 : -- ISBN 0-08-036454-3 (soft) :
    1. Behavior therapy. I. Title. II. Series.
    [DNLM: 1. Behavior Therapy. WM 425 W866p]
    RC489.B4W6 1990
    616.89'142--dc20
    DNLM/DLC
    for Library of Congress   90-6786
                                                    CIP

Printing: 2 3 4 5 6 7 8 9 10   Year: 6 7 8 9

Printed in the United States of America

The paper used in this publication meets the minimum requirements of American National Standard for Information Sciences -- Permanence of Paper for Printed Library Materials, ANSI Z39.48-1984

To Stella,
Beacon of grace and courage

Nature, to be commanded, must be obeyed.

Francis Bacon, *Novum Organon*, 1620.

Contents

Preface to the Fourth Edition

For 25 years, I took it for granted that behavior therapists, in treating their patients, followed procedural rules described in *Psychotherapy by Reciprocal Inhibition*. During that period there was a general feeling of harmony in the field. Any differences that arose were on the merits of techniques or fine points of theory. When some dissident viewpoints appeared in print in the 1970s, I attributed them to the misconceptions of small groups of malcontents whose arguments, I thought, would be defused by critical correction (Wolpe, 1976a, 1976b).

In the years that followed, I became increasingly aware that even dedicated behavior therapists often did not properly investigate their cases. I was especially disappointed to find evidence of this several times in patients who had been treated by therapists trained at my own Behavior Therapy Unit at Temple Medical School. Each case had reached an impasse after having improved to a notable extent. None of the therapists had adequately analyzed the stimulus antecedents of the patient's maladaptive anxieties. The Willoughby Neuroticism Questionnaire (Appendix A) and the Fear Survey Schedule (Appendix C) would have been useful in filling important gaps in the information, but had not been used. A consequent survey of questionnaire practices (Wolpe and Wright, 1988) showed that the Willoughby and the Fear Survey Schedule were used by only 19% and 42%, respectively, of the members of the Behavior Therapy and Research Society. Failure to use these instruments is a serious deprivation of data, parallel to a physician's nonuse of the electrocardiogram in suspected heart disease. There was clearly a general neglect of case analysis. To restore analysis to its central role is a major aim of this book.

This edition has been reorganized in a logical way. It has been divided into five parts: basic principles, case analyses and therapeutic groundwork, behavior therapy techniques, complex neuroses, and evaluations. A number of new topics have been included, of which important examples are panic disorder and post-traumatic stress disorder. On the other hand, matters of marginal importance have been omitted altogether or treated only briefly.

The preface to the third edition recorded growing interest in behavior therapy, but falling standards of practice, largely related to fading awareness of the derivation of behavior therapy from experimentally established paradigms. The situation subsequently deteriorated further, to the extent that some people in the field come to regard behavior principles as passé. This retrogression, recounted in chapter 18, was due to the impact of extraordinary outside influences.

There has, however, also been dissatisfaction from within. Rachman (1990), a major behavior theorist, has relinquished "the conditioning theory of fear acquisition as a comprehensive explanation" (p. 175). The lack of comprehensiveness is not in dispute, since one source of fear acquisition is information (see chapter 4). But Rachman also sees problems for conditioning theory in fear-conditioning situations (such as air raids), and aversive stimulation experiments, because they often fail to engender fears. He incorrectly assumes that danger or pain *should* generate fear. The precondition for classical conditioning of fear is not pain or the reality of danger, but fear *arousal*. If an air raid (or a shock) does not evoke adequate arousal, conditioning will not occur. By contrast, if great fearfulness is induced, as by the paralysis engendered by an injection of curare (Sanderson, Campbell, & Laverty, 1963), there is the consequent development of marked conditioning of fear to contiguous stimuli. Second order conditioning is far commoner.

Other concerns of Rachman stem from his widely shared assumption that though fears arise in different circumstances, they are all acquired by the same process and have the same stimulus-response structure. Actually, the mode of development of classically conditioned fear differs from that of cognitively based fear (Wolpe, 1981b); and the dynamic constitution of their stimulus antecedents differs correspondingly, as do the treatments that are required for each of them. Therapists can easily be taught to differentiate between classically conditioned and cognitively based fears (Wolpe, Lande, NcNally, & Schotte, 1985). Not to recognize the dichotomy that exists stretches conditioning theory to the breaking point. Eysenck (1988) also does not recognize this dichotomy, and assumes that fear acquisition is a unitary process (p. 58). Therefore his vigorous and ingenious defense of conditioning flags at times. For example, he resorts to the weak contention that the importance of cognitive factors increases with evolutionary development (p. 58). If physicians had held the mistaken belief that bacterial pneumonia and viral pneumonia had the same causation their understanding of the etiology of the pneumonias and their evaluations of the action of antibiotics would have been severely dislocated.

Recognition of the dichotomy has a vital clinical role. In respect of every maladaptive habit, it requires the therapist to decide, as a first step in the analysis of a case, whether that structure is based on belief or on classical conditioning. Each analysis must provide an intelligible account of the dynamic interplay of immediate stimuli and preexisting habit patterns.

It may now be necessary to institute a certain change in terminology. Behavior therapy of neuroses has always emphasized thoughts and feelings, but the wide use of the term, "cognitive behavior therapy," is often taken to imply that traditional behavior therapy excludes thoughts and feelings — that it subscribes to the view that only public data is worthy of attention, despite the fact that the existence of cognitively based fears was explicitly recognized in the 1950s (Wolpe, 1958, pp. 106 & 199). To sidestep this false imputation, it may be necessary for behavior therapists henceforth to refer to what they do as *comprehensive behavior therapy*, or in some other distinctive terminology.

I am grateful to Leonard Krasner for important strategic and compositional guidance, and to David Wolpe for valuable comments throughout the book, as well as to Stephen D. Lande for comments on the first three chapters; also to Laurel Airica for her exceptional proficiency that expedited the final chapters under the difficult conditions imposed by my move to Los Angeles.

From the Preface
to the First Edition

Before the advent of behavior therapy, psychological medicine was a medley of speculative systems and intuitive methods. Behavior therapy is an applied science, in every way parallel to other modern technologies, and in particular those that constitute modern medical therapeutics. Therapeutic possibilities radiate from the uncovering of the lawful relations of organismal processes. Since learning is the organismal process most relevant to psychological medicine, the establishment of lawful relations relevant to the learning process is the main road to therapeutic power in this field.

However, the scientifically minded behavior therapist need not confine himself to methods derived from principles. For the welfare of his patients, he employs, whenever necessary, methods that have been *empirically* shown to be effective. Colchicum was a well-authenticated and widely used remedy for attacks of gout long before colchicine was isolated or the metabolism of gout understood (Stetten, 1968). In the same way, in present-day behavior therapy, we use mixtures of carbon dioxide and oxygen to alleviate pervasive anxiety without knowing the mechanism of their action. The criterion is the existence of compelling evidence of a relationship between the administration of the agent and clinical change.

A very special difficulty in evaluating how much a psychotherapeutic technique *per se* contributes to change resides in the fact that almost any form of psychotherapy produces substantial benefit in about fifty percent of cases, apparently because of anxiety-inhibiting emotional reactions that therapists evoke in patients (Wolpe, 1958). Therefore, a particular technique must be, *prima facie* at least, effective beyond that level if it is to be even provisionally recommended on empirical grounds. Failure to observe this rule can lead to the gullible acceptance of almost anything that is touted, and back to the prescientific chaos of recipes from which modern technological principles have extricated us.

Two themes have recently been prominent among the criticisms voiced by opponents of behavior therapy. One is that it is "mechanistic and nonhumanistic." The two adjectives are usually combined as though they belonged together like face and beard. Insofar as behavior therapy leans on mechanisms it is indeed mechanistic. But nobody can fairly call it nonhumanistic. No basis exists for the idea that others have more compassion than the behavioristic psychotherapist. Internal medicine is not dehumanized when penicillin replaces bloodletting as a treatment for infections; and no more is psychotherapy when conditioning replaces free association.

I am grateful to those who have helped in the literary side of the book's production—Mrs. Barbara Srinivasan, Mrs. Aviva Wanderer, and my wife Stella; and to my old friend and colleague, Dr. L. J. Reyna, who, as so often in the past, has been a fount of information and ideas.

PART I

BASIC PRINCIPLES

1
Behavior Therapy: Its Character, Origins, and Applications

Recurring responses to particular stimulus conditions are called habits. Habits can be adaptive — that is, they subserve biological or acquired needs or prevent injury, pain, or discomfort. Some habits are maladaptive; their effects are contrary to the welfare of the individual. A great many maladaptive habits are primarily emotional and the emotion is usually fear. Learned fear is central to the neuroses. Its elimination by behavior therapy is the main focus of this book.

Knowledge of the processes of learning and unlearning ought to be the best source of methods of eliminating maladaptive learned habits. Behavior therapy is the fruit of such knowledge, and this distinguishes it from all other psychotherapies. Its formal definition is the "use of experimentally established principles and paradigms of learning to overcome maladaptive habits."

The therapeutic activities of a behavior therapist will, as far as possible, be directed by this definition. But therapeutic practice includes ordinary human interactions. It also includes the gathering of information.

THE NAMING OF THE DISCIPLINE

The term *behavior therapy* was first introduced by Skinner and Lindsley (1954) but owes its general acceptance to Eysenck (1960). Its chief advantage over the labels that competed with it early on — *conditioning therapy* and *behavioristic psychotherapy* — was that it seemed more likely to be acceptable to clinicians than the other terms, which were suggestive of the experimental laboratory. It was also argued that the word *behavior* would draw attention to what was conceived to be the cardinal distinguishing feature of this newcomer to the psychotherapies—the use of behavior to change habits. Behavior of one kind or another, however, is inevitably implicated in all psychotherapy—most commonly, of course, verbal behavior, ranging from incantations and free associations to primal scream, all of which may have emotional effects beyond their own occurrence. Thus, *behavior therapy* was a poor choice of label; *conditioning therapy* would have been both more distinctive and more informative.

But *behavior therapy* is firmly established and we can live with it comfortably if we are reasonably vigilant. On the one hand, we must avoid the temptation to accept any method as behavior therapy just because it involves activity, for example, running (Orwin, 1973). On the other hand, we must not exclude procedures whose impact is primarily cognitive, on the mistaken ground that cognition is not behavior. It is the latter error that has led to what is called *cognitive behavior therapy* whose redundancy has been noted by Krasner (1988).

HISTORICAL ANTECEDENTS

As behavior is the core of all the psychotherapies, the history of behavior therapy is embedded in the history of psychotherapy (Pichot, 1989). Before the emergence of formal systems of psychotherapy, whatever a person did to and for another person to relieve emotional distress could be called psychotherapy. Most of these early activities were based on religious belief or superstition. It is only relatively recently that psychotherapeutic practices were related to definable principles.

The first psychotherapist to base his work on principles was Anton Mesmer (1779), an Austrian physician who had moved to Paris. He rested his therapeutic practices on the idea that emotional illness could be overcome by equilibrating the patient's animal magnetism. To achieve this, he made use of a large, troughlike arrangement of movable iron rods and mirrors that he called a *bacquet*. An assemblage of patients surrounding the bacquet would form a closed circle by holding hands. Mesmer, clad in gaudy robes, would make a dramatic appearance, holding in his hand a "magnetic wand" with which he would touch and stroke the patients at intervals. His methods were highly esteemed by the public, but they became the subject of investigation by a joint committee (in which Benjamin Franklin participated) that issued a disparaging report. Nevertheless, Mesmer had many attested successes (Darnton, 1968). Although the theory of animal magnetism was not sustained by scientific testing, the procedures had some clinical merit and were the precursors of suggestion and hypnosis. (For a wide-ranging account of this, among other precursors of behavior therapy, see Pichot, 1989.)

Suggestion, whether or not in the context of hypnotic induction, uses words to elicit desirable responses where undesirable responses are habitual. It may succeed in changing a habit when a suggested response inhibits a preexisting one. If standard hypnotherapy has not had impressive long-term results, it is because it has not usually brought the suggested response into effective opposition with the one to be eliminated.

An early example of a direct use of competing responses that is remarkably close to some modern practices was unearthed by Stewart (1961) in a book by Leuret (1846). The patient was a 30-year-old wine merchant with a 10-year history of obsessional thoughts that had become so insistent he was unable to carry on his business. After admitting the patient to a hospital, Leuret gave him daily assignments of songs to learn for recitation the next day. The patient's food ration was made contingent upon how much he had learned. In 6 weeks of this regimen, his recitals steadily improved while his obsessional thoughts became less and less troublesome. At the end of this period, he announced that he had not had the thoughts for several days and felt much better. Leuret found work for him as a nurse, and a year later noted that he was still well and had become a very efficient nurse. (For further examples of the innovations of this forerunner of behavior therapy, see Gourevitch, 1968; Wolpe & Theriault, 1971.)

In the conventional psychiatric setting, a large number of clinical experiments were reported by Janet (1925), but they yielded little that was generally applicable. The nineteenth-century psychiatrist, nevertheless, felt quite confident about the standard repertoire of sympathetic support, advice, persuasion, and suggestion because many of his neurotic patients showed lasting improvement, even though the benefit was, as we now know, not attributable to the methods used but to the nonspecific effects of therapeutic interaction (see p. 333).

Sigmund Freud introduced his highly influential system of therapeutic methods at the turn of the century. Psychoanalytic theory is imaginative and colorful, and Freud's presentation of it had an uncanny persuasiveness that brought a new excitement into the field of psychotherapy. Unfortunately, the therapeutic methods that emerged from his theories did not lead to the increase in favorable outcomes for which everybody had hoped, as witness the discouraging reports of Brody (1962) and Kernberg et al. (1972). His theoretical propositions were not empirically supported, either (see, e.g., Bailey, 1964; Salter, 1952). Nevertheless, Freud's work had two indisputably important results: it drew attention to the primacy of emotional as opposed to cognitive events in the causation of neuroses, and it undermined the social prudery that had enveloped the subject of sex.

Important as these contributions were during the first half of the twentieth century, the field of psychotherapy remained untouched by scientific study. No testable hypotheses were put forward, no lawful relations were found, and no therapeutic principles emerged. In retrospect, we can see the reason for this lack of activity. Modern medicine is applied science. An applied science of psychotherapy could develop only when there was something to apply. There had to be a foundation in the form of data-based knowledge of behavior change.

THE EMERGENCE OF BEHAVIOR THERAPY

Since the beginning of the twentieth century, experimental studies, along the lines initiated by Pavlov and Watson, have revealed more and more about the characteristics of habits and the factors controlling learning and unlearning. The lawful relations that were established lent themselves to the development of hypotheses to account for the acquisition of maladaptive behavior and to suggest methods to eliminate or diminish it.

A major contribution in this direction was Watson and Rayner's (1920) experiment on Little Albert. This 11-month-old child, who was generally of a phlegmatic disposition, was observed to be disturbed by the loud noise made when an iron bar was sharply struck behind him. By striking the bar each time Albert touched a white rat, the experimenters progressively conditioned a fear of this animal, which generalized to other furry objects. They proposed four possible strategies by which this fear might be overcome: (a) experimental extinction, (b) constructive activities around the feared object, (c) reconditioning through feeding the child candy in the presence of the feared object, and (d) stimulating erogenous zones in the presence of the feared object. Although Albert's departure from the hospital prevented the implementation of any of these suggestions, it is worth noting that the last three of them accord with the counterconditioning model, which will be discussed in detail later. (Even though Harris [1979] has correctly noted that the magnitude and extent of Albert's fear conditioning has often been overstated in the literature, there is no doubt that some fear conditioning occurred. In any case, the experiment provided a starting point for the later work described below.)

A few years later, the third of these suggestions — reconditioning by feeding — was employed by Mary Cover Jones (1924a) in the treatment of children's phobias. She described her method as follows:

> During a period of craving for food, the child is placed in a high chair and given something to eat. The feared object is brought in, starting a negative response. It is then moved away gradually until it is at a sufficient distance not to interfere with the child's eating. The relative strength of the fear impulse and the hunger impulse may be gauged by the distance to which it is necessary to remove the feared object. While the child is eating, the object is slowly brought nearer to the table, then placed upon the table and, finally, as the tolerance increases, it is brought close enough to be touched. Since we could not inter-

fere with the regular schedule of meals, we chose the time of the midmorning lunch for the experiment. This usually assured some degree of interest in the food and corresponding success in our treatment.

Jones (1924b) detailed the application of this method in the case of a 3-year-old boy called Peter—"one of our most serious problem cases"—who recovered after daily treatment over a period of 2 months. Hunger had a role in the process of overcoming the fear habit, as shown by an increase in the effectiveness of the method when hunger was greater. On the other hand, "the repeated presentation of the feared object, with no auxiliary attempt to eliminate the fear, is more likely to produce a summation effect than an adaptation." As the first to establish such lawful relations in humans, Jones is distinguished as a pioneer in behavior therapy.

At about the same time, Burnham (1924), starting from a mental hygiene orientation, also proposed the use of counteractive behavior as the agent of habit change. The recommendation of graduated tasks in the treatment of neurotic patients seemed to be forgotten until it reappeared years later in the writings of two clinicians, Herzberg (1941) and Terhune (1948). However, neither of them was aware of competing responses as the agent of habit change.

In the meantime, in the field of experimental psychology, the most studied habit-eliminating process was (and has continued to be) experimental extinction—the gradual decrement in strength and frequency of responses when they are repeatedly evoked without reinforcement. Dunlap (1932) probed the therapeutic possibilities of this, and evolved the technique called *negative practice* whereby undesirable motor habits are overcome as a result of their being deliberately evoked again and again. It was not long afterward that Guthrie (1935) drew attention to the general applicability of counter-conditioning methods, such as those Jones had demonstrated, and concluded that the simplest rule for breaking a habit is "to find the cues that initiate the action and to practice another response to these cues" (Guthrie, 1935, p. 138). An indispensable ingredient of the formula is that the cue to the original response be present while the "other behavior prevails." The new response can then inhibit the original one and thereby weaken it.

An unequivocal demonstration of the therapeutic power of response competition was provided by its success in the treatment of experimental neuroses. These are persistent anxiety-response habits that can be deliberately induced in animals, first reported from Pavlov's laboratories (Pavlov, 1941) at the beginning of this century. A dog is placed on a table in a small chamber, held in a harness that restricts its movements. A high level of anxiety is elicited in the animal either by noxious stimulation or by a strong motivational conflict. The anxiety is conditioned to the sights and sounds of the experimental situation. By repeating the procedure, a rising level of anxiety is conditioned to the experimental chamber, a level that is eventually high indeed. A striking feature of the anxiety is its extreme persistence, and it is not diminished in intensity either by prolonged exposure to the experimental cage or by prolonged removal from it. In contrast is the calm behavior of the animals in their living cages. Some anxiety, however, is manifest in environments that include stimuli resembling those in the environment of the experimental cage, as might be expected. A notable series of experiments performed by Pavlov's pupil, W. Horsley Gantt (1944), showed that untreated animals would remain afflicted with their neuroses for the rest of their lives.

In experiments that I completed in 1948, I found that experimental neuroses could be overcome by employing the same response-competition concept that Mary Cover Jones had applied to children, and, as she did, by using feeding to compete with small evocations of anxiety. These experiments led to the formulation of the reciprocal inhibition principle of psychotherapeutic effects. In human adults, feeding is not an effective competitor with anxiety. A substantial number of other competing responses are available. These and their manner of use are the main substance of this book. Much more will be said about experimental neuroses in chapters 3 and 4.

THE SCOPE OF BEHAVIOR THERAPY

Psychiatry is the study of maladaptive human habitual behavior and its treatment. Behavior is adaptive when it actually results in satisfying the individual's needs, brings him or her relief from pain, discomfort, or danger, or avoids undue expenditure of energy. In everyday life, there are inevitably some actions that fail to meet with success: the number one has dialed does not answer; the shop one has entered does not have the desired item. Unsuccessful behavior is usually soon abandoned (extinguished). But sometimes it persists, and if it is burdensome it calls for treatment.

Psychiatry is unique among the subdivisions of medicine in that its syndromes have two different kinds of origins. Some are organically based (on lesions or biochemical abnormalities). Others are based on learning. Behavior therapy, in general, is relevant only in those syndromes that owe their existence to learning. The syndromes fall into five categories discussed below.

Neuroses

Neuroses are persistent maladaptive habits that have been acquired in anxiety-generating situations and in which anxiety responses are almost invariably central. They are "pure" learned habits in the sense that no special organic state is necessary for their occurrence. Almost everybody acquires some neurotic habits. Known predisposing conditions include high innate emotionality (Eysenck, 1957) and preexisting learned anxiety in the same stimulus area (sensory preconditioning).

In giving this term its traditional role, I am, of course, disregarding its omission from the Diagnostic and Statistical Manual of Mental Disorders–Third Edition, Revised (DSM-III-R). The main reason given for that omission is that there is no consensus about the definition of the term (p. 9). But it is better to go where the evidence points than to wait for a consensus. As will be seen below, there is abundant experimental and clinical evidence of the existence of a large class of maladaptive behaviors united by the definition of neurosis given here. It is useful to continue to employ the word to denote that class even though the continuing influence of psychoanalytic theories leads psychiatrists to ignore the evidence.

Maladaptive Learned Habits Not Associated with Anxiety

Maladaptive habits that fall into this category include nail-biting, trichotillomania, enuresis nocturna, extreme stinginess, chronic tardiness, and some cases of tantrum behavior.

Psychopathic Personality

A diagnosis of psychopathic personality (also known as antisocial personality disorder – DSM-III-R) applies to people who habitually perform asocial or antisocial behavior regarding which they feel no guilt. Rebukes, chastisements, and even the major penalties that society imposes have little or no corrective effect. While there is apparently a biological predisposition to the development of psychopathic behavior (Eysenck, 1957), the particular patterns of behavior are learned and are therefore in principle subject to unlearning. Unfortunately, very little research has been done in this area.

Drug Addictions

Anybody may take a drug to relieve pain, stress, or anxiety. If the drug taking continues after the cessation of the original cause, an addiction may be said to have developed. Addiction is characterized by a craving that compels the person to seek the drug. There are biological changes that underlie such craving, and this is what makes drug habits different from other maladaptive habits. Recent research (Lubeskind & Paul, 1977; Snyder, 1978) has shown that these changes are due to the effects these drugs have on the binding of endogenous analgesics (endorphins) to pain receptors. If the experience of craving is a response to a biological state, it might be possible to inhibit it by aversive stimulation. An experiment is reported later in this book that obtained some evidence of the effectiveness of this strategy (Wolpe, Groves, & Fischer, 1980). An interesting incidental finding was that narcotics addicts have little motivation to be cured. They are evidently reluctant to relinquish the gratifications they obtain. Only when this obstacle is overcome will treatment programs have the possibility of wide success.

Learned Behavior of Schizophrenics

Although it is now clear that schizophrenia is at bottom a biological illness, some of the maladaptive habits that patients display are due to learning, and these can often be eliminated by operant conditioning schedules (Ayllon, 1963; Ayllon & Azrin, 1968; Kalish, 1981; Paul & Lentz, 1977).

Under the influence of psychoanalytic theories, the view that there is a continuum between neuroses and schizophrenia is still widely prevalent. It is believed that neurosis and schizophrenia are functionally related and that transitions occur between them (see, e.g., Arieti, 1974). The transitions are often referred to as borderline states.

In a survey of 13 different areas of comparative research (Wolpe, 1970), I found that the evidence uniformly pointed to neurosis and schizophrenia having separate and unrelated etiologies. The following are some of the differences. (a) The genetic factors in schizophrenia do not coincide with those of neurosis (Eysenck & Prell, 1951). (b) A variety of physiological features are found in schizophrenics that are absent in both normal people and neurotic subjects. (c) Grossly abnormal pupillary reactivity appears to be invariable in schizophrenics and persists even when they are in remission (Rubin, 1970). (d) The early symptoms of schizophrenia are distinct from those of neurosis (Chapman, 1966). (e) Neurotic behavior is lastingly modifiable by conditioning procedures in a way that schizophrenic behavior is not.

The biology of schizophrenia is directly responsible for most of the symptomatology but also sometimes predisposes to the selective learning of bizarre patterns of behavior. Such patterns are the only part of the psychosis modifiable by learning procedures (see chapter 12).

NEUROTIC ANXIETY AND ITS SECONDARY EFFECTS

Of the categories of maladaptive learned habits listed above, only the neuroses are substantively dealt with in this book. The formal definition of neurosis is "a persistent maladaptive habit that has been acquired by learning in an anxiety-generating situation (or a succession of such situations) and in which anxiety is usually the central component." (For a discussion of the definition of anxiety, see pp. 23–25.)

A great many neurotic patients present themselves purely as having inappropriate fears; in others it is consequences of the fear that bring them to treatment. The most common neurotic fears are social—of criticism, rejection, and disapproval. Often bound up with the last is the idea of behaving unacceptably, which is the commonest basis of interpersonal timidity. Fears of public speaking or, more broadly, public scrutiny, are probably the most common of all neurotic fears. One step removed from these is the fear of taking responsibility.

Considerably less common—though one would not think so on the basis of their prominence in behavior therapy research—are the phobias. These include fears of a vast array of animals, such as dogs, mice, or spiders, and other configurations or aspects of things or places that objectively include no danger of any kind. Among these we have fears of darkness, blood, open wounds, injections, elevators, flying, deformities, hospitals, and heights. Of special interest is agoraphobia. Patients who are given this diagnosis all share a fear of being separated from a safe place or safe persons or both; but as will be seen in chapter 14, other kinds of fearfulness often lie behind the manifest agoraphobia. In addition to, but separate from, specific fears there may be pervasive ("free-floating") anxiety, in which anxiety is experienced continuously for days or months, even in the absence of any specific anxiety-arousing stimulus. Apparently, such anxiety has been conditioned to space, time, bodily sensations, and other virtually omnipresent stimulus aspects (see chapter 14).

Anxiety, especially if it is severe, and even more if it is both severe and either continuous or frequent, is a very serious source of human suffering. But, in addition, anxiety often has secondary effects which in some cases are a more important source of suffering than the anxiety that causes them. For example, there may be shyness, blushing, or stuttering. Shyness, besides being an embarrassment in itself, hampers the initiation and development of relationships and may seriously thwart a person's lovelife. Anxiety is also the main cause of sexual inadequacy in men (most often in the form of premature ejaculation), as well as in women, who are affected in degrees that vary from total absence of sexual response to the inability to have coital orgasms. It is also the usual cause of such antisocial habit patterns as kleptomania, exhibitionism, and fetishism, and is the underlying cause of most obsessive and compulsive neuroses. I have left to the last, for emphasis, the fact that anxiety is the basis of neurotic depression (see chapter 15).

Some of the consequences of maladaptive anxiety are illustrated in table 1.1.

Table 1.1. Consequences of Neurotic Anxiety

PHYSIOLOGICAL EVENT	COMMON CLINICAL CONSEQUENCES
A. Autonomic Event	
1. General autonomic response predominantly sympathetic	Feeling of anxiety, panic, dread, etc. Feeling of depression Feeling of threat of losing control or of insanity
2. Hyperventilation	Dizziness Fainting attacks Headaches Paresthesia Tachycardia Panic attacks
3. Automatic discharges especially channeled into one organ system	Psychosomatic symptoms, e.g., Neurodermatitis Asthma Vasomotor rhinitis Peptic ulceration and peptic ulcer syndrome Irritable bowel syndrome Frequency of micturition Dysmenorrhea Hypertension Migraine
B. Motor Event	
1. Prominent muscle tension, general or localized	Motor disturbance, e.g., Tremor Stuttering "Fibrositic" pain (e.g., backache) Ocular dyskinesia
2. Motor avoidance conditioning (may be conditioned to be either simultaneous with anxiety or secondary to it)	Avoidance of anxiety-evoking stimuli
3. Inhibition of complex functioning	Impaired vocational function Impaired social interaction Impaired sexual function
4. Complex motor behavior in combination with anxiety or related to anxiety reduction	Compulsions Character neuroses, e.g., Promiscuity Aimlessness Sexual deviations, e.g., Homosexuality Pedophilia Exhibitionism Voyeurism
C. Cognitive Event	
1. Cognitive focus on anxiety responses	Hypomnesia due to "nonregistration" of external events Impairment of learning and performance
2. Inhibition of a segment of experience by intense anxiety	Circumscribed amnesia (Wolpe, 1958, p. 94)

2
Stimuli, Responses, Learning, and the Nature of Cognition

This chapter provides fundamental facts about stimuli, responses, and learning which often are not common knowledge among practitioners of behavior therapy. Most nonmedical psychotherapists have had only cursory exposure to the findings of experimental psychology, and most medical psychotherapists practically none. Such knowledge is essential to an understanding of behavior therapy and provides a basis for seeing the weaknesses of other theories — for example, the theory that all neurotic problems stem from wrong beliefs (see p. 131).

STIMULI AND RESPONSES

All nervous system functioning, even the most complex — what Pavlov called "higher nervous activity" — consists of stimulus-response sequences. A *response* is either the activation of a particular set or system of neurons or a consequence thereof, such as a perceived image or a muscle contraction. A *stimulus* is the antecedent of a response. A sensory stimulus is an extrinsic source of energy that produces activation of afferent neurons. Each member of a sequence of responses can be regarded as a stimulus in relation to the responses that follow it. Thus, a movement is a response both in relation to the nerve impulses that have immediately preceded it and to the sensory stimulus that triggered those impulses (see Wolpe, 1958, pp. 3–6).

For the sake of clarity, I will depict stimulus-response sequences as occurring in single chains of neurons, always remembering that even the simplest reflex involves the activation of thousands of neurons. Every sensory stimu-

lus has a multiplicity of neuronal consequences that lead to motor, autonomic, and perceptual responses; and many responses produce new stimuli
that elicit further responses — response-produced stimuli (Hull, 1943). For
example, the forward extension of the right leg in walking produces pro-
prioceptive stimuli that stimulate flexion of the left leg. Again, every change
in position changes the visual field and thus provides new stimuli and a new
range of response possibilities. Figure 2.1 is a diagrammatic representation
of the network of simultaneous and successive stimulus-response events that
go on at all times during our waking lives.

Granted that there is always a degree of variability, the behavior of an
organism to a particular stimulus situation tends to be constant within a
range of physiological conditions. The empirical constancy of a stimulus-
response relationship is what we call a habit. Habits are of all degrees of
complexity — from a simple movement, to a disposition (e.g., to listen, to
look, to imitate, or to solve problems), to a complex set of skills (e.g.,
playing tennis or chess, doing eye surgery, or playing the violin). Bandura
(1969) has described some of the intricacies involved in the development of
many social habits. Generally, our habits favor our welfare; it is when a
habit is significantly disadvantageous, that is, maladaptive, that there is
cause to change it.

BASIC PRINCIPLES OF LEARNING
AND UNLEARNING

Some people will find it strange that we deal with learning before dealing
with cognition; but this is the correct sequence. As will become apparent,
cognition is based on perception, and perception is a product of learning.

Learning and the Role of Reinforcement

Learning is the process that initiates or increases the ability of a stimulus
to elicit a response. Experiments by Thorndike (1932) and by Pavlov (1927)
showed that learning a response to a stimulus is often related to reward
following the response. This effect of reward is called *reinforcement*. The
amount of the reward and its timing in relation to the response have an
important role in determining whether and to what extent learning is established. This link has been abundantly shown with respect to a great many
motor habits and some autonomic habits (Pavlov, 1927; Razran, 1971; Skinner, 1953). External reinforcers are of many kinds; eating food and receiving
money or praise are the most widely recognized.

There are many instances, however, in which learning occurs in the absence of any evident external source of reinforcement. One does not need an

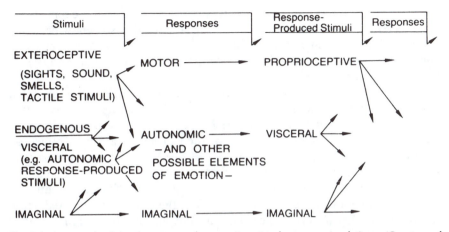

Fig. 2.1. A network of simultaneous and successive stimulus-response relations. (Courtesy of Graphic Communications, Eastern Pennsylvania Psychiatric Institute, Philadelphia.)

external reinforcement to learn from a dictionary that a podium is a high table used for lecturing, or that the German word for sky is *himmel*. The mere presentation of these pairs of symbols in juxtaposition may result in the presence of the one consistently evoking the image of the other. Does this mean that reinforcement is absent in these instances? Actually, internal sources of reinforcement can be found.

Stimulus-response sequences have long been known to depend on the functional connections between neurons (Dale, 1937; Eccles, 1975; Lloyd, 1946). Many years ago I showed how a neuronal model can unify the conceptualization of many instances and aspects of earning (Wolpe, 1949, 1950, 1952a, 1952c, 1953, 1958, pp. 6–31). The model is based on evidence that learning depends on the development of conductivity (synaptic function) between neurons whose endings are in apposition (Culler, 1938; Olds et al., 1972; Olds, 1975; Woody & Engel, 1972). The processes that engender conductivity are beginning to be defined (Huttunen, 1973; Olds, 1975; Young, 1973, 1975) (see below). One may legitimately use what is known about learning at the neuronal level as a framework for suggesting what might be happening at synapses in relation to events at the behavioral level.

To begin, we may ask how external reinforcement might influence the development of conductivity at the synapse. As Hull (1943) observed, a feature common to all external reinforcements is that they reduce "drive" — states of bodily need, such as food or water deprivation, or strong external stimulation, such as noxious stimulation. Central neural excitation above a certain level of strength results in overt motor activity. Reduction of this excitation (of which one indication is reduced motor activity) results either from the reduction of the need-induced stimulation, or from the removal of external stimulation. It seems that stimulation reduction somehow produces a "cementing" effect at active synaptic points: real consummatory behaviors and brain rewards are both correlated with a cessation of firing in "a special kind of drive neuron" (Olds, 1975, pp. 386–387).

Given that external reinforcement is a source of drive reduction in much, but not all, learning, we must inquire whether other modes of drive reduction are at work when learning occurs in the absence of external reinforcement, as in the earlier-stated instance of the learning of a word. In fact, all responses, including perceptual responses, are ipso facto correlated with some measure of central neural excitation: When the perception of an object stops, so does the excitation — and this must mean that drive reduction occurs. Although of lower magnitude, this is the same as a drive reduction following the alleviation of a need such as hunger. The strength of cognitive learning will naturally be enhanced if at the same time there are other arousals in addition to those that are reduced by the particular perception. For example, a greater measure of reinforcement of cognitive learning will occur if the perception allays curiosity (Berlyne, 1960). The same is true if the perceived stimulus happens to arouse aesthetic pleasure (Berlyne, 1971). (The pleasure is the subjective correlate of additional neural excitation.) The reinforcements correlated with ongoing experience are the apparent basis of the learning that goes on continuously through our waking lives. One product of these is the registration of the sequences of experience that are the basis of memory.

While drive reduction is probably the commonest source of reinforcement, drive increment may effectuate it as well. This has been demonstrated by experiments that show that raising the level of stimulation is reinforcing — for example, the addition of light (Hurwitz, 1956) or sweetness (Sheffield & Roby, 1950) — as well as by experiments that show how reinforcement is procured by hypothalamic stimulation (Olds, 1962, 1975). It is thus credible that in the formation of cognitive habits, reinforcement can be provided either by the excitations underlying the cognitions or by the reduction of these excitations, or both. Presumably, either can lead to cessation of firing in Olds' (1975, p. 386) "special kind of drive neurons."

The so-called automatic nature of conditioning has recently been called into question. Researchers have observed that if pairings of a conditioned stimulus and an unconditioned stimulus are each interspersed with several unaccompanied presentations of the unconditioned stimulus, learning does not occur. Rescorla (1988) tries to explain these observations in terms of information that the experiment provides. But if one agrees that learning takes place at a synaptic locus, an explanation must be given in terms of that. Various factors, such as reward, can enhance the synaptic process; others can diminish it, such as, clearly, unaccompanied occurrences of the unconditioned or conditioned stimulus. Conditioning is not governed by "the informational relation" but by the dynamics of the physiological events. In the context of unlearning, it is not that the organism "learns that there is a negative relation" but that a negative effect occurs at the relevant synapses.

While this argument cannot be taken much further here, it is relevant to mention an instance of conditioning which precludes any appeal to cognitive processes. Baeyens, Eelen et al. (1988) tested Levey and Martin's (1987) proposal that, unlike signal learning, evaluative learning does not require and is not influenced by contingency awareness. Furthermore, once established, evaluative conditioning cannot be extinguished by nonreinforcement (Baeyens, Crombez et al., 1988). This practically rules out the possibility that propositional knowledge about the relationship between the conditioned stimulus and the unconditioned stimulus has any relevance to evaluative conditioning. Therefore, the general proposition that information must have a role in classical conditioning is untenable.

Unlearning

Unlearning is the weakening of a previously learned habit of response. The usual context is experimental extinction, in which a habit is weakened when the response is repeatedly evoked without being followed by reward. For example, behavior that has been established by food reinforcement becomes progressively weaker if its elicitations by a stimulus cease to be followed by food. There is evidence of the operation of two distinct habit-weakening processes in the circumstances of nonreinforcement. One is the fatigue-associated reactive inhibition mechanism described by Hull (1943) (for the putative neurophysiological basis of this mechanism, see Wolpe, 1958, p. 27). The second is the occurrence of frustration responses that compete with and inhibit the unreinforced responses (Amsel, 1962, 1972; Asratian, 1972; Gleitman, Nachmias, & Neisser, 1954). Both of these mechanisms are evidently involved in the extinction of motor responses.

But the unlearning of some kinds of response cannot be accounted for in terms of nonreinforcement. The failure to elicit a learned verbal response to a particular cue (which may be another word) can scarcely be attributed to nonreinforced articulations of the word, since the extinguished word may have been articulated only once or twice after being learned. The weakening of the verbal response tendency is much more reasonably explained on the basis that other verbal responses that have also been conditioned to the same or similar stimuli compete with that response and thereby diminish its liability to be evoked (see McGeogh, McKinney, & Peters, 1937). The process involved is evidently reciprocal inhibition (Osgood, 1946, 1948), which is also the likely basis for most deconditioning of anxiety (see chapter 4).

Another context in which the elimination of undesirable behavior occurs without its unreinforced elicitation is one in which the behavior is under the control of emotion. To take a clinical example, a woman's habitual shoplifting of 18 years' duration was revealed on analysis to result from anxiety at the prospect of surrendering anything of value. The shoplifting habit was eliminated by systemic desensitization of the anxiety. The elicitation of shoplifting did not figure in the treatment. It ceased when the anxiety that was its controlling antecedent was eliminated.

It is apparent that either reactive inhibition or inhibition by a competing response is involved in all the above examples of response weakening. The elimination of unadaptive classically conditioned autonomic responses can also involve a variety of modes of response inhibition. It seems to be a rule that inhibition of the response is prerequisite to the weakening of the habit, just as elicitation is prerequisite to conditioning it. Of course, it is at the *neural* level that inhibition has its impact on the habit. Peripheral inhibition of the response does not change the habit (Black, 1958). Baeyens et al. (1989) have provided impressive evidence in respect to affective evaluative conditioning, to show that while it is resistant to extinction, it can be overcome by counterconditioning.

COGNITION IN HUMAN BEHAVIOR

Our perception of things and situations in the world around us is a prime determinant of our actions. In this sense, thought has a central role in human behavior. But thought obeys the same mechanistic laws as other behavior. It does not belong to an entity separate from the mechanism-controlled organism. Not only the moment-to-moment content of thought, but its very faculty is, as will be seen, comprehensible as an organismal function.

It is strange that even within the behavioral field there are many who believe that cognitive processes belong to a domain that is distinct from the physiological and beyond the sway of biological rules (Bandura, 1974; Beck, 1976; Mahoney, 1977; Meichenbaum, 1975). The separate domain, which they believe makes humans partially free from physical causality (Bandura, 1974, p. 867) is what Ryle (1949) called "the ghost in the machine." Ryle showed that belief in the "ghost" is a consequence of regarding different aspects of the same phenomenon as different entities. The dogma of the ghost maintains "that there occur physical processes and mental processes; that there are mechanical causes of corporeal movements and mental causes of corporeal movements" (p. 22). The cognitivists do not face, let alone solve, the problem of explaining how a nonmaterial process can have effects on nerve tissue. No such problem exists when the physical and the mental are both seen as functions of the nervous system. The following passages from Ryle's book crystallize some of the key points of his analysis of the relationship between the physical and the mental:

> When a person talks sense aloud, ties knots, feints or sculpts, the actions which we witness are themselves the things which he is intelligently doing. He is bodily active and he is mentally active, but he is not being synchronously active in two different "places," or with two different "engines." There is the one kind of activity, but it is one susceptible of and requiring more than one kind of explanatory description. (Ryle, 1949, p. 50)

If we take the example of talking aloud, the need for more than one kind of explanatory description is plain. There may be no physical or physiological difference between one person gabbling and another talking sense, but the logical differences are enormous. It is not sounds, but the sequences of meaning that matter.

> I discover that there are other minds in understanding what other people say and do. In making sense of what you say, in appreciating your jokes, in unmasking your chess-strategems, in following your arguments and in hearing you pick holes in my arguments, I am not inferring to the workings of your mind, I am following them. Of course, I am not merely hearing the noise that you make, or merely seeing the movements that you perform. I am understanding what I hear and see. But this understanding is not inferring to occult causes. It is appreciating how the operations are conducted. (Ryle, 1949, pp. 60–61)

A person's knowledge of the world consists entirely of private events. An individual's first response to an object is the perception of it, and that is a private event. Images evoked in the absence of objects — for example, the architectural image evoked by the word *Parthenon* — are conditioned perceptions, in line with what Skinner called "conditioned seeing" (1953, p. 266). Together, immediate perceptions and conditioned perceptions make up cognitions.

The Ontology of Cognition

Since perceptions are the basis of cognition, the ontology of cognition is at bottom the ontology of perception. This matter has received very little notice from psychologists, despite the long availability of a brilliant monograph on the subject by James G. Taylor (1962). Taylor starts from the proposition that perception is not just vision. Take a simple object like a teacup. It does not matter what aspect is held up before you, nor the angle nor the distance — you recognize it as a teacup. Clearly, from different angles and distances, the stimuli impinging upon your retina are different, just as photographs from the various positions would be different. Yet, you see the object as the same. How does it happen? Why is there perceptual constancy? We take for granted what really should not be taken for granted.

Most psychologists regard perception as a kind of photographic process, consisting of the following sequence of events: light rays from the seen object produce an inverted image of the object in the retina where it arouses neural impulses that eventually reach and excite the occipital cortex. The structure is then supposed to generate, right-way up, an image of the object. But how can neurons generate imagery? It is easy to see how a nerve cell can secrete acetylcholine but not how it can secrete images. In any case, there is no explanation for why we see this object that the retina receives in many different ways as the same teacup.

Taylor (1962) showed that visual perception is the outcome of a specific sequence of conditionings. The modifiability of perception is conveniently illustrated by the case of a person who has had bilateral cataracts for which the crystalline lens has been removed. While light can now penetrate to the retina, the images are out of focus, and the person must be fitted with correcting lenses. When looking through these lenses for the first time, the objects seen will be magnified by 30% and the person will find that straight lines in the periphery of the visual field are curved. But these distortions will disappear after a time. The true shapes of objects will return, and ultimately the enlarged world will contract to its true size. Obviously, it is impossible to explain these changes if one believes that images going into the retina are mechanically replicated by the occipital cortex. The change in the image must be due to modifications that have been occurring in the nervous system as a function of visual input through the spectacles.

Certain experimental findings confirm this observation. Stratton (1897) had a subject cover one eye and wear on the other a prism that reversed left and right. The effect of a visual world that is distorted in this way is to discourage mobility. If the subject does try to get around and adapt himself, things improve within about 2 weeks. Not long afterward, a remarkable transformation occurs: the visual world rights itself even though the subject is still wearing the prism! This transformation can be understood as a function of conditioning. Consider a person with a left-right reversing prism over the left eye, sitting at a table on which a watch lies to the left. The watch will be seen *to the right*. If the person wants to pick up the watch, she will reach out to the right where it appears to be, and it will not be there. She will then move her hand hither and thither and eventually make contact with the watch, and will see the contact made. There will at that instant be a coincidence of activity in those neurons subserving the seen image and those subserving the action taken. That coincidence is reinforced by the moment of successful contact. All this will be repeated each time the situation recurs, with the result that the hand goes leftward with increasing readiness. Similar visual and tactile coincidences with numerous objects in various positions eventually have the global result that the visual world is reversed, in conformity with the realities of spatial relations. How and where we see things is the result of conditioning based on the success of previous interactions between visual inputs and movements.

An experiment that further illustrates the point was done by one of Taylor's collaborators, who wore reversing prisms constantly for about 2 weeks. He learned to walk and to do many other things successfully, including riding a bicycle. He then started to ride the bicycle on alternate days with and without the prisms. After a few days he could ride the bicycle and see the world correctly, with or without the prisms. The two functional systems were differentially cued by such differences as prismatic aberration.

When a child is born it has practically no conditioned responses, only unconditioned responses. Taylor postulated that when children can only lie on their backs, they have a rather undifferentiated visual field and reach out with their arms in an aimless fashion. Let us say that there is a horizontal bar in front of a child. If, in reaching out he by chance touches the bar while looking in its direction, he makes a grasping response to whose association with the visual stimuli the tactile sensations provide an element of reward. The movement thus becomes conditioned to the visual input of that movement. This process is repeated in numerous contexts. Besides the conditioning of the central visual stimulus, there is also some degree of conditioning of peripheral stimuli on each occasion, indicating an involvement of the visual world within the limits of the visual field.

When children are able to sit, objects that were previously out of reach become accessible to them. There is thus an extension of the world of potential conditioning. A still more dramatic expansion of the perceptual world occurs with the inception of locomotion. When children crawl and later walk, they acquire responses to directions and distances of objects that were previously beyond their reach. The most important visual effects of locomotion are related to the fact that the retinal image of an object changes as a continuous function of its distance.

A whole crop of perceptual constancies emerges. Although there is a one-to-many relationship between each position of an external object and the patterns of stimulation to which it may give rise, conditioning establishes a one-to-one correspondence between each position of the object and the terminal response conditioned to it — the grasping of the object. Many experiences with many objects at different distances leads to the establishment of general perceptual constancy for three-dimensional objects in general so that a stable object such as a cup or bowl is seen as the same from any distance or angle.

The foregoing is only a soupçon of Taylor's profoundly important research. The interested reader should consult the original monograph (Taylor, 1962).

An interesting phenomenon that was recently brought to light seems at first glance to suggest that perceptual organization is developmentally established. It has been found that children around the age of 2 months show precocious responses. They seem to recognize people, to smile, and to reach for objects. This behavior, however, fades out in a matter of weeks. It does not seem unreasonable to suggest that it has a phylogenetic explanation—a kind of recapitulation of the complex instinctual behavior of lower animals. After a few weeks, apparently, the responsible nerve structures atrophy or lose their function. Only much later, at the age of 6 to 9 months, does one see the beginnings of learned perceptual behavior (Bower, 1976, 1977).

A major advantage in thinking of learning as occurring in the place where it actually happens, the nervous system, is that it insures against trying to apply mentalistic explanations when one is confronted with unexpected data. For example, Rescorla (1988), who, in an otherwise excellent exposition of recent data on the conditions of learning and unlearning, resorts to explaining in terms of "the learning of relations among events so as to allow the organism to represent its environment." This description locates the learning in the mind of the organism—a theory that we have contested above (p. 16).

Our knowledge of the world is a function of the activation of engrams that are the product of repeated occasions of learning in varied spatial relations to objects. The engrams are complex, integrated neural-response systems, arousable by systematically variable combinations of sensory inputs, providing, within specifiable limits, constancy of perception despite variations in sensory stimulation. As there are constancies with regard to all parts of all perceptual fields, consciousness of the environment involves a simultaneous activation of engrams related to all objects present at a given time.

The learning process can connect any engram to any other in such a way that activation of the first leads to activation of the second. Imagery without perception thus occurs, and this is the basis of thinking.

3
The Causation of Neuroses

THE DEFINITION OF ANXIETY

In chapter 1, neuroses were defined as persistent maladaptive learned habits in which the foremost feature is anxiety. The word *anxiety* (for which *fear* is a synonym) must now be defined. I continue to define it operationally as the individual organism's characteristic pattern of autonomic responses to noxious stimulation (Wolpe, 1958). A noxious stimulus is a painful stimulus. It tends to evoke escape or avoidance behavior, together with autonomic responses, predominantly of the sympathetic division of the autonomic nervous system. The responses to the noxious stimulus are conditionable and are the template for all learned anxiety responses, whether adaptive or maladaptive.

Because this definition of anxiety has objective referents, it lends itself to practical application and at the same time provides a firm base for discourse. It bypasses most current controversial issues, such as the synchrony or desynchrony of the autonomic responses with motor and experiential correlates (Lang, 1970; Rachman, 1976). An unequivocal operational definition like this is in every way preferable to regarding anxiety as a variable "entity," loosely tied to antecedents and made up of shifting autonomic, motor, and cognitive components. Meanwhile, it allows for the observation that the profile of autonomic responses to noxious stimulation varies from person to person but tends to be constant for the individual (Engel, 1972; Lacey, Bateman, & Van Lehn, 1953; Lacey & Lacey, 1958).

The definition also necessitates a much broader view of the physiological profile of anxiety responses than is customary. The usual conspectus is limited to the galvanic skin response, respiratory responses, and a variety of peripheral vascular and muscle tension responses (Lader, 1975; Martin,

1961). But there is a wide range of additional autonomic components of anxiety. Subjective anxiety is correlated with elevations of blood pressure (Hall, 1927; Malmo & Shagass, 1952), alterations in gastrointestinal activity (Rubin et al., 1962), pupillary responses (Rubin, 1964), and characteristic changes in evoked electroencephalograph potentials (Shagass, Roemer, Straumanis, & Amadeo, 1978; Shagass & Schwartz, 1963). Variations of "autonomic balance" (Eppinger & Hess, 1915; Wenger, 1966) also warrant attention, as do an extensive array of endocrine changes (Lader, 1976). The implication of such observations is that unless one has a comprehensive knowledge of an individual's autonomic response profile, one cannot speak of his emotions as being independent of autonomic activation. When I was involved in clinical psychophysiology, I occasionally found subjects who either had no changes in skin resistance or no changes of pulse rate, or both, while responding to stimuli that evoked strong subjective anxiety. There are probably subjects who respond in none of the standard modalities, but it is not plausible to suppose that feelings of anxiety can ever be totally without physiological correlates.

Discourse about anxiety has been clouded and complicated by the "shifting sands" view of anxiety favored by Lang (1970) and Rachman (1974, 1978), two leading contributors to behavior therapy. They believe that a firm definition is precluded by the variable makeup of anxiety, sometimes even in the same person. They argue that the autonomic responses of fear are only imperfectly related to cognitive and motor responses. Rachman provides the illustration of a claustrophobic patient who, despite marked behavioral improvement in the sense that he becomes able to travel in underground trains, denies that he has benefited from treatment. Sometimes, moreover, even though the physiological reactions to real and symbolic presentations of a feared object have diminished after treatment, the patient still complains of excessive fear (Hersen, 1973). In line with these findings, Fenz and Epstein (1967) reported a lack of correspondence between physiological measures of emotional distress and subjective reports of fear in veteran parachute jumpers, in contrast to novices in whom the subjective and psychophysiological reactions corresponded.

The operational definition of anxiety used here anticipates a varied "mix" of components. Various incidental factors can influence the makeup of anxiety. Therapist demand or social expectation (Bernstein, 1973; Geer, 1965) can make patients do things fear would otherwise prevent them from doing though their experience of fear remains undiminished, as do their psychophysiological fear responses. The findings of the Fenz and Epstein (1967) study can be explained on the basis that different people mean different things by the "experience of fear." It seems apparent that experienced parachute jumpers do not feel fear in the same way that novices do; to some extent, they may be reporting their *evaluation* of the danger involved in the situation of jumping. It is relevant that they were reported as seeming to enjoy the activity, and that "the absolute magnitude of fear of the experienced parachutists at no point approaches the magnitude of the fear experienced by novice parachutists shortly before a jump." In a somewhat similar way, a person who has a phobia may avoid the relevant situation and report that he does so because he is afraid, when what is actually happening is that he is anticipating the certainty of being afraid were he to enter the situation, but not actually feeling any fear.

Altogether, there is good reason to favor the operational definition of fear given above. Rachman himself (1974, p. 20) concedes that a very substantial degree of cohesion does exist, despite the narrowness of conventional psychophysiological monitoring. Self-reports of fear correlate well with each other and moderately well with the ratings of fear made by external judges and with the avoidance behavior observed in the fear test. Self-reports also correlate with physiological indices of fear, and the usual physiological indices correlate modestly with each other. Sartory, Rachman, and Gray (1977) have obtained some indications that the correlation is greater at high than low arousal, but according to Lande (1982) this is not invariably so.

HOW FEAR IS LEARNED

It is important to note that our definition of fear is based on an unconditioned response. A person who is having a painful experience is usually not aware of the simultaneous autonomic responses because the pain has overriding sensory intensity. Other unconditioned stimuli that also elicit anxiety are sudden loss of support (Watson, 1970, p. 153), very strong auditory stimulation (Watson, 1970, p. 152), and conflict (Fonberg, 1956). In addition, children show fear of unfamiliar faces when they first become able to distinguish them from their parents' faces, perhaps, as a function of dissonance.

Neutral stimuli making impact on the person when fear is evoked are liable to be conditioned to fear. For example, if a mother's voice takes on a certain tone whenever she slaps her child, the fear stimulated by the slap will come to be conditioned to that tone of her voice. This conditioning can theoretically occur to any kind of contiguous stimulation — sounds, things, people, words, ideas — anything seen or heard or felt, anything perceived by the person. Then, second-order conditioning may spread the fear to further stimuli.

It used to be thought that all stimuli are equally susceptible to being conditioned to fear. Seligman (1971), building on his important exposition (1970) of the limited generality of the laws of learning, put forth the proposition that only certain stimuli such as darkness and furry objects are readily connected to fear responses. He called these "prepared" stimuli, and suggested that their special liability to fear conditioning has a phylogenetic basis. His supposition was that such stimuli have had some kind of special significance in the evolutionary history of the species. DeSilva, Rachman, and Seligman (1977) carried out a retrospective study of 69 phobic subjects and found that in the great majority of them the stimuli conformed to certain criteria of "preparedness." Öhman, Erixon, and Löfberg (1975) exposed normal human subjects to pictures of supposedly prepared phobic stimuli (human faces) and supposedly neutral objects (houses) as conditioned stimuli in a classical conditioning experiment with shock as the unconditioned stimulus and the skin conductance response as the dependent variable. Equal acquisition of conditioning was shown to both sets of stimuli. During extinction, however, there were lasting conditioning effects only in the case of the prepared stimuli.

Clinical experience certainly indicates that enclosed spaces, animals, and insects are much more likely to be phobic stimuli than are houses, flowers, clouds, and electric outlets; but a phylogenetic explanation cannot be taken for granted. Another possibility is, quite simply, that in the normal course of life objects like flowers and houses become strongly associated with pleasant or at least neutral responses, and that this inoculates them against anxiety conditioning. Persuasive evidence of this happening has been provided by Davey (1989). In a study of 101 subjects, he found that those who did not acquire a fear of dentistry after a painful treatment had a history of painless dental treatments. He explained this on the basis of the development of latent inhibition (Lubow, 1973; Rescorla, 1969). In contrast, the development of fear may be facilitated by a background of unpleasant or fearful associations, from folklore, fairly tales, or the witnessed fearful behavior of other people.

There is no evidence that human beings have any purely developmentally based responses complex enough to be called "instinctive" (Gesell, 1946). The more complex the organization of an animal's nervous system, the less maturation has to do with complex stimulus response sequences (Carmichael, 1946). To take an example, whereas male rats raised from birth in isolation are able to copulate at their first encounter with a receptive female (Beach, 1942), chimpanzees have to learn how to copulate (Yerkes, 1939). The only example of complex human behavior that seems to be phylogenetically determined is the transitory perceptual responses of infants referred to above (p. 22). The absence of evidence of any lasting instinctive behavior in humans also renders implausible the suggestion of Marks (1969, p. 13ff) that some human fears are innately determined.

In the above example of a child who becomes fearful at a certain tone in the mother's voice, the fear is the result of classical conditioning based on the contiguity of that sound and the autonomic accompaniments of pain. There are many incidents in the life of a growing child that result in the classical conditioning of fear responses. Approaching the stove becomes a conditioned stimulus to anxiety after the hand has been burnt; immersion in water becomes fearful after the child has inhaled some of it after falling into a pool; fears of thorny bushes or of stinging insects may follow the experience of being pricked or stung. We have already noted how Watson and Rayner (1920) deliberately induced in Little Albert a fear of a white rat and related stimuli—rabbits, fur, and fluffy masses of cotton—by repeatedly associating the touching of a rat with a frighteningly loud noise. As language develops, warnings or threatening statements become additional stimuli to which classical conditioning can occur.

Once a repertoire of conditioned fear responses exists in the young child, there is a basis for further spread of fears through second-order classical conditioning. This repertoire is also the foundation for the spread of fears in a different way—on the basis of information—which, as Rachman (1977) commented, "has been strangely overlooked—despite the fact that it is obvious, or perhaps because it is too obvious." A person fears lightning, or contaminated food, or having a pistol pointed at him, not because of classical conditioning but because of information. This is facilitated because the use of language results in the association of fears in general with ideas of danger. Of course, this mode of fear learning has not been overlooked by the cognitivists. They regard it as the only mode (see chapter 7).

THE ETIOLOGY OF NEUROTIC FEARS

Much confusion about the etiology of neurotic fear comes from the assumption that it is quite different from that of normal fear. As I shall show below, however, there is no basic difference. Just as some normal (i.e., appropriate) fears develop on the basis of classical conditioning and some on the basis of information (cognitive learning), the same is true of neurotic fears. Unlike experimental neuroses, classically conditioned clinical neuroses almost always start from anxiety aroused by conditioned stimuli. They are based on second-order conditioning. This is apparent in every example below including the "traumatic" war neuroses.

Classically Conditioned Neurotic Fears

The classical conditioning of human neurotic fears may originate from a single occurrence (single-trial learning) or may be progressively built up in the course of a series of related events. The classic example of single-trial fear conditioning is the war neurosis. A soldier who is driven frantic by the carnage around him develops conditioned anxiety to surrounding stimuli. If in the causal situation a particular stimulus, such as the sound of machine-gun fire, is particularly prominent, that sound or anything that resembles it, such as a motorcycle at full throttle, will subsequently evoke anxiety. Other stimuli—the sight of blood, the sound of screaming, the pouring rain—

would be less strongly connected with fear if they happened not to be at the center of attention at the critical time. The specificity of the reactions to the most prominent features of the individual's battle experience is well brought out by Grinker and Spiegel (1945a, p. 16):

> Those who have withstood prolonged dive bombing and strafing from the air are intolerant of all aircraft, and in the worst cases, of the sound of any motor. The knowledge that all aircraft in the vicinity of the hospital are friendly planes is of no comfort. The patients react automatically to any plane overhead with fear and suspicion and seem to be continually listening for the sound of an airplane engine. On the other hand, those who have experienced adequate support from the air on the part of their own planes, but who have been subjected to heavy fire from artillery and mortar shells, have no fear of planes; however, they cannot tolerate sudden loud noises, such as the dropping of a dish or the banging of a door. In those who have had mortar shells land very close by and have seen the flash of the explosion and felt the concussion, almost any sudden stimulus will produce the fear and startle reaction. This is especially true of sudden flashes of light, such as are made by the striking of a match or a cigarette lighter, or by the opening of the blinds in such a way as to flood the room suddenly with light.

We may note that the anxiety is automatically aroused by the stimuli: no cognitive error is involved. The person does not for a moment believe that danger threatens in the sound of an engine or the sight of a friendly plane. Civilian examples of single-trial fear conditioning are also common.

Case 1

A 34-year old man had a severe fear of being in an automobile. This had started 4 years previously when his car had been struck from behind while he was waiting for a red light to change. He had been thrust forward so that his head, striking the windshield, had sustained a small laceration. He had not lost consciousness, but a surge of panic had swept over him, brought on by the thought, "I am about to die." The fear became connected to the car's interior, with generalization to all car interiors. During these 4 years he had been unable to enter a car without great anxiety. Driving was out of the question. That fear was entirely due to classical autonomic conditioning. He had no expectation of danger when he sat in a motionless car.

Case 2

A 40-year-old businessman had been an enthusiastic spelologist until an incident 7 years previously. During an expedition to a labyrinth of caves, while he was deep underground and separated from his companions, a gust of wind blew out his light. He had no matches and in the utter darkness was beset by a feeling of being entombed there forever. Terror engulfed him. He shouted for help, uncertain that he could be heard. When his companions arrived a few minutes later, his fear receded somewhat, but subsided fully only when he reached the open air. From that time onward he had a fear not only of caves but also of any situation in which he felt confined: traveling in an airplane, driving through a tunnel, riding on a train, and even lying in a tightly made bed.

Case 3

Agoraphobia in the male is relatively uncommon. Mr. S. was an industrial engineer, aged 52, who, when first seen, had been severely afflicted with this condition for 16 years. He was almost completely unable to venture out of his apartment alone. He had adjusted to the problem in a way by moving to an apartment one block from his office, but he could not walk even that distance without becoming very anxious. His work naturally was seriously disrupted.

Twenty years earlier his wife, whom he had dearly loved, had died of lung cancer and he had watched her literally suffocate to death. Gradually he had recovered from the trauma of that experience, and after a year had begun to form relationships with women. Three years later, his trouble started. At that time he had a steady girlfriend who would often spend the night at his apartment. One night, after an orgasm, she began breathing with difficulty and making movements that reminded him of his wife gasping when she was dying. Becoming extremely distressed, he told the woman to dress quickly so that he could take her home. In the car, Mr. S. began to notice that he was having dyspnea that worsened to the point that he felt he was choking; then he panicked. He dropped the woman at a taxi stand and drove home alone. With that single experience, his fear of being away from home began, and later generated a group of satellite fears, including fears of losing his mental stability, of meetings and social gatherings, of unfamiliar places, of being alone in a car, and of dead animals. (Mr. S.'s treatment is described in chapter 11 as case 37.)

Case 4

A 47-year-old housewife, Mrs. A., came for treatment for an extremely distressing fear of mice and rats. She had always been mildly fearful of them, but, in her opinion, "no more than many other women." Seven years previously, when her husband had retired, they moved from the city to a spacious old house in the country. One evening, while she sat in the living room with her husband and parents, a mouse appeared and walked slowly along the wall. She became extremely panicky and screamed loudly, and the mouse disappeared. From that moment she was extremely fearful of these creatures and constantly anticipated their appearance in every strange place. She dealt with the problem in her own home by having it fumigated monthly by a pest control company.

From a pilot study the results of which are summarized in table 3.2 it appears that multiple-event causation of classically conditioned fear is considerably less common than single-event causation. The following are examples of the former. In each case the initial incident resulted in only a moderate degree of anxiety conditioning.

Case 5

Miss S., a woman of 30, experienced a partial blackout while driving on an expressway and guided her car on to the soft shoulder of the road, where she stopped. She felt dizzy and faint for about 30 minutes and also very anxious. She resumed driving when the dizziness and faintness stopped, but the anxiety continued. It gradually subsided during the half-hour drive home.

She avoided driving for a week, but after that she was nervous alone in the car or when she remembered blacking out or had any sensations that were at all suggestive of faintness when driving under any circumstances. The anxiety level was increased by two additional partial blackouts. These were later found to be due to paroxysmal tachycardia.

Case 6

A registered nurse of 35, Mrs. G. came for treatment of a severe fear of public speaking even to very small groups. This was a serious disability because she had to give reports to groups of doctors and nurses at the hospital where she worked.

A mild version of this fear had begun when she was 9 years old. Her father, who was the principal of her elementary school, would often put her on display in front of adults to read or recite poetry. On one occasion, while reciting in front of the school board, she forgot her lines. She became confused, recited the wrong lines, and was greatly embarrassed, but managed to collect herself and finish the recitation. After this, she was always afraid of such performances but did speak in front of the class. The fear was not severe enough to raise the question of therapy.

About a year before I saw her, Mrs. G. had accompanied her husband, a business executive, to a convention in a distant city. She had gone reluctantly, fearing his prominence would lead at some point to her being the center of attention. Despite his assurance that this would not happen, it did, and an enormous amount of anxiety was aroused in her. She was subsequently very much more fearful of any public performance and also afraid to speak to strangers or distant acquaintances on the telephone.

Case 7

This case illustrates that anxiety need not be conditioned to an external stimulus. In a physician whose sexual interest and arousability had always been confined to women, a fear of homosexuality was conditioned in the following way. While reading a description of homosexual behavior in a novel, he became aware of a spontaneous erection (which quite frequently happened to him without any discernible relation to thoughts or circumstances). However, the thought now crossed his mind, "Does the fact that this is happening right now mean that I am unconsciously homosexual?" This thought, based on psychoanalytic "knowledge," aroused great anxiety, and he thereafter had instant anxiety when seeing a homosexual or reading about one, or when making physical contact with any male, as when sitting beside one on a bus or plane, even though except for that one fleeting thought he never believed he was homosexual.

Vicarious Classical Conditioning of Fear

In the classical conditioning of fear discussed above, the fear source is a perceived threat to the subject. But it is also possible for the original fear to be produced by observing the fearfulness of another person. If great upset is produced by seeing someone else's severe fear, as shown by screaming or fainting, to a particular stimulus, fear may be classically conditioned to that stimulus. This corresponds to what Rachman (1977) has called "vicarious fear acquisition." Observational conditioning of fear has been convincingly demonstrated in animals. Miller, Murphy, and Mirsky (1957) described several experiments in which monkeys acquired a fear of snakes by observing a model monkey's fearfulness in the presence of a snake. Mineka et al. (1984) have shown that such acquisition depends on classical conditioning, since the observer monkey acquires the fear only to the extent that it is aroused to fear during the observations. Certain human fears may have the same basis. Solomon (1942) noted during World War II that children's fear of blackouts was directly related to the amount of fear displayed by their parents during blackout periods, and Grinker and Spiegel (1945a) reported cases of combat airmen whose fears originated from observing crewmates express intense fear of flying.

Cognitively Based Neurotic Fears

As stated above, many of our nonneurotic fears—that is, those that relate to real threats—are cognitively based; they have been acquired through information. Misinformation can also bring about fears that are as powerful and enduring as those based on truth. A man may fear masturbation because he has been led to believe that it will injure his health, and a woman may be afraid of sexual arousal because her mother has told her it is bestial or because she has gathered from religious teaching that to be excited by any man who is not actually her husband is a "mortal sin." People may fear worms, flying insects, doctors, or hospitals because they have observed a parent consistently show fear of these things. A woman I once encountered who had fears of many kinds of insects reported that she had two sisters with similar collections of fears. All of these had originated from seeing their mother become distraught every time she saw an insect.

Some wrong beliefs are based on erroneous inferences, rather than on wrong messages. A person who has a bizarre and unusual sensation may infer that his or her order personality is disintegrating.

Case 8

A 29-year-old married woman was afraid to venture out alone because she believed that her frequent attacks of dizziness and tingling of the hands were early signs of "going crazy." Because she had an aunt who had been in a mental hospital and two cousins who were "flaky," she had concluded that she was predisposed by heredity to mental instability. After I demonstrated to her that the dizziness and tingling were due to hyperventilation and then strongly assured her that there was no possibility of her going crazy, she rapidly lost her fearfulness. After seven sessions, she was able to go out comfortably on her own anywhere she wished. She was still well a year later.

Case 9

Not infrequently, the very contiguity of the feared object to the cognitively aroused fear of it leads to the development of classical conditioning of fear of the object. When that happens, adequate treatment requires both cognitive correction and emotional reconditioning.

A 31-year-old computer operator, who had for some time had intermittent showers of sparsely distributed rosy papules on her skin, one day chanced to read in a popular magazine that lupus erythematosus is characterized by rashes. She concluded that she had that dreaded disease and became profoundly anxious. After some months of ineffective insight therapy, she came to me. I sent her to a dermatologist who thoroughly convinced her that she did not have that illness. Nevertheless, whenever she actually saw some papules she still automatically had an anxiety response, which necessitated systematic desensitization.

Fear also spreads by classical conditioning from one inappropriate stimulus to another. For example, a woman with a fear of crowds would go to the movies only in the daytime when few people were present. One afternoon the moviehouse suddenly filled with students, which sent her into terror.

After that she was afraid not only of crowds, but of moviehouses, of restaurants, and of churches—in fact, of any public building, even when it was empty.

Case 10

Sometimes a patient's fear is found to have spread in several different ways.

Mrs. B., an excessively submissive young woman, often endured harsh criticism from her husband and began to dread his return from work. She tried to deal with the problem by working to improve herself so that she might avert his criticisms. Still, she would be gradually more tense when the time approached for him to arrive home, and became increasingly aware of physical symptoms—rapid heartbeat, clammy hands, faintness, and lightheadedness. She did not relate these to her husband but was frightened by them and consulted her physician. When the medication he prescribed failed to diminish her symptoms she decided that she "must be falling apart."

After about 4 months on the downward slope, when her husband was about to depart on a week-long business trip, Mrs. B. went to stay with her parents. Toward the end of the week, she visited a friend who was having a "nervous breakdown." Her friend looked exhausted and haggard, and Mrs. B. asked herself whether the same thing was happening to her. Dwelling on this idea, she became intensely anxious for the last 2 days at her parents' house. When she returned home, she immediately began to improve. But she could not visit her parents' house again because it had become a conditioned trigger to intense fear.

Mrs. B.'s fear had spread in the following steps: first, the fear of her husband's criticisms gave rise to symptoms that included lightheadedness. These symptoms were a further source of fear because they suggested some strange illness. This new fear was greatly intensified when she visited her friend, since she then connected her lightheadedness with the idea of having a "nervous breakdown," which it is quite reasonable to fear. Her preoccupation with this idea caused a continuous high level of anxiety while she was at her parents' house, so that she was afterward afraid of visiting them.

THE DISTRIBUTION OF
CLASSICALLY CONDITIONED
AND COGNITIVELY BASED FEARS

In order to get some idea of the distribution of classically conditioned and cognitively based neurotic fears, I asked an assistant to extract from my files the first 40 cases in which the central complaint was unadaptive fear. In each case, I first decided whether the fear was classically conditioned or cognitively based, and then whether its origin could be traced to single or multiple events. Twenty-six fears were found to be classically conditioned and 16 cognitively based. Both bases were manifest in two cases. The mean age of the subjects was 33.9 years; and the mean age at onset in those in whom it could be dated was 22.3 years. The data are presented in table 3.1 and summarized in table 3.2. As far as possible, similar cases are grouped together in table 3.1.

It is worth noting that only two cases had to be discarded because the precise circumstances of precipitation could not be determined. This is in keeping with the findings of Symonds (1943) on war neuroses, and those of Ost and Hugdahl (1981). Also, Lautch (1971) observed that every one of 34 cases with dental phobia recalled a traumatic dental experience, such as fear of suffocation by an anesthetic mask. These reports are all in sharp contrast to the inability of Marks (1969) to identify precipitating experiences.

Predisposing Factors

When a number of people are exposed to the same anxiety-arousing conditions, only some of them develop neurotic anxiety reactions. Clearly, then, individual differences are of great importance in the etiology of neuroses. Yet, little research has been devoted to their elucidation. The most extensive quantitative study is still that of Symonds (1943) on a consecutive series of 2,000 cases of war neuroses in Royal Air Force personnel. He found a history of stress in 99% of the cases and an inverse relationship between the amount of stress needed to precipitate the neurosis and the degree of preexisting emotional sensitivity.

A few specific facts point to factors that may determine predisposition. First, people differ greatly in innate emotional lability. Shirley (1933) found marked differences of this character in very young infants. It may be expected that an individual who is emotionally highly sensitive would have a greater intensity of anxiety aroused in him under given conditions than one who is relatively phlegmatic.

Second, preconditioning can increase sensitivity. If a stimulus contiguous with anxiety arousal has previously had some anxiety conditioned to it, it will reach a higher level of anxiety conditioning than would be found with a neutral stimulus, as is exemplified in case 6 above.

A third factor seems to be the presence or absence of anxiety-inhibiting stimuli. For example, children who are exposed to an alarming event, such as an air raid, are much less liable to be sensitized to related stimulus situations if they are with people, especially parents, whose effect is to inhibit anxiety (John, 1941). It may be that a person who has once received such support from his elders will also be less affected by later stress, but this remains to be investigated.

Information, or lack of information, is a fourth factor. Many patients report having experienced bizarre sensations at the onset of a neurosis; these led them to conclude that they were "falling apart" or going crazy. Such an experience can elicit secondary fears that are even more severe and disabling than the original ones. Unfortunately, when people consult their doctors about these strange feelings, they usually get very little help. Many a patient finds that "he did not know what I was talking about," and this naturally makes the experience seem unique, and therefore especially ominous.

It is quite likely that physiological factors also have a role in predisposing people to neurotic conditioning — fatigue, infections, drugs, and special conditions of consciousness, such as hypnagogic states. Properly designed studies of the relevance of such factors are very much to be desired.

In the case of cognitively based fears, lack of information obviously has an even more central role. It opens the door wide to the acceptance of anxiety-instilling misinformation. For example, a person who believes that her mother's health is endangered by any opposition is vulnerable to guilt reactions, that with repetition may become very severe.

THE EXPERIMENTAL MODEL OF NEUROTIC ANXIETY

The exploration of human illness is greatly facilitated if the same illness occurs in small animals. We who are involved in the treatment of neuroses have profited greatly from the fact that it is possible to induce longlasting maladaptive fears (phobias) in animals that are indistinguishable from those of humans when due allowance is made for species differences.

Experimental phobias have been a widely recognized phenomenon since they were first produced in Pavlov's laboratories at the turn of the century. They are essentially stimulus-bound states of autonomic hyperexcitability. The bizarreness of some of the manifestations led early experimenters to the erroneous conclusion that experimental phobias were the result of some kind of nervous damage. (For a comprehensive review, see Wolpe, 1952a, 1958). Experiments that I performed between 1946 and 1948 showed beyond any reasonable doubt that these phobias are conditioned anxiety reactions.

There are two basic methods for producing experimental neuroses, and both are dependent on the elicitation of unconditioned anxiety responses. The first is typified by Pavlov's (1927, p. 23a) circle-and-ellipse experiment. At the beginning of the experiment, a luminous circle was projected before a dog that was held in a harness on a table. The projected image was followed by a piece of food placed within easy reach of the animal, leading to the

Table 3.1. Breakdown of 40 Cases of Maladaptive Fear

| | SUBJECT | | FEAR BASIS | | | |
NATURE OF FEAR	PRESENT AGE	AGE AT ONSET	AUTONOMICALLY CONDITIONED	COGNITIVELY BASED	SINGLE-EVENT CAUSATION	MULTIPLE-EVENT CAUSATION
1 Death	31	7		X		X
2 Death	43	39		X	X	
3 Death	10	8	X			X
4 Death	14	8	X		X	
5 Death	46	3		X		X
6 Death and loss of control	39	11	X		X	
7 Being alone	30	29	X		X	
8 Being alone	31	Childhood	X			X
9 Being alone	29	23	X		X	
10 Being alone	26	20	X		X	
11 Being alone	47	24	X			X
12 Driving	45	41	X	X	X	
13 Driving	36	34		X	X	
14 Driving	41	30		X	X	
15 Driving	25	16				(Undetermined)
16 Public speaking	28	25	X		X	
17 Public speaking	39	21	X		X	
18 Public speaking	28	18		X	X	

	Age	Age				
19 Related to health	36	22		X		
20 Self-destruction	42	31	X	X		
21 Harming self	26	12	X		X	X
22 Blacking out	48	39	X	X		
23 Own blood	23	18	X	X		
24 People	31	11	X	X		X
25 Strange men	25	25	X	X		
26 Dentists	25	12	X	X		
27 Eye contact	30	8	X	X		
28 Automobiles	39	37	X	X		
29 Accidents	49	44	X	X		
30 Travel	36	25	X	X		
31 Agoraphobia	28	14	X		X	
32 Going to town	36	32	X		X	X
33 Flying	49	39	X	X	X	
34 Acrophobia	34	4	X		X	
35 Snakes	24	16	X		X	X
36 Mice	45	6	X	X		
37 Storms	58	Childhood			X	X
38 Examinations	22	20			X (Undetermined)	
39 Sexual inadequacy	25	20			X	X
40 War guilt	35	26	X	X	X	

Table 3.2. Analysis of Bases of 40 Neurotic Fears

AUTONOMICALLY CONDITIONED		COGNITIVELY BASED		
Single-event causation	Multiple-event causation	Single-event causation	Multiple-event causation	Undetermined
21	5	7	7	2

Note: The presence of both autonomic and cognitive bases in two cases brings the total to 42.

reinforcement of an alimentary (food-approach) response to the circle. After this, an ellipse with semi-axes in the ratio of 2 : 1 was interspersed among presentations of the circle, but was never followed by food. The result was that the ellipse became a food negative signal — one that elicited inhibition of food-seeking behavior. In subsequent sessions, the ellipse was made rounder in stages. At each rounder stage, the inhibitory power of the ellipse was solidified by interspersing its unreinforced presentations with reinforced presentations of the circle. But a point arrived at which the animal could no longer distinguish the positive and negative shapes. This happened when the ratio of the semi-axes was 9 : 8. The animal showed increasing agitation, which culminated in a state of severe disturbance. The disturbance was thereafter always triggered when the animal was merely put into the experimental chamber. (The induction of neuroses experimentally in children by means of difficult discriminations has been described by Krasnogorski [1925]).

The other basic method for producing experimental phobias is to apply to the spatially confined animal either a large number of weak electric shocks or a small number of strong ones. More than 40 years ago, numerous phobias were produced by weak stimulation at Cornell Animal Farm by Liddell and his associates (Anderson & Parmenter, 1941; Liddell, 1944) who worked with a variety of domestic animals. (For an explication of the subtleties of conditioning underlying the development of these phobias, see Wolpe, 1958, p. 63). Strong noxious stimulation was first used by Pavlov (1927) in dogs, and later by Masserman (1943) in an imaginative series of experiments on cats. Misled by certain features of their experimental arrangements, all these experimenters believed that the phobias and related neurotic reactions were due to conflict. Masserman, for example, ascribed his experimental neuroses to conflict between food-approach motivation and avoidance-of-shock motivation because the shock was inflicted on the animals when they were approaching food in response to a stimulus conditioned to feeding.

However, I demonstrated (1952a, 1958) that experimental neuroses also developed when shocks were administered in the experimental cage to animals that had never been fed there. A study by Smart (1965) revealed that there was very little difference on 16 measures of neurotic behavior between a *shock-only* group of cats and two *conflict* groups—one in which the animals were shocked while approaching food, and another in which they were shocked while eating in the experimental cage.

Smart's demonstration of the irrelevance of conflict controverted the theory that experimental phobias are based on conflict-induced neural damage or strain, removing any serious competition to the view that learning was their basis. Experimental phobias have the following features in common with other learned behavior:

1. The topography of the acquired response is similar to that observed in the precipitating situation.
2. The acquired response is elicited by stimuli that were present in the precipitating situation.
3. The response is also elicited by stimuli similar to those in the precipitating situation. They diminish in intensity as a function of diminishing resemblance, in accordance with the principle of primary stimulus generalization.

REBUTTAL OF RECENT CRITICISMS OF THE CONDITIONING THEORY OF EXPERIMENTAL NEUROSES

In recent years, the conditioning theory has repeatedly been criticized, but always, it appears, the critic has misread or misinterpreted the experimental facts. For example, Mineka and Kihlstrom (1978) propose that the basis of experimental neurosis is "awareness of unpredictability and uncontrollability" in the same way as in Seligman's "learned helplessness" experiments. However, they provide no facts to substantiate this theory. It can be entertained only if, with Mineka (1985), one disregards the facts demonstrating the potency and the central role of autonomic conditioning in animal phobias. For example, she states that in the conditioning experiments the animals were trained only to avoid the unconditioned stimulus. She plays down classically conditioned fears, by pronouncing *ex cathedra*, that in the laboratory they extinguish in a moderate number of trials "even when an intense unconditioned stimulus has been used." It is often true of fears of low or moderate intensity, but quite untrue of the fears of high intensity that characterize experimental neuroses (Appel, 1963; Gantt, 1944; Wolpe, 1952a).

Mineka's therapeutic experiments, which employ the flooding paradigm, contradict her statement that the central part of shock-based training is avoidance learning. She obtained motor extinction but it was later followed by relapse. The explanation, almost certainly, is that the flooding, as commonly happens, failed to extinguish the autonomic responses – about which, however, her experiment provides no data. Also contrary to the experimental literature is her statement (p. 220) that in the overcoming of animal phobias feeding has "a slight facilitatory effect." In my experiments described above and those earlier described by Masserman (1943), the effect was enormous, and it was also clearly evident in a controlled study by Poppen (1970). Mineka disregards these observations, and explains Masserman's therapeutic success as the result of the imposition of "environmental press" on the animals, totally missing the observation that anxiety diminished *only* when the procedure had the effect of making the animal eat. The occurrence of the competing response was a sine qua non for therapeutic change.

Mineka (1985) also gives an erroneous portrayal of the *therapeutic* data. Her statement that the reciprocal inhibition approach to anxiety reduction "has not fared well" will be disputed by a great many behavior therapists. She makes reference to studies that purport to dispute the value of muscle relaxation in desensitization – apparently unaware of Borkovec and Sides (1979) indispensable survey of therapeutic studies employing relaxation, which shows the inadequacy of the relaxation training in those studies. Borkovec and Sides found that whenever relaxation facilitated therapeutic change there had been a mean of 4.57 relaxation training sessions, in contrast to 2.3 sessions in studies in which it had not facilitated change. Of broader significance is the fact that numerous competing responses have been found effective in diminishing anxiety (see chapter 10).

The failure of Bregman (1934) and Hallam and Rachman (1976) to produce conditioned fears in the laboratory has been taken as evidence that classical conditioning is not often a cause of children's fears (e.g., Rachman, 1990, p. 176). But from a study of 50 cases, Kennedy (1971) concluded that "direct classical conditioning or pairing of a neutral object with an unconditioned stimulus is one means of acquiring a fear." Various factors, organismal and situational, play a part in determining whether a fear will be conditioned. Failure of conditioning under some conditions does not negate its success in others. Additional considerations supporting this have been advanced by Delprato and McGlynn (1984).

One clearly important matter is the level of fear the "unconditioned" stimulus must arouse to effect conditioning. Conditioning theory would directly relate the level of arousal to the ensuing magnitude of fear conditioning. This relationship, if confirmed, would dispose of one of Rachman's (1990) reservations about classical conditioning, which stems from his undue focus on strength of stimulation (see p. xii). It should also be noted that the causation of most maladaptive fears is based on second-order conditioning.

4
Principles of the Unlearning
of Neurotic Anxiety

Since, as noted in chapter 3, human anxiety response habits have two different bases — the classically conditioned and the cognitively based — it is hardly
surprising that different principles are involved in their unlearning. Some
systematic support for the dichotomy has been provided by Ost (1985). We
will first address the unlearning of cognitively based anxiety because the
principles here are few and simple, and there are far fewer technical variants
than in the case of classically conditioned anxiety.

UNLEARNING COGNITIVELY BASED ANXIETY
Retroactive Inhibition

Most unlearning of cognitive connections occurs through retroactive inhibition. Retroactive inhibition is defined as the diminution of the learned
response to a stimulus that occurs when a different response is made to
follow the stimulus. For example, if the articulation of a word is the learned
response to a particular stimulus and if thereafter another word is regularly
seen or heard when that stimulus appears, the tendency for the original
word to be evoked by the stimulus will be progressively weakened.

Because cognitively based anxiety depends on the belief that something
actually harmless is dangerous, treatment depends on unlearning that belief.
Thus, retroactive inhibition is the main process involved in the overcoming
of cognitively based maladaptive anxiety. Much more often than not, such
unlearning happens as a matter of common sense and without the therapist's
knowledge of its occurrence.

Retroactive inhibition has long been recognized as the basis for ordinary forgetting. Following the experimental paradigm established by Muller and Pilzecker (1900), Bunch and Winston (1936) showed that after A–B has been learned, the interpolation of A–C produces marked weakening of the A–B bond, in contrast with the interpolation of C–B. It was earlier found by McGeogh and McDonald (1931) and by Johnson (1933) that retroactive inhibition is greater the more closely the learned and the interpolated cues resemble each other in meaning; and Osgood (1946, 1948) noted that if the learned and interpolated cues are identical, interference with the A–B bond increases as the responses differ more in meaning. For a substantial review of this experimental work see Postman (1971).

When therapists have determined that the patient's inappropriate fears are based on misconceptions, they proceed to correct them. This means that they endeavor to replace the erroneous beliefs with facts. For example, a person who is anxious due to the belief that the attacks of dizziness being experienced are an early sign of insanity may be shown that they are in fact due to hyperventilation. When the demonstration is successful, the experience of dizziness ceases to give rise to the anxiety-eliciting idea of insanity, which is replaced by thoughts of the physiological consequences of hyperventilation. This is only a more complex example of the A–C sequence weakening A–B.

Direct Inhibition (Thought Stopping)

Thought stopping (Bain, 1928; Taylor, personal communication, 1955) is a way of dealing with anxiety-evoking thoughts, not by changing meanings but by training the patient to prevent the thoughts from entering his mind. The essence of thought stopping is to teach the patient to develop the habit of switching to another thought whenever the undesirable one threatens to intrude. The tendency to think the undesirable thought is thus directly inhibited. Through constant repetition, a habit of inhibiting the undesirable thought is built up.

The procedural details of cognitive methods are given in chapter 7.

UNLEARNING CLASSICALLY CONDITIONED NEUROTIC ANXIETY

As noted in chapter 3, neurotic anxiety is remarkable for its persistence, often continuing for years and even for life. Almost all other maladaptive behavior is extinguished by the consequences of its own evocation (see p. 17). Clearly, it is important to understand what special features of neurotic anxiety stand in the way of extinction.

More recent studies (e.g., Amsel, 1962, 1972; Gleitman, Nachmias, &

Neisser, 1954) have indicated that the weakening of a response following its nonreinforced evocation depends less on reactive inhibition than on the occurrence of frustration responses that compete with and inhibit that response. We therefore need to know under what circumstances other responses have a weakening effect on anxiety. It is logical to start with an instance in which competition is known without doubt to weaken anxiety — the treatment of experimental neuroses.

OVERCOMING EXPERIMENTAL NEUROSES BY COMPETITION OF FEEDING

Experimentally induced neurotic anxiety responses can reliably be weakened by systematically counterposing to them weak elicitations of an incompatible response. The following is a brief description of the main procedure applied to cats that had been made neurotic in the experiments described in chapter 3. (For fuller accounts see Wolpe, 1958, pp. 55–60; 1976c, pp. 44–80.)

I started from the observation that in all neurotic animals, eating in the experimental cage was inhibited. They would not eat even after 1 or 2 days' starvation. This inhibition was also found when the animals were in rooms that resembled the experimental room. An animal that had been starved for 24 hours would be offered food on the floor of these rooms in descending order of anxiety arousal until a room was found where anxiety was low enough not to prevent eating. The eating was at first delayed and constrained, but later offerings of food were accepted with increasing alacrity, while manifestations of anxiety diminished — eventually to zero. The animal would then accept food on the floor of the room next closer in appearance to the experimental laboratory — a room where it had previously refused to eat. There, too, successive feedings eliminated all signs of anxiety. The same routine was repeated in the other rooms, including eventually the experimental room and the interior of the experimental cage. About 200 pellets of meat had to be placed in the cage over several sessions to eliminate totally its ability to evoke anxiety.

An alternative method succeeded in a few animals. As they were accustomed to having food cast to them by the human hand in their living cages, it seemed likely that the hand had become a conditioned elicitor of approach responses to food. Accordingly, a neurotic animal was placed in the experimental cage and pellets of meat were moved toward its snout on the flat end of a rod held in the experimenter's hand in the hope that the presence of the hand would overcome the inhibition to eating. This technique succeeded in some animals. The animal at first approached the pellets hesitantly, sometimes accepting and sometimes refusing them, but after several pellets, it ate fairly freely from the rod, and soon also began to eat pellets on the floor of the cage. As more and more pellets were eaten, the animals moved about the cage with greater freedom, and showed decreasing anxiety symptoms. Insofar as the eating in this method was made possible by the introduction of an additional food-approach stimulus, we have a clear analogue for assertiveness training in which the therapist's exhortations added to the patient's already present anger, increase the propulsion to assertive acts (chapter 8).

When all conditioned visual stimuli had lost their anxiety-evoking power, the sounding of the auditory stimulus that had preceded the shocks still elicited a high degree of anxiety, not having been included in the therapeutic procedures. One way of overcoming the anxiety due to auditory conditioning made use of auditory intensity as a function of distance. It was necessary to determine by trial and error the closest distance at which an animal would eat while the auditory stimulus (usually a buzzer) sounded continuously. In one animal the distance was found to be 40 feet. Here, with dilated pupils and other signs of distress, it gulped down eight pellets, but would not eat at a distance of 30 feet. The next day, after two pellets at 40 feet, the animal ate 10 at 30 feet. The distance was reduced day by day. After consuming a total of 160 pellets at progressively decreasing distances, he was able to eat two feet away from the buzzer, but at first with considerable anxiety. Four sessions at two feet away, to a total of 87 pellets, removed all evidence of avoidance or anxiety. Regardless of the procedure employed, the question was whether the neurotic reactions had really been eliminated or were merely displaced by a more strongly conditioned feeding reaction. The decisive experiment was to extinguish the food-seeking response to the auditory stimulus and then observe whether the neurotic reactions were reinstated. Each animal was given 30 irregularly massed extinction trials on each of three successive days. Long before the end of the third day's session they all showed complete indifference to the auditory stimulus. At the conclusion of the third day's session the following test was made: a pellet was dropped on the floor of the experimental cage about two feet away from the animal, and as he began to approach it, the auditory signal was sounded continuously to determine whether extinction of eating had reinstated the anxiety. In no instance was there any semblance of the restoration of anxiety responses or any inhibition of eating.

This puts us in a position to understand why neurotic anxiety is so resistant to extinction. The experiments showed that when anxiety is weak enough to permit an animal to eat in the presence of anxiety-evoking stimulation, the anxiety becomes progressively weaker. By contrast, if the anxiety is strong enough to inhibit feeding, no beneficial change occurs and, under certain circumstances, the anxiety spreads to contiguous new stimuli. It seems that when anxiety is intense it inhibits the evocation of almost any other response.

By contrast, low-intensity anxiety can be inhibited and can have its habit strength reduced through the competition of low-level excitation. For example, in an experiment performed by Berkun (1957), rats that were mildly anxious in an alley lost their anxiety after repeatedly running in the same alley (in some cases at first in a somewhat different alley), even without any food reinforcement. It is apparently because they are of low intensity that most laboratory-induced conditioned emotional responses do undergo extinction (Black, 1958). In the same way, human phobias that are relatively weak, most notably many of those of children, fade away seemingly spontaneously. As research on ordinary forgetting attests, time alone does not make learned responses fade. We may confidently postulate that such change is the result of competing responses occurring in daily life.

On the other hand, there has in recent years been much evidence that prolonged evocation of anxiety at relatively high intensities often results in the weakening of anxiety response habits. The basis of this occurrence is discussed in chapter 11. It is worth noting, however, that in experimental contexts the autonomic extinction is often far from complete (e.g., Mineka, 1984). The same applies clinically, despite sweeping generalizations to the contrary; for example, Agras (1985), a strong proponent of this method, states that of patients so treated, few fully recover.

The Reciprocal Inhibition Mechanism in the Elimination of Anxiety

We saw that strong evocations of anxiety were associated with inhibition of eating in food-deprived neurotic cats. By contrast, eating took place when anxiety was relatively weak, and repeated eating resulted in manifest diminutions of the anxiety. A reciprocally inhibitory relationship between the two responses was thus apparent, and it seemed that each inhibition of anxiety resulted in a measure of lasting inhibition — that is, conditioned inhibition. The specific role of feeding in weakening fear responses in experimental animals has also been shown by Gale, Sturmfels, and Gale (1966), and Poppen (1970).

The success of feeding as a reciprocal inhibitor of anxiety in the neuroses of animals led to a search for responses that might be similarly employed in humans. Feeding is effective only in children (Jones, 1924a), but a score of other anxiety-competitive responses have been found useful, as described in later chapters. In addition, the naturally occurring emotional responses of daily life provide an intelligible explanation for the so-called spontaneous cure of fears, observed especially commonly in children (Macfarland, Allan, & Honzek, 1954).

The recent tendency to disparage reciprocal inhibition as a basis for therapeutic change (e.g., Franks & Wilson, 1979; Goldfried, 1980) makes it necessary to redirect attention to its widespread role in the function of the nervous system. Sherrington (1906) was the first to demonstrate that the reflex excitation of a group of muscles is automatically coupled with the inhibition of antagonistic groups. Since that discovery, reciprocal innervation has been found to be constantly at work at all levels and modalities of nervous function (Gellhorn, 1967). Pavlov noted that the first response of a dog to an unfamiliar bell is to make listening movements — to turn its head in the direction of the bell and prick up its ears — but when the bell is repeatedly followed by food, the dog comes to respond to it by food-approach movements, and the listening movements correspondingly fade out. The role of reciprocal inhibition in complex human learning first appeared in research on verbal forgetting (Ebbinghaus, 1913).

Inhibitory conditioning of antagonistic responses is also part and parcel of the conditioning of operants. Consider an animal that has developed the habit of turning right in an alley because that response has been consistently followed by food. The right-turn habit will weaken if one stops delivering food after right turning, but it will weaken more rapidly if one then rewards left turning at that juncture. Presumably, with each left turn there is an inhibition of the right-turn tendency, which results in its being extinguished in conjunction with the new habit's being reinforced.

In recent years, reciprocal inhibition has been studied in new contexts. For example, in the study of behavioral contrast, the reinforcement of one response has been found to have an excitatory effect upon that response, but also an inhibitory one upon another response (Catania, 1963, 1969, 1973). Similarly, the punishment of a response has an inhibitory effect upon that response, and also an excitatory effect on a second response (Deluty, 1976). A number of quantitative models of conditioning (e.g., Herrnstein, 1970; Wagner & Rescora, 1972) have assumed the principle of reciprocal inhibition, although the authors do not use the term *reciprocal inhibition*. For a discussion of these models and their shared assumption of reciprocal inhibition, see Deluty (1977).

In the therapeutic context, the operation of reciprocal inhibition is not confined to anxiety-response habits. It has a vital role in overcoming unadaptive cognitive habits as in Leuret's (1846) case described on p. 5. It is also the basis of the conditioned inhibition of obsessional and compulsive habits by aversive therapy (p. 258). A painful faradic shock, or other strong stimulus, inhibits the undesirable behavior, with the result that a measure of conditioned inhibition of the latter is established. Again, in the process of replacing an undesirable motor habit by a more effective one, the evocation of the new motor response involves an inhibition of the old. For example, when assertive behavior is being instigated, at the same time that the expression of positive feelings reciprocally inhibits anxiety, a new pattern of motor action inhibits the preexisting defensive motor-response pattern. To take a nontherapy example, if one is learning to play a backhand tennis stroke by rotating on the right foot, each correct execution inhibits and diminishes the old inefficient habit of playing off the left foot.

In discussing how active inhibition of a response is necessary to weaken a habit of response, we have considered the instances of fatigue-associated inhibition (reactive inhibition) and inhibition by competing responses (reciprocal inhibition). I shall now draw attention to some other ways of inhibiting anxiety that have the same result.

Intraresponse Reciprocal Inhibition

Competition can occur between the elements within a complex response, so that one element is strengthened and becomes dominant under one set of circumstances while another is weakened, and under opposite circumstances the reverse is the case. Freeman and Pathman (1942) and Haggard and Freeman (1941) long ago reported that motor responses diminished anxiety, an observation confirmed more recently by Rauter and Braud (1969). Mowrer and Viek (1948) showed that conditioned anxiety gradually decreased if, in animals that were repeatedly shocked in a rectangular cage, the shock was consistently terminated when the animal jumped into the air, while greater and more persistent anxiety developed in "experimental twins" who received exactly the same duration of shock that was each time terminated without reference to what they were doing. In the group in which the jumping response was consistently reinforced, that response became progressively stronger. Presumably, upon attaining a certain strength, it produced inhibition and consequent weakening of the concurrent autonomic response. In the "twins," no particular response was reinforced because a different one would be going on each time the shock ended.

Therapeutic application of this idea has so far been made to only a very small number of patients. Once the patient has signaled that he clearly imagines a slightly disturbing situation, the therapist delivers a rather mild faradic shock to the forearm, stopping it when the patient briskly flexes his forearm. In the successful treatment of a particularly severe case of agoraphobia, about 20 forearm flexions were usually needed to reduce the anxiety response to a particular scene to zero (Wolpe, 1958, pp. 174–180).

External Inhibition

Experimenting with mild electrical stimuli on the basis of the published account of the foregoing case of agoraphobia, Philpott (1964) noted that by repeatedly administering weak galvanic stimuli to a patient's forearm, he could often progressively decrease pervasive (free-floating) anxiety. Similarly, if a patient is asked to imagine a scene from a hierarchy (as in systematic desensitization), and if during the scene, two or three weak galvanic stimuli are delivered to his forearm, the anxiety-arousing effect of the scene may noticeably decrease with repetition. As a general rule, it takes between 10 and 30 presentations of a scene to reduce its anxiety-arousing effect to zero. There are some patients in whom very weak stimuli are ineffective, but in whom, if the stimulation is judiciously increased — sometimes to the extent of inducing local muscular contraction — the desired decrements of anxiety are obtained.

The mechanism by which this procedure produces change is seemingly conditioned inhibition based upon external inhibition. If this supposition is correct, then stimuli from other modalities should also be usable in this way for therapeutic purposes. A special virtue of electrical stimulation is the ease with which its strength and duration can be controlled.

Directly Conditioned Inhibition

It has been shown in a variety of contexts that the consistent presentation of a stimulus at each cessation of a response may lead to that stimulus becoming conditioned to the negative of that response. Zbrozyna (1957) conditioned an auditory stimulus to be an inhibitor of eating in this way. Similarly, there are experiments suggesting that a stimulus that coincides with the termination of a noxious stimulus acquires anxiety-inhibiting effects (Coppock, 1951; Goodson & Brownstein, 1955). Many years ago, I investigated the possibility of exploiting these observations clinically in a few patients. I applied a moderately painful faradic shock continuously to the forearm of the patient, who had been told that I would switch it off as soon as he said the word "calm." However, he was to try to bear it for at least 20 seconds. In some individuals the word became conditioned to an anxiety-inhibiting response, so that uttering, or even thinking, "calm" in anxiety-arousing situations produced a decrease of anxiety (Wolpe, 1958, p. 181). This technique was called "anxiety-relief conditioning." In some cases, the systematic use of a word to which anxiety relief has been conditioned has the effect of gradually building a conditioned inhibition of anxiety to the stimulus situations involved. In an electroencephalographic study, Sommer-Smith et al. (1962) demonstrated that schedules of this type produce conditioned inhibition of the characteristic responses to noxious stimulation.

Conditioned Inhibition Based
on Transmarginal Inhibition

If a conditioned stimulus is administered to an animal at increasing intensities, it is usually found that the strength of the response increases until it reaches an asymptote — that is, it remains at its top level no matter how much stronger the stimulus is made. But in some circumstances, after the response has reached a maximum strength, its evocation paradoxically becomes weaker and weaker as the intensity of stimulation is increased. Pavlov (1927) called this kind of inhibition of response "transmarginal inhibition" or "protective inhibition." Gray (1964, p. 173), summarizing recent work in Russia by Rozhdestvenskaya (1959), redefined the phenomenon by saying that when the threshold of transmarginal inhibition is passed, response magnitude diminishes progressively as stimulation continues to increase in intensity.

The phenomenon has obvious possibilities as an explanation of the effects of flooding (see chapter 11). Unfortunately, almost no research has been done on the lasting effects of transmarginal inhibition on habit strength. However, a fact that favors this explanation is that its beneficial effects clearly depend on insistent and prolonged exposure to the anxiety-evoking stimulation.

It is clear from the foregoing that there are several ways in which anxiety can undergo inhibition, and in respect of most of them, there is evidence that the inhibition is followed by diminution and even extinction of anxiety-response habits. Nobody appears ever to have been able to show that classically conditioned anxiety habits can be weakened without the occurrence of such inhibition.

CRITIQUE OF OTHER THEORIES OF ELIMINATION OF CLASSICALLY CONDITIONED ANXIETY

Nevertheless, several rival theories claim to explain how anxiety is weakened by therapy. These theories invoke extinction, habituation, exposure, changed expectancy, and raised self-efficacy. All are inadequate, as will be shown below.

Extinction

Extinction, broadly discussed in chapter 2, is the name for the procedure to weaken a conditioned response by repeatedly evoking it without following it by reinforcement. It is the standard method for bringing about the decline and elimination of conditioned responses. With respect to neurotic fears, the original protagonist of extinction was Malleson (1959). He was followed by Stampfl and Levis and their collaborators (Levis & Boyd, 1979; Levis & Hare, 1977; Stampfl & Levis, 1967) and later by Eysenck (1976, 1979). According to them, the weakening of maladaptive anxiety response results from presenting the conditioned stimulus alone. This is a defensible proposition in some cases — for example, where lasting decrease of anxiety follows prolonged exposure to relatively strong anxiety-evoking stimulation. But weakening of anxiety responses does not always result from exposure to CS alone. It never seems to do so in animal neuroses, and it often does not in human neuroses. Clearly, then, some other factor or factors must account for the inconstancy of weakening in relation to CS alone.

Eysenck (1976, 1979) argues that there are circumstances in which repeated presentations of the conditioned stimulus alone result in enhancement of anxiety. This happens both experimentally (Napalkov, 1963); and clinically (Campbell, Sanderson, & Laverty, 1964; Wolpe, 1958, p. 99). Eysenck (1976, 1979) explains it by postulating that in the special case of nociceptive conditioning, the conditioned response acquires part of the character of the unconditioned response — in contrast to all other conditionings. He contends that this is because conditioned anxiety is "painful." While all anxiety is painful in the sense that it is unpleasant, the physical pain of the unconditioned stimulus (which Eysenck implies) is not present. Eysenck provides no evidence for supposing the presence of a fraction of the unconditioned response that is not present in the evocation of other conditioned responses. The only support to which he points is in the build-up of strong conditioned anxiety responses on the basis of weak unconditioned responses (Liddell, 1944) and the conditioned phenomena that follow repeated daily narcotic injections. But neither of these examples is valid, since unconditioned responses are involved in both.

The truth is that the increments of anxiety responding that may follow presentations of a conditioned stimulus to anxiety are easily explained without resorting to the artifactual assumptions of Eysenck. The increments of conditioned anxiety noted by Liddell (1944) when he used weak electrical stimuli were explained by Wolpe (1958, p. 63) as based on the summation of anxiety from unconditioned and conditioned sources. Increasing levels of anxiety are summated, and these eventually greatly exceed the level due to the unconditioned stimulus alone.

Absent from the accounts of Stampfl and Levis and of Eysenck is any mechanism for extinction. Eysenck points out that response enhancement is more likely when the anxiety is strongly and briefly elicited. But this, though true, is not seen in the frame of a model. The key question concerns what happens in the topography of arousal to make the difference between the strengthening and the weakening of a habit. Nothing is offered that parallels in substance the answer proposed in terms of response competition (pp. 42–44).

Habituation

Lader and Wing (1966) proposed that the anxiety-response decrements obtained by systematic desensitization were better explained by habituation than by reciprocal inhibition. Their theory was subsequently elaborated by

Lader and Mathews (1968). Habituation is defined as the diminution of the response to a stimulus when the stimulus is repeatedly presented. This definition is indistinguishable from that of extinction. Contrarily, as Evans (1973) observed, in the experimental phenomenon called habituation, the response that has disappeared reappears after rest or stimulus change (Sokolov, 1963).

These considerations should suffice to dispose of the habituation theory. Attempts have been made, however, to argue for some kind of deep down difference from extinction. Gray (1976) has claimed to be able to set apart from other stimuli "novel stimuli that elicit orienting responses and stimuli that have been paired with punishing stimuli and arouse anxiety." They are supposedly unique in their ability to inhibit ongoing behavior and to increase arousal. Even if one could accept that they were distinctive in this way, it would not justify the inference that repetition acts on them by a process that is different from whatever effectuates ordinary extinction.

A still more complicated proposal is the dual-process habituation theory of Groves and Thompson (1970). This postulates that observable response decrement is the summation of two inferred processes: habituation and sensitization. Such speculations do not create a viable separation of habituation from extinction in their common meanings. The reader who is interested in the ins and outs of habituation theory should consult a scholarly review by Watts (1979).

Exposure

Exposure to the fearful stimulus has been vigorously promoted by Marks (1969, 1975, 1976, 1981) and Agras (1985) as the basis of psychotherapeutically induced diminution of anxiety. The result of the exposure is that the patient becomes accustomed to the stimulus, by a process they do not specify. Since, as every psychologist knows, all classical conditioning and deconditioning necessarily involves the organism's exposure to the conditioned stimulus, to say that one is using exposure is to say nothing noteworthy unless one indicates what else is happening to strengthen or weaken the habit. Marks recognizes that not all exposure is therapeutic, and that sometimes sensitization is its result, but he has no explanation for this, either.

In the ordinary course of a patient's life, repeated exposure to maladaptive anxiety-evoking stimuli has not weakened the anxiety, since clearly the conditions for weakening have not been present. The anxiety *could* be weakened by various procedures such as systematic desensitization, the basis of which is response competition. Marks and Agras have disputed this conclusion on the basis of various experiments, but all of these are flawed in different ways. For example, Benjamin, Marks, and Huson (1972) found no difference between desensitization with and without relaxation, but their relaxation patients had received only one session of relaxation training.

Borkovec and Sides (1979), in a survey of therapeutic studies, found that for relaxation to make a significant therapeutic difference there must be at least four training sessions. But it is important to remember that the emotional response to the therapist is also a source of response competition (see chapter 17) that must be taken into account in interpretations of therapeutic effects.

It is noteworthy that Agras (1985), after a number of experiments that led him to reject other mechanisms of fear reduction, reached the conclusion that the only thing that works is exposure. Yet, of his patients so treated "few had fully recovered." This being so, exposure therapy can scarcely be called an advance, when compared with the 88 patients treated by reciprocal inhibition (Wolpe 1958, p. 216), of whom 28 were apparently cured and another 50 much improved.

Expectancy

Kazdin and Wilcoxon (1976) proposed that the basis of anxiety reduction was changed expectancy, but proffered no evidence that expectancy per se is ever therapeutically beneficial. They based their proposition on Rosenthal and Frank's (1958) statement that behavior change can be "due to faith in the efficacy of the therapist and his or her techniques." But Rosenthal and Frank did not provide any supporting evidence, either. Kazdin and Wilcoxon surveyed a number of experiments that were meant to examine the role of expectancy in successful systematic desensitization. These did not on the whole show expectancy to be much of a factor.

The expectancy theory of psychotherapeutic change has recently been more assertively promoted by Kirsch (1978) and Reiss (1980). Reiss's position has been presented in detail by Reiss and McNally (1985). A neutral stimulus, having arisen in temporal contiguity with an aversive stimulus, becomes a conditioned stimulus to acquired fear. Subsequently, fear is aroused by the conditioned stimulus, and when the subject has experienced the sequence several times, he or she expects the conditioned stimulus to be followed by fear. (The expectancy depends, however, on an association which would be broken by deconditioning the fear.) The authors state, quite correctly, that some fears are based, not on classical conditioning, but on various kinds of cognitive learning. These are reducible by cognitive relearning (see chapter 7), which can often be said to imply changing expectations. Not content with this, Reiss and McNally argue that all fears, including those that are classically conditioned, are reducible by changing expectations. This would need to be demonstrated, but is not. They claim to find support in a study by Kirsch, Tennen, Wickless, Saccone, and Cody (1983) that compared the effects on snake phobias of systematic desensitization, systematic ventilation, and waiting list control. Although systematic ventilation is described as a credible expectancy modification procedure, it is difficult to see with what justification. It actually consists of having the patient relive childhood experiences, and this might well produce emotional competition as emotive imagery does. The effects of the treatments were similar. Comparative outcome studies like this, are, in toto, almost meaningless, since they do not separate classically conditioned and cognitively based cases, and do not take into account the nonspecific therapist effect (transference).

The weakness of the expectancy theory is that in relation to classically conditioned fears it watches the hole instead of the doughnut—the expectancy instead of the fear habit that is its basis.

Raised Expectations of Self-efficacy

Raised expectations of self-efficacy is a more elaborate form of expectancy theory. According to Bandura (1977), treatments that succeed in eliminating neurotic anxiety do so not by directly weakening anxiety-response habits but through the mediation of expectations of self-efficacy. This proposition must obviously be true of fears that are based on low coping expectations, such as certain fears of public speaking. But Bandura's contention is that it is true of all fears—that in effect there are no classically conditioned fears, no fears that are automatic responses to a particular perception. This conclusion is difficult to support in the face of both experimental and clinical data. For example, how could self-efficacy be relevant to the fear aroused by a bloodstained bandage, by a dead bird in a glass case, or by the patient's own tachycardia? "Coping" is not relevant to the reality of such instances. It is only possible not to see this if one is unshakably convinced that to feel fear implies awareness of a threat to be coped with.

Bandura derived his theory of psychotherapeutic change from observations in experiments in which phobic subjects were treated by having them observe fearless models (Bandura, Blanchard, & Ritter, 1969; Bandura, Grusec, & Menlove, 1967). The most pertinent findings were as follows: in subjects with persistent behavioral patterns of fear of avoidance—for example, of harmless snakes—the repeated experience of observing a film of a person who is fearless of snakes (which is called "symbolic modeling") was about as effective as systematic desensitization. In another form of treatment, called "modeling with guided participation," the subject, after watching the therapist handle snakes, was aided by him to make progressively closer approaches to them. This method was significantly more successful than the other two treatments. Bandura's (1977) explanation is that seeing others perform threatening activities without adverse consequences generates expectations in observers that they, too, will improve if they intensify and persist in their efforts.

This explanation has outward plausibility, but careful scrutiny reveals two major flaws: (a) Bandura assumes that the fears of his subjects all have the same basis, being apparently unaware of the dichotomy between classically conditioned and cognitively based fear (see chapter 5). Though the symbolic modeling and systematic desensitization treatments achieved similar results, each was probably effective in different subjects. Symbolic modeling provides corrective information about harmless snakes; systematic desensitization provides little or no information but accomplishes reconditioning of classically conditioned fears. Thus, if Bandura's experimental populations contained, in more or less equal numbers, subjects who believed snakes to be dangerous, and subjects with classically conditioned fear of them, the two treatments would have fared about equally well (as they did). (b) Bandura fails to note that more than modeling goes on in modeling treatment. Reduction of conditioned anxiety would occur in some subjects receiving symbolic modeling based on the interpersonal anxiety-inhibiting impact of the therapist (chapter 17).

Participant modeling treatment is the most effective of the three because it conveys even more information than symbolic modeling, and it also contains elements that might actively decondition conditioned anxiety. The subject interacts more closely with the experimenter, a condition that would augment the interpersonal anxiety-inhibiting effect. Then, in its systematic gradual approach to the snake, participant modeling has all the ingredients of *in vivo* desensitization, with these same interpersonal emotional responses acting as the counterconditioning agent.

In summary, Bandura's experiments do not provide the supposed support for his theory. They should be rerun with groups that have been subdivided by skilled behavior analyses. A later experiment (Bandura & Adams, 1977) purporting to show that systematic desensitization works by raising self-efficacy is subject to the same criticism (Wolpe, 1978b).

Meanwhile, we must also look at the self-efficacy theory of psychotherapy more broadly. The following statement (Bandura, 1977, p. 194) expresses its essence:

> People fear and tend to avoid threatening situations they believe exceed their coping skills, whereas they get involved in activities and behave assuredly when they judge themselves capable of handling situations that would otherwise be intimidating.

The phrase to note is "coping skills." A skill always involves motor performance, whether it is sawing logs or rebutting arguments. People certainly do avoid situations that exceed their skills, often and wisely. People who avoid threatening situations do not usually do so because they lack performance skills. They usually have the motor capacity to enter the situations and become involved in activities. It is fear that prevents the activities. When a person does act in spite of his fear—does force himself (for business reasons, say) to fly, when he fears flying—then he is enduring the fear, and it could be said that, in a sense, he is coping with it. As long as the fear of flying is felt, however, a therapeutic problem remains. Only when the person can fly without fear can the problem be said to have been resolved.

And this is what psychotherapy should achieve—the elimination of the fears that cause the disabilities. Increases in self-efficacy expectations should and will follow fear diminution. (For a detailed critique of Bandura's theory, see Wolpe, 1978b.)

At a more fundamental level of analysis, Smedlund (1978a, 1978b) has observed that expectations of self-efficacy are intrinsically related to coping skills. The relationship is of the same logical type as "all normal elephants have trunks," when having a trunk is part of the definition of a normal elephant. Relationships that are definitional are not appropriate subject matter for empirical testing.

A trenchant analysis of the self-efficacy concept by Lee (1989) leads to the conclusion that while it has a certain amount of predictive and descriptive value, its ability to explain human behavior is largely illusory. It postulates that behavior arises from interactions between vaguely defined, unobservable variables. Therefore, it cannot generate unambiguous predictions; and it is impervious to scientific testing.

PART II

CASE ANALYSIS AND THERAPEUTIC GROUNDWORK

5
Behavior Analysis: The Study of Case Dynamics

Objectivity, empathy, and sensitivity to suffering are intrinsic to the behavior therapist's approach to his patients. The objectivity follows from the knowledge that all behavior, including cognitive behavior, is subject to causal determination no less than is the behavior of falling bodies or magnetic fields. The person is a composite of physical endowment and the effects of experience. Attitudes, thoughts, verbal behavior, and emotional behavior have all been shaped by interactions with the environment. To have had experiences that resulted in the learning of maladaptive habits is the patient's misfortune. Realizing this, the behavior therapist is sympathetic and supportive. He goes out of his way to dislodge any self-blame that may have been engendered by social conditioning or by the pronouncements of friends or previous therapists. To explain how the patient's neurosis arose out of a combination or chain of particular events helps understanding.

Behavior analysis is the process of gathering and sifting information for use in the conduct of behavior therapy. It is always necessary at the outset to be satisfied that the patient's complaints do not have an organic basis; if the problem does have an organic cause, behavior therapy is not likely to be appropriate. A psychosis or any other organic illness calls for a biological form of treatment. An indicator of organic illness is the occurrence of episodic attacks to which no constant stimulus antecedents can be attached. Common organic causes of anxiety are paroxysmal tachycardia, hypoglycemia, including relative hypoglycemia (Salzer, 1966), and hyperthyroidism.

The vast majority of patients who find their way into the behavior therapist's office do in fact have problems that are attributable to learning, and the bulk of these problems are neurotic — based on maladaptive anxiety. The patient's presenting complaint may feature maladaptive anxiety, or may consist of its secondary effects. The anxiety has been established by learning, and the therapeutic aim is to effect its unlearning. A necessary preliminary is the accurate pinpointing of the stimuli that are its triggers.

People are infinitely varied, and so are their complaints and the ways in which these are tied to stimulus conditions. These relationships constitute the dynamic structure of the case. That is why it is important for the therapist to be able to question probingly, and if necessary to repeat questions in different ways in order to establish particulars beyond reasonable doubt. The way to develop this ability is through supervised work with patients. Formulas and schedules for behavior therapy assessment (Mash & Terdal, 1976) can be helpful, but they can never suffice. The characteristic mode of procedure is described and exemplified below.

BEHAVIOR ANALYSIS PROCEDURE

Having obtained from the patient such personal details as name, address, telephone number, age, and occupation, the therapist proceeds to explore the patient's fears and other complaints. The circumstances surrounding the onset of each of these are meticulously examined in order to obtain a coherent picture of its determinants. It is necessary to identify not only the circumstances of the origin of a fear but also how it may have been modified by later events, including its possible transfer to other stimuli, by second-order conditioning or by cognitive generalization.

This historical information provides a background for subsequent steps designed to reveal the dynamic structure of the case. It can provide important clues to the maladaptive stimulus-response connections that are currently operative. To loosen these connections will be the chief function of therapy. The most careful scrutiny will therefore be given to their makeup. If, for example, the patient is anxious in social situations, it is necessary to find out exactly what aspects of these situations upset him or her. Perhaps the patient has a conditioned anxiety reaction to being looked at. Then, with what factors does it vary? Possible controlling factors are the number of people looking at the patient, the degree of speaking-performance-demand that the situation seems to hold, or a feeling of not being able to get away. The correct identification of the stimulus antecedents of reactions is indispensable to effective behavior therapy. It depends mainly on the questioning of which cases 12, 13, and 14 provide examples. A list of consequences of anxiety is given in table 1.1.

It is easy to be led astray either by the patient's assumptions or by one's own too facile interpretations. For example, one patient attributed her severely disabling anxieties to the anesthesia for an operation she had undergone. Close questioning revealed that social stresses were their true cause and that the anesthetic was irrelevant. The two etiologies pointed to two totally different treatment strategies. The following is an example of therapists' countertherapeutic prepossessions.

Case 11

A man's fear of symptoms had started after an occasion when he had felt an insufferably strong urge to defecate while driving through a suburban area. He had stopped at a house where his request to use the toilet had been granted. On resuming his journey, he felt very tense and became aware of rapid heartbeat and tremor, which led him to think that some bodily damage might have resulted from his severe stress. Thus began a chronic cycle of symptoms and fears. A succession of treatments, including one that was behaviorally oriented, focused on the physiological events but yielded little benefit. Only several years later, when he came to the Behavior Therapy Unit, was a detailed analysis made of the precipitating event. This revealed that the cause of the man's great emotional upset was his embarrassment at having to ask for the use of a toilet. The overcoming of social anxiety thus emerged as the indispensable goal of treatment. The physiological responses were secondary.

The task of stimulus-response analysis is further complicated when there is a presenting complaint other than anxiety — for example, a stutter, a compulsion, or a psychosomatic illness. In asthma and other presumed psychosomatic conditions, a purely organic etiology is common. It is only in some predisposed individuals that the reactions are consequences of neurotic anxiety responses (see chapter 15). We need to know how the anxiety is related to the stutter, the compulsion, or the asthmatic attack. Usually the relationship is clear and straightforward. For example, a stutter may be found to increase as a function of the intensity of felt anxiety, which in turn depends upon features of the audience — their strangeness, their number, and their demeanor. But sometimes it is difficult to detect the relationship between the emotional upset and the psychosomatic reaction. I once treated a man with asthma whose attacks took place regularly 4 hours after a stressful event. This became apparent only after the patient had kept an hour-by-hour diary for several weeks.

One of the first decisions to make about any fear is whether it is based on classical conditioning or on misinformation (see chapter 3). With reference to figure 5.1, consider a person who has a fear of harmless snakes. When a snake (S_1) comes into his line of vision, it produces the neural effects that yield a perception (image) of the snake (rS_1). The consequence of this is to excite the efferent processes as shown as ra that elicit anxiety and avoidance of the animal (R_a). There are two pathways through which rS_1 may lead to

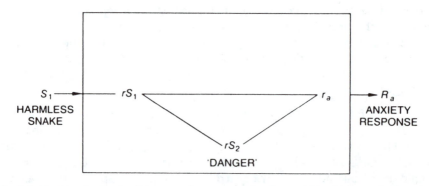

Fig. 5.1. The harmless snake (S_1) causes the perceptual response (rS_1) which may lead to the molecular responses for anxiety (r_a) either immediately or through the intermediary of the idea of "danger" (rS_2). (Courtesy of Graphic Communications, Eastern Pennyslvania Psychiatric Institute, Philadelphia.)

R_a. One possibility is that, if the person believes that all snakes are dangerous, the perception of the snake will evoke the idea of danger or death (rS_2). Eliminating this anxiety response habit entails breaking the connection between rS_1 and rS_2, which means dislodging that (incorrect) belief.

The other possibility is that the perception (rS_1), immediately and without any further cognitive mediation, evokes the anxiety response. The fear is based on conditioning. In that case, cognitive correction is irrelevant since there is no wrong idea to dislodge. Deconditioning is necessary. Sometimes, however, the patient has both a misconception of the implications of the perceived object and an automatic, nonrational anxiety response to it, as exemplified by case 9 (p. 32), a woman who greatly feared eruptions of red pimples on her neck and shoulders, because she had come to believe that they signified lupus erythematosus. Her fear was greatly lessened when the misconception was overcome with the help of a dermatologist, but she continued to have anxiety whenever the macules appeared, and this anxiety had to be treated by systematic desensitization.

BACKGROUND HISTORY

After the patient's presenting problems have been investigated, the therapist obtains the basic facts about his or her past and present life. First to be covered is early family life about which the patient is asked a number of questions: How many siblings do you have? What are their ages? Are your parents alive, or how and when did they die? What kind of person was your father? Did he show personal interest, did he punish, and if so, moderately and justly? The same questions are asked about the mother. Then there are other questions about the family: How did your parents get along with each other? Were there any other important adults in your early home life? Who were they and what was their influence on you? How did you relate to your siblings? How important has religion been early on and now? Did you have any childhood fears and what became of them?

Next to be explored is the patient's education: Did you enjoy school? If so, what did you like about it; if not, why not? How well did you do academically? Did you make friends and, in particular, close friends? Were there any people, either among teachers or students, whom you feared or disliked especially? At what age did you leave school? Did you graduate from high school? What did you do next—go to work or continue your studies at a university or other institution? How did you get on academically and socially? What is your occupational history, in terms of function, satisfaction, and social interaction? How do you get along with employers, underlings, and peers? Have there been changes of employment, and if so for what reasons?

The patient's sex life is then traced from first awareness of erotic feelings: At what age and in what context were you first aware of sexual arousal? What were the experiences that followed? Did you masturbate and was this associated with any feelings of fear or guilt? At what age did you commence dating? When did you have your first important relationship? What attracted you to the girl or boy, and what brought the association to a close? The same questions are asked about subsequent associations: What attracted you to your spouse? How did the courtship go? Were there obstacles from either family? How have you and your spouse gotten along together over the years? How has the sexual side of the marriage been? At least as much attention is given to love and emotional warmth as to sexual behavior as such.

The patient is then asked about present social relationships: Do you have difficulties with any of your friends? Do you have any particularly intimate friends? How do you get on with acquaintances?

For a very illuminating example of case analysis with discussion by a professional audience, the reader is referred to the case of Mrs. H. (Wolpe, 1976, pp. 101–147).

Data-Gathering Instruments

After the history has been taken the patient fills out three questionnaires that have been found useful sources of information for the planning and conduct of behavior therapy. They are (a) the Willoughby Personality Schedule, (b) the Fear Survey Schedule, and (c) the Bernreuter Self-Sufficiency Scale. These are reproduced as appendixes to this volume.

The Willoughby Personality Schedule (Appendices A and B) has relevance for subjects with neurotic problems, as established at its inception by

Willoughby (1932, 1934). Its forerunner was a questionnaire of 223 items compiled by Thurstone and Thurstone (1930) and administered to a large university population. A substantial number of the subjects gave indications of suffering from neurotic illness. The authors used these data to estimate the likelihood of a positive response from a neurotic subject to each question. The Willoughby questionnaire consists of the 25 questions that received the highest weightings in Thurstone and Thurstone's study.

The Fear Survey Schedule (Appendix C) (Wolpe & Lang, 1964) lists a large number of stimulus situations to which fear is unadaptive. Patients indicate on a five-point scale how disturbed they become in each situation. This schedule is an exceedingly useful clinical instrument that frequently brings to the therapist's attention neurotic sensitivities that would not otherwise have been suspected. A revised schedule containing 108 items (Wolpe & Lang, 1969) is commercially available from Educational and Testing Materials, P.O. Box 7234, San Diego, California 92107.

The Bernreuter Self-Sufficiency Inventory (Appendix D), which is a list of 60 questions, is used less consistently than the two foregoing schedules. A normal score is generally between 24 and 42. A score of less than 20 shows marked lack of self-sufficiency. Low scores are indicative of overdependency, which is often associated with agoraphobia. People who are low in self-sufficiency often find it difficult to follow instructions in self-assertion. Very high scores (45 and over) are obtained by some normal people and by the common run of psychopaths.

When there is a question of psychopathic personality and when there are ambiguous manifestations of hysteria, the introversion-extraversion scale of the Maudsley Personality Inventory (Eysenck, 1962) often provides decisive information.

In spite of the obvious relevance of the routinely used data-gathering instruments, and although their importance was stressed during the 18 years of the existence of the Behavior Therapy Unit at Temple Medical School, they are widely ignored even by many of those who received their training in the Unit. In neglecting their use, the therapist often does a disservice to the patient, as in the following case.

Case 12

A 42-year-old woman, whose main presenting complaint was agoraphobia, had, after 20 years of unsuccessful psychodynamic therapy, consulted a well-accredited behavior therapist. By using in vivo exposure therapy and paradoxical intention the therapist had significantly reduced the level of her agoraphobia. However, as progress did not advance beyond a certain point, she left after two years to see another behavior therapist. The latter concentrated on problems of living and achieved further gains for the patient, both in respect to the agoraphobia and more generally, but progress slowed down and halted, leading her after many months to terminate therapy. I found that she had a network of maladaptive social anxieties, dominated by fears of being alone and of the disapproval of other people. A Willoughby score of 67 showed how much still needed to be done. Neither of the behavior therapists had been aware of the social anxieties. They had not used the Willoughby Personality Questionnaire or the Fear Survey Schedule, which displayed them to the full. Only after overcoming the social anxieties could the agoraphobia finally be resolved. Her Willoughby score a few weeks before the end of treatment was 23.

Such experiences raised the general question of the extent to which behavior therapists make use of these systematic questionnaires. The question was answered in a study conducted by Wolpe and Wright (1988), based on a questionnaire sent to all Clinical Fellows of the Behavior Therapy and Research Society. The 134 replies revealed that the Willoughby was routinely used by only 19% and the Fear Survey Schedule by only 42% of those on the Society's roster of behavior therapists. There are two possible explanations for these findings. The first is that the crucial importance of pinpointing sources of anxiety is not widely realized. The second is that even among those who do understand its importance, many are not aware of the facilitative value of the questionnaires. This incognizance must be regarded as a major failure in the teaching of behavior therapy.

EXAMPLES OF INITIAL INTERVIEWS

The presenting complaints in the cases given here are a phobia for sharp objects, a problem of interpersonal anxiety, and sexual inadequacy. Yet, the same action is to be noted in each: a concentrated effort to secure the greatest possible definition in determining the dynamic relations between neurotic behavior and its antecedents.

Case 13. First Interview in a Case of Phobia for Sharp Objects (Mrs. P., age 32)

In this interview the behavior therapist does not simply accept the circumscribed phobia for knives that the patient presents. The therapist follows the routine of uncovering broad areas of the patient's history and current circumstances. The reader should attend to the manner and content of the questioning procedure, in particular noting how the therapist goes out of the way to be permissive—to condone acts and attitudes that the patient regards as natural to deplore—and then tries to define with precision matters that may require therapeutic action.

The one benefit initially expected from therapy was the removal of the phobia. An outsider might have expected a behavior therapist to plunge into systematic desensitization, but the second interview (not given here) led in another direction. Exploration of factors currently controlling Mrs. P.'s fear of knives revealed that it was particularly strong when other people's children were unruly inside her house. This reaction was related to her extreme inhibition in almost all interpersonal situations and her habitually suppressed anger because of fear of disapproval. (Note that direct questioning during the first session failed to elicit the suppressed anger.) Her Willoughby score was 66. The first therapeutic undertaking was assertiveness training. It was postulated that by developing an ability to express her feelings freely and appropriately, she would remove the feeling of helplessness that was a major element in the dynamics of her phobia. Assertiveness training was rapidly effective and diminished the phobia. Nevertheless, desensitization to knives eventually had to be carried out.

THERAPIST: Dr. N. has written to me about you, but I want to approach your case as though I knew nothing about it at all.[1] Of what are you complaining?

MRS. P.: I'm afraid of sharp objects, especially knives. It's been very bad in the past month.

THERAPIST: How long have you had this fear?

MRS. P.: It began 6 years ago when I was in the hospital after my first child was born. Two days later, my husband brought me some peaches and a sharp knife to cut them with. I began to have a fear that I might harm the baby with it.[2]

THERAPIST: How long had the knife been with you when it occurred to you that it might harm the baby?

MRS. P.: I don't believe I let him leave it overnight, that night; I think you could say I told him to take it home. I can't remember exactly; I know I just didn't want it around. From that day to this, I don't mind using knives as long as I'm with someone, but when I'm alone with the children I just don't want them around.

THERAPIST: Can you remember in what way the thought first came into your mind that you might hurt the baby?

---

[1]It is always a mistake to rely upon the version of a case provided by a psychiatrist or psychologist whose orientation is not behavioristic since a good deal of information that interests them does not interest us, and vice versa.

[2]One does not have to be a Freudian to suspect from this that the baby might have been a resented intrusion in her life — and, as will be seen, it was.

Mrs. P.: I can't remember.[3]

Therapist: Now since that time, generally speaking, has this fear been the same all along, or has it got better or worse?

Mrs. P.: Well, right after we moved to Richmond about 5 months ago I felt a little better about it. At first, when I got home from the hospital I made my husband take all the knives away from the house. I didn't want them around, so he took them to my mother's. I brought a couple back from her house when we moved to Richmond. But I couldn't—after I brought them—I couldn't use them. I couldn't keep them out where I could see them and might pick one up and, you know, use it sometime.

Therapist: So what do you say in general—that the fear has been much the same?

Mrs. P.: It seems the same. In fact, mostly I think it's gotten worse.[4]

Therapist: Is there anything—any situation—that you can associate with it getting worse?

Mrs. P.: No. Only it just seems to be on my mind I guess. If you don't mind me going back to something that Dr. N. said that I just didn't want them around, that it was a habit, and I mean I guess I've been thinking about that and—it's hard to admit—the children. I don't know why they make me nervous and I just am afraid that—that sometime it may get the better of me.

Therapist: Are the children making you more nervous—in the past month?

Mrs. P.: Well, you know in the summertime they stay outside; but in this kind of weather they can't get out, and, of course, they like to run and when they run in the house it does kind of get me.[5]

Therapist: When you were in the hospital that time after your baby was born, what was your general feeling about the situation?[6]

Mrs. P.: Well, I wasn't too happy in the first place because we had just built a house. I had just started to work and had been working about 6 months when I got pregnant and I wasn't too happy about it, because I liked my job and, building a house, we wanted new furniture and all. Well, I guess

---

[3]It did not seem advisable to exert pressure on her memory at this point when she was not yet comfortable with the therapist.

[4]Frequent recurrence of emotional disturbance owing to the destructive idea could have resulted in the conditioning of various new stimuli to that disturbance.

[5]The worsening was related to the noise and activity of children.

[6]A return to the quest for information regarding the circumstances of the onset of the phobia.

neither one of us was happy about it. And then just before the baby was born I said, "If it's a girl, a dark-headed girl with brown eyes it will be fine"; but it turned out that it was blonde and a boy. (*Laughs*)

THERAPIST: Was that important?

MRS. P.: That it was a girl or boy?

THERAPIST: Yes. Or were you just joking?

MRS. P.: Well, no, I don't think I was joking, because I really didn't much want it to look like my husband and his side of the family (*laughs*). But it turned out to be the image of his Daddy.[7] But I think that was a selfish . . .

THERAPIST: Well, that's all right.

MRS. P.: . . . on my part. It's probably a selfish way to look at it. I wanted a dark-headed girl.

THERAPIST: Well, you were expressing how you felt about the child at that time. It was just your feeling, and there's no question of right or wrong. It was your true feeling.[8] . . . Don't you like the way your husband's family looks?

MRS. P. (*laughing*): I could never like their looks. I know they like me because of the way they act and . . . I wouldn't do anything against them.

THERAPIST: It is quite possible not to like the way some people look.

MRS. P.: I must have liked the way my husband looked or I wouldn't have married him.

THERAPIST: Then why was it important to you to have a child look like your family?

MRS. P.: Well, as I said, I think it was just selfish on my part.

THERAPIST: But you had a preference. It is not a matter of being selfish. You had a preference.[9]

MRS. P.: Well, I felt I had to go through having and caring for the baby and all, and I felt like I sort of wanted it to look like me since I had to go through it all.

THERAPIST: Sort of reward for your trouble?

MRS. P.: That's right.

THERAPIST: Did you ever have this kind of feeling before this child was born?

MRS. P.: Never.

---

[7]Not only had the pregnancy been unwelcome, but when the child arrived, it was physically displeasing.

[8]Note the matter-of-fact acceptance of her account and the strong rejection of the suggestion of moral turpitude that the patient implied when she used the word *selfish*.

[9]The idea of selfishness was again combated.

THERAPIST: Well, when I said that, I wasn't thinking only about this feeling about knives, but has it ever happened before that you had a feeling of wanting to smash up things, maybe, if you were cross about them?[10]

MRS. P.: I've always been sort of, you know, perfectionist, I guess you'd say, particular about my things. I had two younger sisters and I know if they meddled with any of my things . . . I would get awfully mad about that . . . but I never wanted to hurt anybody.

THERAPIST: Would you ever want to hit them?

MRS. P.: I don't think so.

THERAPIST: Would you ever want to hit anybody who annoyed you? Or when situations worked out the way you didn't like?

MRS. P.: I don't think so. I can't remember it. . . .

THERAPIST: Well, it doesn't have to be a matter of hurting anybody physically, but just a feeling of anger and expressing anger towards people. Well, now let's get your background. Where were you born?

MRS. P.: Norfolk.

THERAPIST: How many brothers and sisters?

MRS. P.: Four sisters and one brother.

THERAPIST: And where do you come?

MRS. P.: I'm in the middle. There's two sisters and a brother older and two sisters younger.

THERAPIST: Will you just tell me how much older than you your eldest sister is?

MRS. P.: She was 47 in October . . . and I've got one who will be 45 in January and my brother will be 43 in December, and then 18 months younger there's a sister, and one 2 years younger than her.

THERAPIST: Are your parents alive?

MRS. P.: Yes.

THERAPIST: What kind of person is your father, especially as you remember him in your childhood?

MRS. P.: Sweet and easy-going.

THERAPIST: Did you feel he was interested in you?

MRS. P.: You mean what I did at school and like that?

THERAPIST: Was your father interested in you personally and in what you were doing?

MRS. P.: Not too much.

THERAPIST: Did he ever punish you?

---

[10]This raised the question whether, in general, she had a tendency toward anger and aggression when thwarted. According to her statements, she did feel angry but did not react violently. The possibility of verbal expression of anger was not pursued at this point, though it might well have been.

Mrs. P.: No.

Therapist: And what about your mother?

Mrs. P.: Well, I could say the same about her. They were both good — you know — provided. She . . . well, she was interested, did things like driving us to school. She didn't seem to be too interested in how we got along or what we did; or if I failed; and I made awful grades in school. She never talked to the teacher to find out if I could have done better. She never helped with homework or anything like that. Of course, I guess she always had too much else to do.[11]

Therapist: Aside from the fact that your parents were rather similar people, would you say they liked each other and also behaved towards you as though they liked you?

Mrs. P.: Well, they tried to see that we did right and I can remember they always took us to Sunday School and to church.

Therapist: Did they get on well together?

Mrs. P.: Well, yes. As far as I know. They had arguments.

Therapist: Did they have lots of arguments?

Mrs. P.: Well, no, after all they lived together some 40 years.

Therapist: Were there any other adults who played any important part in your early home life — like grandmothers, aunts, or nurses?

Mrs. P.: No, I don't remember any grandmothers or aunts.

Therapist: How did you get on with your brother and sisters?

Mrs. P.: Well, pretty good, I guess. Of course, when you are children I think you fuss and fight lots of times. Now I think we all get along good.

Therapist: Did you have any particular fears when you were a child?

Mrs. P.: Well no, not that I know of. But when I was eight years old our house burned down. I was on my way home from school and the fire trucks passed us. It was in January and it was snowing like anything and somebody told us that our house was on fire. And there was a fear. . . . My parents lost almost everything they had. For . . . 5 or 6 years after that, every time I would hear a fire engine I would get so nervous if I was in school I would have to get up and leave. I wouldn't leave the school, but I would have to get out of the class — but things like that don't bother me now.[12]

Therapist: Did you have any other such experiences, or any other fears at all when you were a child?

Mrs. P.: No.

Therapist: Well, now, you said that you didn't get on very well at school.

---

[11]Having had such uninvolved parents, it is hardly surprising that Mrs. P. was unenthusiastic about having children.

[12]It is usual for childhood phobias to be deconditioned by the experiences that life provides, and without formal treatment.

Apart from the fact that your studies were difficult, how did you like school?

MRS. P.: I liked it fine. I mean I just played right along.

THERAPIST: Well, did you always do badly at your classes?

MRS. P.: Yes.

THERAPIST: What about sports? How were you at them?

MRS. P.: I might have taken after Father in sports. I did well.

THERAPIST: Did you make friends at school?

MRS. P.: Yes, I had plenty of friends at school.

THERAPIST: Did you have any close friends?

MRS. P.: Well, yes. There were about six or eight of us that always chummed around together, girls and . . .

THERAPIST: Were there any people at school you were afraid of? I mean either among the girls or teachers?

MRS. P.: No.

THERAPIST: How far did you go in school?

MRS. P.: I finished high school.

THERAPIST: How old were you then?

MRS. P.: 18.

THERAPIST: And then what did you do?

MRS. P.: I worked for a doctor for 3 years.

THERAPIST: As a receptionist?

MRS. P.: I did his lab work and typing, shorthand . . . helped with his patients.

THERAPIST: Did you like that work?

MRS. P.: Yes, very much.

THERAPIST: And then what did you do?

MRS. P.: I worked for a power company for 5 years, as a clerk-stenographer. I liked that too.

THERAPIST: And then?

MRS. P.: Got married. I didn't work for about 10 months. Then I worked for a plastic firm in Norfolk until the first child was born — as I told you.

THERAPIST: And since then?

MRS. P.: Housewife.

THERAPIST: How do you like being a housewife?

MRS. P.: Fine.

THERAPIST: Is there anything you don't like about it?

MRS. P.: That things don't stay clean when cleaned. (*Laughs*) No, I like it fine, I wouldn't go back into public work for anything. Unless I could work in a hospital, something like that. I should get something like that when my children are through school.

THERAPIST: How old were you when you first had any kind of sexual feelings?

Mrs. P.: Well, I . . . (*Desperate gesture*)

Therapist: Well, roughly — were you 10 or 15 or 20? More or less?

Mrs. P.: Well, I can't remember. I have no idea.

Therapist: Well, then, was it before 10?

Mrs. P.: I wouldn't think so.

Therapist: Was it before 15? . . . Before 20?

Mrs. P.: Well I would think it was before 20.

Therapist: Say about 17?

Mrs. P.: Well, yes, maybe.[13]

Therapist: In what kind of a situation did you have your first sexual feeling? Was it out with boys, or at the movies, or what?

Mrs. P.: Well, I never dated too much. And when I was in school, well, in my class in school there just wasn't any boy. And . . .

Therapist: So, you started to date when you were 18 or so, after you left school?

Mrs. P.: That's right.

Therapist: At that stage did you go out with lots of different boys or just one at a time? Did you go to parties? What was the pattern?

Mrs. P.: Well, I went around with several. I belonged to the choir at church and whenever there were things like Sunday School parties we'd usually take somebody with us.

Therapist: Well . . . when did you first become especially interested in anybody?

Mrs. P.: Well, let's see. I started going with my husband, Charles, when I was 24. And after I started going with him I never did go out with anybody else.

Therapist: There has been nobody else ever in whom you have been really interested?

Mrs. P.: Well, when I was working at my second job, there was a boy there, but he was married, and I never did go out with him.

Therapist: What did you like about him?

Mrs. P.: Well, just everything. (*Laughs*) And, ah, well he showed me a lot of attention too. Then he quit and went to Richmond to work and I never did see him again.

Therapist: So you didn't have any kind of going out with him or any physical contact?

Mrs. P.: I know a lot of people wouldn't believe this, but it's absolutely true.

Therapist: I believe it. What did you like about Charles?

---

[13]Note the therapist's insistence on at least an approximate answer, and that, once it has been obtained, details are pursued.

MRS. P.: My husband is just . . . the way he . . . well, just everything I guess. He was nice and the thing that impressed me with him most was the way he treated his mother. His father had been dead for a few years and he was good to her, and he always phoned her, and I felt like anybody who would be that good to his mother might be a good husband.

THERAPIST: Well, when did you feel that you were ready to marry him?

MRS. P.: I don't know if I ever did feel like I was. I went with him for 7 years.[14]

THERAPIST: Well, was he interested in marrying you earlier?

MRS. P.: Uh-huh. Every time I would put it off. And I would say okay and then I would get nervous and upset and couldn't sleep and would say, well, I can't go through this again. So we would put it off again, until he got fed up with that. He was working, and when he got fed up he said he was going to quit his job and go to college. And he did.

THERAPIST: He went to college?

MRS. P.: Uh-huh. From January '53 to June '56. And then he went to Tennessee and got a job at _____. When he left, of course, it left me sitting at home by myself and I nearly died. I lost 20 pounds; I couldn't eat; I couldn't sleep.

THERAPIST: Well, can you tell me what the other man you mentioned had that Charles didn't have? What points were important as far as your feelings were concerned?

MRS. P.: Oh, he was good looking. But I was thinking of my husband's blonde hair and blue eyes. He had dark hair and dark eyes.[15]

THERAPIST: When you had the prospect of marriage to Charles before you, and you felt nervous, what did you feel nervous about? Was there any particular aspect of the relationship that made you feel nervous?

MRS. P.: The whole thing, I guess. I just wasn't ready to get married.

THERAPIST: In 1954 Charles went to study?

MRS. P.: Yeah, he went to Baltimore.

THERAPIST: So eventually you got married. When?

MRS. P.: In August of 1956.

THERAPIST: At that stage, were you satisfied about being married?

MRS. P.: Well, he first of all, he called me from Tennessee and said, "If you don't marry me now," he says, "we're through. I'm leaving the country."

---

[14]It seems that the choice of a husband was made on rational grounds, and not because of his emotional appeal—in contrast to the married man previously mentioned.

[15]Further evidence of the emotional importance to her of the appearance of close relatives, which accounted largely for the strength of her negative reaction to her newborn child.

So it was then or never, so I said, "Okay." So we got married the next autumn.

THERAPIST: Well, how do you get along together?

MRS. P.: We get along fine. I knew I would never marry anybody else. Well, I guess I'm just the type of person, you know, someone sort of has to say well, we are going to do it now or never.

THERAPIST: How is the sexual side of your marriage?

MRS. P.: Fine; I hope he'd say the same (*laughs*).

THERAPIST: At this moment I'm only interested in your side.[16] Do you have climaxes?

MRS. P.: Yes.

THERAPIST: Always?

MRS. P.: Well, no, I don't always, but I do at least part of the time.

THERAPIST: So you're quite happy in general about the marriage?

MRS. P.: Well, I wouldn't be any other way.

THERAPIST: What do you mean by that?

MRS. P.: Well, I mean I wouldn't be single again.

THERAPIST: But you have no complaints about the marriage?

MRS. P.: No.

THERAPIST: How many children have you now?

MRS. P.: I have two. The girl will be three on the 16th of this month.

THERAPIST: Do you like your children?

MRS. P.: Well, I should say I do.

THERAPIST: Except when they make a lot of noise and get on your nerves?

MRS. P.: Well, that's to be expected. I wonder sometimes what my mother did when there were six of us. Of course, we weren't all there at the same time.

THERAPIST: Your children are quite well?

MRS. P.: Yes.

THERAPIST: Do you like living in Richmond?

MRS. P.: Better than I expected. I'd heard that the people were not too friendly, but I found out that they are.

THERAPIST: Is there anything you're not satisfied with?

MRS. P.: Well, I would like to have a new house. We had to buy an old house and there wasn't anything to rent or to buy right when we had to move so we bought this old house and it still needs a lot done to it.

THERAPIST: What's your religion?

MRS. P.: Methodist.

THERAPIST: Is religion important in your life?

---

[16]This statement expresses the central orientation of a behavioristic history. Everything has to be seen from the standpoint of the sufferer, for it is she who needs to be changed.

MRS. P.: Yes, it is.

THERAPIST: Well, in what way?

MRS. P.: Well, I don't think you can get along without it.

THERAPIST: Do you spend a lot of time with church activities?

MRS. P.: Oh, no, no. I haven't been to church in Richmond. We have taken the children to Sunday School.

THERAPIST: Well, do you worry much about what God is thinking about what you're doing?

MRS. P.: I do the best I can.

THERAPIST: Well, I've got enough of the important background information. I will give you one or two questionnaires to do as homework and then next time you come here we'll talk of the treatment procedures.[17] We'll probably be doing a special kind of treatment, called desensitization. It involves deep muscle relaxation and other special procedures. That is all for now.

Case 14: First Interview in a Case of Interpersonal Anxiety (Miss G., age 21)

This is the transcript of the first of two interviews in a filmed demonstration of basic procedures in behavior therapy of neurosis.[18] The reader should note the therapist's insistent endeavors to define the stimulus sources of the anxiety reactions that the patient reported in certain kinds of social situations. After some initial probing, he turned his attention to the patient's life history, but interrupted the chronicle repeatedly to follow clues that promised to throw further light on anxiety-eliciting stimuli. Toward the end of the interview, he abandoned the uncompleted life history to renew his investigation of these stimuli. Finally, he made an examination of some situations in which self-assertive behavior (see chapter 8) would be appropriate; but it emerged that the anxiety Miss G. would have in response to the consequences of assertion was so great as to render futile any attempt at assertiveness training at this stage. It would first be necessary to desensitize her to being looked at and to disapproval.

---

[17]Already, at this interview, the patient was given the message that active therapy would begin very soon. As noted on p. 65, however, the first active treatment was assertiveness training.

[18]A film, which is technically excellent, and which consists of excerpts from these interviews, is available from Psychological Cinema Register, Penn State University, State College, PA, under the title *Behavior Therapy Demonstration*. The viewer should, however, know that it is a 35-minute condensation of almost 2 hours of interviewing which gives it a misleading impression of cursoriness.

THERAPIST: So your name is Carol Green? How old are you?

MISS G.: 21.

THERAPIST: What is your complaint?

MISS G.: I am very, very nervous all the time.

THERAPIST: All the time?

MISS G.: Yes, all the time.[19]

THERAPIST: How long has this been so?

MISS G.: Since I was about 14.

THERAPIST: Can you remember what brought it on?

MISS G.: No, not really. I wish I could.

THERAPIST: But, are you not saying that before you were 14 you were not nervous?

MISS G.: Well, I was, but not to this extreme. I remember being . . . especially in elementary school when I would have to read something in front of the class, then I would get very nervous about that — giving speeches or answering in class. That would bother me.

THERAPIST: Well, that is a special situation.

MISS G.: Yes, but now all the time. When I go out of the house, or walk out the door.

THERAPIST: Well, let's try to build up a picture. You say in elementary school you were only nervous when you had to get up and speak in front of the class. Only then?

MISS G.: Yes.

THERAPIST: And then in high school?

MISS G.: It got worse. When we would go out with boys I would be very nervous.

THERAPIST: Do you mean that you became more nervous in front of the class?

MISS G.: I wouldn't sleep for nights worrying about giving a speech in front of class or something like that.

THERAPIST: And you also said you became nervous about going out with boys.

MISS G.: Yes. You know, I was afraid, especially if I would have a blind date I would be scared to death.

THERAPIST: Well, isn't that to some extent natural?[20]

MISS G.: I guess so, but not to the extremes that I would go to.

---

[19]It is important to establish the presence or absence of continuous anxiety. Its sources are various — the most common being ongoing conflicts, ruminations about possible catastrophes, and free-floating anxiety (see chapter 14). Here, it turned out later that Miss G.'s statement about being always anxious was incorrect.

[20]This was said to imply that her reaction was really not so "far out."

THERAPIST: And if you went out with somebody you knew. What about that?

MISS G.: Well, after a while I would be a little calmer, but still nervous.

THERAPIST: And what about if you went out with girl friends?

MISS G.: Not as much. I wouldn't be quite as nervous, but still a little bit.

THERAPIST: Were there any other situations in which you developed nervousness while you were in high school?

MISS G.: No others that I can think of, just basically when I would walk out of the house everything would just bother me.

THERAPIST: Everything? Like what?

MISS G.: Well, you know I was afraid to take tests or things like that or make speeches like I said before. Just to be with people would scare me.

THERAPIST: Just being with any people?

MISS G.: Yes, it would bother me more if I was with people I didn't know too well.[21]

THERAPIST: What about at times of vacation?

MISS G.: Vacation? I don't understand what you mean.

THERAPIST: Well, I mean you have to take tests and so on at school, but during vacation there are no tests. So would you still be nervous going out of the house?

MISS G.: A little bit. But not quite as much.[22] Because I wouldn't be thinking of that.

THERAPIST: What year did you graduate from school?

MISS G.: 1963.

THERAPIST: And what did you do then?

MISS G.: I went to school and became a technician.

THERAPIST: What kind of technician?

MISS G.: X-ray.

THERAPIST: Do you like this work?

MISS G.: Not really. It's just because I didn't know really what else to do. I thought it would be interesting and the only reason I went into it is because I thought it was interesting, but once I got there I was very nervous about everything. It scared me to be with patients.

THERAPIST: Patients scared you?

MISS G.: Well, especially the sick ones. If something would happen to them.

THERAPIST: You were scared that something might happen to them?

---

[21]This tells us that her interpersonal anxiety varies directly with the strangeness of other persons.

[22]When the threat of tests was present the general level of anxiety was increased.

MISS G.: Yes, like they would have an attack or something.[23]

THERAPIST: Has this ever happened?

MISS G.: No, not really.

THERAPIST: Well, it is now about 5 years since you became a technician.

MISS G.: It is about 4.

THERAPIST: During those 4 years, did you become more nervous or less nervous or stay the same?

MISS G.: Definitely more.[24]

THERAPIST: You have been getting gradually more nervous?

MISS G.: Yes.

THERAPIST: All the time?

MISS G.: Yes. My mouth tightens up all the time.

THERAPIST: I see. Now, are there any special things that make you nervous nowadays?

MISS G.: Special things?

THERAPIST: Well, let's start off by considering your work situation.

MISS G.: Yes.

THERAPIST: You said that sick patients make you more nervous.

MISS G.: And my boss.

THERAPIST: Yes?

MISS G.: He makes me extremely nervous. I am afraid of him.

THERAPIST: Why, is he very strict?

MISS G.: Um, yes, he gives that appearance.

THERAPIST: Does he carry on? Does he scream and so on?

MISS G.: Never at me. But I am always afraid that will happen.

THERAPIST: And what about nurses?

MISS G.: Not really. I am not in too much contact with them.

THERAPIST: And who else scares you?

MISS G.: Men.

THERAPIST: Men?

MISS G.: If I go out with them.

THERAPIST: Yes. What about men who come in where you are working, like medical students?

MISS G.: Yes, they scare me, too. They do.

THERAPIST: They scare you, how?

MISS G.: I am afraid to . . . I don't know. I am not afraid of them really. I am just afraid of how I'll act . . . that my nervousness will show through. And I think about it so much.

---

[23]Here we have anxiety from an entirely different source.

[24]This makes it important to know in what directions reactivity has spread.

THERAPIST: Well, is it correct to say that you are sort of scared of being watched?[25]

MISS G.: Yes, I think everybody is always watching me.

THERAPIST: Now, that is at work. What circumstances scare you when you are away from work?

MISS G.: Just going out. I am afraid, you know, that they'll see the way I am. I am afraid to pick something up, because I am afraid that I am going to shake, and my mouth is all tightened up. I am afraid to look at people directly in the eye.[26]

THERAPIST: Are you only afraid of looking at your escort in the eye, or anybody?

MISS G.: Anybody.

THERAPIST: So looking at a person face to face increases your nervousness?

MISS G.: Yes.

THERAPIST: Suppose that you were walking down the street and there was a bench across the road with some people waiting for a bus. Now those people would be sort of vaguely looking across the street. Would you be aware of their presence?

MISS G.: Yes, definitely.

THERAPIST: Even though they might not be particularly looking at you?

MISS G.: Yes.

THERAPIST: I must be quite certain of this.[27]

MISS G.: Yes.

THERAPIST: If you are completely by yourself, are you absolutely calm and comfortable?

MISS G.: Yes, I am. The same way I am at home. I feel all right.

THERAPIST: Well, that means there are some people who can look at you and not bother you.

MISS G.: Yes, at times. But I don't know why this happens.

THERAPIST: Well, what about your mother?

MISS G.: No, it doesn't bother me at home.

THERAPIST: Your mother can look at you as much as she likes?

MISS G.: Yes. It's silly but . . .

THERAPIST: Well, that's not silly.[28] It is just the way things have developed.

---

[25]Being watched by people means greater contact than when they are not watching.

[26]This maximizes the effect of the being-looked-at stimulus.

[27]Many patients will initially report moderate distress as "completely comfortable."

[28]The patient is to accept her reactions as matters of fact. They are neither "wrong" nor "stupid."

Miss G.: I know.

Therapist: And who else can look at you without bothering you?

Miss G.: My whole family.

Therapist: Who is in your family?

Miss G.: My father, my mother, my sister, my grandmother.

Therapist: Besides these people, are there any others at all who can look at you without disturbing you?

Miss G.: No.

Therapist: What about a little baby?

Miss G.: No, that doesn't disturb me. And an older person who is senile or something — that doesn't bother me.

Therapist: What about a little boy of 4 years?

Miss G.: No.

Therapist: 6?

Miss G.: No.

Therapist: 8?

Miss G.: No. It's when they get older, I get nervous.

Therapist: 12?

Miss G.: Around in their teens.

Therapist: About 12? They sort of begin to bother you?

Miss G.: Yes.

Therapist: I take it that a boy of 12 wouldn't be as bad as one of 18?

Miss G.: No.

Therapist: Let's go back to the street where you are walking and there are three people sitting on a bench across the road. Would it make any difference to you whether they were three men or three women?

Miss G.: No, it wouldn't. I would feel worse if I would see somebody very handsome.

Therapist: When you see him, even if he is not looking at you?

Miss G.: Yes, that's correct.[29]

Therapist: If you go to a movie and see a very handsome film star, does that bother you?

Miss G.: No, not really, because I know he is not there looking at me.

Therapist: And if there is a handsome actor on the stage?

Miss G.: Yes, it would.

Therapist: It would bother you even though he was not looking at you?

Miss G.: Unless it is very dark and he could not see me.

Therapist: Well, then, it is only if he can see you that you feel afraid — because you think that he might see you.

---

[29]At first glance this is an exception to her rule. But on the indications of the succeeding conversation, it seems clear that she was reacting to the anticipation of being looked at by this potentially strongly anxiety-evoking figure.

MISS G.: I think he might.

THERAPIST: Besides looking at you, what else can people do to make you nervous? You have, I think, mentioned one thing. They can be critical of you. You are scared of your boss criticizing you.

MISS G.: Any criticism gets me upset even if I know that I am right. I can't talk back and tell them that I am right[30] in this case; I just get all choked up and feel like I am going to cry.

THERAPIST: Is there anything else that people do to upset you?

MISS G.: Well, let them just tell me I'm wrong—if I am wrong or if I'm right, it still bothers me. It upsets me.

THERAPIST: That's a kind of criticism. Supposing people praise you?

MISS G.: That makes me feel good.

THERAPIST: It makes you feel good. Okay. Who is older, you or your sister?[31]

MISS G.: I am.

THERAPIST: By how much?

MISS G.: Three years.

THERAPIST: What sort of person is your father?

MISS G.: He's on the quiet side, and both of my parents are on the nervous side. My sister, too. The whole family, really.

THERAPIST: Was your father kind to you when you were a little girl?

MISS G.: Yes.

THERAPIST: And your mother?

MISS G.: Yes, she's the stronger one. I'm more like my father and my sister is more like my mother.

THERAPIST: In what way is your mother stronger?

MISS G.: Well, things don't bother her, at least outwardly, as much as they do my father and me. She sort of makes decisions.

THERAPIST: What does your father do?

MISS G.: He sells insurance.

THERAPIST: Did either of your parents punish you when you were young?

MISS G.: They used to hit me once in a while. My mother did. My father hardly ever did.

THERAPIST: Did your mother hit you often?

MISS G.: Not that often.

THERAPIST: Well, did she do anything else to discipline you?

MISS G.: No, that's all. She would have little talks.

THERAPIST: Did you feel when your parents punished you that it was unreasonable?

---

[30]Another major anxiety source.

[31]This begins the questioning about general background.

Miss G.: Sometimes I did.

Therapist: Were there any other adults who played any important part in your home life—grandmothers, aunts, nurses?

Miss G.: Yes, my grandmother—she lives with us.

Therapist: Okay, well now—what about her? What kind of a person is she?

Miss G.: She is very good to me. I am her first grandchild, so she pays more attention to me than to my sister, but she doesn't understand a lot of things because she wasn't born in America and she did not have an education.

Therapist: How do you get along with your sister?

Miss G.: We used to fight an awful lot, but lately we have been getting along better than we used to, but we are not really close because she is completely different.

Therapist: What is she like?

Miss G.: She's more talkative than I am—more outgoing. I'm on the quiet side.

Therapist: Did you go to school in Philadelphia, Carol?

Miss G.: Yes, I did.

Therapist: Did you like school?

Miss G.: Not really.

Therapist: What did you dislike about it?

Miss G.: I was afraid of getting up in front of the class.[32]

Therapist: Yes, is that all?

Miss G.: Yes.

Therapist: How well did you do?

Miss G.: I was a B average.

Therapist: Did you take part in sports?

Miss G.: No.

Therapist: Did you make friends?

Miss G.: Yes, I have a lot of friends.

Therapist: Any close friends?

Miss G.: Yes, one in particular.

Therapist: You say that you don't like being an X-ray technician. What would you like to be?

Miss G.: I would like to be a kindergarten teacher. I like to be with children.

Therapist: Apart from this fear of getting up and speaking, did you have any other fears when you were small?

Miss G.: No.

---

[32]This has already been noted and partly explored. It will shortly be pursued further.

THERAPIST: Like, maybe, insects, darkness?

MISS G.: I was afraid to take a shower because I had claustrophobia.[33]

THERAPIST: When was that?

MISS G.: I was about 12 or 13. I was afraid to be closed in. Somebody locked me in a closet and I couldn't stand it. It scared me.

THERAPIST: How old were you when that happened?

MISS G.: I really don't remember. I guess about 10 or 11.

THERAPIST: After you were 12, that fear disappeared?

MISS G.: Well, I would still be afraid if someone would lock me in a closet. I am not afraid to take showers.

THERAPIST: Do you like going into elevators?

MISS G.: I used to be afraid; I am not anymore.[34]

THERAPIST: You're quite okay now?

MISS G.: Yes, I take the elevator.

THERAPIST: Do you remember any experience at all when you were at school that was particularly frightening in relationship to getting up and talking in class?

MISS G.: Yes, when I was in sixth grade I had to read something in front of the class. I was holding the paper and I started shaking. And the teacher said "What's the matter?" and I couldn't really talk.[35] And from then on if I had to read something I'd put it down on the desk and look at it. I would still be nervous.

THERAPIST: Before this happened were you already nervous?

MISS G.: Yes.

THERAPIST: And after this, you were much worse?

MISS G.: Yes.

THERAPIST: Let me ask you how you would react to certain everyday situations.[36] Supposing you were standing in line and somebody got in front of you, how would you feel and what would you do?

---

[33]Once again the therapist's persistence yielded some fruit.

[34]Especially in childhood, many fears are overcome by life experiences. Miss G. still had some degree of claustrophobia (in closets), but it was not evidently related to her present serious neurosis.

[35]This seems to have been a critical conditioning event. The tremor of her hands suggests that there may have been a preexisting anxiety conditioning, but since it had not happened before in this situation, some intercurrent physiological cause such as hypoglycemia seems likely.

[36]The answers to these questions throw light on interpersonal anxieties of the kind calling for assertiveness training (see chapter 8).

Miss G.: I wouldn't do anything, but I would feel I would be ready to explode because I would think it was wrong.

Therapist: Yes, certainly it would be wrong.

Miss G.: But I can't say anything about it. I can't get up the nerve to say anything.

Therapist: And does that apply to every situation of that type?

Miss G.: Yes. There's a man who gets on the same bus and he limps and he hasn't gotten in front of me, but he pushes and slides and nobody says anything to him and it really upsets me because everybody always complains, but nobody says anything.

Therapist: Well, why would you not say something to him?

Miss G.: I would be afraid to. He has a mean temper.

Therapist: Well, supposing it wasn't him? Supposing you were standing in line at the Academy of Music box office and somebody you don't know got in front of you?

Miss G.: I probably still wouldn't say anything.

Therapist: Why not?

Miss G.: Just because I'm afraid to. I'm afraid to open my mouth.

Therapist: Does this have anything to do with the idea that if you were to say something, people would start looking at you?

Miss G.: Maybe.

Therapist: Let me try to put the question in another way. I would like you to think very carefully before you answer. Supposing you didn't care if people looked at you, would you say something?

Miss G.: I really don't know. It's just that I can't get it out. The words just won't come out.

Therapist: Well, all right. You realize that if somebody does a thing like that, getting in front of you, he is doing you a wrong. One of the things you are going to learn to do when you are treated here is to take action about that kind of thing—to stand up for yourself and not allow people to do you wrong.

Miss G.: How do you go about planning that?

Therapist: Essentially what you do is to express the annoyance that you rightly feel.[37] It is very hard at first, but if you make a special point of doing it, you find that it gets easier and easier.

Miss G.: I have tried but I can't; if the situation arises, the words just don't come out and I start stuttering.

Therapist: Well, I will help you. Later on, each time you come here, I will say, "Carol, did you have any situations of this sort last week?" You will say, maybe, "Yes," and I will want to know what you tried to do about it; and

---

[37]A basic principle in assertiveness training (see chapter 8).

we will play-act what you ought to have said and done. But in the meantime, I know it is difficult for you because of the very special fear you have of being the center of attention. If you told someone to get back in line, he would look at you and other people would look at you. And that makes it more difficult.[38]

MISS G.: Yes.

THERAPIST: So one of the things we will have to do is to break down this fear that you have of being looked at. In order to do this, we need to know more about it. Let's use as a kind of basic situation the one we mentioned in which you are seen from a bench across the road.[39] Now, would it make any difference to you how wide the street was?

MISS G.: Yes—if they were closer to me I would feel worse.

THERAPIST: I see. Now I find it very useful to have some kind of quantitative way of expressing how much afraid a person would be. One way to do it is to ask you to think of the worst fear that you ever had and call that 100; and then you think of being absolutely calm, as when you are at home, and call that zero.[40] Now, consider that the street is as wide as Broad Street (about 100 feet) and there is just one person sitting on that bench; how much anxiety would you feel? Would it be 5, 50, or 20 or what?

MISS G.: I guess around 50.

THERAPIST: Now, supposing that the street was twice as broad as Broad Street and there is just this one person?

MISS G.: I guess about 25.

THERAPIST: Now, if you see two persons, would it still be 25?

MISS G.: Yes.

THERAPIST: It doesn't matter how many?

MISS G.: Well, if there is a whole group it's worse.

THERAPIST: Supposing that you are standing at one side of a football stadium that is twice as wide as Broad Street, and there is one man sitting on one of the stands right across the other side; how much anxiety would that cause you?

MISS G.: Around 25.

THERAPIST: And if, instead of being a man, it is a boy of 12?

MISS G.: It wouldn't be as large . . . 5, 10.

THERAPIST: With a boy of 15, would it be in between 10 and 25?

MISS G.: Yes.

---

[38]Assertiveness training is for the time being precluded by her reaction to being looked at.

[39]What follows is the beginning of a hierarchy construction (see chapter 9).

[40]For a discussion of this scale, see p. 91.

THERAPIST: Well, we can use that information in your treatment. But first we have to prepare you. Your problem, as you know, is that you have anxiety where you shouldn't have it. In order to combat the anxiety, we have to use emotions within you that can fight anxiety. One very convenient one is the calmness brought about by muscle relaxation. Now, you have probably never learned how to relax your muscles, have you?

MISS G.: No.

THERAPIST: Next time I will start to show you.

In the first of the foregoing two interviews we saw that the basis of a woman's fear of knives lay in interpersonal dissatisfactions, for which, (eventually) assertiveness training was the first and foremost therapeutic need, and not systematic desensitization, as might at first glance have been expected. In the second, widespread social fearfulness called in the first place for desensitization to social scrutiny. Both cases were relatively simple, yet without the details that the interviews provided, treatment could very easily have been misdirected.

These cases were selected as demonstrations of initial interviews partly because the directions of therapy were so easily apparent. It is by no means always so easy. Sometimes a dozen sessions or more are needed to unravel a patient's web of reactions. And sometimes, as therapy proceeds, new information changes the therapeutic strategy. This information may arise from the patient's day-to-day experiences or from the therapist's observations of his response or lack of response to the measures being applied. The following cases illustrate this.

Case 15

For 2 years, Mr. D., a lawyer, aged 44, had experienced difficulty in achieving or maintaining an erection although for the previous 12 years he had enjoyed an excellent sexual relationship with his wife, to whom he was strongly attracted. Working at first from the information he had supplied that his first failures had occurred on occasions when he had been unusually tired, I treated him by the *in vivo* method of gradual approaches described on pp. 299–300. At first he seemed to improve, but after a few weeks, his sexual performance was quite erratic. He continued to have "a nagging feeling of uncertainty" about his capacity to make love. This made me examine his relationship with his wife more closely. What emerged was that she had for the first 10 years of the marriage subordinated her life to his. Then she had become dissatisfied with her situation, and 2 years before her husband's sexual difficulties began, had consulted a therapist who encouraged her to be her own person instead of an appendage. After some months, she had begun to rebel in various ways. For example, she had started to resist catering and playing hostess at the very frequent parties he had her give in order to make and consolidate his professional contacts. Her resistance gave him a feeling of having been rejected and abandoned. It was this feeling that interfered with his erotic responses and impaired his sexual function. (The subsequent treatment of this patient is described as case 59.)

Case 16

Miss E. was an attractive 33-year-old research worker in the field of sociology. She came for treatment because of an absolute inability to make a marital commitment despite many opportunities, and despite a number of intense and prolonged affairs. The initial behavior analyses, though they revealed some unadaptive social anxieties, seemed to indicate the existence of the usual basis for this complaint — a fear of being tied down (which is often intertwined with claustrophobia).

When some tests of this hypothesis proved to be negative, I went into an exceptionally detailed probing of her lovelife from childhood onward. From this it emerged that her parents had instilled in her a great fear of doing the wrong thing, and her avoidance of marriage was bound up with this in a rather complicated way. It became clear from an examination of Miss E.'s relationships with men that the obstacle to her forming permanent relationships was a fear of disappointing someone. Her social inadequacies and her avoidance of marriage were really one problem. If she merely refused a request to borrow a coat, the other person would be only slightly disappointed, and Miss E.'s anxiety would be relatively slight. This fear was miniscule in comparison to what she would feel if she disappointed someone in an important love relationship. If she met a man whom she could envisage as her life's partner, she would back away, thinking, "I really can't be certain; I might have to back out later. Then I'll be disappointing him. . . . "

Treatment consisted of desensitization to a hierarchy of situations in which Miss E. disappointed people, starting with mild kinds of social refusals. With respect to relationships with marriage-worthy men, the strength of the fear varied according to two factors: how deeply the man cared about Miss E., and how long the relationship had lasted. It was the latter that chiefly determined how strongly she felt committed to him, and consequently, how much stress there would be in disappointing him. After 16 sessions, all known areas of useless anxiety had been covered, and therapy was completed.

A year later she reported being almost entirely free of her inappropriate anxieties and the resulting inhibitions. She had been having a very satisfying affair with a man she intended to marry after solving some financial problems. She no longer feared involvements that might lead to marriage. (For a full account of this case, see Wolpe, 1976c, p. 199ff.)

Case 17

Miss Y., a 21-year-old psychology student, complained of a lifelong fear of spiders for which she sought treatment because it had become much more severe during the past few months. The larger the spider, the greater her fear. At least once a week she had nightmares in which spiders were involved; for instance, they were thrown at her or surrounded her on a beach.

Miss Y. would often feel that there was a spider on her when there was none. No other creature affected her in this way. She had been married 2 years earlier, and during the 5 unhappy months of the marriage, her nightmares had ceased. On her return to her parents' house, they had recurred. The significance of this piece of history was not immediately clear. I decided to treat the spider phobia by systematic desensitization in parallel with a variety of social anxieties.

It became apparent some weeks later that the spider fear and nightmares were due to her mother's relentless grip on her life. What finally overcame the fear of spiders was not its direct desensitization, but the overcoming of her fear of rebelling against her mother through a combination of assertiveness training and systematic desensitization. The spiders had in a sense become equated with the mother: the same feelings were aroused by the dream spiders and the real mother. The equation was confirmed by the disappearance of the peripheral (symbolic) fear when the central one was eliminated.

The occasional occurrence of such symbolism does not justify dream interpretation as it is commonly practiced. Nor does it provide a warrant for incorporating psychoanalytic practices into behavior therapy, as suggested by Feather and Rhoads (1972). These authors reported some cases in which, as in the case of Miss Y., the true source of disturbance was something other than the main complaint. In one case, a woman's fear of cockroaches was found to be mainly an expression of severe marital tensions. There is really nothing psychoanalytic about this and, in fact, in Feather and Rhoads' own thoroughly appropriate therapeutic interventions, no procedures of a psychoanalytic type were actually involved.

6
Therapeutic Strategy

There is a therapeutic change process that often takes place without planning, and it occurs in every kind of psychotherapy. Emotional responses other than anxiety may be aroused in the patient by the therapist's reputation, appearance, or demeanor. These emotions include feelings of hope, faith, and confidence in the therapist. Added to them are emotional responses to the behavior of the therapist, such as attending seriously to what the patient says instead of dismissing it as of no consequence. If such nonanxious emotions are present at times when anxiety-evoking topics are being aired there may be reciprocal inhibition of the anxiety, resulting in therapeutic change (see Wolpe, 1958, p. 193). While all therapists profit from occurrences of this kind, the behavior therapist does not rely solely on them, but obtains through behavioral procedures additional weakening of anxiety response habits.

There are two preliminaries to the use of behavior therapy techniques: (a) preparing the patient, and (b) deciding on the strategy appropriate to the individual case.

PREPARING THE PATIENT
FOR BEHAVIOR THERAPY

Orientation to Neurotic Anxiety

The patient should have some understanding of what is special about neurotic anxiety. Most patients are aware from the start that inappropriate fear is their central problem, except, very often, those with such complaints as stuttering, headache, or obsessions (see table 1.1). The therapist should then give emphasis to the causal role of fear. For example, he or she should point out to a stutterer how the level of anxiety determines the severity of the stutter. The special features of neurotic fears, and how they are caused, can be brought out in a statement like the following—of which, however, only parts are usually necessary:

> Fear is appropriate under circumstances of real danger—for example, walking alone at night in an unsafe neighborhood, learning that one's firm is about to retrench its staff, or being confronted by a poisonous snake. Fear is not appropriate when elicited by situations that contain no real threat—such as seeing somebody receive an injection, entering a crowded room, or feeling disapproved of by someone who has no importance in one's life. Inappropriate fear is called neurotic fear.
>
> How do neurotic fears begin? If a severe fear reaction occurs in particular circumstances, those circumstances become fear-connected so that their later appearance in some form will automatically trigger fear. For example, an American lieutenant "went through hell" in the bursting of high explosives in a pass in Vietnam. After he returned to the United States, when he and his wife were one day walking to a wedding in New York City, a truck backfired near them. He reacted with instant panic, and "rolled up next to the parked car, cringing in the gutter." Your own fears likewise (as your story shows) originated in unpleasant experiences. They became conditioned, or connected, to aspects of the experiences. That is why exposure to similar situations automatically arouses fear. Now, because this fear is the result of learning, the best possible way to eliminate it is by reversing the learning.

In cases where anxiety is not the presenting complaint, it is desirable repeatedly to draw attention to the connection between level of anxiety and severity of the complaint, whether it is asthma, headache, stuttering, or bingeing. Awareness of this link facilitates the patient's cooperation in the anxiety-weakening procedures.

Explaining How Behavior Therapy Works

The patient is given a general outline of what behavior therapy attempts to do. He or she is told that since neuroses are a matter of emotional learning, it makes the best sense to treat them by using scientific knowledge of how habits are made and broken. The procedures that come from this knowledge are called behavior therapy. But to be as effective as possible, the therapist must know exactly what things, or thoughts, or feelings are the triggers to the neurotic fear responses. The triggers differ from person to person, and the therapist applies his or her expertise to determine their make-up by careful questioning, combined with the information from the questionnaires that the patient has been given.

The Subjective Anxiety (*sud*) Scale

It is important to any psychotherapist, and most of all to a behavior therapist, to know how anxious the patient is at a particular time and in relation to what circumstances. The usual probe is the question, "How anxious are you?" to which the usual response is verbal, for example, "Very anxious," "Fairly anxious," "A little uneasy." These responses are only vaguely informative. The *sud* Scale is a superior means of putting the therapist in touch with the magnitudes of anxiety experienced by the patient. This scale is introduced as follows:

> Think of the worst anxiety you can imagine and assign to it the number 100. Then think of being absolutely calm — that is, no anxiety at all — and call this zero. Now you have a scale of anxiety. At every moment of your waking life you must be somewhere between 0 and 100. How do you rate yourself at this moment?

Most people are able to give a numerical response, such as "20" or "50" immediately, and with practice become increasingly adept. The range adopted is obviously arbitrary. The 0 to 100 scale is favored because it provides a great deal of flexibility; but anyone who prefers a more compact range (e.g., 0–10) can easily be accommodated.

An important matter is the extent to which the subjective scale correlates with psychophysiological parameters of anxiety. Thyer et al. (1984) found, in 20 subjects, significant correlations between the subjective anxiety scale and two physiological indices — peripheral vasoconstriction and heart rate. This correlation broadly agrees with earlier studies relating autonomic indices to subjectively ranked items of fear hierarchies (Gray, Sartory, & Rachman, 1979; Lang, Melamed, & Hart, 1970).

The subjective anxiety scale has many uses. It enables the patient to report his or her anxiety level on arrival in the office and at any point thereafter on request. The patient may also use it to record fluctuations of anxiety in the course of an hour, a day, or a week. Anxiety levels over time may be recorded graphically, and increases or decreases correlated with antecedent stimuli.

The scale comes into play in several ways in systematic desensitization programs. In the construction of anxiety hierarchies, it is used to elicit how much anxiety the patient believes he or she would have in response to different stimuli on a theme. A person who is made anxious by human blood may have five *suds* at seeing a slightly blood-tinged bandage, 100 *suds* at the sight of a person with blood-soaked clothing, and intermediate levels to intermediate stimuli, such as a syringe full of blood. In making up a hierarchy, one uses the numerical values to obtain relatively even differences between adjacent items, usually aiming to have them separated by 5 to 10 *sud*s (see chapter 9).

During the actual desensitization procedure, the subjective anxiety scale has a number of applications. To begin with, it is used to indicate the baseline level of anxiety. Deep relaxation often achieves a zero baseline level, but not always. It is nevertheless often feasible to embark on desensitization with a baseline 5 or 10. The *sud* scale is also employed during desensitization to indicate how much anxiety is aroused by each presentation of a scene. The patient is asked after the termination of the scene to state by how much it raised the *sud* level. Typically, there is a progressive decline in *sud* level from one presentation to the next and when the *sud* level to the treated scene has reached zero or near zero one moves up to the next item on the hierarchy.

CUSTOMARY SEQUENCE OF THERAPEUTIC INTERVENTIONS

The first deliberate intervention consists of making the patient comfortable in the therapeutic situation. This is achieved partly by behaving in a generally friendly and permissive manner, and partly by communicating to the patient that he or she is accepted as the victim of circumstances and is in no way blameworthy. One possible consequence of this approach is to facilitate the nonspecific effects mentioned at the beginning of this chapter.

Since the patient already understands (p. 90) that his maladaptive behavior patterns have been learned, he can readily see that the crux of therapy is to reverse the process, that is, procure unlearning, and is pleased to hear that behavior therapy consists of applying knowledge of the learning process to bring about this unlearning.

With the stage for action set in this general way, therapeutic action follows a logical order. It is reasonable to pay first attention to misconceptions since they lend themselves to the most simple and direct treatment. It is, for example, appropriate to make a direct attack on the proposition that masturbation is dangerous. Misconceptions should be corrected as soon as possible, whether they are socially based, as in the masturbation example, or iatrogenic (e.g., "I have symptoms because they are useful to me"). Case 22 illustrates the massive impact of the correction of an iatrogenic misconception.

Assertiveness training, if indicated, should be introduced as soon as possible because the therapeutic events take place in the course of life outside the sessions. However, assertiveness training must be postponed if there are marked anxiety reactions to some aspect of it, such as being the center of attention. These require desensitization beforehand (see case 14).

Standard systematic desensitization is generally the technique of first choice for treatment of maladaptive anxiety response habits to whose stimuli no motor response is relevant, in contrast to anxiety in situations that call for assertiveness training. Standard desensitization has the usually overriding advantage of being conducted entirely in the office without any need for objects or physical manipulations, but sometimes it is rendered impractical by the patient's inability to imagine scenes realistically, or by relaxation efforts failing to counter anxiety. In such cases one may either employ an alternative anxiety inhibitor or else turn to one of the variations of systematic desensitization described in chapter 10, or to flooding (chapter 11). The last-named is the treatment of choice for most cases of obsessive compulsive neurosis that center on fear of contamination.

Other syndromes that require special methods are discussed under their particular headings.

HOW CASE DYNAMICS INFLUENCE STRATEGY

The chapter on behavior analysis showed that human neurotic problems have various dynamics, which makes it indispensable for the stimulus response structure of each maladaptive habit to be accurately assessed. Response similarity in maladaptive habits provides a convenient basis for placing them in diagnostic pigeonholes — for example, anorexia, claustrophobia, stuttering — but common pigeonholes do not imply common treatments because the stimulus antecedents and their dynamic interactions are unique to each case. To obtain optimal results, the clinician must be skilled not only in behavior therapy techniques but also in the analysis of dynamic relations.

Illustrative Cases

The following cases illustrate how greatly thoroughgoing assessment influences therapeutic strategy, and how much this may differ from what might at first glance have been expected.

Case 18

Miss J., aged 27 and single, complained of lack of confidence and low self-esteem. Just walking in the street made her feel that everybody was looking at her critically. This sensitivity dated from the 12th grade, when she unexpectedly received a sharply negative evaluation from her teacher. Thereafter, she was very fearful of negative attitudes, but later also became uncomfortable with admiration. Although she was an attractive person, she had very little social life and hardly ever dated.

Miss J.'s only previous treatment had taken place 2 years earlier, by a "behavior therapist" of the recent vintage that has discarded conditioning theory and that leans heavily on cognitive methods and exposure (see chapter 18). The therapist started with cognitive therapy, and tried to convince her that the derogatory thoughts she imputed to others were not justified by the evidence. Although she was intellectually persuaded by the therapist's arguments, her sensitivity was undiminished. The therapist then had Miss J. confront the social situations that disturbed her. For example, she was instructed to endure prolonged periods in the company of a person who she felt was thinking of her disparagingly. With no improvement after 4 months, she terminated therapy.

The therapist had not really analyzed what Miss J. found disturbing in her interactions with others. Careful questioning disclosed that it was not their scrutiny, attitudes, demeanor, or what they said. Rather, she was disturbed by disapproving thoughts that she imagined them to have and that she projected into their minds. The cognitive correction was bound to fail because the most it could do was to establish that it was highly unlikely that the other person was thinking of her in the way that she feared. The key to her recovery was enabling her to accept that people might have negative thoughts about her without being distressed by that fact. This could be achieved by the use of systematic desensitization (chapter 9).

In order to desensitize Miss J. to these thoughts it was first necessary to specify them, and to rank them in order of the distress they produced coming from various people, who were ranked according to the importance of their opinions. The product was a two-dimensional hierarchy, with thoughts intersecting with their personal sources. Table 6.1 is made up of 12 items excerpted from the actual 45-item hierarchy to illustrate this. The numbers in the table indicate how much anxiety Miss J. expected to have on the subjective anxiety scale at each point of intersection.

In the actual desensitization, Miss J. was deeply relaxed and asked to imagine herself sitting at an open window on the ground floor of a public library. The window was 12 feet from the ground. She could hear people talk outside, but could not see them, nor they her. First she imagined the voice of the doorman saying, "Miss J. is a very nice person but she doesn't dress in good taste." This produced only a little anxiety, which at the third repetition was down to zero. Next the doorman described her as aloof, and then Anne, Ron, and Mr. Black were heard making critical statements in ascend-

Table 6.1. Projected Disapproval Hierarchy

	MR. BLACK	RON	ANNE	DOORMAN
Miss J is nervous	80	60	50	15
Miss J is aloof	65	50	35	10
Miss J has poor taste	40	30	20	5

Note. This is a condensation of what was actually a 45-item hierarchy whose essence it faithfully conveys. The numbers indicate the anxiety levels the patient expected to have at each intersecting point. Thus, she would have 35 units of anxiety if she overheard Anne describe her as aloof, and 60 units if Ron described her as nervous.

ing order of evoked anxiety. Miss J.'s disturbances to the whole two-dimensional hierarchy were overcome in the course of five sessions. Several related hierarchies were later constructed and their treatment handled in similar fashion. An admiration hierarchy (table 6.2) was treated by progressively more fulsome praise *in vivo*. In effect, Miss J. became less affected by what people might be thinking. After 26 sessions she was less anxious overall and was socializing freely. She had been dating steadily, and was considering marriage.

At a follow-up 10 months later, Miss J. reported that the improvements achieved during treatment had not only been maintained but had shown some further increase. She described her life as "absolutely normal." Her "mutually loving relationship" was continuing.

Table 6.2. Praise Hierarchy

1. "You're beautiful"
2. "You played that well"
3. "That was very considerate"
4. "You're so sweet"
5. "You're a good friend"
6. "You look pretty or good"
7. "You did a good job"
8. "Your food was delicious"
9. "Your house looks nice"

Case 19

The vision of Mr. A., a man of 50 and an artist by profession, had progressively deteriorated to a complete blur over a 2-week period 6 months before I saw him. Two opthalmologists had been unable to find any physical pathology. Their agreed diagnosis was hysterical blindness. From Mr. A.'s history, it was apparent that he had a great deal of social anxiety, reflected by high scores on the questionnaires to hurting the feelings of others, rejection, making mistakes, and losing control. In particular, he was very fearful of incurring disapproval, and the blindness had begun under circumstances where he felt himself excoriated. He had been the executor of his father-in-law's will. One day he was notified that his mother-in-law had started suit against him for "failing in fiduciary responsibility" in handling the will. This distressed him beyond words. When he pictured the arraignment in court, he became even more disturbed and then found it increasingly difficult to bring objects into visual focus.

The treatment that was indicated by this array of facts was not of vision, but of maladaptive social sensitivity. It was necessary to specify the areas of vulnerability and to organize each of them into hierarchies to be treated by systematic desensitization. The derivation of a low-level hierarchy item reveals the extremity of his social fearfulness. If he was dining out and the first course was tasteless soup, he would consume the whole bowl to please the hostess; if she were to offer him a second, he would not be able to refuse for fear of offending her. The hierarchy item consisted of politely refusing the soup. Desensitization was carried out to this and a wide range of related situations grouped in several hierarchies. He also received assertiveness training, requiring a good deal of behavior rehearsal. These measures progressively diminished his social sensitivity. After 6 months, when he was "over the hump" emotionally, his vision began to revive for increasingly longer spells, and returned completely and permanently after 8 months. The final breakthrough was marked by his driving alone to my office — a distance of 25 miles. Recovery has now lasted 4 years.

Case 20

This case illustrates how behavior therapy falls short if its focus is restricted to a sector of neurotic responding instead of the whole spectrum of maladaptive habits.

A physician, aged 47, had been treated several years earlier by a psychologist whose behavior therapy training had been rather patchy. The patient's complaint was that he experienced intolerable stress in the conduct of his profession. He felt hard pressed to get things done because he was anxious "not to let anybody down." His life was ruled by the clock. The psychologist gave him assertiveness training, taught him progressive relaxation, and enabled him to handle the clock. He also did some desensitization in the context of making demands, for example, asking a friend to repay a loan. The patient and his therapist both felt that he had benefited greatly after 4 months of treatment.

However, when I saw him 4 years later he was experiencing increasing anxiety. Investigation showed that the treatment program had neglected a broad range of anxious sensitivities. His feelings were easily hurt and he was especially vulnerable to humiliation, to criticism, and to being watched at work. He had had all these sensitivities at the time of the original treatment, but the therapist had not looked beyond the area of complaint. To overcome the whole range of maladaptive social anxieties required weekly systematic desensitization sessions over 3 months.

Patchwork treatment, such as this case illustrates, based on inadequate analysis, besides being a disservice to patients, gives fuel to the allegation that behavior therapy is superficial. One may speculate that it is association with therapists who work in this way that has led some people (e.g., Franks et al., 1984; Thompson & Williams, 1985) to state that individuals with existential problems of life should look elsewhere than to behavior therapy for treatment. Actually, there is reason to contest this advice (Wolpe, 1985a).

For an informative account of the analysis and treatment of a cognitively complex case, see Mansueto (1988).

PART III

BEHAVIOR THERAPY TECHNIQUES

7
Cognitive Therapeutic Procedures

Cognitive therapeutic interventions are the first to be considered here for two reasons: (a) there may be problems of daily life that require immediate attention, either because they have an urgency that takes precedence over therapeutic action or because they contribute to the anxieties for which the patient is seeking treatment; and (b) when the behavior analysis reveals a cognitive basis for maladaptive anxiety, this, strategically, should be treated first.

LIFE GUIDANCE

Problems of living may be serious enough to obstruct therapy and should if possible be cleared up in advance. The main tools are logic and persuasion. Typical problems are involvement in unwise business operations and difficulties related to marriage or divorce. Sometimes the inadequate handling of a social situation may lead to a conflict of great severity that either exacerbates ongoing neurotic behavior patterns or precipitates new ones. This situation is exemplified by the following case.

Case 21

Mr. B., 41 years old, complained of panic attacks of which the first had occurred 6 months earlier. Investigation showed that a major factor was his inadequate handling of life circumstances in the context of the terminal phases of the chronic illnesses of both of his parents. He had married a few months before the initial panic attack. At first his wife had been very kind to his parents and had given his mother a good deal of practical help, including the administration of physical treatments; but months of unremitting continuance of the demand wore her down. Each weekend they traveled 40 miles to his parents' house and spent 2 days there. The ultimate effect was to make his wife increasingly resentful and finally openly antagonistic to her in-laws.

This state of affairs naturally constituted a major conflict for Mr. B.; besides contributing to his first panic attack, it was an ongoing source of day-to-day anxiety. One aspect of it was that it generated a threat to the marriage. When I first saw Mr. B., he had done nothing to resolve the conflict, largely, as it turned out, because he could not bring himself to remove his parents from the surroundings in which they were comfortable. However, when we discussed the matter he saw the advantages of persuading them to move to a smaller house in his neighborhood, which would obviate the burden of the weekly excursions. Their subsequent move rapidly ameliorated the marital stresses and increased the amount of attention he could give his parents during the week. Only after the move was it possible to take action toward overcoming the neurotic anxieties that were the underlying basis of the conflict and the cause of the panic and of many more problems.

THE TREATMENT OF COGNITIVELY BASED NEUROSES

Even when complex in structure, cognitively based neurotic fears are usually overcome in a few sessions, as is strikingly exemplified by case 22. In cases in which there are both cognitively based and classically conditioned fears, one must take advantage of this, and at first give main attention to the cognitive causes. In addition, in cases that call for classical reconditioning, the stage for operations must often be set by establishing an appropriate cognitive perspective. For example, many timid people believe that it is right always to turn the other cheek. Before they can be taught assertiveness they must realize the futility of following that principle in most circumstances (see chapter 8). But the realization by itself does not cure the timidity.

As noted in chapter 4, there are two basic modes of cognitive therapy — one used commonly and one occasionally. The common mode is the correction of the wrong beliefs that are the source of maladaptive fears. The occasional mode is thought stopping, the application of which is limited to certain obsessional cases.

The conceptual differences between behavior therapists and cognitivist therapists such as Ellis and Beck (discussed at the end of this chapter) are manifested in radical differences in the therapeutic use of cognitive methods. Behavior therapists see a cognitive locus in only some maladaptive anxiety response habits. These are cases in which there is clear evidence of anxiety that is misconceptually based, and the revealed details of the misconceptions led to a definite corrective program. This is apparent in the following interview segments (Wolpe, Lande, McNally, & Schotte, 1985), which illustrate in microcosm how this evidence is obtained.

Example 1 — Fear of Losing Control

THERAPIST: You said that you suffer from attacks of dizziness and tingling of the hands and that because of this, you are afraid of going out alone. How does that work?

PATIENT: I think that if these feelings got worse, I would lose control and go crazy.

THERAPIST: What makes you think that?

PATIENT: Because I have no control of these feelings and I have an aunt who was in a state hospital. I think I will go the same way. I also have a cousin who is flaky.

Example 2 — Fear of Rejection

THERAPIST: What makes you so tense around people.

PATIENT: (an attractive young woman): I'm so ugly that no one could like me.

THERAPIST: What makes you believe you are ugly?

PATIENT: I have ugly freckles on my arms, face, and chest.

THERAPIST: Do you believe that these freckles make you look ugly?

PATIENT: Yes.

THERAPIST: Do you also believe that people are repelled because of these freckles?

PATIENT: Yes. I'm sure they are.

Example 3 — Hypochondriacal Fear

THERAPIST: What are you afraid of?

PATIENT: I'm afraid that these cysts in my breast are cancerous and I will have to have my breast removed.

THERAPIST: Have you had the cyst checked by a physician?

PATIENT: Yes, I have had two mammograms.

THERAPIST: What were the results?

PATIENT: My doctor told me I didn't have cancer.

THERAPIST: Do you believe him?

PATIENT: No. I've read stories about doctors who lie to their patients so that they won't be upset.
THERAPIST: Do you think your doctor is lying to you?
PATIENT: I'm not sure, but I'm convinced my cysts are cancerous.

The following example leads to the contrary conclusion—a diagnosis of classically conditioned anxiety.

Example 4—Hypochondriacal Fear

THERAPIST: What is your complaint?
PATIENT: I am terrified by my symptoms.
THERAPIST: What symptoms?
PATIENT: At times I become weak and shaky, my mouth becomes dry and my neck becomes stiff and painful.
THERAPIST: Are you afraid of what the symptoms may develop into.
PATIENT: No. I have had them very many times in the past 18 months, and I don't believe that they mean anything serious.
THERAPIST: Are you saying that the appearance of these symptoms automatically triggers off a fear in you—a fear that is totally out of keeping with the consequences of the symptoms?
PATIENT: That is exactly what I am saying.

Once it is clear that some or all of a patient's fears are based on false beliefs, the behavior therapist gives corrective information about each of these. For example, the patient who fears elevators because he believes that he would exhaust the air and suffocate if the elevator door failed to open, will require education about the ventilation of elevators. In most cases, verbal instruction suffices, but in others, actual demonstrations by an elevator technician may be necessary. The provision of information is similarly the key to overcoming such fears as those of flying and of harmless creatures like spiders or bats. The same is true of many hypochondriacal fears. Fears of palpitations or of pains in the chest are usually resolved by the information provided by a thorough medical investigation. And the demonstration that hyperventilation is the cause of nervous symptoms such as dizziness or light-headedness may overcome an associated fear of insanity as exemplified in example 1 above.

It is obviously more difficult to deal with wrong beliefs that are part of a deeply ingrained system. I have usually found it impossible to dislodge completely fears based on strong religious indoctrination—for example, in women who have been led to believe that any sexual arousal or erotic thought about a man to whom they are not married is a mortal sin.

THE ANALYSIS AND TREATMENT OF A COMPLEX CASE OF COGNITIVELY BASED HYPOCHONDRIACAL ANXIETY

There are many cases in which the exact features of the wrong belief are not obvious and need to be teased out, and for which treatment involves a good deal of instruction and argumentation. Such efforts must always be based on information supplied by the patient, and not imposed *ex cathedra*. This is illustrated by the case that follows, in which the analysis warrants as much attention as the treatment. The cognitive basis of the main presenting complaint took shape in the course of the analysis.

Case 22

Lisa was an intelligent 35-year-old woman who had suffered for more than 10 years from marked irritability, severe depressions, and tantrums that were sometimes violent. She had never had a coital orgasm, and had repeatedly been told by friends, her husband, and her family doctor that she was constitutionally incapable of normal sexual function, a view that was confirmed in her mind when almost 10 years of psychoanalysis failed to produce any change. This assessment of herself, coupled with the impression that her husband had lost interest in her, filled her with despair.

Since the falsity of this derogatory assessment was quickly apparent to me, I began, during the history-taking, to undermine it at every opportunity. I used the facts Lisa provided to argue that she was a well-integrated person who had, through learning, acquired some unadaptive habits. As the questioning proceeded, the central problem that emerged was a fear of trusting people, a problem that was particularly adverse in the context of the most deeply felt sexual experience—the orgasm.

Once she accepted this diagnosis, Lisa experienced tremendous emotional relief, and from the third session was never again subject to depressions or tantrums. She cooperated eagerly in the measures subsequently applied to normalize her sex life.

The transcript consists of excerpts from Lisa's first three interviews. During the first half of the initial interview, I saw Lisa alone, and at several points disputed her contention that her disability was a sickness and that she was to blame for the marital trouble. Ed participated in the second half of this interview, which gave him the opportunity to try to correct Lisa's impression that he did not care for her. At the conclusion of the interview, they were both given the Willoughby Schedule as homework. A few days later, Ed called to say that Lisa, having gone into an emotional crisis, had taken 30 tablets of Librium the previous day. I at once arranged a brief emergency session, during which it emerged that Lisa's Willoughby score of 51 in contrast to Ed's 16 had convinced her that she must be a hopeless case. As the excerpts from the second session show, I persuaded her that the difference in scores was due purely to emotional conditioning. This was the turning point. The third session extended the conceptual clarification, resting partly on some of Lisa's background history.

THERAPIST: I gather from Ed that there is a lack of harmony in certain ways between you.[1] The question is whether there is any practical possibility of straightening out your relationship and making it mutually desirable.

LISA: I think we're very different people. Of course, most people are different, but I think that I married my husband for very neurotic reasons, and I'm sure there had to be something like that on his side, too. I've spent 10 years in therapy. You're the third doctor my husband has made me come to — not made me come to. I shouldn't phrase it that way.

THERAPIST: Well, sometimes it's not a matter of therapy.[2] Anyway, before we make any decisions, let's get some facts. When did you first meet him?

LISA: I guess I knew him casually when we were in our teenage years. I was a freshman at college when he was a senior. I didn't start dating him until after my first marriage dissolved.

THERAPIST: What did you like about Ed?

LISA: He was entirely opposite from my father.[3]

THERAPIST: How old were you when your first marriage dissolved?

LISA: 20.

THERAPIST: You liked the fact that Ed was different from your father.[4] Well, what was the difference?

LISA: He was quiet and more stable, certainly emotionally more balanced. He was the type of man that I've always been attracted to — protective, I guess.

THERAPIST: Well, he was stable and elicited a feeling of protectiveness. Is that the essence of it?

---

[1]The statement referred to a telephone conversation I had with Ed before the interview. It was deliberately phrased in these extremely general terms so that the patient could state the issues as she saw them without constraint.

[2]Some marital incompatibilities cannot be resolved by psychotherapy. This is true, for example, of intellectual differences and wide divergencies of interest. This idea was now introduced in order to suggest to the patient that she might, after all, not be "sick," as had always been assumed. As it turned out, this was the key move in the treatment of the case.

[3]The importance of this became very clear later.

[4]The history of the first marriage was passed over at this point in order to avoid breaking the flow of the story of her relationship with Ed.

LISA: I don't know. I never thought about it that way.

THERAPIST: Did you feel very strongly attracted to Ed at that time?

LISA: Yeah.

THERAPIST: How long after this did you get married?

LISA: Six months.

THERAPIST: And how did you get along with him during those 6 months?

LISA: Ah—it was sort of a topsy-turvy relationship.

THERAPIST: What do you mean?

LISA: Well, there were certain periods of stress and strain. It was never what I would call a quiet courtship period.

THERAPIST: What were the causes of the stresses and strains?

LISA: Me, I guess. I was a very emotionally sick person at the time and I—

THERAPIST: Something must have upset you.[5]

LISA: I don't know. I guess his background.

THERAPIST: I'm not asking you in that sense. I'm not asking you what caused the upset. I'm just asking what upset you.[6]

LISA: Oh, I don't know. I guess I was demanding and insecure and jealous of the amount of time he spent with me. I never go along on an even keel. I'm always up or down or—

THERAPIST: Still, what are the kinds of things that upset you?[7]

LISA: When he gives attention to another woman, that upsets me.

THERAPIST: Well, that's clear enough. Was that the sort of thing that used to happen?

LISA: It's so long ago, I can't remember. I was in such a state of complete unreality when Ed and I were dating. I don't even remember what my behavior was like.

THERAPIST: But you liked to be with him and you were happy with the relationship.

LISA: Yeah.

THERAPIST: But there were just some things that upset you?

LISA: Yeah. Well, I was living at home with a small baby[8]—not exactly an ideal set-up.

THERAPIST: What was the sexual relationship[9] like at that period?

---

[5]Further deflecting from the idea of "sickness" and suggesting accountable reactivity.

[6]Patients who have had psychoanalytically oriented therapy are characteristically more ready to provide causal hypotheses than facts.

[7]The pressure on her continued as she had still offered no facts, only explanation. Her next response had factual content, but it was unrelated to the time in question.

[8]The offspring of her first marriage.

[9]It should be noted how casually this crucial topic was introduced.

LISA: I don't know. For me there never has been any sexual satisfaction, but I guess I have tried very hard because I want to hold on to him.

THERAPIST: So there wasn't any real sexual enjoyment for you?

LISA: There never has been with anyone.

THERAPIST: You know some women will say they don't reach a climax, but they enjoy sex. You don't even enjoy it?

LISA: Oh, I guess I enjoy it. Yeah, to a point.

THERAPIST: Yes?

LISA: Yes, I guess I never really tore it apart like that.

THERAPIST: Well, do you get stimulated up to a point and then feel left high and dry? Do you feel frustrated?

LISA: No, the anger has completely faded out of it for me. I'm no longer angry about it or demanding of it. I become very irritable and hostile toward Ed.

THERAPIST: Well, that's what I mean.

LISA: But I don't feel that this is my fault because—

THERAPIST: It's not important whose fault it is.[10]

LISA: No, but I mean, there isn't any sexual relationship—unless it comes from me, there isn't any.

THERAPIST: I see. Anyway, going back to that time. At that time, you were having some sex with him?

LISA: Yeah.

THERAPIST: And, you were enjoying it up to a point—

LISA: Oh, yeah.

THERAPIST: And then you were left irritated afterwards?

LISA: Yeah.

THERAPIST: So that tended to make you keep away from him because it was sort of punishing.

LISA: Well, I think eventually, yes. Especially after you're married and you're legally bound to one another, you're safer and you can turn it off, so to speak, emotionally. When I went to the first psychiatrist, and Ed found out there was a problem, he completely dropped sexual approaches. In the last 10 years—if I didn't initiate it, there was nothing. Last year, we went the entire year without any sex at all. But I do feel that my therapy has been— it's been long, but it has served the purpose.

THERAPIST: What purpose has it served?

---

[10]I seized every opportunity to assuage guilt and diminish self-blame. It does not matter that in this instance the patient's next remark showed me that I had missed her intent.

LISA: Well, I have found out, I think, the reasons for my problems. I consider myself a controlled neurotic[11] now. I'm afraid to do anything.

THERAPIST: You're afraid to do anything?

LISA: Right. I don't do anything—at all. If I know it's dangerous to my—

THERAPIST: This is very important. Take this sexual situation. If you find that sex leaves you very upset and irritated, then it's reasonable to avoid it. It doesn't necessarily mean that your failure to respond sexually is itself neurotic. It may be; I don't know. But it may not be.[12]

LISA: Well, it's a different feeling now. But since I returned to Ed—I'm sure he explained to you—following the circumstances of last fall,[13] he made an effort and I made an effort. But he has backed off and this makes me more irritable—

THERAPIST: He has backed off in what way?

LISA: He doesn't make advances toward me any more. He tried for a while—I never rejected him in this entire period; and I was cooperative and enjoyed it and—

THERAPIST: So today you would like him to make advances?

LISA: But he doesn't. And this is when I started questioning him. I said, "Ed, I am not going to any more psychiatrists because it's a two-way street." And I said, "I am tired of always being the aggressive one in our relationship." I can never be subordinate in my mind if I'm the only one who's aggressive.

THERAPIST: In the beginning, you were the one to avoid intercourse and now he avoids it.

LISA: Well, he avoided it during the entire 8-year period. The doctors questioned about it.[14] They felt that Ed had dropped it much too quickly when he found out that I had a mental block concerning—well, they called it an oedipus complex, a father complex, you don't have the ability to have an orgasm.[15] It's so beyond me. A lot of girls adore their fathers—so what? After 10 years of therapy, there certainly should have been some change.

---

[11]Her therapy had led to an acceptance of intractable inferiority.

[12]Like the referent of footnote 2, a thrust in the direction of throwing doubt on the assumption of the patient's "sickness."

[13]The reference was to an affair with a student that Ed had described to me on the telephone and that she later detailed.

[14]Without, however, dispelling the belief that the primary blame was Lisa's.

[15]This dogmatic equation would preclude any exploration of the evolution of Lisa's sexual behavior on the part of the analysts.

THERAPIST: I agree with you.[16]

LISA: Here we are in the same situation and, for some reason, these women are still very upsetting to me — his mother, his sister — it doesn't make any difference; it's just women in general. My mother was my competitor, so any woman is my competitor.[17]

THERAPIST: Well, do you think you would feel this as much if Ed were making advances to you?

LISA: No, I wouldn't. I would feel more secure.

THERAPIST: That makes sense.

LISA: As it is now, I feel very insecure. I feel any woman is a threat to me. There are certain kinds of women that are very feminine, who seem secure enough in their own life. They don't pose a threat. But then there are those that all of a sudden bleach their hair and are dissatisfied with their home situations. To me they are threatening.

THERAPIST: But there's a basis for this. Ed is a person and has needs. If he doesn't come to you, maybe he feels these dissatisfied people are more accessible.[18]

LISA: Well, if it's that, I've disguised it to myself. Perhaps that would be too horrible for me to face.

THERAPIST: But you are acting as if you were feeling that way, aren't you?

LISA: I guess.

THERAPIST: Apart from this sexual business, how do you get along?

LISA: Terribly. I'm constantly irritable — we're just like two people grating against each other.[19] I do love Ed and we have three of the loveliest children. They're very stable, healthy in body and spirit. It's amazing to me. I look at them and think, "With my mental condition, how could these children possibly be the way they are?" Ed has never been around for 12 years. I guess to escape me, he throws himself into work. I don't know. I guess a lot of men do. Maybe it's just a pattern of behavior. It runs in his family. His own sister never stays home and she has four children; and she is constantly going. And his brother has been through three divorces at 38. I look at all these things and I think, "Is it all me?" I've said to Ed, "I'm through with the therapy. I

---

[16]Reinforcing her questioning of the analytic theory, and augmenting the statements referred to in footnotes 2 and 5.

[17]The reason being, as it emerged, that no other woman suffered from her "abnormality."

[18]Because they are looking around outside of their home situations.

[19]In the light of what has been said, it could scarcely be otherwise.

feel like I've been placed under doctor's care so I couldn't make waves[20] so you could go on your merry way and enjoy life while I was trying to keep the lid on, plus raise the children." I guess you get to a certain point where you just don't care.

THERAPIST: Have your thoughts ever turned to other men?

LISA: Last year, I went away with a college student for a few days. He was unhappy with his personal life. His family are our neighbors. He came to speak to me and I got involved. Reality just seemed to leave me. I look at it now and I think it couldn't possibly have happened. But it did.

THERAPIST: Was it an emotionally satisfying situation?

LISA: Emotionally satisfying, yes. It fulfilled a need. I guess I've been looking and looking for years, but I just didn't think it would be a boy of 20.

THERAPIST: Well, that doesn't matter.[21] Did you have orgasms?

LISA: No.

THERAPIST: Well, did you get close to them?

LISA: No.

THERAPIST: What do you think is lacking—preventing you from having an orgasm?

LISA: Well, I've been told it's an oedipus complex.

THERAPIST: Never mind that.[22] What do you think?

LISA: I just don't think that I feel adequate. I don't know.

THERAPIST: Can you picture any circumstances in a relationship that would let you—

LISA: Oh—I feel that I have a fear of losing touch with reality.

THERAPIST: Sort of a fear of letting go, is it?

LISA: This is what it is. I don't trust anyone enough.[23]

THERAPIST: Of course, really, if you have an orgasm, you're not losing touch with reality. You are engrossing yourself very very much in reality.[24] I can see that you might feel the other way, though. We find people who are afraid even to relax.

LISA: Well, I never relax either. I don't mean just in sex, I mean in any-

---

[20]While this was not the purpose of "doctor's care," it was certainly a consequence of it.

[21]A few words to dispel any thought of censure.

[22]A further rejection of the sickness diagnosis and a suggestion of self-exploration.

[23]This remark opened a new direction of investigation. What did she mean by "trust"? How did fear of it begin? What factors were involved?

[24]I reverted to this topic because, before going further, I wanted the basic facts of sexual responding to be clear in her mind.

thing. And they tell me, "Don't be nervous." It's very fine to tell somebody, don't be nervous, but—

THERAPIST: Well, I would like to ask Ed to come in and see if we can get some further clues.

(*Ed is summoned and enters.*)

ED: Good morning, sir.

THERAPIST: Do sit down. We've had a brief conspectus of the marital problem from Lisa's point of view and it seems to me that there are both general and situational factors. One situational factor that seems very important to me is that, according to her account, you don't make any sexual approaches to her. Can you comment on that?

ED: I'd say that generally it's true.

THERAPIST: Uh-hum. Well, there must be a reason for it. What prevents you?[25]

ED: There's been a particularly bad spectacle, so to speak, between us over this thing. I was just turned off somewhere along the line.

THERAPIST: Perhaps there has been some bad communication between you. Long ago,[26] Lisa became negative towards sex because she was irritable after not having orgasms. But her feeling is different now. She now looks for signs of affection from you and would respond to them. I guess that you're not aware of that.

ED: Well, she's told me that. Perhaps I have a block now, because of past bad experiences with her.

THERAPIST: Well, do you like her?

ED: I love her.

THERAPIST: Do you like to be close to her?

ED: Very much so.

THERAPIST: Well, how do you get there without approaching her?

ED: I'm not following your question.

LISA: He means how to get to first base, honey, if you don't try.

ED: Oh, I see. Well, it's a good question, but I don't have an answer.

THERAPIST: It's very understandable that you've become scared, like a child who has had his knuckles rapped quite a number of times. To be perfectly frank with you, a situation can become so powerfully aversive that

---

[25]This is a characteristically behavioristic question, seeking the antecedents of behavior. It is to be contrasted with other kinds of therapist responses at a juncture like this—for example, responses such as moralizing, directing, interpreting, reflecting, and the like.

[26]A thumbnail résumé of the history as background to discussing the present situation.

the approach movement cannot be made.[27] There will then be a therapeutic problem. But, before trying therapeutic solutions, I want to see if I can persuade you to make approaches. The fact that the three of us have been discussing the matter openly may already have facilitated action, because you now know in advance, Ed, that you are going to be accepted. Would you welcome it, Lisa?

LISA: I think it would take some effort. I've become angry to the point that I just can't predict an answer. I mean, you can become so completely turned off that it would take a longer period of time to be aroused. But I'd welcome it, sure.

THERAPIST: I think, Lisa, a lot depends on what we mean by an approach. An approach can take many forms. It can be just holding your hand. It can be walking into the kitchen and giving you a hug. At this stage, Ed is sort of hesitant and you are sort of resentful. But since affection is mutual, action should start.[28]

LISA: I think that I would be very suspicious. I would feel that he was initiating it because you told him to.

THERAPIST: Well, that's true, but he also wants it.

LISA: I'm not convinced of that.

THERAPIST: Well, how can we find that out?

LISA: I don't know. I've spent 10 years in therapy and I haven't found out.

THERAPIST: I really don't see how that therapy could have helped you find this out. You said that you would be pleased if he were to approach you. If he didn't want you, he could just leave you, couldn't he?

LISA: Yeah. Sure.

THERAPIST: What would be the point in his lying? Why should he pretend he wants you? Why should he endure the dissatisfaction, unless he really hopes that something will work out?

LISA: Well, I think this is true.[29]

THERAPIST: Therefore, I think there's a primary reason for accepting him. There is what we might call ground for an experiment. I would like to see him making approaches, small approaches, many approaches. He would be uncertain at first, but you would reward him. Then it would become easier for him to do it.

LISA: I have been forthcoming since Christmas time, since I went back to Ed.

---

[27]By raising the possibility that emotional factors might render action impossible, I freed Ed from the belief that I was pointing an accusing finger at him.

[28]The degree of affection was, of course, questionable.

[29]The purpose (and evident result) of the foregoing argument was to shake Lisa's firmly held conception of Ed's attitude toward her.

THERAPIST: Yes, but I mean when he makes an approach.

LISA: I have.

THERAPIST: But you said he never makes an approach.

LISA: He tried. He read this book by Masters and Johnson, and then he dropped it again.

THERAPIST: Why did you drop it again, Ed? Did you feel unwelcome or what?

ED: Yes, to a great extent, I did. I felt that it was a failure, although at first we did have a good relationship on occasion. But then after that, if I did reach an orgasm—it was premature and Lisa said, "Why are you so fast?" Sometimes the act just was a failure.

THERAPIST: What is foremost here is not sex, but love of which the sexual act is an outward expression, but not the only one.[30] There are also many small things that happen between people—small approaches where sex needn't happen, and perhaps couldn't happen. If Ed will do these things and Lisa responds positively, a strong feeling of mutual assurance will build up, from which sex is a natural offshoot, though it will not necessarily be an enormous success from the beginning. Lisa's fear of letting go may make it impossible now for her to have coital orgasms. But I'm pretty sure she will eventually have orgasms with you.[31]

LISA: I don't think we accept each other as individuals.[32] Therefore, I don't see how we can possibly have a satisfactory sexual relationship.

THERAPIST: Let's consider that. Sometimes people don't accept each other because they really are terribly different and incompatible. Sometimes they don't accept each other because of a succession of wrong messages. I don't really know what the situation between you is. Let's explore these things. I'll ask each of you some questions. Do you, Ed, feel attracted to Lisa physically?

ED: Yes.

THERAPIST: Do you feel attracted to Ed physically?

LISA: Yes, definitely.

THERAPIST: Do you have a substantial number of common interests?

ED: We have a number of them; we have golf, we have our children.

LISA: I took up golf to be with you.

THERAPIST: But it's there now.

---

[30]The expression of affection solely in the context of sexual intercourse is amazingly common, and a major source of marital trouble.

[31]This speech exaggerated the potentialities of the situation in order to encourage the approach experiment as much as possible, and to reveal the obstacles.

[32]Now, though granting mutual goodwill, she expressed the idea that a fundamental incompatibility comes between them.

ED: It's there, yes.

LISA: We enjoy it.

THERAPIST: What else are you interested in?

LISA: Not very much anymore.

THERAPIST: What could you be interested in?

LISA: Creative things. Anything creative; I sew a lot. Things that Ed isn't interested in.

THERAPIST: Well, you don't have to share everything.

LISA: Don't you have to share some things?

THERAPIST: Some things.[33] You have golf and you have the children.

LISA: But golf only came about in the last 4 years.

THERAPIST: That doesn't matter. It's here now. What about movies and books and so on?

LISA: We don't like the same movies at all.

THERAPIST: I think the most important thing is a feeling of mutual participation in living itself. That is more important than movies and books, to the extent that you can feel yourselves capable of building a life together, in which your house and children are an important part. Do you have any such general feeling?

ED: Of being able to build a life together?

THERAPIST: Yes.

ED: Oh, certainly I have.

LISA: I thought you said "participation."

THERAPIST: Yes. I mean emotional participation in building a life together.

ED: Well, I think that — I think we both really want that. I think this is —

THERAPIST: All right, Lisa, what are the things that you would like that Ed doesn't provide?

LISA: Well, I think the most important thing is to be able to see somebody's needs. And when they need you, you've got to be there.[34]

THERAPIST: I'll tell you what I'd like you to do. Would you each make a list of the things that you feel come between you? As many as you can. Then I would like you to give each other these lists and indicate whether you think that anything can be done to reconcile each particular objection. I would also like each of you to fill in one of these Willoughby Questionnaires.

The second session was an emergency session that took place 4 days later, three days before the next one was scheduled. Ed telephoned to tell me that Lisa had been in a state of great emotional distress, and that she had

---

[33]There was a reasonable amount of mutual interest to build on.

[34]She saw Ed as insensitive and unresponsive to her needs.

swallowed 30 tablets of Librium the previous day. I asked him to bring her to see me without delay. The following is the relevant part of the brief, but important, interview that followed:

THERAPIST: You seemed rather hopeful at the end of the last session. Then there was a collapse. What happened?

LISA: Those Willoughby tests we did showed that I am the sick one and that Ed is the normal one. My answer to practically every question is the opposite to his. He was right all along. His answers show stability and mine show instability. I feel hopeless.

THERAPIST: That test measures social neuroticism. That means the extent to which there is excessive anxiety or nervousness in relation to other people. Your score of 51 in contrast to his of 16 shows that you are much more vulnerable than Ed is to people's statements and their attitudes toward you. But this anxious reactivity is not organic. It is not inherited. It was acquired by learning. It is a matter of emotional learning. What has been learned can be unlearned.

LISA: But how? All these years of psychotherapy!

THERAPIST: Well, we have methods that are based on our knowledge of how learning takes place. Your previous therapists did not use such methods because they operated on the theory that your troubles are caused by emotional complexes deeply buried in your supposed unconscious mind. Since that theory, though very widely held, has no scientifically acceptable support, it is not surprising that their efforts have not helped you.

LISA: I never could understand how all the analyzing of my childhood was supposed to help. But what else would help?

THERAPIST: If we take a laboratory animal and make him fearful by means of a mild electric shock in a particular room or in the presence of a particular sound, such as a gong, that room or that gong will become attached to the fear—associated with it. It acquires independent power to arouse fear. The fear reaction to the gong can last for years even if the animal is never again given a shock in its presence. But we can do things with him that we know will break the habit. I am sure that when we examine your history we will find that you have had experiences that led to your reacting fearfully to various social situations, including certain aspects of sex. Different kinds of experiences can be arranged here that can disconnect fear from these situations.

LISA: I get the idea.

THERAPIST: We'll begin to develop that kind of program when you come here on Thursday as arranged. How do you feel now?

LISA: Happier. Very encouraged.

The third session occurred 3 days later.

THERAPIST: How have you been feeling in the last 3 days?

LISA: I felt very, very good. Better than I've felt in a long time. It's a strange feeling when somebody offers you a hug and you're ready to grab it.[35] I feel like I'm sort of halfway home.

THERAPIST: Well, we have to proceed systematically now. What have your complaints been?[36]

LISA: All of them? You mean my complaints of my marriage or of my personality?

THERAPIST: You had psychiatric treatment. What has been the trouble in that area?

LISA: The fact that I haven't been able to produce since I was about 13 years of age. My studies started to fail. I was a very bright student — bright enough to have skipped sixth grade. Then I started to slip. I became grossly overweight, and then I was sent to a fine girls' school, but it wasn't fine for me. I became heavier and my work failed. I was taken out and sent to public high school for the last year where I didn't produce either. I was accepted at the Philadelphia Museum School of Art, but I wasn't permitted to attend. I was sent to Penn State University. I still could not produce.

THERAPIST: Okay, you were unproductive. What do you think was the reason for this?

LISA: I refused to compete because I didn't want to fail. My father only has one measuring stick, and that's the top; there's no in-between. It's either A+ or nothing. And I was tired of my mother as a competitor. I always came out second-best anyway.

THERAPIST: Now, there was a time when you were doing very well.

LISA: Uh-hum.

THERAPIST: And then you stopped doing very well. Something must have changed. What changed?

LISA: I don't know. Me. I had a sexual attitude, I guess. I don't know.

THERAPIST: Why do you say a "sexual attitude"?

LISA: I don't know. It must have been. Isn't that the age when you start to have—[37]

---

[35]The elucidation of the nature of her illness at the second interview had given her a feeling of my complete acceptance and convinced her that her troubles were not only understood, but also remediable. The emotional crisis that preceded that interview was the last of its kind to date. She subsequently had "normal" upsets to ordinary frustrations and difficulties, but no more of the helpless distress that had previously been more or less constant.

[36]It was necessary to pose this question anew because we had previously concentrated on the sexual problem and its repercussions.

[37]The explanation presumably came from her psychoanalytic mentors.

THERAPIST: Maybe, but I want to know what actually happened to you.

LISA: Nothing. Not a thing.[38] It was just a period of — I started to change.

THERAPIST: Well, there was a time when you did your work and a time when you didn't. What was it that prevented you from doing your work?

LISA: A lack of desire.

THERAPIST: You lost interest in work?

LISA: It was a way of getting complete attention because I didn't do it.[39]

THERAPIST: No, that's theory. Don't give me any theory. We have lots of theories.

LISA: I don't know. I can't tell you. It was so many years ago. I was so nervous. Maybe I couldn't concentrate.

THERAPIST: What made you nervous? What were you nervous about?

LISA: Maybe of being accepted into a world I didn't want any part of. I don't know. I guess I had seen a bad relationship between my mother and father. Maybe I didn't wish to grow up.

THERAPIST: You are full of psychoanalytic indoctrination, and when I ask you to tell me what happened, you give me theory. I don't want theory.

LISA: But I don't know what happened.

THERAPIST: I'm just asking you what were the events. I don't want to know motives or things like that. I want you to give me a kind of story. The details will be yours. The kind of story I'm expecting from you now is this: "I was doing fine until the age of 15 and then my grandmother began to live with us. There are things about her that I find disturbing and I got into a nervous state and I couldn't do my work." These would be facts; that's the kind of story I want.

LISA: There had been a great big Halloween Party in fourth grade and we had all run off in the woods.[40] And I can remember the boys starting to tease us and call us by dirty names, you know. And then in junior high school, boys who had also transferred from the other school continued to ride me.

THERAPIST: They continued to ride you?

LISA: Yeah, about these episodes that had happened when we were in fourth grade. They kept calling me names. I can remember how tremendously upsetting it was. Some days I didn't even want to go to school.

THERAPIST: You were very distressed by the attitude of these boys?

---

[38]This is not credible. Something must have happened. The patient may truly be unable to recall it. The therapist must do all he can to jog her memory — but gently, not derogatorily.

[39]She had either been told this or deduced it from standard psychoanalytic thinking. I continued to press for facts from her own experience.

[40]Lisa having finally understood what I meant by *facts*, we began to get some.

LISA: Mortified. Just absolutely horrified.[41]

THERAPIST: This went on all through the seventh grade?

LISA: Eighth grade and part of ninth.

THERAPIST: Now you're telling me the kind of thing I want to know. Were you sensitive to other things that people might say?

LISA: Oh, yes. I had my nose straightened a few years ago. I had a pug nose, not large, but enough that I looked like my mother. They used to tease me about this nose and it upset me.

THERAPIST: How would you defend yourself?

LISA: By retaliating or saying something harsh about some other person—which I didn't do.[42] I usually was so wounded that I never said anything. There was also no doubt about my parents being critical of me. I mean it was a life of criticism: "Sit straight"—"Put your napkin on your lap."

THERAPIST: Are your parents alive?

LISA: Yes.

THERAPIST: What sort of a person is your father?[43]

LISA: Brilliant—unfortunately. He's always a perfectionist.

THERAPIST: How did he treat you when you were a little girl? Was he good to you?

LISA: Oh yes—yes, very good—very generous. He didn't have very much time, because of his business, to give to me, but he was very generous materially. He never doled out any punishment—my mother gave it all. He always wanted to be the good guy.

THERAPIST: And he always wanted to see high standards from you?

LISA: Oh yes—completely. He gave me everything he lacked when he was raised in the semislums of Philadelphia.

THERAPIST: What about your mother?

LISA: Possessive — critical — domineering — competitive — negative — but she tried to do everything for me. I mean I never lacked anything. She was always there to drive me or take me or pick me up.

THERAPIST: Well, what was your general feeling toward her?

LISA: I didn't like her—I still to this day can't bear to have her near me or

---

[41]Possibly a key conditioning experience in the development of the "fear of trusting," a result of which was the inhibition of her sexual response.

[42]Patients are often aware that they should behave assertively, but usually cannot do so without help.

[43]This began the formal background questioning. Topics previously covered were, of course, not repeated.

touch me. I didn't want either of them to touch me as a child.[44] It even distresses me to think about it—that's how hostile I was towards both of them.

THERAPIST: Something must have happened to make it unpleasant.

LISA: She was just critical—it was just one constant criticism.

THERAPIST: What in particular did she criticize?

LISA: I don't mean criticizing me as a person—I mean critical of my actions—if I didn't put my napkin on my lap at dinner time—corrective measures. It was just a constant sort of thing. My father had a very destructive side. He used to get me pets and if they didn't please him, then he would have them given away or destroyed, which was extremely upsetting to me as a child.[45]

THERAPIST: That is extraordinary.

LISA: It's a little cruel, isn't it? When I went away to school and wasn't a good student, when I came home for vacation my dog was gone. When I first got married, I had played the piano for 14 years. I came back and my piano was gone. There were lots of little things like that. When I wouldn't divorce my first husband during a very rocky marriage, I was disowned. It's amazing to me that I've lasted 12 years with Ed. To me it's just incredible; that he's seen all of me and he still doesn't hate me.

THERAPIST: Well, why should he?

LISA: I guess because maybe I hate myself and I'm sure everyone else will, too. I mean in total picture; oh, there are lots of things I don't desire to change at all.

THERAPIST: You mean you expect to be hated?

LISA: Maybe, yes—disliked.

THERAPIST: But you might be quite wrong in thinking that you should be.[46]

LISA: I don't know.

THERAPIST: Well, I rather think that's true. At what age did you have your first sexual feelings?

LISA: Toward boys—I guess about—

THERAPIST: Did you have them towards girls?

LISA: No. I guess around nine—eight or nine.

THERAPIST: Did you engage in masturbation?

LISA: Yes.

---

[44]It is possible that this negative conditioning to touching was a factor in the development of her sexual inhibitions. She had, however, always enjoyed erotic touching.

[45]It is easy to see how this would have increased her fear of trusting people close to her.

[46]Putting a spoke in the wheel of this belief.

THERAPIST: At what age?

LISA: About nine.

THERAPIST: Did you have any feelings of guilt about it?

LISA: Yes.

THERAPIST: What did you think would happen?

LISA: I was afraid someone would discover me.[47]

THERAPIST: You didn't think it would do anything terrible to you?

LISA: I didn't know.

THERAPIST: Well, some just enjoy themselves and don't care.

LISA: Oh, really?

THERAPIST: And some have been given some sex instruction and they—

LISA: I was given none—ever about anything.

THERAPIST: So you had a sort of fear of discovery. But did you have any fear that you might be doing harm? Did you think that God might punish you?

LISA: There wasn't any God in my life. I had never been taken into the Church.

THERAPIST: When did you start dating and all that sort of thing?[48]

LISA: Well, I went to dancing class when I was about 9 years of age—but dating—maybe 12, 13—you know, little parties where your parents drove you, picked you up—stupid little tea dances.

THERAPIST: Well, when did you become interested in any person?

LISA: I was interested very definitely in one boy when I was—from about the age of 9 on till about 12 or 13 maybe. I thought he was perfectly marvelous.

THERAPIST: What did you think was marvelous about him?

LISA: He was just bright and blond and handsome and athletic.

THERAPIST: Was there anyone important before your first husband?

LISA: No—no one.

THERAPIST: What was your first husband's name?

LISA: Sid.

THERAPIST: What did you like about him?

LISA: He was blond and charming and quiet, pleasant and handsome—all the men in my life were quiet.

THERAPIST: Well, what happened?

LISA: It was one constant harangue—one violent fight after another.

THERAPIST: What were the causes?

---

[47]This early fear was another etiological factor in the development of her sexual inhibition, in which the production of fears of being revealed and of trusting seemed to have combined.

[48]Further inquiries into her sexual history were now begun in a very open-ended way.

LISA: I guess I was hostile and irritable. Sexually we weren't compatible — I knew something was wrong with me.

THERAPIST: With you?

LISA: Yes — I mean I couldn't achieve orgasm and, of course, this started to disturb me greatly.

THERAPIST: Was this the main thing that disturbed you?

LISA: Oh, I think so, yes.

THERAPIST: This is terribly important. Are you telling me that if you had had orgasms no trouble would have arisen in this marriage?

LISA: I think I would have been able to adapt. I really don't know. I mean if you're irritable and hostile because your sexual relations aren't right — how do you know how you'd react to everyday living?

THERAPIST: Well, tell me, actually what used to happen?

LISA: It just was a tempestuous sort of relationship. I think he was a perennial sophomore college type and, of course, I was trying to do all the little things to make a marriage hold together. He wanted a playmate and I wasn't it.

THERAPIST: Before you married did you get on well?

LISA: Oh, yes. I can never remember one bad fight that we ever had.[49]

THERAPIST: Then, when you got married and there were attempts at sex, you would get aroused and you wouldn't have an orgasm?

LISA: We had sex a few times before we were married and of course, when I didn't have any orgasm, he said, "Well, that's all right because it's unnatural circumstances and you're not relaxed," etc. Of course, after you get married, you're supposed to be relaxed, aren't you?

THERAPIST: Are you saying that not having orgasms had a very strong physiological disturbing affect?

LISA: Definitely it did. It was so disturbing I went to see a strange doctor down in Memphis, Tennessee. All he did was look at me and say, "Well, I'm sure it will right itself in time — don't worry about it."

THERAPIST: Can you say why you didn't have orgasms? Could it have been anything to do with him?

LISA: No — it's me.

THERAPIST: No, wait a minute — that's sort of —

LISA: An assumption — I shouldn't —

THERAPIST: I'd just like to know why you say that — could it be that if he had handled you differently, you might have had orgasms?

LISA: No. There have been many men in my life since my first husband. It's me.

---

[49]This strongly suggests that they might have "made out" if there had been no sexual problem.

THERAPIST: Has your pattern of response to each of them been the same?

LISA: Exactly.

THERAPIST: What is that pattern of response?

LISA: Pleasure to a certain degree and wanting to be closer to somebody; and yet when it comes to the act of intercourse — nothing. You know I've always made a joke, saying I want somebody to hold my hand — period. Maybe I'm still waiting to go back to adolescence.[50]

THERAPIST: That's rubbish.

LISA: Well, I don't know — may not be.

THERAPIST: You say you get pleasure up to a degree. Tell me what the pattern is in detail?

LISA: I don't dislike it. I find the intimacy pleasurable and I like to be close to Ed — but there's no sensation there at all. I become a little edgy about it — uncomfortable — it makes me feel bad — sad — melancholy — not irritable, as in the past — I accept the pleasure that I do get to a certain degree, and accept the fact that there is nothing else. I have accepted this.

THERAPIST: Well, what actually happens — first of all, there's petting, etc. Do you find that pleasurable?

LISA: Yes — I find everything pleasant.

THERAPIST: Do you get excited?

LISA: Oh, yes.

THERAPIST: Do you get really strongly excited?

LISA: Yes.

THERAPIST: And then it's only during the actual act of intercourse that you get no sensation?

LISA: No sensation whatsoever.

THERAPIST: What happens if your clitoris is stimulated?

LISA: Nothing.

THERAPIST: Nothing at all?

LISA: No.

THERAPIST: But you said to me at an earlier stage that you had masturbated.

LISA: Yes.

THERAPIST: Does that mean that an orgasm can be induced by digital stimulation?

LISA: It hasn't so far — no.

THERAPIST: And by you yourself?

LISA: No.

THERAPIST: When you were a child?

---

[50]Even if there had been some evidence to support this proposition, it had no practical implications, suggested no direction of action for change.

LISA: No.

THERAPIST: You never had an orgasm?

LISA: Yes I have, but I don't touch myself.[51]

THERAPIST: How do you have an orgasm?

LISA: By crossing my legs and applying pressure on my muscles.

THERAPIST: Well, what does that stimulate?

LISA: I guess my clitoris, I don't know. I mean medically I don't know.

THERAPIST: I'll try not to impose the answer on you.

LISA: Well, I don't know the answer.

THERAPIST: But if it's compressed by hand, that doesn't have any effect?

LISA: No.

THERAPIST: How often can you have an orgasm that way?

LISA: How often? What do you mean how often?

THERAPIST: Well, can you do it every day?

LISA: Oh, certainly.

THERAPIST: Can you do it repeatedly?

LISA: Four or five times in a row.

THERAPIST: You regularly do that sort of thing?

LISA: Not every day—no, but when I do I can have orgasms. So I'd say I'm a pretty healthy woman. But for some reason I cannot build up an intimacy with another person. And it's not just Ed. It's anybody.

THERAPIST: Why do you say it that way? You say you can't build up an intimacy. Do you mean that in a general way or just in a physical sense?

LISA: I mean in any way.

THERAPIST: You spoke of this kind of thing happening when you were at school. There was a sort of fearfulness about persons. Do you still have that?

LISA: Yes.

THERAPIST: Well, that might be the clue. Let me just pursue it one step further. Suppose you have been stimulated sexually and you haven't had an orgasm in the usual way, can you or do you then go ahead and give yourself one by compressing your thighs?

LISA: No.

THERAPIST: Now, why is that?

LISA: Because Ed is there.[52]

THERAPIST: Oh, I see.

---

[51]Once again demonstrating the value of insistent questioning. Her ability to have masturbatory orgasms was crucially important.

[52]This answer was the "open sesame" of the case. It was now plain that all efforts directed at giving Lisa coital orgasms must fail as long as she could not bear to be seen having even masturbatory orgasms.

LISA: I told you it was an embarrassing thing with me when I was a child and it still is. I guess it became a personal withdrawn sort of action.

THERAPIST: How terribly interesting. Next week we'll begin treatment.

LISA: You mean there's treatment for this?

THERAPIST: Oh, yes. We do have to have a little more history — but not much.

"The good feeling" that Lisa reported at the beginning of the third session persisted thereafter. The undercurrent of misery that had been present for many years, with frequent spells of high anxiety, anger, and depression, had evidently been overcome. The crux of the problem had been seen to be the belief that her inability to have coital orgasms indicated an irremediable constitutional deficiency. She had learned the falseness of this belief — partly by being shown that it was not logically justified, and partly by the provision of an explanation that accorded with her own experience. She could see how her inhibited sexual responses were related to emotional responses learned in the course of unfortunate experiences, combined with the assurance that what has been learned can be unlearned. Thus, by cognitive correction the foremost goal of therapy had been rapidly achieved.

It remained necessary to overcome Lisa's fear of being observed having an orgasm. Although the treatment needed was reconditioning and not cognitive correction, it is given here to round off the account. (It is difficult to see how it could have been overcome by any cognitive input.) When Lisa planned to masturbate, Ed's geographic proximity made her anxious, even if he were visiting three houses away, and it increased when he was nearer. Accordingly, desensitization on a distance dimension was planned. But the first time she was asked to close her eyes for the purpose of relaxing, she became very anxious at closing them in my presence — another manifestation of her fear of trusting people. She was then instructed to close her eyes only until she felt the slightest anxiety, and then to open them and keep them open until the anxiety subsided. The period of closure then progressively lengthened, and before the session ended she could close her eyes indefinitely without anxiety in my presence — an interesting instance of *in vivo* desensitization. Thereafter, standard desensitization was used to overcome the anxiety related to Ed's proximity during masturbation, by having her imagine herself masturbate while he was in places progressively closer.

When Lisa was able to masturbate without anxiety in Ed's presence, it was possible to organize a series of steps through which the masturbatory orgasm was integrated into coitus in a way that both of them found satisfying. The jealousy reaction faded out as sexual progress continued. Five months later, Lisa wrote: "My days continue to be filled with sunshine and my evenings begin with a million stars." There has not been a shadow of recurrence of the original emotional turmoil in a 16-year follow-up, despite numerous stresses, including divorce from Ed in the second year.

THE FAMILY OF HYPOCHONDRIACAL ANXIETIES

Lisa's was an unusual case of hypochondriacal anxiety—meaning anxiety aroused by symptoms that are mistakenly attributed to a grave pathological state. Although no statistical breakdown is available, it appears that most hypochondriacal anxieties are cognitively based.

The commonest form of hypochondriacal anxiety is baseless fear of heart disease. The symptoms from which the wrong diagnosis is deduced are usually tachycardia, palpitations, and pain in the front of the chest—in various combinations. It is necessary as a first step in every case for a physician to eliminate the existence of actual pathology. Quite often, his reassurance quells the fear (for example, case 23). But some patients, not unreasonably, require in addition a positive explanation for their symptoms. Chest pain is often caused by gastrointestinal distension or skeletomuscular conditions of the chest wall. In many gastrointestinal cases the characteristic pain can be elicited by drinking a glass of orange juice to which a teaspoonful of sodium bicarbonate has been added. This proves that the pain is gastric and not cardiac.

In contrast, proof is irrelevant when fear is not misconceptual, but classically conditioned. A person may react fearfully to a certain quality of pain as a function of its location on the trunk. It will require systematic desensitization to a hierarchy of positions (see chapter 9).

Also very common is fear of mental disintegration. This may be due to misinterpretation of any of a variety of symptoms—e.g., dizziness, light-headedness, giddiness, tremor, or paresthesia. The symptoms seem more ominous when the patient's physician is unable to explain them. They are frequently due to hyperventilation (whose effects extend beyond panic disorder). Its role can be confirmed by noting the effects of voluntary hyperventilation. I reinforce reassuring findings by firmly telling the patient that he is not of the "right" constitutional type. Some sophisticated patients may be told of physiological criteria (Wolpe, 1970), and a few may be offered the ultimate reassurance of a pupillography that detects predisposition to schizophrenia (Rubin, 1970).

The following cases are examples of the treatment of anxiety-response habits based on false beliefs.

Case 23: Fear of Heart Attacks

Mr. S., a 43-year-old car dealer, was sitting in an office doing routine work when suddenly he felt flushing of his face, shortness of breath, and a constriction in his chest. He became very anxious, thinking that he was about to die because his father and brother had both died of heart attacks, and his sister had died of high blood pressure. Even though a medical checkup showed that he was in perfect health, he was left with the feeling that something was wrong. From then on, he was continuously anxious whenever he was alone. He also occasionally had inexplicable, frightening attacks like the first one. These could have been panic attacks, but paroxysmal tachycardia could not be ruled out.

When I first saw Mr. S., this fear had been with him for 5 years. I began by carefully explaining to him that the major attacks were typical of a kind of rapid beating of the heart that occurs in normal people. It starts suddenly, stops just as suddenly after minutes or hours, and produces strange sensations like those he had experienced. While it is an unusual state of heart function, it is not harmful. It took six sessions and the help of medical textbooks to convince him that he was in no danger. Through losing his fear of these symptoms, he lost his fear of being alone. On a later occasion I saw Mr. S. during an attack and confirmed the diagnosis of paroxysmal tachycardia.

Case 24: Fear of Cancer

Mrs. T., 60 years old, had had an obsessional fear of cancer for 20 years that had not been helped by numerous treatments, including psychoanalysis and insulin-shock treatment. When she was 17, her parents had persuaded her to marry a kindly man of "good family" to whom she was not attracted and who was not as bright as she. The marriage was an emotional disaster, but she was unable to leave her husband because she was afraid that her parents would disapprove. As time went on, the anxiety caused by her conflicting emotions increased, generating "terrible depressions and attacks of panic."

When Mrs. T. was 51, she had a hysterectomy for benign myomata of the uterus. On coming around from the anesthesia, she asked the nurse, "Did I have cancer or didn't I?" The nurse replied, "A friend of mine had cancer and lived to be 70." Mrs. T. was terrified, and even when the surgeon showed her reports that the tumors were not malignant, she remained unconvinced. She began probing for cancers, especially in her breasts, and then as time passed, she moved to suspecting other parts of her body on the flimsiest grounds. When Mrs. T. came to see me, she was obsessed with the thought that she had cancer of the intestines. She scrutinized her bowel movements and panicked at any slight diarrhea or constipation. She was under the impression that cancer could develop in a day or a week; consequently, she had had repeated x-rays and other examinations.

Realizing that it was her wrong thinking that had to be changed, I presented her with pathological evidence that cancer of the bowel takes a year to double its size. She had recently had a sigmoidoscopy that had shown no abnormality of the bowel wall. "If," I reasoned with her, "you have cancer of the bowel now that is so small that it cannot be seen with this instrument, it will still be of negligible size a year from now. Even then it may be too small to be detected. And a cancer of the bowel that small cannot produce diarrhea or any other symptoms. So cancer is the one thing that *cannot* be their cause. A once-a-year checkup with this instrument is more than enough." This argument repeated in different ways over several sessions markedly diminished her fear. (Her extensive social fears called for a combination of assertiveness training and systematic desensitization, with which, unfortunately, she did not persist.)

It is often not enough just to reason with a patient if his thinking is to be changed. An activity in which he participates can play a vital role in changing what he perceives to be the source of fear. The activity may be quite elaborate, as illustrated in the unusual case of Mr. E. who had an all-engulfing fear of rabies.

Case 25: Fear of Rabies

Mr. E.'s fear of rabies had begun 2 years previously when, having been scratched by a stray cat, he had seen a doctor who had asked him, "Do you reckon that cats may be rabid?" Two months before he came to see me, the fear had become much worse after he had read of a child who had died of rabies after being bitten by a bat in daylight. Because he knew that bats fly most often after dark, Mr. E. had become afraid of being out at night. He had blocked his chimney and locked all the doors and windows, but since reading about the boy, he had become reluctant to go out even during the day.

I therefore had to convince him that he had an impregnable defense against rabies. At the time, only a painful and temporarily effective vaccine was available, but he was willing to put up with the discomfort of the vaccine in order to become free of his fear. Since serum examination at the university's laboratories showed no antibodies to rabies, we went ahead with the vaccination. A few days later a second examination showed significant antibodies. Both reports were shown to Mr. E., who, upon reading them, felt very relieved. His family doctor in his home town agreed to provide booster injections as often as necessary. Mr. E.'s belief that he now had nothing to fear from any rabies-infected bite (no matter how remote the possibility), put an end to his fearful obsession. Nevertheless, he was enjoined to consult his doctor at once if by chance he were bitten (mainly because of the danger of sepsis).

Follow-up information was obtained through the family doctor over a period of 8 years. The phobia did not recur, and the treatment was later facilitated by the development of a less painful vaccine with more durable effects.

Thought Stopping

Thought stopping is a method of changing cognitive behavior that, unlike the cognitive correction procedures described above, does not depend on changing the meanings of words or the implications of situations. It is a way of eliminating day-to-day preoccupations with useless thoughts. It consists of training the patient to exclude at the earliest moment—even, if possible, before formulation—every undesirable or unproductive thought.

Thought stopping was introduced to me by James G. Taylor in 1955 (see Wolpe, 1958), but, unknown to him, it had already been described by Alexander Bain (1928). Rosen and Ornstein (1976) reported a still earlier usage by Lewis (1875), who treated a man who was preoccupied with thoughts of nude women by having him switch his thoughts whenever a sexual idea entered his mind, a program that proved very effective. Taylor regarded the method as parallel to his successful treatment of a case of compulsive eyebrow plucking of 31 years' duration by training the patient to inhibit the chain of movements leading to the compulsive act (see Taylor, 1963). If motor habits can be overcome by inhibiting the relevant response, so can thinking habits.

Unrealistic, unproductive, and anxiety-arousing, perseverating trains of thought are a common clinical problem. If chronic, they are called obsessions. Many are only episodic. A businessman, for example, constantly brooded upon the possibility of a fire breaking out in one of his warehouses after a friend of his suffered a severe financial loss.

An essential preliminary to training in thought stopping is to reach agreement with the patient that particular categories of thought are indeed futile and therefore worth the trouble necessary to eliminate them. The training in thought stopping typically begins by asking the patient to close his eyes and verbalize a typical futile thought sequence. During the verbalization the therapist suddenly shouts, "Stop!" and then draws the patient's attention to the fact that the thoughts actually do stop. This is repeated several times, and then the patient is urged to try stopping the thoughts by saying "Stop!" himself, subvocally. He is warned that the thoughts will return, but every time they do, he must interrupt them again. Effort is later directed at trying to stifle each unwanted thought at its birth. The moment it looms, the patient must quickly inhibit it by concentrating on something else. The thoughts in many cases return less and less readily and eventually cease to be a problem.

Modifications of the method are applied to patients with whom the standard procedure fails. A fairly uncomfortable faradic shock accompanying the "stop" signal may successfully disrupt the negative thought sequence. Or the patient may be asked to keep his mind on pleasant thoughts and to press a button which activates a buzzer each time a useless thought intrudes.

Whenever the buzzer sounds, the therapist instantly shouts, "Stop!" Usually, in the course of the session, there is a progressive decline in buzzer pressing, which may be steep, for example, from 20 times per minute to once every two minutes in the course of a 15-minute treatment period.

Some years ago, I took advantage of an opportunity to observe the effects of this procedure on myself. I had been involved in a legal dispute that was finally settled at a meeting of principals and lawyers. Later that day, reflecting upon the proceedings, I became very disturbed when I realized how ineptly I had handled an important interchange. Dwelling continuously on the matter, I became increasingly distressed. I decided to try the thought stopping that I so readily recommended to patients. I found it very difficult to do, for the thoughts were seemingly borne along by the anxiety that they themselves had stirred up; but I worked at it assiduously, and after an hour, I noticed that the general anxiety level was distinctly lower. After 2 more hours, I was no longer troubled by the thoughts. Even when my anxiety was high, it seemed that the successful exclusion of a thought slightly diminished it; and when the anxiety was low, this effect was quite marked.

While thought stopping has its most frequent use for episodic preoccupation or brooding, it is also occasionally of great value in the treatment of true obsessions. In an obsessional neurosis of 8 years' duration reported by Yamagami (1971), it was the sole agent of recovery. The patient was a 24-year-old male graduate student whose obsession consisted in verbalizing in thought the names of colors, counting numbers, and typing words in fantasy. The color obsession was predominant, occurring an average of 110 times per day. Colored sticks, which could trigger the color obsession, were placed in front of the subject. He was told to look at them and not to try to suppress whatever obsessional thinking came to mind. He was to signal the onset of the obsessive thoughts by raising a finger. At this point the therapist would shout, "Stop," which he was instructed to repeat. By the fourth session, the obsession had diminished by about 80%. Treatment was continued for a total of 17 sessions, in the course of which three variations of the technique were used. In one of them an electric shock was substituted for the shouting of the word "Stop." At the time of the 17th weekly session the obsession had decreased to about five occurrences per day; and the patient could control it easily by saying, "Stop," subvocally, on any occasion. A month after the end of treatment, the color obsession disappeared completely. At a 7-month follow-up, it had not recurred, and the other obsessions were reported to be progressively decreasing.

From the personal experience described above, as well as the testimony of patients, there is reason to believe that thought-stopping procedures work by reinforcing thought inhibition through the anxiety-reducing consequences of each successful effort at thought inhibition. This hypothesis could be tested by psychophysiological monitoring.

COGNITIVISM: A RETROGRESSIVE
THEORY OF THERAPY

Through most of human history, mental events—perceiving, feeling, thinking, and deciding—were regarded as functions of the "mind," an entity that is supposedly separate from the body and that obeys its own rules—our old friend, the "Ghost in the Machine" (chapter 2). Only with the emergence of an objectively based science of human behavior could psychology be integrated with biology. As the result of investigations that began with Sechenov a century ago (see Sechenov, 1965) and culminated in the work of Taylor (1962), it became apparent that even the most complex human behavior could be understood in organismal terms. This was, for psychology, a revolution and a rebirth. In psychotherapy, behavior therapy was the logical offspring of this revolution, and the logical successor to the preexisting mentalistic theories.

Recent years have witnessed a strong resurgence of mentalistic thinking. It is widely held that cognitive errors or distortions are, after all, the sole cause of neuroses (see, e.g., Beck, 1976; Ellis, 1974; Goldfried & Goldfried, 1975; Mahoney, 1977; Meichenbaum, 1975; Raimy, 1976). Mahoney (1977) has labeled this viewpoint "the cognitive revolution." If neurotic problems were all due to wrong ways of thinking, then thought correction would always indeed be what was needed to overcome them. While the cognitivists unflinchingly assert that this is the case, it should be noted that in practice they frequently use behavioral procedures such as assertiveness training and systematic desensitization, employing cognitive interpretations for their success (e.g., Beck, 1976).

For the cognitivists, emotional conditioning and, more specifically, learned automatic triggering of fear responses do not exist. To take the example of a person who has a fear of being the center of attention, they suppose that between the perception of the situation of being the center of attention and the fear that follows, some kind of thought-out rationale is necessarily interposed, for example, "being the center of attention is dangerous, because it will expose my ignorance." Essentially, then, an idea of danger is seen as the universal mediator of fear. But they claim that the mediating thought is there even when there is no evidence of it, ignoring the evidence (outlined in chapter 3) that it is common to observe fear unmediated by thoughts of danger.

The cognitivists' insistence that all maladaptive fears are cognitively based leads to a major divergence between their practices and those of behavior therapy. Whereas behavior therapists use cognitive methods only in cases in which anxieties have evident misconceptual sources, cognitive therapists use them in all cases. This means that when a misconceptual basis for anxiety is not presented by the patient (as illustrated in example 4, p. 104), the cognitivists invent them. They do this in different ways. Ellis routinely imposes on the patient an array of irrational thoughts that he assumes all patients have—such as "awfulizing," or adhering to an irrational system of "musts" and "must nots" (Dryden & Ellis, 1987; Ellis, 1962, pp. 126–128). Beck projects six types of "cognitive errors" into the mind of the patient (Beck, 1976; DeRubeis & Beck, 1988). These include seeking out "cognitive errors" (that are often unconnected to the patient's maladaptive fears) and identifying "automatic thoughts." It is noteworthy that when treatment of these cognitive artifacts is added to behavior therapy it does not improve outcomes (Latimer & Sweet, 1984).

Fundamental Objections to the Cognitivist View of Psychotherapy

The following considerations are incompatible with the cognitivist view that the psychotherapeutic task consists of nothing but cognitive correction.

1. Most neurotic patients are afraid of situations that they judge as not objectively dangerous, and this judgment persists, contrary to Beck's (1976) contention, while they are anxious. For example, a woman's lifelong fear of mice began when, at the age of 5, her brother had chased her all over the yard with a mouse he held in his hand. She knew very well that mice were harmless, but even the picture of one aroused fear.

2. When a situation evokes anxiety, not only its picture, but also imagining it usually evokes anxiety (Wade, Malloy, & Proctor, 1977), though the subject can scarcely believe that the image is dangerous. This fact cannot be handled by cognitivist theory and thus disconfirms it. By contrast, anxiety that is a conditioned response is arousable by both real and imaginary images of the stimulus.

3. Standard desensitization does not include corrective information. Beck (1976) has argued that the patient gets better because he realizes in the course of the procedure that he is having little or no fear, but the realization is merely a reflection that desensitization has diminished the fear response to the given stimulus. This differs from the cognitive case, in which the elimination of fear occurs secondary to realization that what was thought to be dangerous is not so.

4. Rachaim, Lefebvre, and Jenkins (1980) showed that changes in behavior altered cognitions, rendering unnecessary any adjuvant cognitive strategy. Cognitivists strain the facts to fit their explanations. This is the same in principle as Weitzman's (1967) effort to explain the effects of systematic desensitization on the basis of psychoanalytically derived propositions. As I pointed out in a critique of Weitzman (Wolpe, 1971), it is always possible to explain particular phenomena on the basis of almost any ad hoc idea. One

might, for instance, explain gravity as the action of angels seizing objects and pulling them downward. It is logically possible, but unpersuasive without evidence of the angels.

5. A patient who is continuously anxious may be found to have a specific persistent fear, for example, of going insane. Strong reassurance may convince him to the contrary, yet his anxiety may not materially diminish. A few inhalations of a mixture of carbon dioxide and oxygen (Wolpe, 1973, pp. 157, 183) may lastingly remove that anxiety (e.g., Latimer, 1977; Steketee & Roy, 1977). The success of this treatment cannot be explained as a matter of cognitive correction. The procedure removes the anxiety response habit, and subsequently the patient realizes that he is no longer liable to anxiety.

6. A clinical experiment that inadvertently provided data contradicting the "pure cognitive theory" was reported by Seitz (1953). He encouraged 25 patients with psychocutaneous excoriation syndromes to express, during his interviews with them, their hostile feelings toward other people, while explicitly discouraging them from acting out their aggressions in their life situations. Eleven of the 25 disobeyed him, and in these 11 alone the skin cleared up. As we often also find when we are teaching assertiveness, emotional change does not follow a change of viewpoint but is related to new outward behavior based on the new viewpoint.

7. A recently vaunted strong point of cognitivist theory has been the proposition that panic attacks are caused by catastrophic misattributions (e.g., Clark, 1986). Misattributions are very common in panic, though not invariable (Rachman, Levitt, & Lopatka, 1987), but when they occur they do add to the severity of the panic. However, a study by Wolpe and Rowan (1988) found that in every first panic, if there was a misattribution, it *followed* the panic. The first panic is evidently an unconditioned fear response. (For further discussion see chapter 14.)

8. It has been claimed (e.g., Beck, 1976) that nonpsychotic depressions are cognitively based and respond particularly well to cognitive therapy. This claim is invalid for at least two reasons: (a) the claim is based on studies of nonpsychotic depression, which is a mixture of endogenous and neurotic depressions (Akiskal et al., 1979); (b) totally ignored are the nonspecific effects of the therapeutic relationship, which would contribute to overcoming those depressions that are anxiety-based, just as they contribute to all psychotherapy of neuroses (see chapter 15).

Ellis (1986) has argued against the considerations given earlier for the existence of anxieties that do not depend on misconceptions and that can be seen as classically conditioned. However, all he really does is to sidestep the issues. To begin with, he misattributes to me the statement that if neurotic individuals can be upset by imagining a fearful situation, that is an indication "that cognitive therapy often does not work." This is not my point. The point is that if a person is upset by imagining a fearful situation it cannot be because he believes that the image can hurt him. The same is true of fear of a picture of a fearful thing.

Ellis's response is that a neurotic individual may "partly know" that a situation is not objectively dangerous but also "know" that it is. What is this but a play on words? Where are the data to show that a person really believes that the picture of a thing he fears is dangerous even when he declares that there is no danger in the picture. In the absence of data, it is both parsimonious and elegant to attribute the fear to conditioning, rather than to insist that it must have a cognitive basis, merely because Ellis must stick to his theory at all costs.

Anxiety at the sight of a test-tube full of blood is another disconfirming example. Since here, too, the person can point to no danger, Ellis attempts to deal with it also on the "partly know" theory. He states that while individuals may know that there is no danger of "pain of bloodletting they may also know that it reminds them of their anxiety of bloodletting." But this reminder is manufactured by Ellis. The patients concerned do not speak of bloodletting.

The purport of the foregoing critique of cognitivism must be clearly understood. It is not an attack on cognition. Cognition is part of all that we do and participates in all therapeutic action. The target of the critique is *cognitivism*, the theory that all maladaptive fears are due to misattributions or cognitive distortions, and that therefore the function of all psychotherapy is the correcting of wrong thinking. The considerations in the above critique decisively disconfirm that theory.

8
Assertiveness Training

This is the first of several chapters that deal with specific methods of eliminating classically conditioned anxiety-response habits. Although systematic desensitization is the most widely used method, assertiveness training will be considered first. Its change-inducing operations occur mainly outside the consulting room, which makes it advantageous to introduce at a very early stage. It is frequently initiated on the basis of relatively simple instructions, leading, in many cases, to significant change in a matter of weeks.

Assertive behavior is the socially appropriate verbal and motor expression of any emotion other than anxiety. Assertiveness training is indicated when a person finds it difficult to express his feelings in social contexts because anxiety inhibits him. Thus, the primary target of the training is to decondition maladaptive social anxiety responses, exploiting the competition of other emotions that are present at the same time. The therapist's role is to enhance the expression of the emotions. Since these are subserved by bodily responses that are different from those of anxiety, they are potentially competitive with it. Their intensity, and therefore their competitiveness, is increased by encouraging their motor expression.

The contexts in which assertiveness training is appropriate are numerous. In all of them the patient is inhibited from the performances of "normal" behavior because of neurotic fear. The fear factor distinguishes them from the less common cases in which there is primarily a lack of social skill — such as how to make an approach or how to break away gracefully. Fear inhibits the patient from saying or doing things that would seem reasonable and right to an observer. He or she may be unable to complain about poor service in a restaurant from fear of hurting the waiter's feelings; unable to express differences of opinion to friends from fear that they will not like him or her; unable to get up and leave a social situation that has become boring from fear of seeming ungrateful; unable to ask for the repayment of a loan or to administer a legitimate reproof to a subordinate out of fear of losing the image of being a "nice person"; or unable to express love, warmth, admiration, or praise because such expressions are embarrassing. Besides the behaviors that fear prevents, there may be others that a person cannot restrain because of it. For example, the patient may compulsively reach for the lunch check on every occasion to ward off a fear of incurring an obligation, or talk too much because silence creates anxiety. In the context of such anxieties as the latter two, assertiveness training is either irrelevant or secondary. One cannot be assertively silent if one is anxious about what the other person is thinking about the silence. Systematic desensitization is a necessary preliminary to assertiveness training in such cases.

A common history in patients who have difficulty in asserting themselves is of early teaching that has overemphasized social obligations, engendering the feeling that the rights of others are more important than their own. An extreme example was a 36-year-old man whose parents had strongly insisted on polite submissiveness. During World War II, at the age of 8, he had gone to live for 2 years with an uncle and aunt who had encouraged self-expression. The behavior learned during that time was severely punished when the child returned to his parental home, a circumstance which led to a profound and enduring habit of timidity, especially toward authority figures.

The therapist's interventions are aimed at augmenting every impulse toward the elicitation, under appropriate circumstances, of such anxiety-inhibiting responses as the expression of legitimate anger. The expectation is that each occasion of expression will result in some degree of weakening of the anxiety-response habit. Meanwhile, the motor behavior that is the vehicle for the anger is reinforced by its favorable consequences, such as awareness of the attainment of control of the social situation, reduction of anxiety, and, later, the approbation of the therapist. The counterconditioning of anxiety and the operant conditioning of the motor act take place simultaneously, facilitating each other. (For a fuller discussion, see Wolpe, 1958.)

Operant conditioning of assertive behavior is employed alone in a person who lacks it not because of anxiety but because he or she simply has not acquired the appropriate motor habits for certain social situations. Such a person literally needs what is called social skills training (see below). Unfortunately, the latter is often used where assertiveness training should be given.

Like all other methods of behavior therapy, assertiveness training is applied only in relevant contexts. Some patients are unassertive in a very wide range of personal interactions; to these, Salter's (1949) appellation, "the inhibitory personality," is descriptively apt. Here, almost any social interaction provides grounds for assertiveness training. Other people need such training only in particular contexts. There are those who are able to handle tradesmen and strangers competently, but who are timorous and submissive with anybody who is important to them, like a mother, a wife, or a good friend. Others are comfortable with close associates and may even dominate them, but are fearful, awkward, and ineffective with the "outgroup."

The quintessence of assertive behavior is to do toward others what is reasonable and right. It is well brought out in the following extract from a written statement by a patient who was a journalist (Wolpe, 1958, 118):

> I have been given the assignment of winning emotional victories in daily life. . . . This is the important discovery I have made — and it is a satisfying one emotionally. Other people's opinions and feelings count — but so do mine. This does not mean that I have become aggressive, unpleasant, or inconsiderate to other people. . . . This new method of coping with interpersonal situations simply boils down to doing the things which, if you were an onlooker watching the situation, would seem fair and fitting.

The interrelations between assertive and other categories of behavior are illustrated in figure 8.1. Assertiveness encompasses many categories of emotional behavior. The most common category is oppositional behavior (e.g., standing up for reasonable rights). But not all oppositional behavior belongs to the assertive category. Behavior that is provocative, aggressive, violent, or even sarcastic, is outside the definition of assertiveness given above. A second major category of assertiveness is the expression of affec-

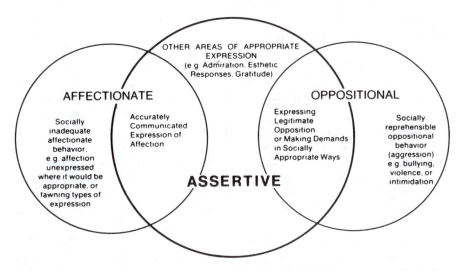

Fig. 8.1. Interrelations between assertive, oppositional, and affectionate categories of behavior. (Courtesy of Graphic Communications, Eastern Pennsylvania Psychiatric Institute, Philadelphia.)

tion of all kinds or degrees. There is also a wide group of miscellaneous assertive responses that include admiration, gratitude, the expression of opinions and questions, and various modes of humorous expressiveness.

There has been relatively little psychophysiological research on the inter-relations between the various emotional states since the early survey by Leschke (1914). Arnold (1945) marshaled evidence of physiological antago-nism between anger and anxiety. Ax (1953) expressed doubts about this, although his own data to some extent supported it. Arnold (1960) later collected further supporting data. Soviet research (Simonov, 1967) has yielded impressive evidence of the existence of separate and reciprocally inhibitory centers for anger and anxiety in the midbrain. When either of these sources of emotional responses is put out of action by drugs or by ablations, the other is facilitated. A study by Izard and Blumberg (1985) obtained evidence of differences between emotions at both psychophysio-logical and neurobiological levels.

PRELIMINARIES TO ASSERTIVENESS TRAINING

Before assertiveness training can begin, the patient must accept its reason-ableness. Sometimes submission to the needs of others is bound up with the general philosophy that it is morally good to place the interests of others ahead of one's own. An extreme example of this is the person who, on religious grounds, makes a practice of turning the other cheek. I tell him or her that this policy is practical only for rare saintly individuals and that from everybody else biology exacts its toll for behavior contrary to the interests of the organism. I add that most people who turn the other cheek do so because they are socially anxious.

There are, however, patients who raise doubts about the morality of as-sertive behavior. A reasoned response to them may start by pointing out that any one of three principles may guide a person's approach to interpersonal relations. One possible principle is to consider one's self only and ride roughshod over others to get what one wants. Psychopathic personalities are the extreme embodiment of this. While they may get away with it to a considerable extent, sooner or later they usually fall foul of society. A sec-ond possible principle is always to put others before oneself. People who follow this policy are frequently emotionally upset, their feelings fluctuating between guilt at falling short of their own standards of selflessness and annoyance at the frustrations of self-abnegation. It is this kind of person the Talmudist had in mind when he wrote, "If I am not for myself, who will be for me?" This question expresses an awareness of the reality that the welfare of the organism begins with its own integrity. But the Talmudist went on to ask, "But if I am for myself alone, what am I?" Consideration of the latter question leads on to the third possible principle of conduct: the individual puts himself first, but takes others into account. He or she conforms to the requirements of social living while yielding to the demands of biology.

Most patients can readily be brought to recognize the need for appropriate assertiveness. Some have always been aware of it. The insight as such, however, produces no change (Seitz, see p. 133; Rathus, 1972). The therapist must help the patient to translate the insight into action. Simple coaxing and directing are often all that is necessary. This consists in part of emphasizing the disadvantages of nonassertion—its inevitable winlessness, its frequently unpleasant emotional consequences, and the unfavorable image it gives to others—and in part, of promising increasing ease of execution of assertive acts as anxiety diminishes. I tell patients that the power to assert grows with action like a snowball rolling down a slope. Sometimes it is helpful to tell the story of a successful previous case. If assertion results from these interventions, it can be seen as being due to a summation between an already-present action tendency (to protest, for example) and the promptings of the therapist.

A suitable context for starting assertiveness training often emerges in a very natural way from the patient's narration of some recent incident. An alternative starting point may be found in his or her responses to the Willoughby Personality Schedule (Appendix A)—particularly if there are high numerical responses to the following questions: Are your feelings easily hurt? Are you shy? Does criticism hurt you badly? Are you self-conscious before superiors?

To take the first of these as an example, the therapist asks for an actual situation that hurts the patient's feelings, and follows this up by inquiring how he or she would handle the situation. If the proposed handling is unassertive, the therapist proposes an assertive substitute. A route to the initiation of assertion in "outgroup" contexts takes off from asking the patient how he or she behaves in one or more set situations, such as the following:

1. What do you do if, after having bought an article in a shop, you walk out and find that your change is a dollar short?
2. What do you do if, arriving home after buying an article on the way, you find it slightly damaged?
3. What do you do if somebody pushes in front of you in line (e.g., at the theater)?
4. At a shop, while you wait for the clerk to finish with the customer ahead of you, another customer arrives and also waits. What do you do if the clerk subsequently directs his attention to that third customer?
5. You order a steak rare and it arrives well done. How do you handle the situation?

In each of these situations, people ought to be able to stand up for themselves and right the wrong. If they are unable to do so, a context for assertiveness training exists. These examples all relate to interactions with strangers. It is necessary also to explore unassertiveness with people involved in the patient's life. A useful inventory for identifying areas of inadequate assertiveness has been provided by Gambrill and Richey (1975).

THE CONDUCT OF ASSERTIVENESS TRAINING

Let us trace how assertiveness training may begin out of the third of the above questions:

THERAPIST: What do you do if you are standing in line for theater tickets and somebody gets in front of you?
PATIENT: I don't do anything.
THERAPIST: Well, how do you feel?
PATIENT: I feel mad. I boil up inside.
THERAPIST: So, why don't you do anything?
PATIENT: I'm afraid of hurting the other person's feelings.
(Thus, it is the fear of distressing the intruder that prevents the patient from taking action. But at the same time, the patient is angry. The therapist must try to get him or her to augment this anger by giving vent to it in a socially appropriate way. Then the level of anger may rise to a level sufficient to inhibit the anxiety.)
THERAPIST: People are taking advantage of you. This person is taking advantage of you. You should not allow it. You must say to the person, "Will you kindly go to the back of the line?" In doing this, you will be expressing your anger in a way that is appropriate to the situation and socially acceptable.

Each time the patient, by expressing anger, inhibits anxiety, the anxiety habit is weakened in some measure. But emotion is not the only component of the instigated behavior. There is also new verbal behavior: the patient for the first time tells another person to go to the back of the line, and will probably be rewarded by the approval of others in the line, and by the intruder's moving to the rear. These rewards will reinforce the patient's tendency to speak up, not only in this specific situation, but in all similar ones.

Progress in assertion depends on success. Therefore, the therapist must be aware of the details of the situations for which the counseling of assertive action is being given. The therapist would not, for example, advise the patient to insist on his or her rights standing in line in a tough neighborhood.

Case 26: Initiation of Assertiveness with Strangers

The following transcript provides a more detailed example of the initiation of assertiveness, taking off from another of the set situations on p. 139. Dorothy, a schoolteacher, was 40 years old.

THERAPIST: Suppose that you went into a shop to buy a pair of gloves and when you came to the glove counter there was somebody else standing there. Naturally you would wait. Now suppose that while you were waiting, another customer arrived. After a time the assistant finished with the customer who was there before you and turned her attention to the one that came after you. What would you do?

DOROTHY: It happens all the time. I would not say anything.

THERAPIST: What would your reason be?

DOROTHY: Well, I remember as a child my mother being very hard on salespeople and I was always embarrassed, and I tend to be the opposite. I'll stand there forever sometimes.

THERAPIST: Well, what does this actually mean? How would you feel?

DOROTHY: I would be angry. Probably more than anything angry with myself for not speaking up.

THERAPIST: So, you think that really you ought to speak up?

DOROTHY: Right.

THERAPIST: Then what prevents you?

DOROTHY: I feel tense and unhappy at making a scene.

THERAPIST: Well, I certainly agree that you should speak up. Obviously, it's a fear that is preventing it. There's the anger that you feel at the same time because of the injustice. But the fear is dominant, and that is why you've never spoken up. Now, if you do speak up, if you make it your business to speak up, you will express the anger. And each time you do that, you will push the fear down a little and each time as a result somewhat weaken the fear habit.

DOROTHY: I see.

THERAPIST: Gradually, through repetition, you will find that you don't have this fear any more and then you will naturally and easily stand up for yourself. Of course I'm not just talking about this single situation. There are all kinds of similar ones. So, I would like you to go out of your way to try to do things like that—expressing your legitimate feelings towards people. What we have been talking about is the expression of angry feelings that are appropriate. Do you have any difficulty with the expression of appropriate *positive* feelings?

DOROTHY: Yes. Sometimes I do. I notice it with my children. When they were tiny it was very easy to cuddle them. Now I find that although I love them as much as ever, it's hard to give even a little hug.

THERAPIST: As we saw in the situation where you wanted to buy gloves, it was fear that prevented the expression of feelings. In the same way, we usually find that when a person doesn't express affectionate feelings or feelings of admiration, it's also because of a kind of fearfulness. I want you to make an effort to express your affection. To the extent that you do, you'll find that it gets progressively easier, as the fear lessens. What about another kind of expressiveness? Sometimes you have a need to ask for somebody's help. Do you have any difficulty in doing this?

DOROTHY: No. I have some close friends and we reciprocate. It works out well.

THERAPIST: And you don't have any problem?

DOROTHY: No.

THERAPIST: You can make reasonable demands of people?

DOROTHY: Yes I can.

(At the next session it was seen that the instructions were already having an effect.)

DOROTHY: I more or less followed your advice and said what was on my mind on a few occasions without holding back.

THERAPIST: Very good. Give me an example.

DOROTHY: I have a very good example. I was chaperoning a swim party of 90 junior-high-school children, with five mothers to cook their meals and everything. I was the only mother who was a member of the club. So, during dinnertime a lifeguard came up to me saying the children weren't behaving very well — you're a member — do something about it. So I said, "Well, you're the lifeguard — you were hired to take care of the people in the pool, not to oversee the children's behavior."

THERAPIST: Very good. That's a very encouraging performance.

DOROTHY: Yes.

THERAPIST: Any other examples?

DOROTHY: I noticed a number of small things that occur daily — for instance, driving the car and being overly polite and letting five cars get into line when one is sufficient really. So I put a stop to that.

THERAPIST: Well, you certainly have the idea, and you are commendably on the lookout.

The examples of Dorothy dealt mainly with strange persons in public places. The following is an example of the initiation of assertiveness with significant figures in the patient's life.

Case 27: Initiation of Assertiveness With Mother-in-Law

THERAPIST: Let us talk about your mother-in-law.

MRS. A.: She is a bully, says a lot of things and does a lot of things to me that I sit back and take. I really should open my mouth and not be big about it. Personally, I don't care if the woman does not like me. I feel more for the guy in the line than I do for her, because she has done a lot of things that I feel are not right. She steps all over me and I let it boil up inside.

THERAPIST: Now what would happen if you let it out on your mother-in-law—which is what you really want to do, isn't it? Let us take an actual example.

MRS. A.: Well, she is always telling me for instance that my mother did not raise me properly.

THERAPIST: That is an insulting remark.

MRS. A.: Yes, it is, and I never say anything.

THERAPIST: Well, do you mind the remark?

MRS. A.: It cuts me, like you would stab me.

THERAPIST: And you let her get away with it. What should you do?

MRS. A.: I should say, "It is my mother. Please don't talk about her."

THERAPIST: Right. And the effect will be to increase her respect for you.

MRS. A.: My in-laws don't like the way I behave, by the way; they really don't.

THERAPIST: That's not surprising. Let me give you a contrast. Suppose you are visiting at somebody's house and you notice two men there. They are your hosts' two sons-in-law. One of them is meek and ingratiating all the time, while the other one speaks up to his in-laws. Which one gives you a better impression?

MRS. A.: The one that speaks up. You don't have to make up an example. This new fiancee of my sister-in-law is living at my in-law's house right now with them and he speaks up. They love him.

(A little later in the interview, Mrs. A. expressed concern that her husband might object to her new behavior to his mother.)

MRS. A.: Suppose my husband starts up with me, "You shouldn't talk like that to my mother. You are not cementing relationships; you are putting them farther apart." How do I handle that situation?

THERAPIST: You have to say, "If your mother makes unjust remarks I have to tell her and I will tell her. If your mother makes reasonable criticisms, I will be very interested in what she has to say. But she is always at me, and she has gotten into the habit of it because I have been allowing her to say whatever she likes. I am not going to have it any more."

The following are two random lists of assertive statements; the first list expresses opposition, the second commendation. The former are more numerous because they come up more frequently in assertiveness training.

Oppositional Assertive Statements

1. Would you please call me back? I can't speak to you now.
2. Excuse me. You're obstructing my view.
3. Will you kindly stop talking during the play/movie/music?
4. This is a line. Please go to the back of it.
5. You have kept me waiting 20 minutes.
6. Do you mind turning down the heat in the restaurant?
7. It's too cold for me to go outside.
8. Please put those heavy packages in a *double* bag (at a supermarket).
9. Your behavior disgusts/annoys me.
10. I hate your duplicity/intolerance/unreasonableness.
11. Your nagging bores me.
12. If it is not inconvenient, will you pick up my parcel?
13. I'm sorry, but it won't be possible.
14. Would you ask the pilot to radio ahead to my connecting flight? (To the stewardess on a flight that is late for a connection.)
15. I would rather not wait.
16. If you persist in coming late, I will stop making appointments with you.
17. I insist that you come to work on time.
18. How dare you speak to me like that.
19. Pardon me, I was here first.
20. I enjoy talking to you, but please be quiet while I am reading/writing/thinking/listening.

Commendatory Assertive Statements

1. That's a beautiful dress/brooch, etc.
2. You look lovely, terrific, ravishing, glamorous.
3. That was a clever remark.
4. What a radiant smile.
5. I like you.
6. I love you.
7. I admire your tenacity.
8. You handled him very skillfully.

With a reasonable amount of pressure and encouragement, most patients begin to be able to assert themselves in a matter of days, or a week or two. At each interview, they report what they have done in the intervening time and the therapist commends their successes and corrects their errors. They must be warned not to rest on their laurels but to be alert for every opportunity that offers for assertion. As interpersonal anxiety decreases, acts of assertion become easier to perform. One rule must always be observed:

Never instigate an assertive act that is likely to have punishing consequences. For example, it is unwise to be assertive with an employer or with a tough character in a tough neighborhood.

For patients who have a great deal of anxiety about assertion, it may be necessary to grade the tasks in order of difficulty. Actually, it is good practice to make this a rule, but not a rigid one.

Some patients have great difficulty performing any assertive act. The therapist must ascertain why. He may discover a "phobic" reaction to some aspect or implication of assertion. Patients may have a conditioned anxiety response to perceiving themselves as selfish or to the idea of having behaved assertively (i.e., guilt about assertion). A preliminary program of systematic desensitization to the relevant stimulus configurations is then needed. As an example, a young man was unable to begin to behave assertively until he was desensitized to a range of situations in which he placed his own interests ahead of those of others. Excessive fear of hostility from others (which is always a possible response to assertiveness) similarly requires desensitization.

When the patient finds assertive behavior difficult not because of inhibiting fears but as a matter of principle, a more vigorous reiteration of the arguments that were initially given is necessary. One may increase motivation by contrasting the negative and unprepossessing effects of timidity with the benefits that assertion is expected to yield. (A good demonstration of assertiveness training is to be found in a sector of a film entitled *Behavior Therapy: An Introduction*, IL: MTI Teleprograms.)

BEHAVIOR REHEARSAL

In the great majority of subjects, satisfactory assertive behavior (and consequent diminution of interpersonal anxiety) results from instructions followed by monitoring of reports of performance from session to session. There are, however, a considerable number of people who find it difficult or impossible to carry out their assignments. In some cases, although the requisite words are uttered, it is with inadequate expressiveness; in others there is so much anticipatory anxiety that the performance of assertive behavior cannot even be initiated. Behavior rehearsal has its most important role in the treatment of such cases, although it is also often used to accelerate assertiveness training in run-of-the-mill cases.

Behavior rehearsal was originally called "behavioristic psychodrama" (Wolpe, 1958). It consists of the acting out of short exchanges between the therapist and the patient in scenes from the patient's life. The patient represents himself, and the therapist takes the role of someone toward whom the patient is unadaptively anxious and inhibited. The therapist starts with a remark, usually oppositional, that the other person might make, and the patient responds as if the situation were real. His initial response will usually be variously hesitant, defensive, and timid. The therapist then suggests a more appropriate response, and the exchange is run again in a revised form. The sequence may be repeated until the therapist is satisfied that the patient's utterances have been suitably reshaped.

The ability of pretended behavior to bring about real therapeutic change is in accord with some observations on actors reported by Simonov (1967). Especially (but not only) when the actor has been trained by the Stanislavsky method (which requires him to try to *live* each part), he evinces autonomic responses in the direction of the emotions that he is simulating. Simonov states, "The actors were asked to pronounce certain words under various mentally reproducible conditions. . . . The changes in the heart rate, recorded in the actor when he was fulfilling the task, confirm that he was actually reproducing an emotionally colored situation and was not copying intonations formerly noticed in other people. This conclusion was confirmed by comparison with the results of analyzing speech in natural situations." However, there are differences, too, because if the actor is doing his part well he gets a pleasurable feeling intermixed with the anxiety or anger that he is enacting. A detailed account of this work is, unfortunately, available only in manuscript form (Simonov, 1962).

It is necessary, in behavior rehearsal, to take into account not only the words the patient uses but also the volume, firmness, and emotional expressiveness of voice, the use of eye contact, and the appropriateness of accompanying gestures and other bodily movements. Serber (1972), who placed great importance on these features of assertive behavior, advocated giving the patient videotaped feedback of his or her behavior — a device that I have occasionally used with excellent results in difficult cases. The aim of modeling, shaping, and rehearsing is partly to give the patient motor skills to deal with the real adversary, and partly so that the anxiety the rehearsal evokes may be reciprocally inhibited and weakened by other emotions simultaneously present.

Case 28

This case affords a typical example of the shaping that is done during behavior rehearsal (Wolpe, 1970). The patient had been brooding over having been unfairly criticized by her father for lacking in family feeling and wanted to rectify the matter.

THERAPIST: Well, let's do an experiment. Let's sort of act it out. Suppose you just go ahead and pretend I am your father and say to me what you think you would like to say to him.

PATIENT: About the other night, I would like to say that I think you were exceptionally unfair in assuming that I did not want to come up and that I was the one who was being unjust or the villain because I wasn't coming up to make the family happy. The family hasn't been much of a family actually for a number of years and, when it comes down to it, the family doesn't mean that much to me. I would be much happier spending Christmas by myself. And then he would probably say, "Well, you just go ahead and do that."

THERAPIST: Wait a minute. Don't you worry about him. I am he, so don't put words in my mouth. Besides this, in general I would like to correct your approach. You are doing it in a way that leaves you too vulnerable. First of all, it is very unsatisfactory for you to complain to somebody that he is unfair, because if you do that you are really in some sense putting yourself at his mercy. A better line would be: "I want to tell you that you had no right to assume the other night that I had no intention of coming for Christmas. You know very well that I have always come. You accused me of lacking feeling. I have a great deal of feeling, and perhaps too much. Your attack was absolutely unwarranted." In saying this, you are not asking for justice or fairness, you are simply stating what you feel was wrong in his behavior. Now, do you think you could redo it in some fashion?

PATIENT: Okay. I would like to set some matters straight—about your call the other night. When you called me I just couldn't think of this right away. I was so taken by surprise, but I have been thinking about it and I would just like to say a couple of things.

THERAPIST: I must interrupt you again. You started fine—the first sentence was fine, but when you began to explain why you didn't say it the other night, that weakens your position. For example, it might invite him to say "Yes, that is like you, isn't it? You never answer at the right time. You always have to brood for three days before you can say anything." He could say something of that sort. But in any case, it is a kind of underdog statement, and we don't want that.

PATIENT: All right. About the call the other night, I had not entirely given up on the idea of coming up to have Christmas with you and Mom. I was doing what I thought was best according to what I gathered from the conversation I had with Mom. I felt that Mom wanted me to have Christmas with Grandma and Grandpop—have Christmas dinner, and I wanted to be both places, but I just felt that the drive might be too much.

THERAPIST: I am sorry, but I must interrupt you again. You see, you are explaining yourself. You are giving a kind of excuse. Actually, the important part of this conversation is to bring out the point that it was not right for him to plunge into a criticism that assumed that you had made up your mind not to come.

PATIENT: How about—I don't think it was right for you to call me last night, and say what you did, because I don't think you had the facts straight from Mom. I think you should have checked with her first and be sure you understood the situation. I had talked with Mom earlier and felt that this was what we had worked out and I think you should have checked with her and made sure that —

THERAPIST: That's enough. The fact that you keep on suggests that you are not very confident; so stop. Now, let him say something.

Behavior Rehearsal as a Medium for Desensitization

As noted above, assertiveness training has the deconditioning of anxiety as its primary goal. In cases where progressively more difficult assertive tasks are assigned, the parallel to desensitization is close. In the usual run of cases, it is the anxiety elicited by the confrontation with other persons that is the target of treatment. Whenever the patient is assertive, the anxiety elicited by the confrontation is inhibited by the expression of anger (or whatever other emotion is relevant) with resultant weakening of the anxiety response habit.

There are, however, fairly frequent cases in which the anxiety that lies behind a person's unassertiveness is elicited by aspects of social interaction other than confrontation. The anxiety may be triggered by feelings of being pushy or inconsiderate, for example. Carefully conceived programs of behavior rehearsal can be used to overcome such anxiety in what amounts to a variant of systematic desensitization (see chapter 9). Cases 29 and 30 exemplify this.

Case 29

Irma was a librarian of 42, with a wide array of phobias and social anxieties (Willoughby 64). Lack of expressiveness being a prominent feature of her behavior, she was, as is usual, introduced at an early stage to the rationale for assertive behavior and given some relatively easy assignments. However, she was totally unable to take the first step toward carrying out any of them. The reason, as it turned out, was the anxiety she had at the thought of inconveniencing anybody. Only with her closest friends could she make any demands at all.

Questioning revealed that the major variable controlling this anxiety was the magnitude of the inconvenience she saw herself imposing on another person. Thus, a hierarchy of imposition was arranged on the theme of making demands.

In applying behavior rehearsal to treat this hierarchy the first scenario consisted of my taking the role of a library colleague who lived a block from her. She was required to ask him for a ride home on a day when she had injured her ankle and could barely walk. Although it was agreed that this would take him only one block out of his way, she was totally unable to articulate this modest request in the play-acted rehearsal. I therefore gave her this sentence to use: "If you are going home after work, would you mind giving me a ride home?" Her first attempt was very awkward, and it evoked a good deal of anxiety (70 *suds*). My reply was, "I will take you with pleasure." With repetition, she articulated the sentence with greater ease and better expression, while the level of her anxiety progressively fell. After a total of eight repetitions in two sessions, she could request that ride with practically no anxiety. During subsequent sessions, the distance she was taking me out of my way was progressively increased. These "rehearsals" enabled the patient comfortably to make reasonable requests in reality.

9
Systematic Desensitization

Systematic desensitization is one of a variety of methods used to break down neurotic anxiety-response habits in piecemeal fashion on the model of the therapy of experimental neurosis. After a physiological state inhibiting anxiety has been induced in the patient by means of muscle relaxation, the patient is exposed to a weak anxiety-arousing stimulus for a few seconds. If the exposure is repeated, the stimulus progressively loses its ability to evoke anxiety. Successively stronger stimuli are then similarly treated.

Employing a counteracting emotion to overcome an undesirable emotional habit step by step has a precedent in everyday experience: a person may be desensitized to a situation he or she fears by being exposed to small doses of it in circumstances in which other emotions are also present. For example, if a child is afraid of playing in the sea, the parent will take him by the hand to the fringe of the approaching waves and lift the child up when a wave is close; then, when the child has become comfortable about this, the parent encourages him to dip a foot into a wave, and later the ankle, and so on. The excitement of the situation and the comforting impact of the parent combine to inhibit the fear and weaken it. The eventual result is that the child plays at the edge of the sea with pleasure.

THE HISTORY OF SYSTEMATIC DESENSITIZATION

The systematic desensitization technique had its roots in the experimental laboratory (Wolpe, 1948, 1952a, 1958). As described in chapter 3, I had found that experimentally induced anxiety responses were extremely resistant to the normal process of extinction. The animals, however hungry, could not be tempted to eat pellets of fresh meat scattered on the floor of the experimental cage. The anxiety produced total inhibition of eating. But if one arranged for the feeding impulse to exceed the anxiety in strength, anxiety was inhibited reciprocally. The animals showed less anxiety in the experimental laboratory outside the cage and still less in other rooms, according to how closely the rooms resembled the laboratory. Sooner or later, one found a room where the anxiety was not great enough to inhibit feeding. The animal ate successive pellets of meat there with increasing readiness while anxiety receded and finally disappeared. The same behavior sequence took place in the room next in resemblance to the experimental laboratory. Through a succession of stages, eating eventually eliminated all anxiety from the experimental cage (see pp. 43–45).

The technique of systematic desensitization emerged from the following succession of events. From 1947 onward, I endeavored to overcome anxiety in patients by getting them to perform acts that were antagonistic to anxiety in their daily lives. These were mainly assertive acts, in which I was greatly encouraged by the appearance of Salter's *Conditioned Reflex Therapy* (1949); in fact, I was moved by his enthusiasm to prescribe it for all patients. I did this even though I could not see why it should benefit neuroses in which the controlling stimuli were not present in the interpersonal situations in which the assertive behavior figured. After a time, I realized that these cases were actually not improving. Conditioning theory requires that, in order to weaken a reaction to a stimulus, that stimulus must be present in the deconditioning situation. Assertion toward persons clearly cannot diminish anxiety that is evoked by nonpersonal stimulus constellations, such as enclosed spaces, animals, heights, or the sight of blood—particularly if these are absent at that time.

A case that was a turning point for me was a woman who was severely anxious at manifestations of illness in other people. Successful schooling in assertive behavior having failed to diminish her anxiety, I had sorrowfully abandoned her as a failure. I knew of no way to inhibit anxieties aroused by something the patient could not change.

Therapeutic potential was greatly expanded when I learned about progressive relaxation (Jacobson, 1938). Here was an anxiety-inhibiting procedure that could be used against practically any anxiety source. I was particularly interested in the potentialities of relaxation for neuroses in which assertion was not applicable. One major problem was how to get relaxation to inhibit the anxiety evoked by real life exposures to anxiety-eliciting situations. It was apparent that if some of Jacobson's patients were able to control such anxiety it was because of intensive training and diligent practice.

Since Jacobson's relaxation program is time consuming I tried to find a way to counterpose relaxation to anxiety-evoking stimuli controlled by the therapist. As it is difficult to control real-life situations, I began to explore the possibility of using imaginary ones, which can be graduated at will. I was delighted to find that anxiety diminished progressively, eventually to zero, when a patient repeatedly imagined a situation that was weakly anxiety arousing. Increasingly "threatening" imaginary stimuli could, in this way, one by one, be divested of their anxiety-evoking potential, with transfer of change to the corresponding real situations. At first, influenced by a procedural rule of Pavlov, I presented only one stimulus of a class at a session, but later made cautious trials of multiple presentations and found no disadvantage.

THE DESENSITIZATION PARADIGM

In animal neuroses, feeding can inhibit only weak anxiety responses; the same is true of relaxation in humans. If the anxiety response to a stimulus in a relaxed person is weak enough, it diminishes further, eventually to zero, with repetition of the stimulus. (However, many observations, including those of Wolpe and Flood [1970], indicate that response decrement often does occur if stronger stimuli are administered insistently enough. This is discussed under the rubric of flooding [chapter 11]). Then, when the next stronger stimulus is presented to that person, it evokes less anxiety than it would have previously. Successive presentations under relaxation reduce that anxiety also to zero. Increasingly strong stimuli are thus brought within the anxiety-inhibiting capacity of the subject's relaxation.

This method is illustrated in figure 9.1. In an acrophobic subject who has one unit of anxiety when looking out a second-floor window, and two units looking out a third-floor window, reduction to zero of the amount of anxiety from the second-floor window has the effect of diminishing to only one unit the amount evoked at the third-floor. Then, when anxiety at the third floor is zero, there is only one unit at the fourth floor, two at the fifth, and so forth. (This linear relationship is used for clarity of exposition. The actual relationship is a simple power function; see p. 177f.)

It is appropriate at this point to note that although it is usual to refer to the weaker anxiety-evoking stimuli as "generalized stimuli," this is not always accurate. A generalized stimulus incorporates some feature of the conditioned stimulus, and the magnitude of the shared feature is the basis of a generalization gradient (Hull, 1943). But sometimes, weaker anxiety evocation is a function of stimuli that have been conditioned to anxiety through being on the pathway to the central conditioned stimulus. These pathway stimuli owe their anxiety-evoking power to their location, and not to any resemblance to the central conditioned stimulus. The difference is illustrated in figure 9.2.

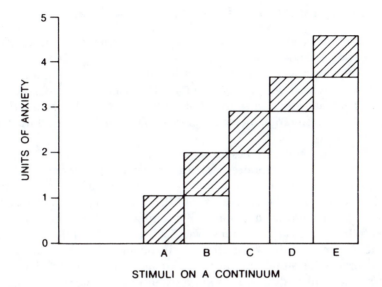

Fig. 9.1. Effects on anxiety evocation of anxiety. When A's ability to evoke anxiety goes down from 1 unit to 0, B evokes 1 unit in place of an original potential of 2 units; and when B's evocation is 0, C evokes 1 unit, and so forth.

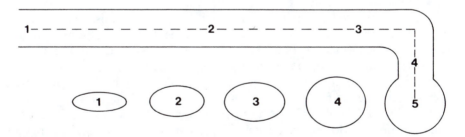

Fig. 9.2. Two stimulus continua: shape generalization and pathway stimuli. If there is a conditioned anxiety response to a circular enclosure, less anxiety is evoked by exposing the subject to a shape that is less than circular, or by placing the subject at points on the accustomed pathway to the enclosure. In the latter case, anxiety increases with decreasing distance. (Courtesy of Graphic Communications, Eastern Pennsylvania Psychiatric Institute, Philadelphia.)

The Anxiety-Inhibiting Effects of Muscle Relaxation

The autonomic effects that accompany deep relaxation are diametrically opposed to those that are characteristic of anxiety. Jacobson (1939, 1940) long ago showed pulse rate and blood pressure to be diminished by deep muscle relaxation. It was subsequently demonstrated (Clark, 1963; Drvota, personal communication, 1962; Wolpe, 1964a) that skin resistance increases and respiration becomes slower and more regular during deep relaxation.

More thoroughgoing studies subsequently appeared. Paul (1969b) showed that muscle relaxation produces effects opposite to those of anxiety on heart rate, respiratory rate, and skin conductance. Obvious effects were obtained even by simple instructions to relax, but they were significantly enhanced if the instructions were given in a hypnotic setting and even more significantly if they followed relaxation training. Van Egeren, Feather, and Hein (1971), in an elaborate psychophysiological study involving skin conductance, heart rate, digital pulse amplitude, and rate of respiration, found that relaxed subjects showed less decrease in skin resistance to phobic stimuli than subjects who were not relaxed. The calming effects of Jacobsonian relaxation appear to be concomitants or consequences of the voluntary efforts made by the subject to diminish the tonus of his muscles. They cannot be secondary to the relaxed state of the muscles: the complete or almost complete relaxation induced by drugs like curare may elicit severe anxiety (Campbell, Sanderson, & Laverty, 1964). That relaxation inhibits aversively conditioned autonomic responses has been directly demonstrated by Grings and Uno (1968) and Grings and Schandler (1977).

Not only are the effects of relaxation opposite in kind to those of anxiety, but, if counterposed to anxiety-evoking stimuli, they diminish the anxiety responses that these stimuli evoke. A pilot investigation by Wolpe and Fried (1968) provided evidence that the galvanic skin response (on Lathrop's [1964] variability measure) decreases during desensitization parallel to the decrements of anxiety that are reported by patients. Figure 9.3 shows the averaged changes of four patients to whom hierarchical phobic scenes were each presented three times in each of two sessions. The decrease of response from one presentation to the next should be noted, as well as the "savings" between session 1 and session 2 on the same scene.

Van Egeren, Feather and Hein (1971) reported that with repetitions of the phobic stimuli, the magnitude of effects decreased progressively in relaxed subjects but remained much the same in the unrelaxed. In a nontherapeutic experiment comparing the effects of presenting hierarchical stimuli in a standardized repetitive way to relaxed and nonrelaxed subjects, a consistent downward trend of autonomic arousal as measured by galvanic skin

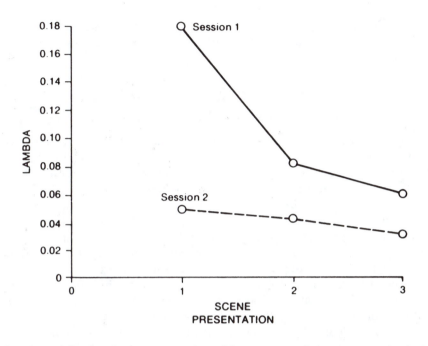

Fig. 9.3. Lambda values for three presentations of the same scene during two successive desensitization sessions. The figure averages the readings for four different patients. Note that reactivity not only declines during each session but the decrement obtained at the end of session 1 is maintained at the beginning of session 2.

response was noted across sessions with respect to each stimulus in relaxed subjects but not in the nonrelaxed (Wolpe & Flood, 1970). In a clinical context, Paul (1969b) demonstrated that autonomic arousal by a stressful stimulus decreases with repetition as a function of the degree to which relaxation has anxiety-inhibiting effects. Conner (1974) made the interesting observation that even when muscle relaxation is insufficient to lower autonomic baseline levels, it can still diminish the anxiety response to a conditioned stimulus.

In the practice of standard systematic desensitization there is also evidence of the potency of relaxation. Working on spider and snake phobias respectively, Rachman (1965) and Davison (1965) found that subjects to whom the whole desensitization sequence of procedures was applied showed significantly more improvement than either those who received relaxation training without scene presentations or those to whom scenes were presented without relaxation. Farmer and Wright (1971) subjected snake-phobic subjects to desensitization under either muscle relaxation or directed muscle activity. Muscle relaxation was significantly effective in reducing fear; muscle activity was less so.

THE TECHNIQUE OF SYSTEMATIC DESENSITIZATION

Generally, systematic desensitization is indicated for the treatment of fears evoked by situations that do not lend themselves to "being handled" — in contrast to those that call for assertiveness training. One cannot handle an elevator or being the center of attention in the way in which one can handle an unfair remark or an inattentive waiter — by speaking out in protest. Systematic desensitization is a resource to be called on in all these situations — in all classical phobias, in such impersonal human stimulus situations as crowds, and in social fears of the many kinds for which assertiveness training is not suitable. For the latter it is an unequalled resource.

At the point at which systematic desensitization is being considered, the problems of the patient will have been evaluated; misconceptions, if any, will have been corrected; and assertiveness training, if required, will have begun. The patient will also have learned the use of the subjective anxiety (*sud*) scale (pp. 91–92). Systematic desensitization will not displace ongoing measures but can be conducted concurrently with them. The technique involves three sets of operations:

1. Training in deep muscle relaxation
2. The construction of anxiety hierarchies
3. Counterposing relaxation and anxiety-evoking stimuli from the hierarchies

Training in Relaxation

The method of relaxation that is routinely taught is essentially that of Jacobson (1938), but instruction is completed in about six lessons, each taking up about one-third of a session, in contrast to Jacobson's very prolonged training (generally 50 sessions or more).

In introducing the subject of relaxation, I tell the patient (who by this time usually has some idea of the nature of conditioning therapy) that relaxation is one of several available methods for combating anxiety. It is a skill that, like other skills, improves with practice — to which the subject will be expected to devote 10 to 15 minutes twice a day. I continue as follows:

> Relaxation works by producing emotional calmness. Even the ordinary relaxing when one lies down often has quite a noticeable calming effect. There is a definite relationship between the degree of muscle relaxation and the produc-

tion of calmness to oppose to anxiety. I am going to teach you how to relax far beyond the ordinary level, and with practice you will be able to "switch it on" and calm yourself for many purposes.

There is no sacred sequence for training the various muscle groups in relaxation, but the sequence adopted should be orderly. My own practice is to start with the arms because they are convenient for purposes of demonstration and because it is easy to check their relaxation. I go to the head region next because the most marked anxiety-inhibiting effects are usually obtained by relaxation there, and then I move downward.

The patient is asked to grip the arm of the chair with one hand to see whether he or she can distinguish any qualitative difference between the sensations produced in the forearm and those in the hand. The patient is told to take note of the quality of the forearm sensation because it is caused by muscle tension in contrast to the touch and pressure sensations in the hand. The gripping action tenses both the flexor and extensor muscles of the forearm. The patient must note the location of those tensions. Next, I grip the patient's wrist and ask him or her to bend the elbow against resistance, thus making him or her aware of tension in the biceps. Then, by having the patient straighten the bent elbow against resistance, I draw attention to the extensor muscles at the back of the arm. I then describe the essential relaxation procedure:

> I am now going to show you the essential activity that is involved in obtaining deep relaxation. I will again ask you to resist my pull at your wrist so as to tighten your biceps. I want you to notice very carefully the sensations in that muscle. Then I will ask you to let go gradually as I diminish the amount of force exerted against you. Notice, as your forearm descends, that there is decreasing sensation in the biceps muscle. Notice also that the letting go is an activity, but of a negative kind — it is an "uncontracting" of the muscle. In due course, your forearm will come to rest on the arm of the chair, and you may then think that you have gone as far as possible — that relaxation is complete. But although the biceps will indeed be partly and perhaps largely relaxed, a certain number of its fibers will still, in fact, be contracted. I will then say to you, "Go on letting go. Try to extend the activity that went on in the biceps while your forearm was coming down." It is the act of relaxing these additional fibers that will bring about most of the emotional effects we want. Let's try it and see what happens.

Gripping the patient's wrist a second time, I have him or her tense and then gradually relax the biceps. When the forearm is close to the horizontal, I release the wrist, allowing the patient to complete the movement alone. I then exhort him or her to "go on letting go," to "keep trying to go further and further in the negative direction," to "try to go beyond what seems to you to be the furthest point."

When the patient has shown, by successfully relaxing his biceps, that it is fully understood how to proceed, he or she is asked to put both hands comfortably on the lap and try to relax all the muscles of both arms for a few minutes. The patient must report any sensations that are felt. The usual ones are tingling, numbness, and warmth, mainly in the hands. After a few minutes I palpate the relaxing muscles. With practice, the therapist can judge in a rough way between various degrees of muscle tension.

Most patients have rather limited success when they first attempt to relax, but they are assured that good relaxation is a matter of practice and are told that whereas, initially, 20 minutes of trying may achieve no more than partial relaxation of an arm, one can eventually relax one's whole body in a few minutes. However, there are some fortunate individuals who from the beginning experience a deepening and extending relaxation, radiating, as it seems, from a particular muscle group and generating marked calmness.

I customarily begin the *second lesson* by telling the patient that because, from the emotional point of view, the most important muscles are situated in and around the head, we will deal with them next. I start with the muscles of the face, demonstrating the tensions produced by contracting the muscles of the forehead. These lend themselves to a demonstration of the "steplike" character of deepening relaxation. I simultaneously contract the eyebrow-raising and the frowning muscles on my forehead very intensely, pointing out that an anxious expression has been produced. I then say: "I am going to relax these muscles in a controlled way to give you an impression of the steplike way in which decrements of tension occur, although the real steps take much longer than my demonstration." I then relax my forehead, making an obvious step down about every 5 seconds until, after about half-a-dozen steps, the forehead is quite smooth. At this point I state that the relaxation is continuing, and that this relaxation 'beneath the surface" is the part that matters most for producing marked emotional effects. The patient is then told to contract the eyebrow-raising muscles and is given a few minutes to relax them as far as possible. The same routine is applied to the frowning muscles. (It is much better to train the forehead muscles separately than together, as I used to do in the past.) Many patients spontaneously report sensations of tingling, warmth, or thickness, as though the skin were made of leather. These sensations are indicative of relaxation beyond the normal level of muscle tone.

The lesson concludes by drawing attention to the circumorbital muscles by closing the eyes tight, to the muscles in the region of the nose by getting the patient to wrinkle the nose, and to the muscles around the mouth by making the patient purse the lips and then smile. All these muscles are relaxed in turn.

At the *third lesson* the patient is asked to bite on his or her teeth, thus tensing the masseters and temporales. The position of the lips is an important indicator of relaxation of the muscles of mastication. When these are relaxed, the lips are parted by a few millimeters. The masseters are definitely not relaxed if the mouth is resolutely closed. On the other hand, an open mouth is no proof of relaxation.

At the same lesson, I usually also introduce the muscles of the tongue. These may be felt contracting in the floor of the mouth when the patient presses the tip of the tongue firmly against the back of the lower incisor teeth. Relaxing the tongue muscles may produce such local sensations as tingling or a feeling of enlargement of that organ.

The *fourth lesson* deals with the neck and shoulders. The main focus in the neck is the posterior muscles that maintain the head's normal erect posture. Most people become aware of them merely by concentrating on the back of the neck. Relaxing these muscles makes the head fall forward, but because the relaxation is incomplete, the head's whole weight is imposed on the fibers that are still contracted, producing discomfort and perhaps pain in the neck. Persistent practice, despite the discomfort, leads to a progressive yielding of these muscles, and usually in a week or so the patient finds that the neck is comfortable with the chin resting on the sternum. Those who find the discomfort of the forward-leaning head too great may practice relaxing the neck muscles with the back of the head resting against a high-backed chair.

Shoulder muscle tensions are demonstrated by the following routine: the deltoid is contracted by abducting the arm to the horizontal, the lateral neck muscles by continuing this movement up to the ear, the posthumeral and scapulo-spinal groups by moving the horizontal arm backward, and the pectorals by swinging it forward across the chest. In relaxing these muscles, the patient is directed to observe their functional unity with those of the arm.

The *fifth lesson* deals with the muscles of the back, abdomen, and thorax. The procedure with respect to the first two areas follows the usual pattern. The back muscles are contracted by backward arching of the spine. The abdominal muscles are tensed as if in anticipation of a punch in the belly. After contracting these muscles, the patient lets them go as far as he can. The thoracic muscles, or, more accurately, the muscles of respiration, are necessarily in a different category — for total inhibition of breathing is not an achievement to be promoted. But the respiratory rhythm can often be used to augment relaxation. Attention to the musculature during a few fairly deep breaths soon reveals that while some effort is involved during inhalation, expiration is essentially a "letting go." Many people find it helpful to coordinate relaxation of other muscles with the automatic relaxation of the respiratory muscles that takes place with normal exhalation.

In making patients aware of the muscles to be relaxed in the lower limbs, during the *sixth lesson*, it has been my custom to start with the feet and work upward. The flexor digitorium brevis is felt in the sole by bending the toes within the shoe, the calf muscles by placing some weight on the toe, the peroneal and anterior tibial muscles by dorsiflexing the foot, the quadriceps femoris by straightening the knee, the hamstrings by trying to bend the knee against resistance, the adductors of the thigh by adduction against hand pressure on the inner aspect of the knee, and the abductors (which include some of the gluteal muscles) by abduction against pressure. These muscles represent a load of information, that the patient should be allowed enough time to absorb.

The assessment of a patient's ability to relax depends partly upon his reports of the calmness that relaxing brings about, and partly upon observing of the patient. By the second or third lesson, most patients report ease, tranquility, or sleepiness. A few experience little or no change of feeling. It is an advantage to have objective indicators of relaxation. Jacobson (1939, 1964) has used the electromyogram but mainly as a corroborative measure. More convenient equipment has become available that translates muscle potentials into auditory signals whose pitch drops as tension decreases (Budzinski, Stoyva, & Adler, 1970). This also facilitates relaxation by providing feedback to the patient. Fortunately, the reports of patients are usually a sufficient guide to their emotional state, especially with the help of the Subjective Anxiety Scale. Quite a number of patients, especially those with little or no ongoing anxiety, report a feeling of calm after only one or two sessions of relaxation training. In many of these, it is possible to do desensitization on relaxation of only the upper half of the body.

The Construction of Hierarchies

An anxiety hierarchy is a thematically related list of anxiety-evoking stimuli, ranked according to the amount of anxiety they evoke. It has been my practice to place the stimulus that evokes the greatest anxiety at the top of the list. While hierarchy construction may be an easy matter, as exemplified in Figure 9.2 it can be very complicated, as Case 64 illustrates.

The theme, or common core, of a family of anxiety-evoking stimuli most often consists of something that is extrinsic to the patient, such as spiders or criticism; but it may be internal, like a feeling of losing control. Sometimes a number of physically disparate extrinsic stimulus situations induce a common internal response. For example, a patient suffering from claustrophobia (Wolpe, 1961b) had the same kind of trapped feeling from irremovable nail polish on her fingers or from a tight ring as she had when physically confined. Such commonality of response is termed *secondary generalization* (Hull, 1943, p. 191).

Hierarchy construction usually begins at about the same time as relaxation training but is subject to revisions or additions at any time. It is important to note that communication with regard to this operation occurs in an ordinary conversational way and not under relaxation.

The raw data from which hierarchies are constructed come from four main sources: (a) the patient's history, (b) responses to the Willoughby questionnaire — Appendix A or B that reveals anxieties mainly in interpersonal contexts, (c) the Fear Survey Schedule (Wolpe & Lang, 1964) — Appendix C (a 108-item inventory [Wolpe & Lang, 1969] is commercially available from Educational and Industrial Testing Service, San Diego, California.) and (d) special probings into situations in which the patient feels unadaptive anxiety, some of which are indicated by responses to the questionnaires. If needed, further information may be sought by assigning to the patient the homework task of listing all situations, thoughts, or feelings that he finds disturbing, fearful, embarrassing, or in any other way distressing.

When all the identified sources of neurotic disturbance have been listed, the therapist classifies them into themes. Usually there is more than one theme. Many themes are self-evident, but there are frequent exceptions. For example, a person's fears of going to movies, parties, and football games may suggest a core fear of public situations and turns out to be claustrophobia or agoraphobia. Frequently, fear of social occasions is at the bottom of fear of criticism or rejection; or it may be a function of being the center of attention, in which the fear worsens with increasing numbers of people. One patient's ostensible fear of social situations proved to be an anxiety response to the smell of food in public places. Another unexpected source of anxiety was in a case of impotence (Wolpe, 1958, p. 152) that was found not to be related to sexual stimuli but to the idea of inflicting physical trauma. (An attempt at defloration had previously aroused high anxiety in this man because he was already vulnerable to tissue damage stimuli.) The treatment that emerged from this analysis was systematic desensitization to a tissue damage hierarchy.

It is not necessary for the patient actually to have experienced each situation that is included in a hierarchy. The question posed is this: "If you were today confronted by such and such a situation, would you expect to be anxious?" To answer this question he has to imagine the situation concerned, and it is generally almost as easy to imagine a supposed event as it is to imagine one that has at some time occurred. The temporal setting of an imagined stimulus configuration scarcely affects the responses to it. A man with a phobia for dogs will usually have as much anxiety at the idea of meeting a dog on the way home tomorrow as when recalling a past encounter with one.

The following list of fears supplied by a patient is used to illustrate some of the intricacies of hierarchy construction. This list is reproduced exactly as the patient presented it.

1. High Altitudes	11. Fire
2. Elevators	12. Fainting
3. Crowded Places	13. Falling Back
4. Church	14. Injections
5. Darkness—Movies, etc.	15. Medications
6. Being Alone	16. Fear of the Unknown
7. Marital Relations (pregnancy)	17. Losing My Mind
8. Walking any Distance	18. Locked Doors
9. Death	19. Amusement Park Rides
10. Accidents	20. Steep Stairways

With a little help from the patient the items were sorted into categories:

A. ACROPHOBIA
  1. High Altitudes
19. Amusement Park Rides
20. Steep Stairways
B. CLAUSTROPHOBIA
  2. Elevators
  3. Crowded Places
  4. Church
  5. Movies (darkness factor)
18. Locked Doors
C. AGORAPHOBIA
  6. Being Alone
  8. Walking any Distance (alone)

D. ILLNESS AND ITS ASSOCIATIONS
12. Fainting
13. Falling Back
14. Injections
15. Medication
E. BASICALLY OBJECTIVE FEARS
  7. Marital Relations (pregnancy)
  9. Death
10. Accidents
11. Fire
16. Fear of the Unknown
17. Losing My Mind

Before considering the neurotic groups A through D to which desensitization is relevant, some remarks must be made about group E. The patient's fears of pregnancy, accidents, death, and fire were all in contexts in which fear can be reasonable, but her apprehensions about these matters were somewhat more than normal. I considered that this might be a function of a generally elevated level of anxiety—which is quite often found in neuroses—and might disappear when the major maladaptive anxieties had been overcome by therapy. Her fear of the unknown was bound up with the idea of death. Her fear of losing her mind was an inference from the bizarre and uncontrollable feelings that characterized her neurosis and was overcome at the cognitive level to which it belonged by the strong assurance that her condition was not related to insanity and could never lead to it. This was reinforced by demonstrating to her that hyperventilation could precipitate many of her symptoms (see chapter 14). (There are people in whom all fears would belong to group E, in which case, of course, desensitization would not be relevant; supplying corrective information, with the addition, sometimes, of thought stopping would be indicated [see chapter 7].)

On scrutinizing the stimulus groups A through D, the reader should observe that the items are merely assorted settings associated with the fears. They are not specific enough or in proper order to constitute hierarchies. Newcomers to behavior therapy often attempt to employ such material in hierarchies. One day, I asked 25 members of a class (none of whom had previously treated more than two or three patients) how they would proceed to build a hierarchy out of the five claustrophobia items of group B. The majority of them were in favor of ranking them, that is, churches, movies, etc., hierarchically. But, as noted above, they are merely settings, each with potential for variations in space constriction.

As one goes up a claustrophobia hierarchy, the essential feature — amount of confinement — must progressively increase as far as appropriate within a single setting. Claustrophobic anxiety increases with diminishing size of the enclosing space and/or with increasing duration of confinement. Desensitization in the above case employed two hierarchical series: first, confinement for a constant length of time in progressively smaller rooms; and then confinement in a very small room (four feet square) for increasing periods.

Similarly, in group A, agoraphobia, each of the three items covered a range of situations. Particularizing within the areas they encompassed provided a range of concrete situations evoking anxiety of rising intensity. Heights were increasingly fearful starting from about 20 feet (or a second-floor window). Group D yielded a lengthy medical hierarchy, some of whose items, ranked in order of diminishing anxiety, were the following:

1. Feeling of being about to lose consciousness
2. Feeling of falling backward
3. Marked dizziness
4. Feeling of lightness in head
5. Moderate dizziness
6. Smell of ether
7. Receiving an injection
8. Racing heart (anxiety increasing with rapidity of heart beat)
9. Weak knees
10. Seeing syringe poised for an injection
11. Sight of bandages

It should be observed that the stronger stimuli (1–5) are all endogenous and most of the weaker ones are exogenous. What is common to all is the arousal of a feeling of personal threat.

In some cases, besides multiplicity of hierarchies, one encounters multiple dimensions within a single hierarchy. For example, in a patient having claustrophobic reactions in social situations, five variables controlled their intensity. The reactions were stronger under the following conditions: the greater the number of people present, the more unfamiliar the people, the greater the difficulties of leaving the room (both physical factors and social propriety being relevant), the shorter the time since her last meal (this factor determining the perceived likelihood of vomiting). The reactions were weaker if she was accompanied by protective persons—husband, mother, or close friend (in descending order of effectiveness). For these variables to be covered by the treatment required about a dozen hierarchies.

In constructing hierarchies one always aims for a reasonably evenly spaced progression. If items are too similar, time will be wasted; if adjacent items differ too widely in anxiety-evoking potential, progress will be halted upon moving from the lesser to the greater. Occasionally, a patient may even be further sensitized if a high level of anxiety has been evoked. Experience with flooding suggests that sensitization would be related to brevity of exposure (see chapter 11). When a hierarchy is based on a directly measurable dimension such as distance, a well-spaced progression is relatively easy to obtain. This is not a linear function: a simple power function is involved, whose index exceeds unity in some cases and is fractional in others. Where fear is a function of number of feared objects, small increments are more potent at low numerical levels. This whole topic is discussed below (pp. 177–182).

Hierarchy construction is greatly facilitated if the patient's emotional responses are quantified on the *sud* scale (pp. 91–92). The standard procedure is to ask patients to rate items according to the amount of anxiety they think they would have upon exposure to them. If the differences between items are, generally speaking, not more than 5 to 10 *suds*, the spacing can be regarded as satisfactory. On the other hand, if there are large differences—for example, 40 *suds* for item number 8, and 10 *suds* for item number 9—intervening items must be found.

Conventional and Idiosyncratic Hierarchies

It is technically necessary to distinguish between two types of hierarchies—conventional and idiosyncratic. Conventional hierarchies are smoothly incremental in one or other of the two ways indicated in figures 9.1 and 9.2—either generalization from a maximal stimulus (the usual state of affairs) or as a monotonic function of distance from a feared object such as a dead bird. Most simple phobias resolve into conventional hierarchies.

Idiosyncratic hierarchies do not display these smooth progressions. There are always irregularities in the stimulus-response relationship. These are related to past conditioning. They produce unpredictable turns in hierarchical sequences. Idiosyncratic hierarchies are characteristic of complex neuroses.

Examples of Conventional Hierarchies

Figure 9.1 (p. 153) epitomizes conventional hierarchy. Although for the sake of simplicity of exposition, the figure portrays a simple arithmetical relationship between magnitude of stimulus and strength of anxiety, the relationship actually conforms to a simple power function. This means that if a person with acrophobia is exposed to increasing heights, it takes greater and greater increases of height to increase anxiety a given amount. To exemplify: going from the second to the third floor increases anxiety by 10 *suds*, but one may need to go from the 15th to the 20th floor for an increase of 10 *suds*. The mathematical aspects of simple power functions and the different exponents found in different kinds of phobias are set forth on pages 177–181.

The following are common examples of conventional hierarchies.

Claustrophobia

1. Locked in a small room (with reading matter) for durations of
    5 hours (asymptote, up to 100 *suds*)
    3 hours
    2 hours
    1 hour
    40 minutes
    25 minutes
    15 minutes
    9 minutes
    6 minutes
    4 minutes
    2.5 minutes
    1.5 minutes
    1 minute
    40 seconds
    25 seconds
    15 seconds
    10 seconds (5 *suds*)

Fear of flying

1. Journeys in planes of increasing durations (up to 100 *suds*)
2. Sitting in airliner taxiing on ground
3. Sitting in airliner with engines running but not scheduled to take off
4. Sitting in airliner with engines off
5. Sitting in airliner at an exhibition
6. Sitting in small passenger plane at exhibition
7. Exploring large model plane in backyard

8. Handling small model plane
9. Hearing a plane overhead

Although conventional hierarchies are unidimensional, they are not always easy to formulate. A 42-year-old woman's 21-year fear of traveling alone was seen on analysis to be a fear of *being alone* away from home. This would have been difficult to quantify in the context of actual travel. A more manageable sequence was derived from using an elevator as the vehicle of her separation from the outside world. The weaker items of the hierarchy were set in a completely open elevator in which she ascended an increasing number of floors up to 100. Then she was "placed" in an elevator that had a single 1-foot-square window, and in this a similar sequence was followed. The same was then done in an elevator with a 9" × 2" window, an elevator with a 2-inch peephole, and finally, a completely opaque one. Desensitization to these items was attended by a progressive increase in her capacity to travel afield, even though distance had not figured at all in the desensitization. The basis of the strategy was the realization of the dynamic role of fear of separation in her fear of travel. After this fear was addressed, a new desensitization series was started, embracing anxiety-conditioned stimuli belonging to journeys of various kinds.

Idiosyncratic Hierarchies

Idiosyncratic hierarchies do not follow the rules of the conventional. Anxiety does not vary along a physical dimension but rather according to variables established in the course of the individual's previous experience. For example, if a person is inappropriately upset by disapproval, the range and magnitudes of disturbing disapprovals are necessarily functions of previous experiences. Thus, one person will be distressed at being regarded as pushy but not at being thought untidy, whereas in another the reverse will be true. The kinds of variation of individual anxious sensibility are limitless. Among the idiosyncratic hierarchies exemplified below it should be noted that there are in some merely irregularities of sequence in the framework of essentially conventional material, for example, in the examination series of Miss C.

Case 30: Four Idiosyncratic Hierarchies Involving People

Miss C. was a 24-year-old art student who came for treatment primarily because her anxiety at examinations had caused repeated failures. Investigation had revealed three other areas of maladaptive fear that yielded the additional three hierarchies. In the examination series it is notable that whereas the bottom seven (weaker) items are in temporal order, the top five are not. Seventeen desensitization sessions overcame all four of these hierarchies, with transfer to the corresponding real situations. Four months later,

Miss C. was able to take her examinations without anxiety and passed in all subjects. Following are the hierarchies developed for Miss C. The numbers in parentheses are *sud* scores.

A. Examination Series

1. On the way to the university on the day of an examination (95)
2. In the process of answering an examination paper (90)
3. Standing before the unopened doors of the examination room (80)
4. Awaiting the distribution of examination papers (70)
5. The examination paper lies face down before her (60)
6. The night before an examination (50)
7. One day before an examination (40)
8. Two days before an examination (30)
9. Three days before an examination (20)
10. Four days before an examination (15)
11. A week before an examination (10)
12. Two weeks before an examination (5)

B. Scrutiny Series

1. Being watched working (drawing) by 10 people (85)
2. Being watched working by six people (70)
3. Being watched working by three people (55)
4. Being watched working by one expert in the field (anxiety begins when the observer is 10 feet away and increases as he draws closer.) (25–55)
5. Being watched working by a nonexpert (anxiety begins at a distance of four feet.) (5–20)

C. Devaluation Series

1. An argument she raises in a discussion is ignored by the group (60)
2. She is not recognized by a person she has briefly met three times (50)
3. Her mother says she is selfish because she is not helping in the house when studying (40)
4. She is not recognized by a person she has briefly met twice (30)
5. Her mother calls her lazy (20)
6. She is not recognized by a person she has briefly met once (10)

D. Discord Between Other People

1. Her mother shouts at a servant (50)
2. Her young sister whines to her mother (40)
3. Her sister engages in a dispute with her father (30)

4. Her mother shouts at her sister (20)
5. She sees two strangers quarrel (10)

A Sampling of Hierarchies about Sickness and Injury

The following examples illustrate individual differences in the content, order, and number of items that make up hierarchies of the same theme in different patients. In most of the cases there was fear of both external and internal stimuli. Again, numbers in parentheses are *sud* scores.

Case 31

Mrs. D., aged 35, was agoraphobic in addition to having the fears of illness shown in the following hierarchy. She had actually experienced the possible events in the series.

Illness in Others

1. Sight of a fit (100)
2. Jerky movements of another's arm (90)
3. Sight of someone fainting (85)
4. An acquaintance says, "That man across the street has some form of insanity" (80)
5. The word "insanity" (70)
6. The word "madness" (65)
7. Insane-sounding laughter (60)
8. An acquaintance says, "That man across the street has an anxiety state" (50)
9. The sound of screaming (the closer, the more disturbing) (25–40)
10. A man with a fracture lying in bed with ropes and pulleys attached to his leg (35)
11. A man propped up in bed short of breath because of heart disease (30)
12. An acquaintance says, "That man across the road is an epileptic" (25)
13. Seeing a man propped up in bed short of breath because of pneumonia (20)
14. A man walks by with a plaster cast on his leg (15)
15. A man with Parkinson's disease (10)
16. A man with blood running down his face from a cut (7)
17. A person with a facial tic (5)

Case 32

Mrs. E., aged 32. External and internal illness fear sources

External Series (Illness in Others)

1. The sight of physical deformity (90)
2. Someone in pain (the greater the evidence of pain, the more disturbing) (50–80)
3. The sight of bleeding (70)
4. The sight of somebody seriously ill (e.g., heart attack) (60)
5. Automobile accidents (50)
6. Nurses in uniform (40)
7. Wheelchairs (30)
8. Hospitals (20)
9. Ambulances (10)

Endogenous Series (Illness in Self)

1. Tense sensation in head (90)
2. Clammy feet (80)
3. Perspiring hands (75)
4. Dry mouth and inability to swallow (70)
5. Dizziness (60)
6. Rapid breathing (50)
7. Racing heart (40)
8. Tense feeling in back of neck (30)
9. Weakness at knees (20)
10. Butterflies in stomach (10)

Case 33

Mrs. F., aged 52, External and internal illness fear sources

External Series (Illness in Others)

1. Child with two wasted legs (85)
2. Man walking slowly — short of breath owing to weak heart (80)
3. Blind man working elevator (70)
4. Child with one wasted leg (65)
5. A hunchback (55)
6. A person groaning with pain (50)
7. A man with a club foot (40)
8. A one-armed man (30)
9. A one-legged man (20)
10. A person with a high temperature owing to a relatively nondangerous disease such as influenza (10)

Endogenous Series (Illness in Self)

1. Extrasystoles (80)
2. Shooting pains in chest and abdomen (70)
3. Pains in the left shoulder and back (60)
4. Pain on top of head (55)
5. Buzzing in ear (50)
6. Tremor of hands (40)
7. Numbness or pain in fingertips (30)
8. Shortness of breath after exertion (20)
9. Pain in left hand (old injury) (10)

Multidimensional Hierarchies

Most hierarchies vary in a single dimension, but a good many are multidimensional. A few of the latter are conventional, but the great majority are idiosyncratic. Multidimensionality is practically invariable in fears of criticism and disapproval. The fear is a joint function of the nature of the negative opinion and the identity of the person who holds it. The hierarchy is set out in tabular form in table 9.1, in which a woman's fears of the negative opinions of others varied with the adjectives applied to her and the identity of the person expressing them. It should be noted that the hierarchical order of the adjectives varied somewhat from speaker to speaker. The way to treat a hierarchy of this kind would be to have the patient imagine herself overhearing the named person attributing an undesirable quality to her while unaware of being overheard.

Pseudoidiosyncratic Hierarchies

Some hierarchies give the appearance of being idiosyncratic because their contents have not been adequately examined for the existence of a common factor. The following example, taken from the literature, is typical:

Table 9.1. Bidimensional Hierarchy Set Out According to the sud Score Resulting from the Interplay of Pairs of Factors

	UNCLE CHARLIE	FLORENCE	SHARON	GERALDINE	SHOPKEEPER SHE BARELY KNOWS
Uses People	95	65	70	50	20
Irresponsible	90	75	50	40	20
Selfish	90	75	40	50	20
Unreliable	80	60	30	40	10
Lazy	60	50	10	20	0
Untidy	50	40	20	10	0
Awkward	40	30	10	10	0

1. At a large university cocktail party talking with strangers
2. At a department luncheon with friends
3. Entering common room of residents where people glance up at you
4. People look at you walking down street
5. Reading in library, glanced at by two men at opposite table
6. At library, conscious of girl looking at you

One apparent feature of this material is anxiety that increases with the number of people looking at her. The increasing audiences could have been placed in a single, arbitrarily chosen setting — for example, a library. As far as can be seen, the hierarchy is conventional. If later exploration shows that different settings add their own anxiety, these can be dealt with in a new hierarchy of places, keeping persons at a constant number.

Desensitization Procedure

The stage is set for desensitization when the patient can calm himself by relaxation and when the therapist has established appropriate hierarchies. Many patients can be adequately calmed when relaxation training has gone halfway or less. While a desensitization program makes it highly desirable for the patient to achieve a positive feeling of calm — that is, some measure of the negative of anxiety — it is not mandatory, and one can be well satisfied with zero subjective units of disturbance. In a fair number of patients who have considerable levels of current anxiety (whether or not this is pervasive — "free floating") it has been found that a substantial lowering of the level — say, from 50 to 15 *suds* — may afford a sufficiently low baseline for successful desensitization. Apparently, an anxiety-inhibiting dynamism can inhibit small quantities of intercurrent anxiety even when it does not fully overcome current anxiety. However, desensitizing effects are very rarely obtainable with levels in excess of 25 *suds* and in some individuals a zero level is obligatory for change to occur.

The therapist naturally hopes for a smooth passage, and such is often the case, but there are many difficulties that may encumber the path. I shall first describe the technique and the characteristic course of uncomplicated desensitization.

The first desensitization session is introduced by saying, "I am now going to get you to relax, and when you are relaxed I will ask you to imagine certain scenes. Each time a scene is clear in your mind indicate this by raising your index finger about one inch."

While the patient sits or lies comfortably with eyes closed, the therapist proceeds to bring about as deep a state of relaxation as possible by the use of such words as the following: "Now, your whole body becomes progressively heavier, and all your muscles relax. Let go more and more completely. We will give your muscles individual attention. Relax the muscles of your forehead and your lower face. (Pause 10 to 20 seconds.) Relax the muscles of your jaws and those of your tongue. (Pause.) Relax the muscles around your eyes. The more you relax, the calmer you become. (Pause.) Relax the muscles of your neck. (Pause.) Let all the muscles of your shoulders relax. Just let yourself go. (Pause.) Now relax your arms. (Pause.) Relax all the muscles of your trunk. (Pause.) Relax the muscles of your lower limbs. Let your muscles go more and more. You feel at ease and very comfortable."

At the first desensitization session, which is always partly exploratory, the therapist seeks some feedback about the state of the patient, asking him to state on the subjective scale how much anxiety he feels. If it is zero or close to it, scene presentations can begin. If the patient continues to have some anxiety despite his best efforts at direct relaxation, various imaginal devices may be invoked. Those most commonly used are the following:

1. "Imagine that on a calm summer's day you lie back on a soft lawn and watch large, fleecy clouds move slowly overhead. Notice especially the intensely brilliant edges."
2. "Imagine an intense, bright spot of light about 18 inches in front of you just above eye level." (This image is from Milton Erickson.)
3. "Imagine that near a river's bank you see a leaf moving erratically on little waves."

The introduction of the scenes at the first desensitization session follows a standard routine. Observations of the patient's responses at this session frequently lead to concordant modifications of technique.

The first scene presented is a "control." It is neutral in the sense that the patient is not expected to have any anxious reaction to it. I most commonly use a street scene. Sometimes it is "safer" to have the patient imagine himself sitting in his living room reading a newspaper, but there is no guarantee of "safety" unless the subject matter has actually been explored beforehand. At one time, I used to employ a white flower against a black background as a control scene. One day, a patient showed considerable anxiety to it because he associated it with funerals, and, as it turned out, had a neurosis about death.

There are two reasons why a control scene is used. First, it provides information about the patient's general ability to visualize. Second, it gives indications of possible contaminating factors; for example, the patient may have anxiety at losing control or about the unknown. In either case, that anxiety, which has nothing to do with the target of the desensitization, must be dispelled before therapy can continue.

For many years, the standard method of introducing scenes was the one that I described in 1954. The patient was asked to imagine the scene and then told to desist after "sufficient" time had passed. The sufficiency had to be guessed and was usually 15 to 20 seconds. He was then invited to raise his finger if the scene had caused even the slightest rise of anxiety; and this was the signal for repetition. The important fact is that the therapist could not tell when visualization had actually begun or what its actual duration was. Moreover, the *sud* values were given only at the end of the session, from memory.

The following method, which is free from these disadvantages, has been consistently used and taught since 1968. Patients are instructed to imagine scenes indicated by the therapist. They are to raise an index finger about an inch when the image is clear. The therapist lets the scene remain for as long as he wants—usually 5 to 7 seconds. He terminates it by saying, "Stop the scene," and then asks the patients to state how much it disturbed them in terms of *suds*; that is, by how much did the scene raise the *sud* level? After a few sessions, many patients give this information automatically upon the termination of the scene. While a verbal report may possibly disrupt relaxation more than would the raising of a finger, the adverse effects have seemed negligible. Any disadvantages are certainly outweighed by dispensing with the need to allow "sufficient time" for the scene and by the immediate and precise *sud* feedback at the scene's ending.

In order to illustrate what is typically said and done, let us make use of the cluster of four hierarchies of Miss C. (p. 167).

THERAPIST: I am now going to ask you to imagine a number of scenes. You will imagine them clearly and they will interfere little, if at all, with your state of relaxation. If, however, at any time you feel disturbed or worried and want to draw my attention, you can tell me so. As soon as a scene is clear in your mind, indicate that by raising your left index finger about 1 inch. First, I want you to imagine that you are standing at a familiar street corner on a pleasant morning watching the traffic go by. You see cars, motorcycles, trucks, bicycles, people, and traffic lights, and you hear the sounds associated with all these things.

(After a few seconds the patient raises her left index finger. The therapist pauses for 5 seconds.)

THERAPIST: Stop imagining that scene. By how much did it raise your anxiety level while you imagined it?
MISS C.: Not at all.
THERAPIST: Now give your attention once again to relaxing.

(There is again a pause of 20–30 seconds, with renewed relaxation instructions.)

THERAPIST: Now imagine that you are home studying in the evening. It is May 20, exactly a month before your examination.

(After about 15 seconds Miss C. raises her finger. Again she is left with the scene for five seconds.)

THERAPIST: Stop that scene. By how much did it raise your anxiety?
MISS C.: About 15 units.
THERAPIST: Now imagine the same scene again—a month before your examination.

At this second presentation the rise in anxiety was five *suds* and at the third it was zero. The numbers given vary with the individual and with the scene. When the initial figure is over 30, repetition is unlikely to lower it. But there are exceptions. There are also occasional patients in whom an initial rise of 10 is too great to be diminished by repetition.

Having disposed of the first scene of the examination hierarchy, I could have moved on to the second. Alternatively, I could have tested Miss C.'s responses in another area, such as the discord hierarchy, which I did:

THERAPIST: Imagine you are sitting on a bench at a bus stop and across the road are two strange men whose voices are raised in argument.

(This scene was given twice. After the patient reported on her response to the last presentation, I terminated the desensitization session.)

THERAPIST: Relax again. Now I am going to count up to five and you will open your eyes, feeling calm and refreshed.

The responses of this patient were commonplace. Since visualization was clear, and there was evidence of decrease of anxiety with each repetition of a scene, it seemed likely that we would make our way through all four hierarchies without much trouble, an expectation that was borne out by the course of events.

Procedure at later sessions takes much the same course as at the first, but the preliminaries take less and less time. Whenever the patient is judged sufficiently relaxed, he is informed that scenes will be presented to his imagination. If at the previous session there was a scene for which repeated presentations diminished anxiety, but not to zero, that scene is usually the first to be presented. But if at the previous session, that scene ceased to arouse any anxiety, the scene next higher in the hierarchy will be presented. There are, however, some patients who, despite no anxiety at all to the final scene at a session, again show some anxiety to that scene—a kind of spontaneous recovery of anxiety. The scene must then be repeated until the anxiety is entirely eliminated. In some of these patients, the need for backtracking can sometimes be eliminated by overlearning, that is, presenting a scene two or three times more after it has ceased to arouse anxiety.

All relevant occurrences during the desensitization session are noted on a card by a concise notation. The following is the record summarizing Miss C.'s desensitization session as described above:

S.D. by rel. Scene 1—corner ([× 1] 0). 2—studying at home one month before exam ([× 3] 15,5,0). 3—two strange men argue across road ([× 2] 15,10).

"S.D. by rel." stands for "systematic desensitization by relaxation." The numbers in square parenthesis show how many presentations were given. Those to their right are the *sud* scores for the successive presentations.

The usual plan followed in assigning numerical indices to scenes is to use an integer to indicate the class of subject matter and letters for variations of detail. For example, in Miss C.'s case, the imaginary situation of being at home working two weeks before the examination was given the index 1 a, one week before the examination was 1 b, and so forth. The advantages of employing these indices are the following: (a) they obviate repetitious writing; (b) they make it easy to find particular scenes when one consults the record; and (c) they facilitate later research work.

QUANTITATIVE ASPECTS OF DESENSITIZATION

There is great variation in how many themes, how many scenes from each, and how many presentations are given at a desensitization session. Generally, up to four hierarchies are drawn upon in an individual session, and not many patients have more than four. Three or four presentations of a scene are usual to bring the responses to zero, but 10 or more may be needed. The total number of scenes presented is limited mainly by availability of time, but sometimes by the endurance of the patient. On the whole, available time increases as therapy goes on, and eventually almost the whole interview period may be devoted to desensitization, so that whereas at an early stage 8 or 10 presentations may be the total at a session, at an advanced stage the number may be 30 or even 50. The usual duration of a desensitization session is 15 to 30 minutes. However, Wolpin and Pearsall (1965) reported totally overcoming a phobia in a single session conducted continuously for 90 minutes and it is not uncommon to hear clinicians make this claim.

While the foregoing generalizations apply to the great majority of patients, there are rare individuals who manifest marked perseveration of even the mild anxiety aroused by a single scene presentation. Yet, anxiety decreases from session to session. In such individuals only one scene should be given at a session. Marked perseveration of anxiety can also occur in the usual run of patients after the presentation of an unduly disturbing scene. When this happens, the session should be terminated.

It has hitherto been the accepted principle in systematic desensitization to use only weakly anxiety-evoking stimuli. While this is obviously prudent when one depends on reciprocal inhibition for change, it is not necessarily always the most economical thing to do. There are clinical reports suggesting that more rapid progress sometimes follows larger steps (Rachman, 1971). There may be a personality factor that determines responsiveness to change, ranging from "desensitizability" at one extreme to "floodability" at the other.

The duration of a scene is usually of the order of 5 to 7 seconds, but it may be varied according to several circumstances. It is quickly terminated if the patient indicates strong anxiety. Whenever the therapist has special reason to suspect that a scene may evoke a strong reaction he presents it with cautious brevity—for 1 or 2 seconds. By and large, early presentations of scenes are briefer, later ones longer. A certain number of patients require 15 or more seconds to construct a clear image of a verbally triggered scene. The character of the scene also necessarily plays a part in determining the time allowed for it. A clap of thunder takes less time than making a speech.

The interval between scenes also varies. It is usually between 10 and 30 seconds, but if the patient has been more than slightly disturbed by the preceding scene, the interval may be extended to a minute or more, during which time he may be given repeated suggestions to be relaxed and tranquil. Until the therapist is well acquainted with the patient's reactions, he should frequently check the basal relaxation level between scenes using the *sud* scale.

The number of desensitizing sessions required depends on the number of scene presentations necessary to overcome the constellations. Relevant factors are the number of such constellations, the severity of each, and the degree of generalization or involvement of related stimuli. One patient may recover in half a dozen sessions, another may require 100 or more. The patient with a death phobia (p. 184), on whom a temporal dimension had to be used, also had two other phobias and required a total of about 100 sessions. To remove the death phobia alone, a total of about 2,000 scene presentations were given.

The spacing of sessions does not seem to matter greatly. As a rule, they are conducted once or twice a week, but may be separated by many weeks, or take place daily. Some patients, visiting from afar, receive two sessions a day, and occasionally as many as four. Whether sessions are massed or widely dispersed, there is practically always a close correlation between the extent to which desensitization has been accomplished and the degree of diminution of anxiety responses to real stimuli in the phobic areas. Except when therapy is almost terminated and nothing remains of a phobia but a few weak reactions that may be expected to fade through the competition of emotions arising spontaneously in the ordinary course of living (Wolpe, 1958, p. 99), very little change occurs, as a rule, between sessions. In one case of severe claustrophobia, a marked but incomplete degree of improvement achieved by a first series of sessions remained almost stationary during a 3½-year interval, after which further sessions led to complete elimination of the phobia. The patient mentioned earlier, who had a disabling fear of cars, had daily sessions for a week or 2 every 5 weeks or so, and improved greatly during the treatment phases, but not at all during the intervening weeks (see case 64, p. 317ff).

Rate of change is neither haphazard nor a purely individual matter. In the case of desensitization of the classical phobias, it follows consistent quantitative laws. A study of 20 phobias of 13 patients (Wolpe, 1963) was prompted by the clinical observation that, during desensitization, the number of presentations of a scene required to bring the anxiety level down to zero is not uniform, but tends to increase or decrease on the way up the hierarchy. The study focused on phobias that vary along a physical dimension. It was found that in claustrophobia and those phobias in which anxiety increases with increasing proximity to the feared object, the cumulative curve relating number of scene presentations to therapeutic progress is a positively accelerating function. In agoraphobias, acrophobias, and those in which anxiety increases with the number of objects, the cumulative curve is a negatively accelerating function. No exceptions were found, as may be observed by studying figures 9.4 through 9.7, each of which portrays the curves of a particular group. In order to make them comparable, the curves were subjected to percentile transformations. The horizontal axes show attained percentage of criterion of recovery, and the vertical axes show scene presentations as a percentage of the total number employed to overcome the hierarchy.

Figure 9.8 illustrates that it is not the personality of the patient but the type of phobia that determines the shape of the curve. The three curves in this figure were obtained from a single patient. That displaying negative acceleration (B) delineates the desensitization of the anxiety response to an increasing number of tombstones at 200 yards. The positively accelerating curves belong respectively to proximation phobias to a dead dog (A) and to a stationary automobile (C), and are strikingly concordant.

Mathematical analysis of the curves reveals that, in general, they express the same kind of functional relation as found by Stevens (1957, 1962) in relating the physical magnitude of a stimulus to its perceived intensity — the "psychophysical law." According to his empirically based law, psychological (subjective) magnitude is a power function of stimulus magnitude. This means that to make one stimulus seem twice as strong as another, the

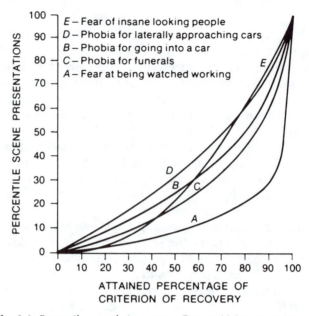

Fig. 9.4. Percentile cumulative curves: Densensitizing operations in proximation phobias in different subjects.

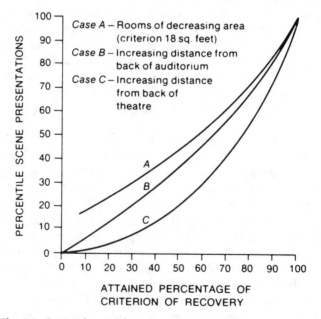

Fig. 9.5. Percentile cumulative curves: Desensitizing operations in claustrophobia.

178

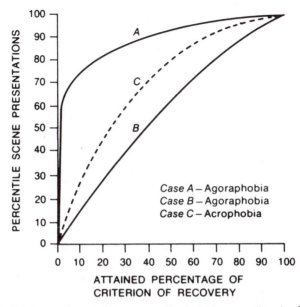

Fig. 9.6. Percentile cumulative curves: Desensitizing operations in phobias involving increasing distance from a safe point: Agoraphobia or acrophobia.

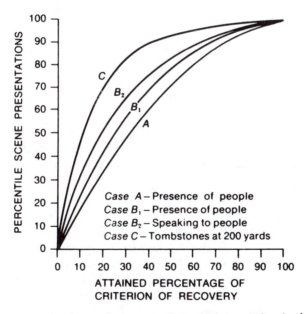

Fig. 9.7. Percentile cumulative curves: Desensitizing operations in phobias increasing with numbers of phobic objects

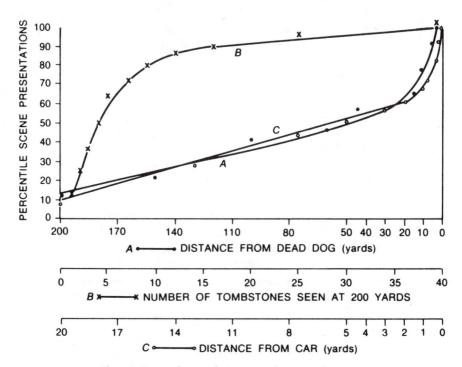

Fig. 9.8. Percentile cumulative curves from a single case.

physical energy must be increased at a fixed ratio, no matter what the initial intensity level. The relationship is expressed by the formula

$$P = kS^n$$

where P stands for perceived intensity (psychological magnitudes), S for stimulus magnitude, k is a constant, and n the exponent of the relationship. The exponent is determined empirically by the formula:

$$n = \frac{\log .05}{\log r}$$

where r is the ratio between the physical magnitude of a given stimulus and the physical magnitude of the stimulus that appears twice as strong as the given stimulus. Insofar as the desensitization curves portray this kind of functional relation, it may be deduced that the amount of work required for each measured unit of progress in overcoming these phobias is a function of the correlated magnitudes of the subject's pretreatment responses. It is desirable to correlate autonomic magnitudes of response at different points in hierarchies before treatment, with the desensitization curves subsequently obtained. No direct comparison has as yet been attempted, but Lang et al. (1970) found that the curve correlating pulse rate change with hierarchical position of the stimulus in snake phobias is very similar to the proximation phobia curves in figure 9.4. For further details, and for a discussion of some deviations from the formula, see Wolpe (1963).

Awareness of these quantitative relations makes it possible to predict the stage, in cases of each class, at which progress will be slowest. It also helps the therapist to decide which dimension to work with first in a multidimensional hierarchy. For example, if fear increases with numbers of feared objects and with proximity to them, the knowledge that the numbers curve accelerates negatively and the proximation curve accelerates positively mandates first presenting increasing numbers at a fixed distance. Then the numerous objects can be gradually brought closer. If the reverse order were adopted, one would ultimately be contending with the steep ends of both curves simultaneously.

When Systematic Desensitization Does Not Succeed

Sometimes, despite having carried out all steps conscientiously, the therapist is chagrined to find that desensitization is not proceeding according to expectation. Either the patient experiences no decrements of anxiety with successive presentations of scenes, or he or she finds no improvement in reactions to real situations despite apparent progress during sessions. To remedy the situation, the therapist must discover what accounts for the failure. The usual reasons are of three kinds:

1. Difficulties of relaxation
2. Misleading or irrelevant hierarchies
3. Inadequacies of imagery

Difficulties of Relaxation

Relaxation is generally deemed inadequate when it fails to lower anxiety to less than 10 *suds*. It may sometimes be effectively enhanced by doses of such drugs as diazepam or codeine an hour before the interview. Which drug to use is a matter of trial and error. When pervasive (free-floating) anxiety impedes relaxation, the use of carbon dioxide-oxygen mixtures by the single inhalation technique (see chapter 14) is of the greatest value, and with some patients comes to be used before every desensitization session. Inhalations are given until anxiety stops decreasing—usually by the fourth inhalation.

Relaxation is sometimes enhanced by hypnosis, for which I employ the levitation technique described by Wolberg (1948). In difficult subjects the procedure is soon abandoned. But in some patients who cannot relax effectively, attempts at desensitization may nonetheless succeed, presumably because therapist-induced emotional responses (see chapter 17) inhibit the anxiety aroused by the imagined stimuli. Much effort can be wasted if the therapist has the impression that the patient is well relaxed when in fact he or she is not. The use of the *sud* scale guards against miscommunications of this type. Questionable cases may require psychophysiological monitoring, usually by auditory feedback from muscle potentials (Budzinski, Stoyva, & Adler, 1970; Leaf & Gaarder, 1971).

There is an important group of subjects in whom muscle relaxation causes fear instead of calmness. It seemed to me long ago (Wolpe, 1969, p. 139) that this was essentially a fear of letting go, which I treated in each case by using another source of inhibition of fear. In recent years, attempts to understand relaxation-induced fear were initiated by Heide and Borkovec (1983, 1984). Unfortunately they approached the problem by offering speculative proposals instead of examining the dynamics of individual cases. Norton et al. (1985), in analyzing the psychological characteristics "of people who show a paradoxical increase in anxiety during relaxation training," made the unjustified assumption that the phenomenon has the same basis in all cases.

The handling of patients who react with anxiety to attempts at relaxation varies with the individual. Sometimes it is possible to achieve a state of calm adequate for desensitization simply by telling patients to calm themselves in their own way, without any talk of "letting go." In other cases, one may resort to other methods of counteracting anxiety such as described in chapter 10, including in their use desensitization to the fear of letting go.

Misleading or Irrelevant Hierarchies

When the therapist finds himself making no headway, another possibility is that the hierarchies are off track. This often happens because a common context of the patient's fears is mistaken for the trigger. For example, after a man had been treated for 20 sessions with minimal benefit for claustrophobia and agoraphobia it was found that in both constricted space and separation from a safe place he had a fear of dying, because in each of these circumstances it would be difficult to get help if he should collapse.

Not infrequently, hierarchies not amenable to desensitization are found in unhappily married women who are low in self-sufficiency (see chapter 14). Apparently simple phobias that have originated in the course of the marriage turn out to be fear reactions to stimulus situations that are related to some distressful aspect of the marriage. This was independently noted by Fry (1962). Many of these cases present as agoraphobia.

Case 34: Fear of Assertion With Husband Displayed as Fear of Conversing With Strangers

This is a nonagoraphobic example. A 34-year-old woman complained of a feeling of being closed in and an urgent need to escape when engaged in conversations with adults, except in interchanges of the most casual kind, such as asking the time. The problem had begun 8 years previously during the patient's first pregnancy. When I first saw her, I could elicit no satisfactory precipitating cause. I trained her in relaxation and took the phobic stimuli at their face value. The first hierarchy I used for desensitization was on the theme of being stared at, on her statement that anxiety increased with the proximity of the starer. The scenes I presented to her imagination initially aroused little anxiety until a distance of 15 feet was reached, and then there was a severe reaction. Various other dimensions were then tried in turn—number of people at a distance, age of starer, duration of stare, and intensity of illumination—in each instance with the same consequence. It was obvious that something was being missed, but I could not tell what. I was about to abandon the case when the patient, whom tranquilizers had helped only a little, asked, "Is there *nothing* that could diminish my distress?" I replied, "At times of special stress you might try a little alcohol." After a long pause she said, "My husband doesn't let me drink." This was the first time I had heard her make an adverse remark about him, but it was the thin end of a wedge that pried open long-suppressed anger and frustration at his absolute domination over her. The first pregnancy had precipitated the neurosis because it had seemed to block forever a way out of the marriage, which to the outer world and partly to herself she had pretended was a great success.

The phobia was now seen to be primarily a fear of others peering or prying. In relevant situations this summated with the impulse to escape, chronically engendered by the marriage. Thus, an unacknowledged tension was the real basis of the phobia. Teaching the patient assertion, especially with her husband, became the foremost therapeutic tactic.

Since some might infer that in these circumstances of hidden information, psychoanalysis might have been the treatment of choice, it must be said that the patient had previously had 2 years of psychoanalysis without any success. The patient's true feelings about her husband had not emerged during its course, in which major attention was given to oedipal attitudes and the like. The guiding rules of psychoanalysis often prove to be a straitjacket, prohibiting the full and free exploration of a case. In any event, the insight about the marriage was not itself therapeutic.

Sometimes, the inadequacies of a hierarchy become evident only after attempts at desensitization have begun, when it may be seen that the anxiety level does not diminish after repeated presentations of the weakest scene contained in the hierarchy, even though relaxation is manifestly good. The problem is then to find stimuli whose evoked anxiety is weak enough to be inhibited by the patient's relaxation. In many cases, it is obvious where to look for such stimuli. In a patient who had anxiety on the theme of loneliness, the weakest item in the original hierarchy — being at home accompanied only by her daughter — was found to evoke more anxiety than was manageable. In order to obtain a weaker starting point, all that was needed was to add to the situation more companions. But it is not always so easy, and the therapist may have to innovate a way of procuring weak stimuli.

For example, following an accident 3 years previously, a woman had developed severe anxiety reactions to the sight of approaching automobiles. I had been led to believe that her anxiety began when a car was two blocks away, and increased with proximity. This seemed straightforward enough; but at the first desensitization session an imagined distance of two blocks from the car aroused anxiety too great to be inhibited by the relaxation. Further questioning revealed that the patient had considerable anxiety at the prospect of even the shortest journey by car, since the whole range of threatening possibilities was present the moment a journey became imminent; but she had "not thought this amount of anxiety worthy of report." Desensitization could not succeed until the "general danger" was removed. What was required was rigorous control of the "danger." An imaginary enclosed field, two blocks square, was drawn on paper. The patient when relaxed imagined that she sat in her car in one corner of the field while a trusted person drove his car up to an agreed distance from her, and then to ever-closer agreed points as the anxiety declined. The danger was thus always circumscribed. Many other details of the treatment of the case are given under case 64, p. 317ff.

Another case in which it was difficult to find stimuli weak enough to start desensitization was a woman with a death phobia, whose anxiety-arousing areas in descending order of intensity were human corpses, funeral processions, and dead dogs. Imagining dead dogs produced marked and undiminishing anxiety, even when they were at distances of two or three hundred yards. A solution was found in the use of "temporal distancing," beginning with the historically inaccurate sentence, "William the Conqueror was killed at the Battle of Hastings in 1066." After desensitization to this, we moved progressively closer over the centuries; then through narrowing intervals of years, months, and days to the present.

Temporal distancing was used in a different way with a woman who had severe reactions to the idea of anybody fainting or "losing power." Imagining even the most trivial sign of weakness in a person or an animal produced more anxiety than her relaxation could counteract. The first scene to be successfully used in her desensitization was in the context of her being shown around a campus. Her imaginary escort pointed to a platform and said, "That is where, 5 years ago, an animal was given an injection that paralyzed it for 5 minutes." Desensitization involved first making the incident more recent and then increasing the duration of the paralysis.

Inadequacies of Imagery

Most patients are able to project themselves into imagined anxiety-evoking situations in a way that elicits something of the reality of the situations and a corresponding amount of anxiety. I have found this in about 85% of patients in both South Africa and the United States. When I spent a year in England, the percentage seemed to me to be lower in that country, in line with the observations of Meyer (1963). Perhaps the traditional English training to control displays of feeling also impairs the ability to evoke emotion by imagery.

A few patients are unable to conjure up the visual or auditory images required by the therapist. Far more commonly, images are formed but have little or no sense of reality. Occasionally, the therapist can overcome this problem by describing in great detail the situation to be imagined, especially in good hypnotic subjects, or by having patients verbalize what they imagine. Darwin and McBrearty (1969) found that in speed-anxious subjects, significantly more rapid progress was made during desensitization if the patients described the scenes out loud instead of merely imagining them. An apparently effective program for enhancing the capacity to imagine realistically was put forward by Phillips (1971). If such efforts fail, therapeutic change will require the use of the real stimuli or physical representations of them (chapter 10).

Occasionally, patients who have visualized satisfactorily cease to do so when they have advanced to a "dangerous" point. They then seem to detach themselves from the imagined situations, viewing them from the standpoint of a disinterested spectator. An example is case 65, who had an extreme cleanliness compulsion, based upon a fear of contamination with his own urine. When the imaginary situations got close to actual contact, they lost their realism. Relaxation was then counterposed to real stimuli. On this basis, the neurosis was finally fully overcome.

RESULTS OF SYSTEMATIC DESENSITIZATION

A Clinical Study

In a statistical study (Wolpe, 1961b), I used as subject matter 39 patients whose case records had been extracted in random fashion from my files. Many of these patients also had other neurotic habits that were treated by other methods deemed more appropriate.

The details of the study are tabulated in table 9.2, in which outcome of treatment is indicated on a five-point scale ranging from four-plus to zero. A four-plus rating means complete or almost complete freedom from the fear of the relevant class of stimuli encountered in actuality. A three-plus rating means an improvement of response such that the fear class is judged by the patient to have lost at least 80% of its original strength. A zero indicates that there is no definite change. It will be noted that only four-plus, three-plus, and zero ratings were given to the patients in this series.

Table 9.3 summarizes the data given in table 9.2. There were 68 anxiety-response habits among the 39 patients, of whom 19 had multiple hierarchies. The treatment was judged effective in 35 patients. Forty-five of the anxiety-response habits were apparently eliminated (four-plus rating) and 17 more markedly ameliorated (three-plus rating), making 90% in all. It is probable that many of the latter group would have reached a four-plus level had there been additional sessions. In patients 16 and 32, progress had tailed off when sessions were discontinued, but not in any of the others.

Among the failures, patients 8 and 18 were unable to imagine themselves within situations; patient 21 could not confine her imagining to the stated scene and repeatedly exposed herself to excessively disturbing images. She was later treated with complete success by the conditioned motor response method outlined on page 197. Patient 24 had interpersonal reactions that led to erratic responses and, having experienced no benefit, sought therapy elsewhere.

The mean number of sessions per fear was 11.2; the median number of sessions per patient, 10.0. It should be noted that a desensitization session usually takes up only part of a 45-minute interview period, and some of the cases also had other neurotic problems for which there were interviews in which a desensitization session did not occur, and these are not included in the tally.

An important point to note about this data is that of the 68 fears treated, only 14 can be classed among the classical phobias. That number includes five cases of agoraphobia which, as will be seen in chapter 14, is frequently based on social fears. The others are claustrophobia (4), snakelike shapes, bright light, crowds, storms, and tissue damage in others. The inclusion of the last as a phobia is probably questionable. Although in clinical practice the predominating use of desensitization is in the treatment of social fears, the popular belief continues to be that its applicability is confined to phobias.

Controlled Studies

In a brilliantly designed experiment, Paul (1966) compared desensitization with two other methods in the treatment of students with severe fears of speaking in public. He enlisted the services of five experienced psychothera-

Table 9.2. Basic Patient Data

PATIENT SEX, AGE	NO. OF SESSIONS	HIERARCHY THEME	OUTCOME	COMMENTS
1 F,50	62	a Claustrophobia	+ + + +	
		b Illness and hospitals	+ + + +	
		c Death and its trappings	+ + + +	
		d Storms	+ + +	
		e Quarrels	+ + + +	
2 M,40	6	a Guilt	+ + + +	
		b Devaluation	+ + + +	
3 F,24	17	a Examinations	+ + + +	See Case 25
		b Being scrutinized	+ + + +	
		c Devaluation	+ + + +	
		d Discord between others	+ + + +	
4 M,24	5	a Snakelike shapes	+ + + +	
5 M,21	24	a Being watched	+ + + +	
		b Suffering of others	+ + + +	
		c "Jealousy" reaction	+ + + +	
		d Disapproval	+ + + +	
6 M,28	5	Crowds	+ + +	
7 F,21	5	Criticism	+ + + +	
8 F,52	21	a Being center of attention	0	No disturbance during scenes
		b Superstitions	0	Was in fact not imaging self in situation
9 F,25	9	Suffering and death of others	+ + +	
10 M,22	17	Tissue damage in others	+ + + +	
11 M,37	13	Actual or implied criticism	+ + + +	
12 F,31	15	Being watched working	+ + +	
13 F,40	16	a "Suffering" and eeriness	+ + + +	This case has been reported in detail (Wolpe, 1959)
		b Being devalued	+ + + +	
		c Failing to come up to expectations	+ + + +	
14 M,36	10	a Bright light	+ + + +	
		b Palpitations	+ + + +	
15 M,43	9	Wounds and corpses	+ + +	
16 M,27	51	a Being watched, especially at work	+ + +	After treatment, no anxiety, while being watched at work
		b Being criticized	+ + + +	Anxious at times while playing cards
17 M,33	8	Being watched at golf	+ + +	
18 M,33	8	Talking before audience (stutterer)	0	No imagined scene was ever disturbing
19 M,40	7	Authority figures	+ + + +	
20 M,23	4	Claustrophobia	+ + + +	
21 F,23	6	a Agoraphobia	0	Later successfully treated by conditioned motor response method
		b Fear of falling		

(*continued*)

Table 9.2. Basic Patient Data (*continued*)

PATIENT SEX, AGE	NO. OF SESSIONS	HIERARCHY THEME	OUTCOME	COMMENTS
22 M,46	19	a Being in limelight	+ + +	
		b Blood and death	+ + + +	
23 F,40	20	Social embarrassment	+ + + +	
24 F,28	9	Agoraphobia	0	
25 F,48	7	Rejection	+ + +	
26 M,28	13	a Disapproval	+ + +	
		b Rejection	+ + + +	
27 M,11	6	Authority figures	+ + + +	
28 M,26	217	a Claustrophobia	+ + + +	
		b Criticism (numerous aspects)	+ + +	Finally overcome completely by use of flooding
		c Trappings of death	+ + +	
29 F,20	5	Agoraphobia	+ + + +	
		b Masturbation	+ + + +	
30 M,68	23	a Agoraphobia	+ + + +	
31 F,36	5	Being in limelight	+ + + +	
32 M,26	17	a Illness and death	+ + +	
		b Own symptoms	+ + +	
33 F,44	9	a Being watched	+ + + +	
		b Elevators	+ + + +	
34 F,47	17	Intromission into vagina	+ + +	
35 M,37	5	a Disapproval	+ + + +	
		b Rejection	+ + + +	
36 F,32	25	Sexual stimuli	+ + + +	
37 M,36	21	a Agoraphobia	+ + + +	
		b Disapproval	+ + + +	
		c Being watched	+ + + +	
38 M,18	6	a Disapproval	+ + +	
		b Sexual stimuli	+ + + +	Instrumental in overcoming impotence
39 F,48	20	a Rejection	+ + + +	Stutter markedly improved
		b Crudeness of others	+ + + +	

Table 9.3. Summary of Data in Table 9.2

Patients	39
Number of patients responding to desensitization treatment	35
Number of hierarchies	68
Hierarchies overcome	45 } 91%
Hierarchies markedly improved	17
Hierarchies unimproved	6 9%
Total number of desensitization sessions	762
Mean session expenditure per hierarchy	11.2
Mean session expenditure per successfully treated hierarchy	12.3
Median number of sessions per patient	10.0

pists whose "school" affiliations ranged from Freud to Sullivan. Nine subjects were allotted to a therapist, so that he could use three different methods, each in three subjects. The methods were (a) the therapist's own customary type of insight therapy, (b) a stylized procedure involving suggestion and support called "attention-placebo," and (c) systematic desensitization which the therapist had to be trained to administer. Each patient had five therapeutic sessions. The results showed significantly superior effectiveness for systematic desensitization on a variety of measures: cognitive, physiological, and motor performance. On the conventional clinical criteria, 86% of the patients treated by desensitization were much improved and 14% improved (table 9.4). This compares with 20% much improved and 27% improved for the insight group, and with none much improved and 47% improved for the attention-placebo group. In a follow-up 2 years later Paul (1968) found that the differences had been maintained.

Lang was the chief architect of an excellent series of controlled studies beginning with Lang and Lazovik (1963) and Lang, Lazovik, and Reynolds (1965). Their subjects were students who had severe phobic reactions to harmless snakes. They treated some groups by systematic desensitization and compared the results with those obtained in control groups who either received no treatment or else "pseudotherapy" (i.e., relaxation training followed by interviews focusing on problems of "living," with the subject in a state of relaxation). The desensitized students improved much more than either of the control groups, as shown by a snake avoidance test, and by the patient's self-rating of fear reactions to snakes (table 9.5). The difference was significant at the .001 level when 15 or more hierarchy items had been desensitized.

Moore (1965) described a controlled investigation on asthmatic patients at a clinic. She used a balanced, incomplete block design (in which the subjects were their own controls) to compare the effects on these cases of three forms of treatment: (a) reciprocal inhibition (systematic desensitization) therapy, (b) relaxation therapy, and (c) relaxation combined with suggestion. During

Table 9.4. Percentage Breakdown of Cases in Traditional "Improvement" Categories from Stress-Condition Data*

TREATMENT	N	UNIMPROVED	SLIGHTLY IMPROVED	IMPROVED	MUCH IMPROVED
Desensitization	15	—	—	14%	86%
Insight	15	7%	46%	27%	20%
Attention-Placebo	15	20%	33%	47%	—
Treatment-control	29	55%	28%	17%	—

*From Paul, Gordon L. (1966). *Insight versus Desensitization in Psychotherapy.* Stanford, CA: Stanford University Press. Reprinted with permission.

Table 9.5. T-tests of Mean Fear Change Scores from Pre- to Posttreatment in Snake Phobias

GROUPS	AVOIDANCE TEST	FEAR THERMOMETER	FSS NO. 38	FEAR SURVEY
Combined control vs. Desensitization	2.57*	2.12*	2.19*	1.25*
Combined control vs. 15 or more	3.26†	3.44†	3.99‡	2.52*
Combined control vs. less than 15	0.14	0.41	1.85	0.41
Less than 15 vs. 15 or more	2.33*	3.28*	5.00‡	2.26*
Pseudotherapy vs. no treatment	1.67	0.48	0.58	0.12

*p<.05. †p<.01. ‡p<.001.
Lang, P. J., Lazovik, A. D., & Reynolds, D. (1965). "Desensitization, Suggestibility, and Pseudotherapy." *Journal of Abnormal Psychology, 70*, 395.

the first 4 weeks of treatment, both subjectively and objectively as measured by maximum peak flow of respired air, all three groups improved, but the desensitization group more than the others. After this time, progress continued in the desensitization group, while the other two began to regress. Eight weeks from the beginning of treatment, in terms of maximum peak flow, the superiority of improvement of the desensitization group was significant at the .001 level (Fig. 9.9).

Paul (1969a, p. 63ff) made an analysis of 75 studies of the outcome of systematic desensitization. These involved "more than 90 different therapists and nearly 1,000 different clients." Out of 55 uncontrolled reports, all but nine showed evidence of the effectiveness of systematic desensitization. There were eight controlled experiments that included designs that ruled out intraclass confounding of therapist characteristics and treatment techniques, of which "all found solid evidence for the specific effectiveness of systematic desensitization" (p. 145). Paul concluded that "for the first time in the history of psychological treatments, a specific therapeutic package reliably produced measureable benefits for clients across a broad range of distressing problems in which anxiety was of fundamental importance" (p. 159). Relapse and symptom substitution were notably lacking though most of the authors were on the lookout for them.

REBUTTAL OF SOME CRITICISMS

Systematic desensitization continues to be the subject of much criticism. Some critics (e.g., Sue, 1972) betray their alien orientation by solemnly contesting the statement (which they wrongly attribute to me) that relaxation is indispensable to desensitization. The calming effects of relaxation are only one of numerous responses that can compete with anxiety, many of which are described in detail in chapter 10.

The very notion that systematic desensitization works on the basis of response competition continues to be disputed. While acknowledging that the "package" is therapeutically effective, the critics contend that its success

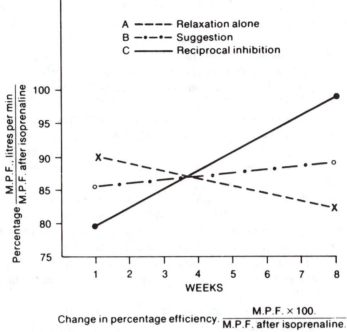

Fig. 9.9. Comparative effects of three treatment schedules on maximum peak flow of inspired air in asthmatic patients (Moore, 1965).

is not a function of competition between its elements, that is, of reciprocal inhibition. As they see it, this competition has as much relevance to the real cause of change as Mesmer's bacquet and wand had to the behavioral changes he reported. Thus, Kazdin and Wilcoxon (1976) claim that desensitization works through expectancy of favorable change. But of the experiments they quote in support of their theory, none provides evidence that expectancy per se ever produces the weakening of maladaptive fear that is the routine outcome of desensitization correctly performed. Kazdin and Wilcoxon simply accept the unsupported assertion of Rosenthal and Frank (1958) that therapeutic change is "due to faith in the efficacy of the therapist and his or her technique." Ford (1978) found evidence to the contrary — that clients' expectations of therapeutic change were not a reliable predictor of long-term improvement.

Advocacy of expectancy theory from a different angle comes from Reiss (1980) and Kirsch et al. (1983). In 36 snake phobic subjects who had responded to a newspaper advertisement, Kirsch et al. compared the effects of systematic desensitization with those of what they termed a highly credible expectancy procedure in which subjects were asked to relive in fantasy and fully associate to a series of childhood events that "clinical research has established as being related" to the target fear. From the fact that the treatments produced no significant differences in outcome it is concluded that favorable expectancies were the basis of change in both treatments.

It has frequently been noted (see chapter 17) that weak fears frequently respond to minimal interventions, so that studies like this are very misleading. The authors totally ignore the inadvertent change processes that are always present in addition to deliberately deployed techniques. These inadvertent processes are the presumptive basis of most of the effects of therapies other than behavior therapy, but also contribute to behavior therapy. The magnitude of the contribution of these processes is indicated by the amount of improvement in Paul's (1964) attention-placebo group (table 9.4). It seems likely that these processes are attributable to intercurrent emotions competing with anxiety. It may well be that optimistic expectations are one source of such emotions. But there is no reason to believe that they are more important than other sources, such as emotional responses to the therapist (see chapter 17).

Another contender with reciprocal inhibition is the theory that the effects of systematic desensitization depend on "therapeutic instructions" (Leitenberg et al., 1969; Oliveau et al., 1969). Snake-phobic subjects who thought they were being desensitized as a therapeutic measure improved significantly more than those who thought they were engaged in a physiological experiment (though the latter group also did better than a control group). This difference in outcomes was not replicated by McGlynn, Reynolds, and Linder (1971). The claims of other explanations for systematic desensitization, such as suggestion (Efran & Marcia, 1967; McGlynn & Williams, 1970), have little force since they are based on experiments that, like that of Kirsch et al. (1983), deal with weak fears. Bernstein and Paul (1971) warned that unless the fears that are the subject of an experiment have the severity that characterizes clinical phobias, they do not constitute an acceptable analogue of clinical problems.

A criticism at a different level alleges that relaxation contributes nothing to the efficacy of systematic desensitization. A great deal of the research supposedly showing this has been summarized by Yates (1975) and by Kazdin and Wilcoxon (1976). However, this research has misinterpreted its data mainly by disregarding the nonspecific effects discussed above. The fact is that the nonspecific emotion is both a potent source of therapeutic change in the control groups and adds to the effects of relaxation in the experimental groups.

Misleading in a different way is a study by Benjamin, Marks and Huson

(1972). The patients receiving the desensitization procedure did equally well whether or not it was administered under "relaxation." The quotation marks are used because those given relaxation had been inadequately trained in it. They had had only one session of training from a psychiatric resident who had himself had only a single training session. Borkovec and Sides (1979), reviewing 25 studies of the physiological effects of progressive relaxation, found that in those studies in which the relaxed group showed greater reduction of autonomic responses than the control group, the subjects had received an average of 4.57 relaxation training sessions, in contrast to an average of 2.30 sessions in studies in which anxiety reductions were not significantly different between groups. They comment that while the role of relaxation in systematic desensitization is "solidly grounded in autonomic notions of anxiety process, numerous studies questioning it have employed brief, taped relaxation training in normal subjects." (For review of these studies, see Borkovec & O'Brien, 1976.)

All the foregoing critical proposals show a curious neglect of accepted scientific procedure. A theory stands until it is refuted by facts incompatible with it (Popper, 1959). The reciprocal inhibition theory of desensitization (and of some other psychotherapeutic effects) was the logical outcome of a considerable number of experimental and clinical observations to which no contradictory facts were apparent. The competing theories are often put forward as inherently better without any data incompatible with the reciprocal inhibition theory; or else the critic regards the mere presence of change in the absence of relaxation as a refutation. He does this because he does not realize that there are numerous sources of competition with anxiety, of which interview-related nonspecific effects are one variety.

10
Variants of Systematic Desensitization

Having a principle to work from provides a framework from which variations of tested procedures may be derived. If standard desensitization is inapplicable to a particular case, attempts can be made to implement in other ways the principle of inhibiting small amounts of anxiety at a time. Several alternative techniques are described in this chapter. Some are used when conventional desensitization cannot or does not succeed. Others have been the subject of experiments that suggest they may be superior to it, at least in some circumstances.

The desensitization variants can be divided into three categories: (a) alternative counteranxiety responses, (b) methods involving the use of real anxiety-evoking stimuli, and (c) technical variations of the standard consulting room procedure. It will be seen that the first two kinds of variants are frequently used in conjunction.

ALTERNATIVE COUNTERANXIETY RESPONSES
Therapist-Evoked Responses

As noted earlier, the psychotherapeutic interview itself evokes emotional responses in many patients. Sometimes the emotion is anxiety, but more often it seems to be a mixture of hopeful expectation, confidence in the expert, and positive emotions that have been previously conditioned to doctors and their offices. Altogether, it corresponds roughly to the psychoanalyst's "positive transference" without the presumed projection of a father-image. When such emotional responses occur, they inhibit some anxiety responses verbally evoked during the interview (Wolpe, 1958, p. 193). The interview-induced emotions are probably the basis for the very similar success of all therapies other than behavior therapy (Eysenck, 1952, 1965. See also chapter 17). Of course, behavior therapy profits from them as well, probably to an extent corresponding to the amount of change found in the "attention-placebo" group in Paul's (1966) study (p. 186).

The therapist-evoked emotions are inadvertent and their effects unsystematic. It is possible, however, to make systematic use of them. In subjects who are unable to learn to relax or who are afraid of "letting go," it is still worth presenting hierarchical scenes in the hope that therapist-evoked emotions will inhibit the anxiety, a hope that is fulfilled now and again. The same emotions are the main therapeutic agency in desensitization in vivo (see below).

Alternative Ways of Procuring Calmness

There are several procedures that produce much the same autonomic effects and subjective calmness as is obtained by muscle relaxation. They are autogenic training, transcendental meditation, yoga, and biofeedback. In a general way, if a person is well practiced in any of the first three of these, that skill can replace muscle relaxation for purposes of systematic desensitization.

Autogenic Training

This procedure, which is widely practiced in Europe, was developed by Schultz and Luthe (1959). It makes use of repeated suggestions of heaviness and warmth. To begin with, the heaviness suggestions are repeated five times by the therapist, and then the subject repeats them several times to himself. Warmth suggestions are incorporated later. There is evidence that the heaviness suggestions produce muscle relaxation, and the warmth suggestions produce vasodilatation.

There have been few studies comparing the effects of relaxation and autogenic training. Nicassio and Bootzin (1974) found that in the treatment of insomnia the two procedures were equally effective and superior to control groups.

Transcendental Meditation

The idea behind this procedure is "to turn the attention inwards to the subtler levels of thought, until the mind . . . arrives at the source of the thought" (Mahesh Yogi, 1969, p. 470). The technique consists of giving the patient a word (e.g., "rama") to attend to continuously while seated in a quiet room with eyes closed. If other thoughts intrude the patient must expel them and return to the word. He or she is encouraged to expect calm and relaxation to result from regular practice of this discipline.

Wallace (1970) reported physiological changes during transcendental meditation, including decreased metabolic rate, increased skin resistance, and diminished heart rate, all of which are also produced by muscle relaxation. Benson (1975) made extensive use of the method, especially in cases of hypertension. Boudreau (1972) reported its use in the treatment of a college student who had several disabling phobias. At first, systematic desensitization was tried without noticeable improvement. Then the patient indicated that he was adept at transcendental meditation. He was instructed to practice meditation following imaginal phobic scenes for a ½ hour every day and also at the actual appearance of fear-evoking situations. Marked improvement followed. Within 1 month, the avoidance behavior to enclosed places, being alone, and elevators had disappeared. Once his tension level had decreased, he ceased to experience abnormal physiological sensations, and this reassured him as to his physical and mental state.

Yoga

This is a broad class of practices of which transcendental meditation is an example. To the extent that these lead to control of autonomic responses, their potential as a means of breaking unadaptive emotional habits is obvious. Boudreau (1972) has described the case of a 40-year-old schoolteacher whose severe suffering from excessive perspiration was only partially alleviated by assiduous practice of muscle relaxation. She then took a summer course of training in yoga exercises. She practiced the yoga exercises for a ½ hour daily, with additional practice during tense moments. After 3 months of this, her mild perspiration decreased to below 1 hour every day while excessive perspiration disappeared.

Electromyographic Biofeedback

The original work in this method was conducted by Budzinski and Stoyva (1969), who observed that it was effective in accelerating and possibly deepening muscle relaxation. Comparative studies of relaxation and biofeedback have yielded conflicting results. Chesney and Shelton (1976) found that progressive relaxation produced superior clinical effects in tension headaches, but Reinking and Kohl (1975) achieved lower tension levels with biofeedback than with relaxation training. From a survey of comparative studies, Qualls and Sheehan (1981) concluded that electromyographic biofeedback compared favorably.

It is really impossible to say which is "better" — for several reasons, one of which is the wide differences in relaxation training schedules in the various studies. What is of practical importance is that electromyographic biofeedback is an additional resource and a reasonably convenient one. And there are certainly some patients who respond better to it than to muscle relaxation. Other modes of biofeedback have special relevance in the treatment of some psychosomatic disorders (p. 284ff).

Responses Triggered by Electrical Stimulation

Desensitization Based on Inhibition of Anxiety
by a Conditioned Motor Response

This technique (Wolpe, 1954) has been used very little, although it has a solid experimental basis in an experiment reported by Mowrer and Viek (1948). They found that if a noxious electrical stimulus applied to an animal was consistently switched off whenever the animal performed a particular motor response (e.g., jumping up in the air), the animal developed conditioned inhibition of the *autonomic* responses that were evoked at the same time. By contrast, the experimental twin that received exactly the same duration of noxious stimulation whose termination was unrelated to the animal's motor behavior failed to develop any inhibition of the emotional response.

In the clinical use of this finding, the patient with an anxiety hierarchy is asked to imagine a scene and to signal when the image is clear. The therapist then passes a fairly mild shock into the forearm, in response to which the patient has previously been instructed to flex his arm. The worst case of agoraphobia that I have ever seen was successfully treated by this method and is described in detail elsewhere (Wolpe, 1958, p. 174). It generally required 15 to 25 arm flexions to bring the anxiety response to a disturbing scene down to zero. In that patient, flexion of the arm seemed indispensable for weakening the anxiety response. But since we now know that weak electrical stimulation without a motor response can also weaken anxiety habits, we may question how much the motor response really contributed to the change that was noted. However, there are some clinical data to suggest that muscle activity can be an anxiety-inhibiting agent (Farmer & Wright, 1971; Wolpin & Raines, 1966).

External Inhibition

The therapeutic use of this phenomenon (Pavlov, 1927, p. 46) for deconditioning anxiety was suggested by William Philpott (personal communication, 1970). The technique is as follows. Weak electrical pulses, each lasting about half a second, are delivered to the forearm of the patient. The level of current correct for the patient is that which is strongly felt without being aversive. In some cases a very weak pulse suffices; in others no therapeutic effects occur until the electrical stimulus is strong enough to produce vigorous contraction of the forearm muscles. (It has also been noted that if the patient has free-floating anxiety, 8 to 10 pulses per minute will gradually reduce it, so that in 20 or 30 minutes it may be brought down from 60 *suds* or more to a low level, sometimes to zero.)

Once the appropriate level of electrical stimulation has been established, the desensitizing procedure can begin. First, the weakest item in the hierarchy is presented alone to the patient's imagination in order to determine how many *suds* it evokes. The patient is then asked to imagine the scene again and to signal by raising an index finger when it is well defined, at which point the therapist administers two brief stimuli of the predetermined strength, separated by about a second. After about 5 seconds, the patient is instructed again to imagine the scene, signaling as before. After a series of 5 to 20 repetitions, a check is made on the status of his reaction to the scene by presenting it without any shock.

An early case to be treated by this method was a woman whose many-faceted neuroses had been largely overcome by the usual behavior therapy methods. An important remaining neurotic problem was a phobia for driving alone. Originally, she had been unable to drive up her own driveway without feeling anxious. With standard desensitization, she had progressed steadily, though slowly, until she was able to drive ¾ of a mile without any discomfort. But a disturbing incident a ½ mile from home had set her back to that distance. Rather than resume the desensitization that had been so tedious, I decided to try external inhibition. Mild stimulation proved to be completely ineffective, but shocks strong enough to cause muscle contraction while she visualized herself at that critical place a ½ mile from home led to decreasing anxiety. With 20 repetitions of the scene, the anxiety decreased to zero. The procedure was then repeated for the ¾ mile point. When she later tested herself at that point, she found herself completely free from anxiety. Continuing with this method produced much more rapid progress than had previously been achieved with standard desensitization.

Responses Evoked by Verbally Induced Imagery

Under the heading of verbally induced imagery are three methods: emotive imagery, induced anger, and direct suggestion. In the first of these, an emotional state counteractive to anxiety is evoked by the setting into which the anxiety-evoking stimuli are to be introduced; in the latter two, the counteractive emotion depends on deliberate and insistent verbal inputs, and the setting is mainly background.

Emotive Imagery

In this procedure, described by Lazarus and Abramovitz (1962), hierarchical stimuli are presented to the patient in an imaginary situation whose other elements evoke responses that are antagonistic to anxiety. One of their cases was a 12-year-old boy who greatly feared darkness. In the room he shared with his brother, a light constantly shone at night next to his bed. He was especially afraid in the bathroom, which he used only if accompanied by another member of the household. Attempts at relaxation training had failed. The child had a passion for two radio serials: "Superman" and "Captain Silver." He was asked to imagine that Superman and Captain Silver had appointed him their agent. Subsequent procedure was as follows:

> The therapist said, "Now I want you to close your eyes and imagine that you are sitting in the dining room with your mother and father. It is nighttime. Suddenly, you receive a signal on the wrist radio that Superman has given you. You quickly run into the living room because your mission must be kept a secret. There is only a little light coming into the lounge from the passage. Now pretend that you are all alone in the lounge waiting for Superman and Captain Silver to visit you. Think about this very clearly. If the idea makes you feel afraid, lift up your right hand."

An ongoing scene was terminated as soon as there was any indication of anxiety. When an image aroused anxiety, it would either be repeated in a more challengingly assertive manner, or altered slightly so as to appear less threatening. At the end of the third session, the child was able to picture himself alone in the bathroom with all the lights turned off, awaiting a communication from Superman. There was complete transfer to the real situation. A follow-up 11 months later revealed that the gains had been maintained.

The technique has also been used with adults. For example, a man with a claustrophobia that was especially manifest in theaters and restaurants was instructed to imagine himself seated in a theater (at the aisle in the back row, initially) watching a striptease. The sexual arousal inhibited the weak anxiety response and was the basis for the beginning of a deconditioning program.

Induced Anger

Goldstein, Serber, and Piaget (1970) found induced anger to be effective in six out of ten cases; it consists of getting the patient to pair anger-arousing imagery (augmented by appropriate verbal and motor behavior) with fear-arousing imagined scenes (or real stimuli in the consulting room). Later, the patient uses the images to arouse anger in spontaneously occurring fear-producing real-life situations. The concern that such treatment might leave patients angry instead of fearful has not been borne out by experience. They merely become indifferent to the previously disturbing stimuli, supporting the viewpoint that the therapeutic achievement is the conditioning of inhibition of fear responses to the relevant stimuli.

One of their cases was Mr. F., aged 23, who complained of fears of riding public conveyances, walking in certain neighborhoods, and being in the presence of seemingly aggressive people. These fears more or less confined him to his home. He ventured out only to attend therapy sessions, taking a roundabout route on foot to avoid public transport and certain streets.

Although some progress was made in systematic desensitization to the fear of buses, none occurred in the area of interpersonal situations. When asked to imagine even very weak interpersonal scenes, Mr. F. would reach near-panic states that completely undid the relaxation. He was then asked to imagine being accosted on the street by an aggressive man (a reconstruction of an actual past event). When he felt afraid, he was to imagine punching the man. Mr. F. found that he was unable to do this effectively. But by starting the imagining simply with talking back to the man, he could gradually increase the amount of aggressiveness until he was eventually able to imagine effectively punching, kicking, and finally chopping the man up with an axe. With each increase of aggression he felt less fear and more anger. At one point, he said, "I feel like screaming and actually hitting something." He was given a large pillow and encouraged to do so and vocalize according to his feelings. After three sessions of ten repetitions per session of scenes appropriate to his fears, Mr. F. reported complete freedom of fear in most of the situations that had previously been frightening and said that he was traveling freely wherever he desired. Further use of induced anger overcame his remaining fears. At a 6-month follow-up he reported that he was free of fears, was planning marriage, and was about to attend graduate school.

Case 35: Induced Anger in a Case of Agoraphobia

Induced anger succeeded where several other methods had failed in the case of Yolanda, a 23-year-old girl who was severely afflicted with agoraphobia. Three months previously, after seeing a play in downtown Philadelphia, she had returned to her car which was parked in the street. She was just about to start it when she felt a bump from the car that had been parked behind her. A moment later, the driver of that car was at her window screaming abuse and threatening to take legal action. Although entirely innocent, she "felt anxious and helpless." She behaved "nicely" and did not protest. On driving away from the scene she noticed that she was extremely nervous. Thereafter she felt some degree of anxiety whenever she drove a car. Two weeks later, driving on a lonely but familiar road, she had a sudden sharp panic, which subsided in a few minutes but left her feeling uncomfortable for the rest of the day. From that time onward, she became increasingly fearful of driving and of being alone. Within a week she could not be alone even at home without anxiety. Its diurnal range was now 50–75 *suds*.

Treatment began with explaining to Yolanda the nature of her illness primarily to counteract her fear of "going crazy." I then introduced assertiveness training, which was clearly necessary, but not expected to help much in overcoming the ongoing incapacitating fear. I taught her progressive relaxation, but could not lower her anxiety enough to make desensitization feasible. The administration of carbon dioxide (chapter 14) showed that about one-quarter of Yolanda's continuous anxiety was free-floating. Next, I attempted to control the anxiety with diazepam, but found that to decrease it significantly required a dose that produced unacceptable drowsiness. During the next 2 months Yolanda became markedly more assertive. Although a certain amount of improvement in her general state was achieved by a systematic program of in vivo desensitization, progress was slow, and her orbit of comfortable movement stopped short at the lawn surrounding the clinic. A program of flooding in vivo during the next 3 weeks produced a great deal of distress and no improvement. It was followed with paradoxical intention (p. 226). Yolanda followed my instructions to the letter; but instead of her anxiety flattening out and diminishing, it rose gradually and distressfully in the course of 1½ hours on each of 2 successive days. The net effect of this was to make her feel extremely angry at me for having subjected her to "torture."

The exploitation of this anger provided a breakthrough. I had Yolanda make increasing excursions away from the clinic on foot, in the course of which she was to express her anger at me, out loud when socially feasible, and subvocally when not. This was gratifyingly effective. Anxiety decreased progressively, enabling her to go farther and farther with comfort. The same strategy was equally successful in increasingly prolonged solo car trips. Within 3 weeks, Yolanda was so much improved that she was able to participate comfortably in her own graduation. Her remaining problems were later handled by an intern using a combination of techniques with complete success.

Direct Suggestion

Rubin (1972) described a variant of systematic desensitization, direct suggestion, that depends on inducing counteranxiety responses by strong verbal suggestion. One of his cases was a 36-year-old woman who had anxiety reactions to numerous situations, including sitting at the dining table, applying cosmetics, sitting down to work, and going to the beauty shop. All of these reactions could be traced to an occasion 2 years previously when she had been seized with trembling of her hands while drinking coffee in a restaurant at the moment when she became aware of a posterior cervical spasm. Anxiety at the thought of cervical spasm was brought into opposition with the suggestion of delicious food. The patient was seen four times and was able to return to work. A follow-up 9 months later revealed that all of the improvement had been maintained.

This technique brings the hypnotist's repertoire to the service of behavior therapy. Instead of the classical ineffective practice of suggesting away symptoms or reactions, it brings suggested responses into opposition with anxiety responses.

Case 36: Suggested Responses Producing Rapid Improvement in a Fear of Flying

I have used suggestion in a few cases. The first case responded markedly in a single session. He was a 45-year-old executive who had just been promoted to a highly paid position that entailed a great deal of flying. During the previous 10 years, however, he had been severely aerophobic following a hair-raising flying experience. Because he had come from Boston and was due to fly to Nashville a few days later, I decided to try counterconditioning by direct suggestion. I elicited from him aspects of being in a plane that he enjoyed — a feeling of freedom, the decor, attractive flight attendants, and the reassuring tones of the captain's voice. I then had him close his eyes and imagine that he was sitting in a stationary chamber with the decor of a plane, strongly responding to those pleasant stimulations. When he indicated that he was having the required feelings at considerable strength, I had him imagine that the chamber was airborne, at first moving slowly near the ground, and then as in actual flight. He was able to sustain this image without any anxiety for about 3 minutes. I then instructed him to practice the image several times a day and told him that when he boarded the plane, he was to focus his attention on the pleasant stimuli and respond exclusively to them. After the scheduled flight, he telephoned from Nashville to say that he had had slight anxiety initially and then none at all. Four months later, he informed a behavior therapist in Boston to whom I had referred him for other problems about the "miraculous cure" of his fear of flying in a single session.

Physical Activity Responses

Physical activity responses refers mainly to Oriental defense exercises. Desensitization based on the activity of reading (Everaerd, 1970; Stoffelmayr, 1970) may belong to the same category. As noted previously (p. 197), Farmer and Wright (1971) found that muscle activity can be used to desensitize some subjects.

In two cases who could not be satisfactorily treated by standard desensitization, Gershman and Stedman (1971) used Oriental defense exercises as the source of reciprocal inhibition of anxiety on the reasonable supposition that "if a therapist identifies a counterconditioner that is idiosyncratic to a patient it is likely to have special therapeutic efficacy." One of their cases was a man who routinely practiced karate to keep himself in physical condition. His fear of flying was treated by having him imagine flying situations in hierarchical order, and, at each presentation, engage in vigorous karate exercises. In two sessions, anxiety to all items was reduced to zero on the *sud* scale. In their other case, Kung Fu exercises were rapidly effective in over-

coming a severe claustrophobia by having the patient initiate them immediately upon being locked in a room. The periods of his confinement were
progressively increased from 10 seconds to 1 hour, and the duration of
"Kung Fu-ing" progressively diminished, though if the patient at any time
felt a twinge of anxiety he could again resort to the exercises to dissipate it.
Six-month follow-ups found both of these patients free from the anxiety
habits that had been treated. It seems that motor competition was the basis
of the changes, but the role of concomitant emotional arousal cannot be
ruled out.

Stoffelmayr's (1970) case was a 30-year-old woman who complained of
retching and gagging in response to the insertion of her dentures. This was
successfully treated by arranging for reading aloud and later other activities
to compete with the retching response. At a 6-month follow-up, the patient
was still able to retain dentures without any discomfort. Everaerd (1970)
described a patient whose anxiety was triggered by awareness of his heart
rate, and in whom standard desensitization and the use of external inhibition had failed. Prescribed reading proved to be an effective means to desensitization to his heart beat. Subsequently, his spoken descriptions of other
disturbing situations seemed also to act as anxiety inhibitors. The patient
was still free of symptoms 18 months after treatment.

Saccadic Eye Movements

Saccadic eye movements (Shapiro, 1989) promise to be a major new resource for inhibiting and deconditioning anxiety. They were originally introduced as a treatment for post-traumatic stress disorder, but they seem to
have a wider range of efficacy. Their use is described on pages 272–273.

Responses Produced by Relief from Distress

Response produced by relief from distress are substitutes for relaxation.
They conform to the anxiety-relief paradigm (Wolpe, 1958, p. 180) that was
suggested by an experiment performed in Poland by Zbrozyna (1953). An
auditory stimulus was presented to an eating animal just before the food was
withdrawn on a number of occasions; the stimulus was subsequently found
to inhibit feeding even in the middle of a meal. It is consistent with this that
a stimulus repeatedly associated with the termination of a noxious stimulus
acquires anxiety-inhibiting properties. In line with this is the observation
that approach responses are conditioned to a stimulus consistently presented
at the termination of electrical stimulation (e.g., Barlow, 1956; Coppock,
1951). The derivatives of this paradigm are anxiety relief, aversion relief,
respiratory relief, and sensory contrast.

Anxiety Relief

The term *anxiety relief* (Wolpe, 1958, p. 181) refers to the deconditioning of anxiety that is obtained by pairing the word *calm* with the cessation of a moderately unpleasant continuous electrical stimulus applied to the patient's forearm. The patient is instructed to say this word aloud when he strongly desires the stimulation to stop. Its termination produces a feeling of relief that, upon repetition, may become conditioned to the word *calm*. This apparently only happens in individuals who experience emotional disturbance in addition to the sensory discomfort from the stimulus. The feeling of relief when the shock stops may be quite marked. The relief may be increased and conditioning facilitated by the administration of drugs that augment sympathetic responses, such as amphetamines (Eysenck, 1963). Subsequently, saying the word *calm* subvocally in disturbing life situations may reduce anxiety and result in conditioned inhibition of the anxiety habit.

Meichenbaum and Cameron (1974) reported two studies in which anxiety-relief conditioning was pitted against verbally cued anxiety responses to reduce persistent fears of harmless snakes. In the first study, compared with a self-instructional rehearsal group and a waiting-list control group, the anxiety-relief subjects showed significantly more improvement. In the second study, there were two anxiety-relief groups, both of which terminated shock by emitting self-statements instead of the single cue word, *calm*. The self-statements of one group were of a "coping" character, for example, "Relax, I can trust the snake; just one step at a time." In the second anxiety-relief group, avoidant thoughts (e.g., "It's ugly, it's slimy, I won't look at it") were paired with relief from shock. The two anxiety-relief procedures — whether they included coping statements or avoidant statements — were equally effective in reducing fears. Thus, the content of the cue statement was irrelevant to the efficacy of the procedure. Each was conditioned to anxiety relief. Yet, Meichenbaum and Cameron concluded that the "plausibility of a conditioning explanation for treatment efficacy is seriously called into question." On the contrary, if the content of the statement was irrelevant to the outcome, a conditioning explanation would seem to have been unequivocally supported.

Aversion Relief

The essence of aversion relief, which was first employed by Thorpe et al. (1964), is to present a phobic stimulus to the subject at the moment that he presses a button to terminate a continuous unpleasant electrical stimulus. Solyom and Miller (1965) and Solyom (1969) later made extensive use of the following modified procedure.

The patient, who had prepared a tape recording consisting of both past and potential anxiety-provoking events, was seated in an armchair, separated from the experimenter by a one-way screen. Items from this tape recording were presented to him one at a time, through earphones. After a silence of about 30 seconds, an unpleasant electric current was applied to the patient's finger. By pressing a button, the patient both shut off the current and obtained an anxiety item from his tape. For example, a cat-phobic patient might hear his own voice saying, "I see a grey cat" simultane-ously with the cessation of the shock. The intensity of shock was set as the midpoint between shock reception threshold and shock tolerance threshold. Solyom and Miller (1965) treated eight patients, of whom six entirely over-came their fears after a mean of 19.5 treatment sessions. There was no relapse or symptom substitution at follow-up.

Respiratory Relief

The respiratory-relief method (Orwin, 1971) consists of asking the patient to hold his breath as long as possible and to signal when he can no longer maintain it. At that moment, the phobic stimulus is presented to the pa-tient's imagination, enabling the relief that ensues on the resumption of breathing to compete with the anxiety. Orwin states that six patients rapidly lost lifelong phobias. Four spider-phobic patients were able to touch a spider in one or two 30-minute sessions. One of them subsequently allowed a large house spider to run over her hands and arms without concern. The phobic constituents of chronic obsessional conditions were also "surprisingly easily controlled by respiratory relief" and all patients showed marked improve-ment.

The simplicity of the method warrants trial but until now, apparently, there have not been other reports.

Sensory Contrast

Cabanac (1971) has shown that physical stimuli can be made pleasurable by applying them against a suitable background state — for example, local-ized cold against general hotness. This observation offers the possibility of a low stress alternative to the foregoing methods. Nobody has as yet tried it out therapeutically. It is mentioned here in the hope that somebody will.

Pharmacological Agents that Inhibit Anxiety

This section describes how two very different kinds of agents — tranquiliz-ing drugs and carbon dioxide — are used to decondition maladaptive anxiety responses habits on the desensitization model.

Deconditioning with Tranquilizers

Lasting recovery from neuroses, or at least improvement, through the prolonged use of bromides and barbiturates, was reported many years ago (Dworkin, Raginsky, & Bourne, 1937; Masserman & Yum, 1946; Pavlov,

1941). However, none of these experimenters arranged for systematic exposure to anxiety-arousing stimuli to occur during the action of the drugs. Nevertheless, nonspecific beneficial effects cannot be ruled out (chapter 17). There have also been some negative experimental results. Cooper et al. (1974) and Gorman et al. (1971) found that benzodiazepines failed to facilitate the overcoming of avoidance responses.

Miller, Murphy, and Mirsky (1957) were the first to organize systematic exposure. Using electric shock as the unconditioned stimulus, they conditioned four groups of rats to perform an avoidance response at the presentation of a buzzer. To study extinction of the avoidance response under different conditions, the researchers injected the animals of two of the groups with saline and those of the other two groups with chlorpromazine on each of four consecutive days. One of the two saline-injected groups (group 1) and one of the two chlorpromazine-injected groups (group 2) received 15 unreinforced presentations of the buzzer on each of the 4 days, while the animals of the other two groups (groups 3 and 4) were simply returned to the living cage after receiving their injections. During these 4 days, group 2 animals made far fewer avoidance responses (less than 5% of trials) than group 1 (more than 70% of trials). On the fifth and subsequent days, all groups were given unreinforced trials without receiving any injections. Whereas the other groups showed an average of about 60% avoidance responses, group 2 showed only about 20%: exposure to the buzzer under chlorpromazine, thus, had lasting effects. The animals were presumably responding to other stimuli in the environment when the buzzer was heard. In animals under chlorpromazine the avoidance response and anxiety were weaker and thus could be reciprocally inhibited by these other responses, with consequent diminution of their habit strength.

Unfortunately, no systematic clinical study has emerged from this interesting experiment. An indecisively supportive straw in the wind exists in some incidental observations by Winkelman (1955). He gave his patients chlorpromazine for 6 months or more in doses sufficient to obtain marked diminution of neurotic symptoms, and then gradually withdrew the drug. He found that improvement persisted for at least 6 months after the withdrawal in 35% of the patients. Unfortunately, there was no control study to show what would have been achieved by a placebo, or to indicate to what extent his own interactions with patients might have been therapeutic.

For many years, I have employed tranquilizers in a way that parallels the experiment of Miller, Murphy, and Mirsky. The patient takes the drug in advance of exposure to a disturbing situation in an adequate dose, and must control exposures (if necessary) so that no substantial anxiety is ever elicited. To take an early example: finding that the severe classroom anxiety experienced by a graduate student was markedly ameliorated by meprobamate, I kept him on an adequate dosage of the drug on every school day for 6 weeks.

Then I gave him a drugfree test day on which he found his anxiety to have diminished by 40% from its original level. A second test after 6 more weeks showed a further 30% decrement of the anxiety—an overall improvement of about 70%. Some cases in which I achieved complete recovery were a fear of physical deformities for which codeine was the drug used, a barber's chair phobia for which I used meprobamate and alcohol (see also Erwin, 1963), and an airplane phobia that was overcome by the use of alcohol on three flights of about an hour's duration each.

There were also reports by others during the 1960s of successful treatments by such means. A case of stuttering treated with meprobamate by Maxwell and Paterson (1958) was a 25-year-old butcher who was eventually able to dispense with the drug and still maintain marked speech improvement. Drugs of the benzdiazepine group are preferable to meprobamate because their tranquilizing effects increase with increasing dosage. One of the earliest reports was by G. E. Miller (personal communication, 1967), who used chlordiazepoxide in four phobic cases. In his first two cases, a woman with a fear of eating in public and a man with agoraphobia, doses of 50 and 75 mg, respectively, were needed. Miller stated, "The medication was taken only for the purpose of desensitization and never on a routine basis. The patients 'planned' a phobic exposure, took the medication, waited until it began to exert its effect and then exposed themselves to the phobic situation (in real life, not in fantasy). The course of the therapy was 4 weeks in one case and 6 weeks in the other." Both patients were completely free of their phobias without using medication when followed up 6 months after the treatment.

Case 37: Diazepam in the Treatment of Agoraphobia

I found diazepam impressively effective in Mr. S., a 52-year-old man (first encountered as case 3) who when first seen had been severely disabled by agoraphobia for 16 years. Its causation is given under Case 3. His anxiety level rose by 50 *suds* if he ventured alone one block from home, and rapidly rose higher if he went further. After seeing psychoanalysts for 10 years without improvement, Mr. S. had gone for 2 years to a "behavior therapist" who had persisted for months with standard desensitization although Mr. S. repeatedly told him that imagined scenes aroused no anxiety. After this, the therapist had him force himself to go out as far as possible to phase out the fear. Numerous stressful excursions accomplished nothing. When Mr. S. came to see me he had to be brought by his mother, since he was too fearful to drive alone. The analysis of the case revealed a classically conditioned fear of separation from base that increased with distance. Since Mr. S. could not imagine realistically, he needed to be treated *in vivo*. The feasibility of using diazepam was suggested by the observation that he had been somewhat calmed by 5 to 10 mg doses that a previous therapist had prescribed. We found that 25 mg of diazepam brought his baseline anxiety down to about 5 *suds*. He was then given the assignment of going one block from home in a particular direction, while under the protection of 25 .ng of diazepam. This raised his anxiety level to 20; but after seven repetitions he was able to walk that distance without anxiety rising above the baseline. Increasing distances were then assigned. When he could walk five blocks comfortably, he began to drive his car alone; and within 3 weeks was able to dispense with the services of his mother as chauffeur. Monitoring his own responses, he thereafter took increasingly long drives, and as he improved found it possible to decrease the dose of diazepam. A trip of 20 miles eventually required only 5 mg. I saw Mr. S. for a total of 26 sessions over 18 months—weekly for 3 weeks, biweekly for 6 months, and subsequently monthly. He was eventually able to go any distance with only occasional mild anxiety, keeping 5 mg of diazepam in his pocket as a precaution. At a 3-year follow-up his recovery had been fully maintained.

Two points must be underlined with regard to in vivo desensitization using tranquilizing drugs. First, the effectiveness of such programs, in contrast to flooding, almost certainly depends upon insuring that high-anxiety evocation never occurs, for whenever it does it may recondition a substantial degree of anxiety and lose hard-won ground. Second, the hazard of addiction is small when the administration of drugs is limited to assignments.

Systematic Desensitization with Intravenous Anxiety Inhibitors

Methahexitone sodium, which goes under the trade names of Brietal and Brevital, used to be quite popular as a means of tranquilization for purposes of desensitization. It was regarded by some of its users (Friedman, 1966; Friedman & Silverstone, 1967) as a primary anxiety-inhibiting agent. Others, such as Reed (1966) and Brady (1966), regarded it as essentially an adjuvant to relaxation, always using it with relaxation instructions. A controlled study by Mawson (1970) suggested that methohexital was a self-sufficient anxiety-inhibiting agent, significantly more effective than relaxation.

Brady (1966) made particular use of methohexital in cases of frigidity and described his use of it with great clarity. After an introductory explanation, he made the patient relax comfortably in a reclining chair before injection of a 1% solution:

> During the 2–4 minutes required for the drug to have its maximum effect, suggestions of calm and relaxation are given such as might be used to induce hypnosis. When a deeply relaxed state is attained, the patient is instructed to imagine the first or weakest scene in the hierarchy. For example, "Now I want

you to imagine as vividly as possible that you and your husband are seated in the living room, fully clothed, and he is kissing you affectionately on the lips. You remain calm and relaxed." The patient is permitted to visualize this scene for about 2 minutes and is then instructed to stop and simply relax. After a minute of rest, the same scene is again suggested for about 3 minutes. After another rest period, and assuming that no anxiety is evident, the next scene in the hierarchy is suggested, and so forth.

Four of Brady's five cases were greatly improved in a mean 11.5 sessions. Follow-ups did not reveal relapse or new symptoms.

Yeung (1968) reported the successful treatment of a subway phobia and of snake phobias on the basis of a single large intravenous injection of diazepam. Pecknold, Raeburn, and Poser (1972) gave intravenous injections of this drug to two patients who were too anxious to calm themselves by muscle relaxation. In each patient the drug-induced calmness was used for desensitization, and after a few sessions it was found that the desensitization could be continued with the calmness of muscle relaxation alone.

Deconditioning by Carbon Dioxide

The ability of carbon dioxide-oxygen mixtures to reduce free-floating (Wolpe, 1958, pp. 166–173 and chapter 14) anxiety suggested that they might also be effective for specific maladaptive fears. Early attempts to use the mixtures for this purpose employing single full-capacity inhalations, were unsuccessful—apparently because it is impossible to bring the sharp and rapid hyperpnea thus obtained into effective juxtaposition with the anxiety aroused by an episodic stimulus. The difficulty is solved by administering the gas continuously through an open mask that the patient holds about ½ inch from his nose and open mouth. When he displays moderate hyperpnea he is asked to imagine (or verbalize) a scene from an anxiety hierarchy for 10 to 15 seconds. The therapist repeats the procedure until the scene ceases to be disturbing, and then advances to the next scene up the hierarchy. It is usually possible to work with more disturbing scenes than is customary with standard systematic desensitization. Progress can also be remarkably rapid; one case of classroom phobia made an apparently lasting recovery in two sessions. In an unusual phobia for certain configurations of the opposite sex that had resisted all other available methods, marked reduction in anxiety responses to the stimuli concerned was obtained in eight sessions by presenting them pictorially during inhalations that lasted from 2 to 3 minutes.

It is important to realize that the stimulus that elicits the fear may be complex. In a case reported by Latimer (1977), the maladaptive fear was elicited by somatic symptoms—rapid heart beats, trembling hands, and hyperventilation—only when these symptoms occurred while the patient was talking to another person *and* having the thought that she might panic. In her treatment, the somatic symptoms were induced by carbon dioxide, but the elicitation of fear required combining them with the image of talking to another person and the thought of panicking. The fear was overcome in eight sessions and recovery persisted at an 11-month follow-up.

EXTEROCEPTIVE SUBSTITUTES FOR IMAGERY

While it is very convenient to conduct desensitization with imaginal stimuli, it is not feasible with patients who do not imagine realistically. Some of them can form images, but these do not elicit anxiety similar to that of the corresponding real situations. Real stimuli must be used either in the form of actual feared objects or else pictorial representations of them, in the context of whatever counteranxiety response is used. Some examples have already been given in earlier parts of this chapter.

Actually, real life exposure is routinely encouraged in coordination with standard desensitization. For example, a person with a fear of driving is asked to go driving up to the last desensitized point. A controlled study by Garfield, Darwin, Singer, and McBrearty (1967) indicated that this actually accelerates desensitization. Somewhat contradictorily, Cooke (1966) found that in snake phobias, desensitization proceeded with the same speed whether imaginary or real stimuli were used.

Desensitization in Vivo

The use of real-life graduated exposures in an inpatient setting was first reported by Terhune (1948), who worked empirically, without awareness of the learning principles involved. The first account of in vivo therapy that was directly based on the desensitization paradigm was in connection with two agoraphobic cases treated by Meyer (1957). It was followed in 1960 by Freeman and Kendrick's report of the overcoming of a cat phobia by getting the patient to handle pieces of material progressively similar to cat fur, exposing her to pictures of cats, then a toy kitten, followed by a real kitten, and eventually grown cats. A phobia for earthworms was treated in a similar way by Murphy (1964), and Goldberg and D'Zurilla (1968) overcame fears of receiving injections by the use of slide projections of the stages of activity involved in an injection. Dengrove (personal communication, 1968) used moving film to overcome phobias for bridges.

The above treatments relied on interpersonal and other "natural" events to evoke anxiety-inhibiting emotional responses, and this often suffices. Graded exposure of the patient occurred to real fear-evoking stimuli while the therapist was present in the double role of guide and anxiety inhibitor. In a case of my own, a woman whose anxiety level was related to distance from a "reliable" person was brought by her husband to meet me in a public park in the quiet of the early morning. In the course of about 10 meetings, I effected increasingly distant separations, the anxiety of separation presumably having been inhibited by her emotional responses to me.

As with standard desensitization, the in vivo stimulus requirements are not always obvious. Special dramatic or technical arrangements may have to be contrived. For example, in treating patients whose fear of public speaking is based on a fear of humiliation, I often have them intentionally give wrong answers to simple arithmetical problems. The anxiety this at first produces fades away with repetition. I then introduce more difficult problems, some of which they are really unable to answer correctly; and then I may increasingly deride the errors. Witnesses may be introduced to watch the sequence of failures.

Case 38: In vivo Desensitization of Tachycardia

A case that called for special measures was a young woman whom I saw in 1967. She was practically confined to her home by the fear that she would die if her heart beat too fast. She was admitted to the hospital, and when conventional desensitization had proved inapplicable, I organized the following series of procedures: (a) the induction of tachycardia by stepping on and off a stool an increasing number of times; (b) tachycardia produced by intravenous injections of increasing doses — up to 1 cc — of epinephrine hydrochloride 1 : 1000; (c) epinephrine injections accompanied by feedback from an oscilloscope that grossly exaggerated the tachycardia; (d) inhalations of amyl nitrite (3 cc capsules crushed in a handkerchief); and (e) locking her up for increasing periods up to 2 hours in an isolated room in the basement of the hospital. Following these measures the patient was greatly improved, though not cured. But she was able to resume working regularly, and in a 7-year follow-up made only occasional telephone calls to boost her confidence. In the last two of those years she phoned only about three times, and after that was not heard from again.

Case 39: In vivo Treatment of Fear of Crowds and Crowding

This was a case in which desensitization in vivo occurred in the first place inadvertently and was later deliberately continued. The patient, who had an 11-year-long fear of confinement in social situations, was being treated in front of 20 members of a training course I was conducting in Heiloo, Holland, in 1966. After he had been trained in relaxation and an elaboration of his hierarchies was prepared, he was asked, at his fourth interview, to visualize being in movie houses with increasing difficulty of egress; but none of this evoked the slightest anxiety. I then told him that it would be necessary for us to work with real stimuli. He replied, "Something remarkable has already happened, doctor. During my first session here I was very nervous in the group, but every day my nervousness has decreased, and today I don't feel nervous at all." He had been unwittingly desensitized (perhaps flooded) to the audience of 20. As it happened, 160 psychologists were expected to be present the next day, and I decided to make use of them for continuing the treatment. Accordingly, the next morning in a large lecture hall, I had the patient at first sit with me on the platform while the original 20 institute members sat in the forward rows of seats. As the patient reported no anxiety, I gave a prearranged signal for 20 more people to enter the hall. When they did so, he reported anxiety and was instructed to relax. After a minute, he stated that he felt comfortable, and then another 20 people were permitted to enter. Again the anxiety that appeared was relaxed away. The same procedure was repeated until all 160 people were seated. The patient spent the remainder of the afternoon seated comfortably in the front row of the audience. Subsequently, further in vivo operations were arranged — such as jamming him in the front row of spectators at a tennis tournament. These tactics resulted in marked improvement of his neurosis in a 10-day period.

Graded exposure that depends on "natural" competition with anxiety is not always successful; "deliberate" competition must then be sought. Usually the calmness of muscle relaxation is used, and occasionally anxiety-relief conditioning is required.

Modeling

The group of methods called modeling, which was introduced by Bandura (1968), is a valuable addition to the behavioral armamentarium, but has been erroneously represented as a cognitive strategy *sui generis*. The methods do have an informational component that is therapeutically relevant in cognitively based phobias. However, they can also effect classical deconditioning, as will be described below, constituting a form of in vivo desensitization. This double-barreled thrust gives modeling special practical value in certain phobic populations. A new analysis of the many processes that contribute to the efficacy of modeling methods is provided below.

The first study of the treatment of maladaptive fears by modeling was reported by Bandura, Grusec, and Menlove (1967). Forty-eight dog-fearful children between 3 and 5 years old were randomly assigned to one of four treatment conditions, each covering eight 10-minute periods. During these periods, two of the groups observed a fearless peer model exhibit progressively more difficult interactions with a dog. One control group saw only the dog during the eight sessions; the second control group saw neither dog nor model. The two experimental groups subsequently displayed significantly greater approach behavior toward the experimental dog and also toward an unfamiliar dog than did the children of the control groups. Sixty-seven percent of the children who had had the modeling treatment and 33% of the controls were eventually able to be alone in the room with the dog without distress.

However, the changes that occurred in the control groups were not negligible and have implications for understanding change in the experimental groups. To begin with, as Bandura et al. note, the improvements in the control groups were related to the exposure of the children to the numerous tests of avoidance behavior that were conducted on them by amiable experimenters. It is significant that the control group exposed to the dog during the eight sessions did significantly less well than the control group not exposed to it, "apparently because the mere presence of the dog had some mild negative consequences." (Presumably, classically conditioned fear was somewhat increased by this experience.) The pleasant responses aroused by the "amiable experimenters" can be seen as reciprocally inhibiting classically conditioned fear, but its effects were partially nullified in those children who were exposed to "the mere presence of the dog."

The experimental groups, too, would have profited from the amiable experimenters, but, in addition, observing the fearless model would have combated the fears of children who believed the dog to be dangerous. (It might be conjectured that at this young age most of the subjects would believe that dogs are dangerous.) At the same time, pleasant *emotional* responses to the model would counteract fear in those children in whom it was classically conditioned. To test this formulation would require an experiment in which it was known beforehand which children had classically conditioned and which cognitively based fears.

In an adult study Bandura, Blanchard, and Ritter (1969) had snake interactions modeled by the therapist, and subjects were then aided, through demonstration and coaxing (guided participation) to make progressively closer approaches themselves to a snake. Two other groups of subjects received, respectively, conventional desensitization and in vivo desensitization to filmed scenes of a snake. The latter was labeled *symbolic modeling* because it showed people in "progressively threatening interactions with a snake." The *modeling* appellation is questionable. Increasingly threatening images without people would probably have achieved the same result, but the necessary controlled study has not been done. Guided participation eliminated the snake phobia in 92% of subjects, in contrast to about 50% for both desensitization groups. However, when the "failed" subjects in these latter groups were then given live modeling and guided participation, snake phobic behavior was overcome in all of them. The likelihood is that these later changes were all in subjects whose fear of snakes was cognitively based.

The guided participation would have provided the corrective information that was absent from both modes of desensitization.

Ritter (1968) earlier obtained similar success in snake-fearful children who received modeling with guided participation as did Rimm and Mahoney (1969) in snake-avoidance behavior in adults.

The most arresting clinical study to date is a comparison of guided participation with in vivo exposure in the treatment of anxiety in agoraphobias by Williams and Zane (1989). The guided participation subjects achieved significantly more reduction of anxiety than the exposure subjects, a result which the investigators attributed to increasing proficiency in activities involved in the fearful situations. The character of the tasks mastered makes this interpretation quite unconvincing. For example, elevator phobics were encouraged to stand in different positions and to vary the fixation of their gaze; driving phobics were instructed to sit back, loosen their grip on the steering wheel, and maintain "a constant and reasonable speed." It is difficult to see the relevance of incidental motor acts for mastering fear.

An explanation consistent with established knowledge of fear and its unlearning can be given. In Williams and Zane's exposure group, the therapist did not accompany her subjects into the anxiety-arousing setting at any time. By contrast, she was constantly present with them during the guided participation treatment, deflecting their attention. Thus, she was a source of emotional competition with fear (like the father of the child afraid of the sea [p. 150]); also, by diminishing the impact of the feared situation by her deflective talk she facilitated reciprocal inhibition of the fear. The relevance of this kind of competition is further supported by Ritter's (1968) demonstration that contact with the subject during participation enhances its effectiveness. What is needed, clearly, is a repetition of Williams and Zanes's experiment with a control group in which a therapist accompanies the *exposure* subjects and distracts them with conversation about sports, movies, or fashion.

In the meantime, much credit is due to Williams and Zane for having pointed to a way of dealing with agoraphobic fear that is superior to standard exposure. Their contribution, if confirmed, will remain important, even if, as here predicted, it is later shown that any other induced behavior would be as effective.

In sum, the guided participation technique has great therapeutic value in the treatment of simple phobias because its different elements have the potential to combat both classically conditioned and cognitively based fears, and in the treatment of agoraphobia as described above. In both contexts, the changes are explicable on the basis of established knowledge and do not require the theoretical structures that Bandura has superimposed on them because he does not realize that different modes of fear learning exist.

ECONOMICAL VARIATIONS OF
STANDARD DESENSITIZATION

Certain therapeutic strategies reduce the amount of time the therapist has to spend with each patient. One way is to automate some operations so that they do not need the therapist's physical presence. The second strategy treats groups of patients with similar neurotic fears.

Automated Desensitization

Lang, Melamed, and Hart (1970) described how desensitization could be successfully accomplished by a machine. Phobias for snakes were overcome by the use of two tape recorders, one carrying hierarchy items and the other relaxation instructions. Migler and Wolpe (1967) used a single, specially modified tape recorder to treat a patient who was severely disturbed by inferred disapproval when speaking to a group. The patient himself recorded the hierarchy items and the relaxation instructions under supervision. He then took the tape recorder home and completely desensitized himself in seven sessions. He was free from his original fears when followed up 2 years later. The primitive equipment of that time necessitated complicated switching arrangements.

Much simpler methods soon appeared. Kahn and Baker (1968) introduced a phonograph record for home use. It contained instructions for scene presentations followed by silences into which the patient inserted his imaginary hierarchical scenes as directed beforehand by the therapist. Relaxation instructions preceded each scene, and the recording was worded in such a way that the patient could repeat a particular scene as many times as necessary.

Modern tape recorders offer far more flexibility than phonograph recordings. Denholtz (1971) described the home use of tape recorders for both relaxation training and the presentation of anxiety-evoking scenes. Each relaxation lesson was recorded during the treatment session on the patient's own tape, which he then took home, having been instructed to play it twice daily until his next visit. At subsequent visits, instructions were taped again, but were progressively abbreviated as the patient became more adept at relaxation. For the purposes of homework desensitization, one to three scenes from each hierarchy were provided at each session. The patient was told to use the tape recording daily until his next session when he would usually report no longer having anxiety to any of the taped scenes; this achievement would mean that he was ready to move upward in the hierarchy. The homework materially reduced the time the therapist had to spend with the patient.

Tape-recorded material is particularly valuable for the patient who is too anxious in the presence of the therapist to be able to let go. Some of these patients, having learned relaxation at home can later do it in the office, where treatment may continue.

Group Desensitization

If several people suffer from the same phobia, it is feasible to attempt simultaneously to desensitize them, even if the slopes of their hierarchies differ. However, the therapist must ensure that the current scene no longer evokes anxiety in anybody before proceeding to the next scene. Obviously, group desensitization can be very time-saving. For example, an average of less than 2 hours of therapist time per client was expended by Paul and Shannon (1966) in the treatment of severe "social evaluative" anxiety in college students, manifested by fear and disablement in public-speaking situations. At a 2-year follow-up, Paul (1968) found that the improvements had been maintained or increased.

It is possible that part of the reason Paul and Shannon's patients were more rapidly desensitized is that exteroceptive stimuli from the other members of the group were involved in the deconditioning maneuvers. This possibility seems to be supported by a miniexperiment I performed in 1966 during a series of behavior therapy seminars. The class had 30 members. I invited all those with fears of public speaking to submit to group desensitization in front of the class. Eight volunteered. The treatment sessions—each lasting 15 minutes—took place at the end of the weekly 2-hour seminar. The group sat before me in the front row of seats. The first session was devoted to relaxation training, with which all were already familiar, and which some had already been practicing. At subsequent sessions, imaginary scenes of speaking in public were presented. The first scene was speaking to an audience of three. By the fifth desensitization session, three subjects had dropped out, but the remaining five were each able to imagine themselves speaking to a group of 50 without anxiety. Evidence of transfer to the real situation was subsequently obtained from two of them. One had given a lecture to a group of 75 without any anxiety at all. The total time spent on the group therapy was 90 minutes, so that for the five who completed the course there was a mean time expenditure per patient per phobia of 18 minutes. As suggested above therapeutic change may have been accelerated by the subjects' awareness of sitting in a group while desensitization to imaginary groups was being carried out—an interesting subject for research.

Successful treatment in group settings has been reported for a variety of phobias, for example, test situations (Cohen & Dean, 1968; Donner & Guerny, 1969; Ihli & Garlington, 1969). Donner and Guerny (1969) used an automated technique and, at a follow-up, Donner (1970) found that the gains had been maintained. Robinson and Suinn (1969) reported successful group treatment of spider phobias using massed desensitization sessions.

11
Procedures Involving
Strong Anxiety Evocation

Contrasting with the desensitization strategies that combat weak anxiety responses are treatments that involve strong responses. The classical example is abreaction; in this technique strong emotional responses are stirred up by recall of distressing experiences in which the neurotic anxiety was conditioned. In recent years, methods have emerged that evoke strong responses directly, by exposing the patient either to real stimuli that are highly disturbing or to corresponding imaginary situations. These methods are the *flooding* techniques.

Flooding techniques belong very properly to behavior therapy because they aim to change the disturbed behavior by directly evoking it. Flooding can be instituted at will and its components can be quantitatively varied. Abreaction, on the other hand, is not strictly a behavior therapy technique because all that the therapist can do is to try to create conditions to trigger its occurrence. When it occurs, both its content and its outcome are unpredictable. Nevertheless, it may turn out that abreaction and flooding work in the same way.

ABREACTION

Abreaction is operationally defined as the reevocation with strong emotional accompaniment of a fearful past experience. Some abreactions are followed by therapeutic changes; others are not and may even leave the patient worse. As matters stand, its induction is unreliable and its effects unpredictable. However, in some neurotic patients the unadaptive emotional responses have been conditioned to stimulus compounds of such complexity that neither current nor contrived stimulus situations can incorporate them; in these cases, attempts at abreaction are justified (Wolpe, 1958, p. 198).

Contrary to common belief, the therapeutic efficacy of abreaction, as Grinker and Spiegel's (1945a & b) experiences with war neuroses showed, bears no relation to whether the abreacted experiences are remembered or forgotten. The one apparent essential for therapeutic effects is that the abreaction take place in the context of a psychotherapeutic relationship (Grinker & Spiegel, 1945a). This circumstance underlies the suggestion (Wolpe, 1958, p. 196) that abreaction succeeds when anxiety is inhibited by emotional responses that the therapeutic situation induces in the patient. It is possible that the same process operates in flooding (see below).

Abreactions sometimes arise unbidden, during history taking or systematic desensitization.

Case 40: Abreaction During Desensitization

Following an accident, a truck driver had a severe fear of driving (in addition to considerable free-floating anxiety). After training in relaxation and the construction of a driving hierarchy, the driver was asked during his first desensitization session to imagine himself sitting at the wheel of a car that was stationary and whose engine was not running. He suddenly began to verbalize the details of the accident, broke into a sweat, and became very agitated. After about a minute, when the reaction subsided, he was asked to open his eyes. When he did so, he appeared tired but relieved, and said that he was no longer afraid to drive a truck. The test of reality proved him right.

Case 41: Abreaction During History Taking

Unplanned abreactions occurred in a 50-year-old lawyer who had been vaguely tense for decades, and who had come for treatment of increasing insomnia. During assertiveness training he began to talk of his childhood and mentioned that though his family had been very poor, he would never take anything from other people. He described a sporting event at school, in which though a foremost athlete, he was the only contestant without spiked shoes. He had proudly refused to accept a pair as a handout from the school. He became very agitated and tearful during this narration. At the next interview, a week later, he said that he was feeling better and that his average duration of sleep had gone up from four to six hours per night. At this interview he abreacted at telling the story of a friend in the Army toward whom he had been aggressive and who had been killed a month later. Under hypnosis, he further abreacted in relation to this story. Each of these abreactions, though weaker than the first one, was followed by improvement. With further assertiveness training and desensitization to receiving praise and favors, an apparently complete recovery was obtained in 15 sessions.

There are several paths to the deliberate induction of abreaction. The therapist may endeavor, either with or without hypnosis, to plunge the patient into a past situation known or suspected to be highly disturbing. A case of successful hypnotic abreaction of a war neurosis after 20 years was reported by Leahy and Martin (1967). It may be worth trying the age-regression technique in which the patient imagines himself back in past phases of his life, starting relatively recently and then going back year by year. I have used this technique very occasionally, but have not seen the dramatic effects reported by others. Barber (1969) has shown that it produces a restimulating, not a reliving.

The most effective way of pursuing abreaction is by means of drugs. The first drug to be widely used for this purpose was pentobarbital (Pentothal), which was introduced by Horsley (1936) and became very popular during World War II. At that time at a military hospital, I was one of several physicians who used it in the hope of obtaining beneficial abreactions; but though abreactions did occur, and were frequently vivid and exciting, we only occasionally obtained marked and lasting improvement. However, some authors, for example, Horsley (1946) and Grinker and Spiegel (1945a & b), had more favorable experiences.

Ether has also been used to induce abreaction (Palmer, 1944; Shorvon & Sargant, 1947). While the patient lies on his back on a couch, the therapist talks to him informally about events that preceded the incident on which it is hoped he will abreact. The ether-soaked mask is held a few inches from the face, and then rather rapidly approximated. In a matter of minutes the patient becomes excited and, in a successful case, begins to recite the events that led to the precipitation of his neurosis. He is encouraged to "cry, shout, and struggle"; an assistant should be at hand to restrain excessive movement. Shorvon and Sargant express the consensus when they state that one is much more likely to produce emotional release in an individual suffering from a recent traumatic neurosis than in one with a longstanding illness. But even with recent cases, they acknowledge that there are many failures. On the other hand there are also pleasant surprises. Little and James (1964) described how a neurosis originating in battle 18 years previously was progressively overcome in five sessions of ether abreactions. During the course of these, the patient pieced together a tremendously disturbing sequence of events that had precipitated the neurosis, beginning with his shooting of two young German soldiers while the three of them were in a ditch taking shelter from artillery shells.

FLOODING

Flooding may be defined as the prolonged exposure of a patient to fear-arousing stimuli of relatively high intensity. The first account of a case that was successfully "flooded" is recorded in *Recent Experiments in Psychology* (Crafts et al., 1938, p. 322). (The case was treated by a physician whom the book does not name.) The patient, a young woman, was afraid to ride in automobiles, except over familiar roads, and had an especially intense fear of bridges and tunnels. One day, the physician ordered her to be driven from her home to his New York office. The distance was nearly 50 miles, and the route took her over a number of high bridges and through the Holland Tunnel. On the morning set for the ride, the woman was in a condition of terror, with violent nausea and faintness. Her terror persisted during much of the ride but diminished as she neared the refuge of her physician's house. The return trip provoked little or no emotional disturbance, and subsequent journeys over the same route became increasingly easy for her.

Systematic development of flooding therapy started with the work of Malleson (1959) and Stampfl (1964). Malleson treated several cases by deliberately evoking intense anxiety on the supposition that experimental extinction of the habit would occur. One patient was an Indian student who was very afraid of examinations. He was asked to describe the awful consequences that he felt would follow his failure — derision from his colleagues in India, disappointment from his family, financial loss. Then he was to try to imagine these things happening — the finger of scorn pointed at him, his wife and mother in tears. At first, as he followed the instructions, his sobbings increased. But soon his distress subsided. The effort needed to maintain vivid imagining increased, and, inversely, the emotion he could summon began to ebb. Within half an hour he was calm. Malleson instructed him to repeat the exercise of experiencing his fears. When he felt a little wave of spontaneous alarm he was not to push it aside, but to try to experience it more profoundly and more vividly. If he did not spontaneously feel fear he was to make a special effort to try to do so every 20 or 30 minutes, however difficult and ludicrous it might seem. He was seen twice a day over the next 2 days until his examination. Malleson states that, being an intelligent man and an assiduous patient, he practiced the exercises methodically and by the time of the examination reported himself almost totally unable to feel frightened. He had, as it were, exhausted the affect of the situation. He passed his examination without apparent difficulty.

Stampfl (1964) called his strategy, which also relies on the patient's imagination, *implosive therapy*. He expressed the view that if the patient were insistently exposed to the conditioned anxiety-producing stimulus situations, and if the anxiety were not reinforced (by an unconditioned stimulus), the anxiety-response habit would extinguish. Continuous exposure to the stimulus was expected to cause it to lose all power to elicit anxiety. The patient was induced to imagine himself realistically in the relevant fear situation while the therapist described in great detail the most vivid horrors possible.

Although in later accounts implosion therapists (e.g., Levis, 1980; Stampfl & Levis, 1967) continued to stress maximal stimulation as a matter of principle, in practice they often employed weaker stimuli in the initial phases. They prescribed an "avoidance serial cue hierarchy," and the hypothesized cues low on this hierarchy (that is, cues that have low anxiety loading) were presented first.

An unexpected feature of the work of Stampfl and his colleagues was that while they based their methods on learning theory, they also assumed the validity of psychoanalytic theorizing and derived some of their scene material from it. Stampfl and Levis (1968) stated that "castration dangers and oedipal time conflicts are not foreign to the implosive theory approach in that they are hypothesized to be a product of primary or secondary aversive conditioning events." Some of the scenes they based upon psychoanalytic assumptions did evoke anxiety that diminished in time. The authors took this as evidence that such material had special therapeutic relevance, but it is quite possible that a variety of other stimulus materials would also evoke anxiety that diminishes.

In the first edition of this book, I expressed reservations about the wideranging success with flooding claimed by implosive therapists (e.g., Levis & Carrera, 1967). I felt also that the method was not without risk. While I am now convinced of the value of this method and that the risks are small, I still advocate caution because prolonged in vivo exposure does exacerbate occasional cases (see case 45).

Meanwhile a strong conviction regarding the superiority of flooding (exposure) over other anxiety-deconditioning methods has become widespread, though it is not warranted by data. The limited success of flooding in agoraphobia is discussed in chapter 14. In simple phobia, a review by Barlow (1988, p. 486ff) finds its comparative efficacy to be equivocal. Exceptionally favorable outcomes have, however, been reported by Ost (1990) in the treatment of specific phobias, mainly animal phobias, in a single session of about 2 hours' duration.

Successful flooding requires prolonged exposure to anxiety-arousing stimulation, but it is prudent to work with only moderately strong anxiety. The stimulation should continue until there is clear evidence of anxiety decrement, for this is the indication that it has produced anxiety-response inhibition. This usually takes 30 to 60 minutes. If the stimulation is removed early, there is not enough time for the inhibitory process to develop, and the anxiety-drive reduction that follows removal may reinforce the anxiety habit.

Some Personal Experiences With Flooding

The following cases illustrate the individual variability that is found in flooding. Success in Case 42 required moderating the stimulus inputs; while in Case 43, it seemed to require maximizing it. Flooding was rapidly successful in case 44, but made case 45 worse. Imaginal stimulation was used in Case 43, in vivo exposure in the others.

Case 42: Multifaceted Experimental Flooding

The subject of the experiment was a woman in her late 20s with long-standing severe phobias for dead birds and bats. She had heard of flooding and believed that it might be a rapid way of overcoming her phobias. At first, an attempt was made to induce it by images based on verbal descriptions, but very little emotion was aroused in this way. The decision was then made, with her full agreement, to expose her to real dead birds.

On the appointed day, the patient sat in a comfortable armchair. Two dead birds, a small blackbird and a pheasant, had been prepared in accordance with the patient's description of what for her provided maximal stress — exposure of the neck by the removal of most of the feathers. The patient was then told that the blackbird would be brought in, and a vivid verbal description was given. This produced a certain amount of manifest uneasiness, and she reported some anxiety, but not much. She was then asked to close her eyes, whereupon the bird was brought in, held by the feet, with head dangling down, and in this position kept about 7 feet away from her. She was asked to look at it, but refused. After 2 minutes, she shot a glance at the bird, and gave vent to a loud shriek and a great deal of generalized movement. She said that she would not look again. After gentle but firm coaxing, however, she did glance at it again with loud screams of terror and much movement. This made me suggest having it moved a little farther away — to about 10 feet. She seemed pleased at this, and after a half a minute or so, opened her eyes and looked at the bird for about three seconds, again screaming and contorting her body. She subsequently opened her eyes for progressively longer periods, and the fifth time was able to scan the bird continuously. Even then, though she was relatively undisturbed most of the time, she would occasionally relapse into screaming. When questioned about this, she said that at those times the bird assumed an aspect which made it seem as though it was getting "under her skin," suggesting a perceptual organization process of turning on and off the impact of the stimulus.

Eventually, these spontaneous outbursts ceased, and then an interesting thing was noticed. Every time the bird was jerked or the angle of presentation changed, there was a further flurry of anxiety. After about 5 minutes, the patient could no longer be stirred up, no matter what was done with the bird at 10 feet, though rating her basal level at 20 *suds*. It seemed as though all the angles and varieties of movement had been deconditioned at 10 feet. The bird was now brought closer through three stages until it was only about three feet from her. Again, at each approximation, there was a need to present the bird at different angles and with renewed movements, but the reactions were smaller and quite quickly overcome. At this point, it was suggested that she stroke the bird's feathers. She resisted this, but allowed herself to be persuaded to move her finger closer and closer, and eventually touched it. Thereafter, she was able to go on to stroking the bird with decreasing anxiety. The next step was to get her to hold the bird herself, which she finally did, without any increase in the anxiety level beyond the 20 *suds* baseline level. At a second session, anxiety fell to zero in 20 minutes.

Case 43: Successful Imaginal Flooding

Imaginal stimuli were employed with Dr. E., a dentist who had had an extraordinarily severe and widespread neurosis that had in most respects responded well to varied and sometimes prolonged applications of assertiveness training and systematic desensitization. But two disabling neurotic constellations remained — an inability to give dental injections because of a fear of the patient dying in the chair, and an extravagant fear of ridicule. Since attempts to desensitize Dr. E. to these were making painfully slow progress, I decided to try flooding. Under light hypnosis he was asked to imagine giving a patient a mandibular block, then, withdrawing the syringe, standing back and seeing the patient slump forward, dead. Dr. E. became profoundly disturbed, sweating, weeping, and wringing his hands. After a minute or so, noticing that the reaction was growing weaker, I terminated the scene and told him to relax. Two or three minutes later, the same sequence evoked a similar, but weaker reaction. The sequence was given three more times, at the last of which no further reaction was observed. Dr. E. said that he felt he had been through a wringer — exhausted, but at ease. At the next session, the fear of ridicule was introduced. Dr. E. imagined that he was walking down the middle of a brilliantly lighted ballroom with people on both sides pointing their fingers at him and laughing derisively. At the fifth flooding session, it was clear that nothing remained to be treated. Four years later, at an interview, Dr. E. stated that his recovery had been fully maintained. The same was true 23 years later.

Case 44: Rapidly Successful in vivo Flooding

Mrs. C., had agoraphobia so severe that she was unable to go on her own more than two blocks by car without anxiety. Attempts at systematic desensitization had failed — apparently because she was unable to imagine scenes realistically. After other measures had also proved ineffective, I persuaded her to expose herself to flooding, which had to be in vivo because of the demonstrated inadequacy of her imagination. Plans were made for her husband to place her, unaccompanied, on a commercial aircraft 1 hour's flight away from the airport where I would await her. When Mrs. C. in due course alighted from the plane, she walked toward me smiling. She had felt increasing anxiety for the first 15 minutes of the flight, and then gradual subsidence of it. During the second half of the journey she had been perfectly comfortable. She flew home alone the next day without trouble. This single experience resulted in a great increase in her range of comfortable situations away from home. She was now able, without anxiety, to drive her car alone 3 or 4 miles from home and to make unaccompanied trips by plane without any anxiety. Plans to build up this improvement by further treatment were foiled by distance and other practical obstacles.

Case 45: Unsuccessful in vivo Flooding

The following is an example of a patient who was made worse by attempts to "flood" him. Dr. K. was a physician with a severe phobia for insane people and insane behavior. He was in military service, and soon after he began to consult me was offered a transfer to a psychiatric hospital. I encouraged this, thinking that the phobia might be overcome by flooding. On my advice, he exposed himself continuously to the presence of schizophrenic patients, sometimes for hours at a stretch. Far from decreasing, his reactions to these patients grew progressively worse; in addition, he developed a rising level free-floating anxiety. By the end of the second day he was so extremely anxious that he had to be relocated. He had become much more sensitive than ever before to "insane stimuli," and only with much effort was his neurosis overcome by desensitization.

How Does Flooding Work?

Though the success of flooding was explained by Malleson and Stampfl on the paradigm of experimental extinction, it seems most unlikely that the attenuation of anxiety occurs by the same process as the weakening of motor habits. One point of difference is that in the extinction of a motor habit the more strongly the response is evoked, the more rapidly it extinguishes (Hull, 1943, p. 279; Mowrer & Jones, 1945), although the relationship is more complex than originally appeared (Lawson & Brownstein, 1957). With conditioned anxiety, by contrast, the experimentally observed relationship is the opposite: when anxiety is relatively weak, repeated elicitation extinguishes it relatively easily; when its arousal is strong, there is little or no response decrement. Experimental neuroses are uniformly resistant to extinction by prolonged exposure to maximal stimulation (see chapter 3). The clinical failures of flooding—such as exemplified by case 45 and by the many aerophobias that do not improve in repeated fear-filled flights—are of a piece with this.

For flooding (or, for that matter, any procedure) to succeed in reducing fear conditioning, it must somehow reduce evoked fear. When flooding reduces fear, by what process does this happen? One straw in the wind is the observation that the therapist's presence facilitates the ability of flooding to diminish fear. There has been only one study to provide data on this point. Sherry and Levine (1980) evaluated, in speech-anxious subjects, the impact of the presence of the therapist on the therapeutic efficacy of two different modes of scene presentation. In the cases in which the therapist was present during the presentations, the outcome was significantly better than when he was absent. Because of the popularity of exposure as an explanation (though it was seen on p. 51 to be a nonexplanation), it is common for the response-competition implications of such observations to be missed. For example, in their scholarly volume on flooding, Boudewyns and Shipley (1983) attribute the advantageous impact of the therapist to his "facilitating increased exposure" (p. 35).

Sherry and Levine's observations are in keeping with those of Butler et al. (1984). They gave one group of social phobics standard flooding, and gave a second group, in addition, cognitive and distractive strategies plus some relaxation training. The second group did notably better, especially at 6-month follow-up. From the dynamic standpoint adopted here, the superior success would be attributable to cognitive input in cognitively based cases, and to response competition due to the relaxation and distractive strategies in classically conditioned ones. Only empirical study can settle the matter.

It is likely that in the weakening of anxiety response habits by flooding, reciprocal inhibition plays a major role. This has not been formally investigated, but there are significant pieces of data. The success of modeling, as stated above (p. 213) appears to depend, in classically conditioned cases, largely on the anxiety-inhibiting role of the therapist, and this may also apply to flooding. Reference was made above to the findings of Butler et al. (1984) that showed increased success in social phobics when exposure was augmented by cognitive and distractive strategies plus some relaxation training. Once again we see the indispensability of individual case analysis, if we wish to know what is really going on, as a preliminary to treatment.

Another possible explanation for the effects of flooding is that continuing strong stimulation may lead, after a varying time, to transmarginal inhibition of the response (Gray, 1964; Pavlov, 1927). The relevance and the mode of operation of this mechanism remain entirely unexplored in this context.

Flooding has deservedly come to be the treatment of choice for the obsessive-compulsive case characterized by fear and avoidance of contamination. This topic is considered more fully in chapter 15.

PARADOXICAL INTENTION

Like flooding, paradoxical intention involves high anxiety, but its intent is different. It was developed by Victor Frankl (1960) from the standpoint of existential theory (Frankl, 1960, 1967a, 1975; Gerz, 1966). The central idea is that if the patient tries to bring on or magnify his symptoms he will find difficulty in doing so, and this will change his attitude toward his neurosis. Frankl (1967b) described the application of paradoxical intention to maladaptive fears as follows:

> It consists not only of a reversal of the patient's attitude toward his phobia inasmuch as the usual avoidance response is replaced by an intentional effort—but also that it is carried out in as humorous a setting as possible. This brings about a change of attitude toward the symptom which enables the patient to place himself at a distance from the symptom, to detach himself from his neurosis. This procedure is based on the logotherapeutic teaching that pathogenesis in phobias and obsessive-compulsive neurosis is partially due to the increase of anxiety and compulsions by the endeavor to avoid or fight them.

There is an interesting similarity between this and Malleson's (1959) description of flooding (reproduced on p. 220).

Rapid recovery is sometimes achieved by paradoxical intention, but treatment may have to be given repeatedly over several months. One of Gerz's (1966) cases was a 29-year-old woman who had fears of heights, of being alone, of eating in a restaurant in case she vomited, and of going into supermarkets, subways, and cars. She was instructed to try to expose herself to the conditions that she feared. She was to try to vomit while dining out with her husband and friends, so as to create the greatest possible mess. She was to drive to markets, hairdresser, and banks "trying to get as panicky as possible." In 6 weeks she had lost her fears in her home situation, and shortly thereafter drove all by herself to Gerz's office, about 5 miles from her home. Four months later, she drove with her husband to New York City, 100 miles away, across the George Washington Bridge, back through the Lincoln Tunnel, and attended a goodbye party on the lower deck of an ocean liner. Gerz states that 2 years later she was free of symptoms.

Paradoxical intention lends itself readily to incorporation into behavioral programs. Its widest use by behavior therapists has been in the treatment of insomnia (Ascher & Efran, 1978). In a controlled study, Ascher and Turner (1979) found that it was as effective as progressive relaxation or *stimulus control*—diminishing the impact of sleep-negative stimuli. Solyom, Garza-Perez, Ledwidge, and Solyom (1972) conducted a pilot study to test the effectiveness of a modified paradoxical intention procedure in the amelioration of obsessive thoughts. Each of 10 patients complaining of multiple obsessions was assigned a *target* thought and a *control* thought from among his own obsessions. Patients applied paradoxical intention (exaggerated attention) to the "target" thought while the control thought remained untreated. Five of the ten subjects reported that the target obsession was greatly reduced or eliminated by paradoxical intention while the control obsession continued unabated.

Ascher (1981a) and Mavissakalian and Michelson (1983) obtained encouraging results from the use of paradoxical intention in agoraphobia. Ascher (1981a) found in a small scale comparison, that it produced significantly more change than graduated exposure in vivo. Mavissakalian et al. (1983) reported that paradoxical intention was superior to exposure as well as to cognitive methods. On the basis of these findings, Michelson and Ascher (1984) proposed that paradoxical intention affects both deconditioning and cognitive correction. But the findings themselves would be more meaningful if classically conditioned and cognitive cases were separated at the commencement of investigations, and more still if the dynamic differences between cases were given recognition. (For a wide ranging symposium on paradoxical intention see the *Journal of Behavior Therapy and Experimental Psychiatry*, No. 3, September 1984.)

12
Operant-Conditioning Methods

It was shown in chapter 1 that there is only one learning process — one process that connects stimuli to responses. What varies is what is connected to what. Therefore, the difference between operant conditioning and respondent conditioning is not in the nature of the conditioning process: in the former, autonomic behavior is predominantly involved; in the latter, the behavior is predominantly motor.

The conditioning of motor responses is "under the control of its consequences" (e.g., reward or nonreward from without). This is also true of some cognitive behavior (Cautela, 1979a & b). The conditioning of autonomic responses is not, as a rule, a function of external rewards. But it does require the occurrence of internal reinforcing states of affairs (see chapter 2). These do, however, sometimes coincide with external reward contingencies (Kimmel, 1967; Lang, 1968; Miller & DiCara, 1968). For wide-ranging modern accounts of operant conditioning, see Mackintosh (1974), Rachlin (1976), and Balsam (1988).

The operant procedures that are used in clinical practice are generally based on paradigms elaborated by Skinner (1938, 1953, 1988). If these paradigms do not figure largely in the treatment of neuroses it is because neuroses are primarily autonomic habits. Nevertheless, operant conditioning of motor responses often goes hand in glove with emotional reconditioning. In particular, it is an integral part of assertiveness training. Appropriate assertive behavior is reinforced, e.g. by the approval of onlookers, at the same time as anxiety is being reciprocally inhibited, e.g. by appropriate anger (see chapter 8). There are numerous other patients in whose treatment operant change is vital: for example, those who have difficulties in interpersonal relations. In addition, operant procedures are widely applicable in a wide range of unadaptive habits that are only sometimes related to conditioned anxiety, such as nail biting, trichotillomania, enuresis, encopresis, chronic tardiness, and inability to stick to work routines. Detailed expositions of operant conditioning treatment were given early on by Ayllon and Azrin (1968), and by Schaefer and Martin (1969), and compilations of cases by Ullman and Krasner (1965), Franks (1965), Ulrich, Stachnik, and Mabry (1966), and recent overviews by Kalish (1981) and Goldstein and Krasner (1987). This chapter gives a summary of the main procedures.

There are six basic operant-conditioning schedules: positive reinforcement, extinction, differential reinforcement, response shaping, punishment, and negative reinforcement. Punishment is discussed in the context of aversion therapy in chapter 13. Differential reinforcement is a selective combination of positive reinforcement and extinction. Shaping is a special application of positive reinforcement. We will therefore focus on the basic elements of positive reinforcement, negative reinforcement, and extinction.

POSITIVE REINFORCEMENT

Any state of affairs that, following a response, serves to increase the rate of responding is called a *reinforcer*. Food, water, sex, money, domination, approval, and affection are all reinforcers when they increase the rate (or probability or strength) of a response in a given stimulus situation. Homme (1965) extended the range of reinforcers to include high-probability (preferred) behaviors on the basis of Premack's (1965) observation that these increase the probability of any low-probability behavior that they follow. (The rate of responding can also be increased by relief from something aversive — such as pain, discomfort, or tension, which is called *negative reinforcement*.)

Examples of the efficacy of positive reinforcement are legion, ranging from pecking habits in pigeons to the most complex ceremonials of mankind. In the field of therapeutic change, we have noted that the motor behavior of assertion is reinforced by such consequences as the achievement of an interpersonal victory or the later approval of the therapist. Examples are easy to find in the behavior problems of children. For example, a child may habitually scream to get what he wants because screaming has repeatedly resulted in this. Now, if the child is told, "You will not get it (e.g., a toy) if you scream; to get it you must say quietly, 'Please, may I have it?'" rewarding the new behavior increases the likelihood of its occurrence, and, with repetition, in its displacing the screaming.

Modification of Schizophrenic Behavior

The therapeutic efficacy of positive reinforcement has been widely demonstrated. Much of the early work was on chronic schizophrenics. Cure of the psychosis was neither expected nor claimed, but only change in particular habits. A variety of evidence—for example, genetic (Kallman, 1953), physiological (Rubin, 1970), and biochemical (Gottlieb & Frohman, 1972)—indicates that schizophrenia is basically an organic illness (Wolpe, 1970). The organic state seems directly responsible for some of the psychotic behavior and at the same time predisposes the individual to the learning of unadaptive habits that are often quite bizarre.

Lindsley (1956) was the first to explore the possibilities of operant-conditioning schedules in psychotic subjects. His work was later vastly extended by Ayllon and Azrin (1964, 1965). One of the clever treatment schedules devised by Ayllon (1963) is worth presenting at length. The patient was a 47-year-old schizophrenic woman who had been in a state hospital for 9 years. Among other strange habits, she always wore an excessive amount of clothing—weighing about 25 pounds. In order to treat this, Ayllon had a scale placed at the entrance to the dining room. The requirement for entering (to receive food reinforcement) was a predetermined weight:

> Initially, she was given an allowance of 23 lbs. over her current body weight. This allowance represented a 2 lb reduction from her usual clothing weight. When the patient exceeded the weight requirement, the nurse stated in a matter-of-fact manner, "Sorry, you weigh too much, you'll have to weigh less." Failure to meet the required weight resulted in the patient missing the meal at which she was being weighed. Sometimes, in an effort to meet the requirement, the patient discarded more clothing than was required. When this occurred, the requirement was adjusted at the next weighing time to correspond to the limit set by the patient on the preceding occasion.
>
> At the start of this experiment, the patient missed a few meals because she failed to meet the weight requirement, but soon thereafter she gradually discarded her superfluous clothing. First, she left behind odd items she had carried in her arms, such as bundles, cups and handbags. Next, she took off the elaborate headgear and assorted "capes" or shawls she had worn over her shoulders. Although she had worn 18 pairs of stockings at one time, she eventually shed these also.

At the end of the experiment, the patient's clothing weighed a normal three lbs and remained stable at this level. One result of dressing normally was participation in social events at the hospital. Another was that her parents resumed taking her out after a lapse of 9 years.

Anorexia Nervosa

Anorexia nervosa is a learned maladaptive syndrome in which positive reinforcement is sometimes the appropriate treatment. I participated in the treatment of the first two successful cases, one of which was reported in detail by Bachrach, Erwin, and Mohr (1965)—a 37-year-old woman whose weight had fallen to 47 pounds despite various medical treatments. For the purposes of the conditioning program, she was transferred from her attractive hospital room to a barren one that was furnished only with a bed, nightstand, and chair. Each of the three authors had one meal a day with her. The reinforcement schedule featured reinforcement of movements associated with eating.

When the patient lifted her fork to spear a piece of food, the therapist would reinforce this act by talking to her about something of interest. The behavior required to elicit reinforcement was progressively extended — to lifting the food toward her mouth, chewing, and so forth. A similar schedule was later applied to increasing the amount of food she consumed. At first, any portion of the meal that was eaten would be a basis for a postprandial reinforcement — a radio, television set, or phonograph would be brought in by the nurse at a signal from the experimenter; if she did not touch any of the food before her, no reinforcement would be given at that meal time. Subsequently, more and more of the meal had to be consumed for her to be reinforced, and she was eventually required to eat everything on the plate. After 2 months, when she had gained 14 pounds, she was discharged to outpatient treatment, and the positive reinforcement treatment was continued at home with the cooperation of her family. Eighteen months later her weight was 88 lb. A 16-year follow-up of this case has been provided by Erwin (1977).

A number of other cases of anorexia nervosa have been successfully treated by operant methods (e.g., Blinder, Freeman, & Stunkard, 1970; Hallsten, 1965; Scrignar, 1971). Unfortunately, the same inattention to case dynamics noted in relation to other syndromes is often apparent with respect to anorexia nervosa. Patients have been placed on operant schedules without any preliminary case analysis. Results are often unsatisfactory and sometimes catastrophic. The procedure used with some operantly treated patients was justifiably the subject of sharp criticism by Bruch (1973), who pointed to the emergence of depression and other unfortunate sequelae, even in cases where the anorexia had responded favorably. The fact is that operant conditioning programs are off target in cases of anorexia nervosa that are emotionally based. However, Bruch went beyond the data to challenge behavior therapy in general. I pointed out in a rebuttal (Wolpe, 1975) that it was *misuse* of behavioral principles that accounted for those results. It is only when behavior therapy is carried out by practitioners who realize the variability of conditioning histories and explore the resultant stimulus-response structures of cases that behavior therapy reveals its superiority.

Operant Methods in Neuroses

Operant procedures have particular importance in overcoming unadaptive fears in whose maintenance physical avoidance plays a major part. Ayllon, Smith, and Rogers' (1970) treatment of a school phobia illustrates this. The problem was redefined as zero or low probability of school attendance. The first step was to get the child's mother to withdraw the rewards of staying at home. Then, a home-based motivational system was used to reinforce school attendance; refusal to attend school resulted in punishment. School attendance increased rapidly and was maintained even after the procedures were withdrawn a month later. No symptom substitution was noticed within the nine months of follow-up.

The masturbatory orgasm appears to be a powerful reward agent for transferring male sexual interest from deviant objects to women (Marquis, 1970). The patient is instructed to masturbate to the point where he feels the inevitability of orgasm, using whatever fantasy is most arousing. Then he is to switch to the female fantasy that has previously been agreed on as appropriate. He is warned that he may experience some difficulty at first, but that he will not lose his sexual arousal. After he has successfully shifted to the appropriate stimulus four or five times, he is instructed to start moving the introduction of the appropriate fantasy backward in time toward the beginning of masturbation. An attempt is made at the outset to get a commitment from the client never to continue picturing the inappropriate fantasy through the orgasm, whether in masturbation or overt sexual behavior. Any decrease in sexual arousal upon switching is seen as evidence that the client has exchanged fantasies too soon, and he is instructed to drop back to the original fantasy and switch at a higher level of sexual arousal. Of the 15 cases Marquis reported, 5 were cured, and 7 much improved. The technique has not been subjected to systematic study, and the clinical reports of its efficacy are partly positive (e.g., LoPiccolo, Stewart, & Watkins, 1972; Van de Venter & Laws, 1978), and partly negative (Conrad & Wincze, 1976; Marshall, 1974).

Operant Methods in Maladaptive Motor Behavior

Operant programs have been particularly widely applied to asocial behavior in children. A prominent context has been uncooperative classroom behavior (Bijou & Ruiz, 1981; Homme et al., 1971; O'Leary & O'Leary, 1977; Patterson & Gullion, 1968), but psychiatric syndromes have also received a great deal of attention (see Daniels, 1974, for many examples). Of special interest is a method described by Kimmel and Kimmel (1970) for treating nocturnal enuresis. The child, who may drink water and other liquids without restriction, is rewarded with cookies or other desired items for "holding in" his urine for increasing durations. At the beginning, the child is given the reward for inhibiting urination for 5 minutes after his first report of a need to urinate, and then the period of inhibition is progressively lengthened. Apparently, a habit of inhibition of urination is established by the positive reinforcement. In three cases in which the method was used, complete cessation of bedwetting was achieved in about a week. Neale (1963) overcame several cases of encopresis by rewarding defecation at the toilet with candy. Similar cases were reported by Madsen (1965) and Tomlinson (1970). Edelman (1971) used a combination of negative and positive reinforcement to the same end.

Important developments in the treatment of autistic children have been reported by Lovaas and Smith (1989). Moving away from the concept of autism as a disease entity, they show that autistic children have individual behavioral deficits that are related to developmental delays. Each case is carefully analyzed and treatment is guided by the findings of the analysis. One necessity is to devise a special environment that is functional for each child, an environment in which he can obtain reinforcement and learn. When this can be arranged, the characteristic behavioral deficits are very often overcome.

Applications of operant-conditioning techniques to delinquent behavior (Burchard & Tyler, 1965; Schwitzgebel & Kolb, 1964; Stumphauser, 1986); have yielded encouraging results. Schwitzgebel and Kolb treated 40 adolescent delinquents by reinforcement procedures. A 3-year follow-up study of 20 of them revealed a significant reduction in the frequency and severity of crime in comparison with a matched-pair control group. Burchard and Tyler produced a marked decrease in the destructive and disruptive behavior of a 13-year-old delinquent boy by systematically isolating him when he performed in an antisocial way and by rewarding socially acceptable behavior.

Thomas (1968) listed a number of rules to enhance the effectiveness of positive reinforcement:

1. The response to be reinforced must first be emitted, otherwise reinforcement is impossible.
2. Reinforcement must not be delayed; in general, the more immediate the reinforcement, the better.
3. Reinforcement of every desired response emitted is most effective for establishing behavior.
4. Not reinforcing every desired response during response establishment (partial reinforcement), while less effective in achieving immediate high rates of responding, is generally more effective in producing responses that endure after reinforcement is terminated.
5. The stimuli suitable to reinforce one individual's behavior may not be the most appropriate for another. Recent research suggests that one important clue to appropriate reinforcing conditions is simply the rank order of activities in which a person engages in his free time (see Homme, 1965; Premack, 1965).

Covert Positive Reinforcement

Cautela (1970b, 1972, 1977; Cautela & Wall, 1980) introduced a procedure that he called *covert reinforcement*. In this, the response to be reinforced and the reinforcer are both presented in imagination. Cautela reported that he had successfully employed covert reinforcement for phobias, obsessions, homosexuality, and obesity. The first step is to identify stimuli that will function appropriately as reinforcers. This can conveniently be done on the basis of the patient's responses to a reinforcement survey schedule (Cautela & Kastenbaum, 1967). Any item to which the patient indicates a high degree of pleasure is tested for visual clarity and for the ease with which the patient can conjure up its image. The patient must be able to evoke the image within about 5 seconds if the item is to be usable as a reinforcer.

The method is well exemplified in a case reported by Wisocki (1970). The patient had a neatness compulsion that included, among other things, the habit of folding articles of clothing again and again, smoothing them down more perfectly each time. In applying the covert-reinforcement procedure, the therapist instructed the patient to imagine herself in various situations involving two types of behavior: (a) refraining from repeating the obsessive-compulsive behavior, and (b) making responses that were antagonistic to that behavior. When the patient signaled imagining the appropriate response, the therapist immediately said "reinforcement," which was the cue for the patient to imagine a predetermined reinforcing item, such as walking in a forest, practicing ballet, or eating an Italian sandwich. Thus, the therapist would induce a reinforcing image when the patient signaled that she was thinking, "I don't care if it is wrinkled; it doesn't matter," or if she imagined folding a laundered item quickly and putting it on top of the finished pile, even though it was a little wrinkled. This patient's obsessive-compulsive behaviors were eliminated in eight 2-hour sessions. At a 12-month follow-up, there was no recurrence of the compulsive behavior.

While the covert-reinforcement procedure is often successful (and certainly gives the therapist much scope for inventiveness), it seems likely that when it is used to decondition anxiety, as in the above case, its mechanism is reciprocal inhibition and not positive reinforcement. In an analogue study on rat-fearful college students, Ladouceur (1974) found that those in whom the reinforcement *preceded* the approach response did as well (in contrast to a control group) as those given the standard sequence. Bajtelsmit and Gershman (1976) made the same observation in students with test anxiety, in a study that contained a more exact replication of Cautela's procedure.

NEGATIVE REINFORCEMENT

Negative reinforcement means increasing the rate or strength of a response by the contingent removal of a source of pain or tension. The therapeutic use of this strategy is sometimes complicated by the fact that the therapist has to introduce the source of pain in the first place, which may have countertherapeutic consequences.

An informative example of the operation of negative reinforcement is afforded by Ayllon's (1963) treatment of another habit of the patient referred to on p. 230 — towel hoarding. This woman would collect and store large numbers of towels which the nursing staff would remove from her room about twice a week. Ayllon instructed the staff to stop the routine towel removal and, intermittently each day, to hand the patient a towel without comment. The patient was delighted at this new policy, and arranged her growing stock in neat piles, first on the dressing table and chair, and later on the floor and bed. When there were several hundred, the piles became unmanageable so that increasing numbers of them began to lie about the room in disorder. The patient now began to ask the staff to stop bringing the towels, but without avail. When the number reached 600, additional towels seemed to become aversive. One day, when there were 625 towels in the room, the patient seized the next towel that arrived and threw it out of the room, presumably to reduce the oppressiveness of the excess of towels somewhat. Since that towel did not come back, there was negative reinforcement of the act of discarding a towel. Thereafter, the patient progressively removed them and no more were given her. During the next 12 months the mean number of towels found in her room was 1.5.

Cautela (1970a) extended his covert-reinforcement idea to include covert negative reinforcement. He states that it is especially applicable to subjects who find it easier to evoke disagreeable images than pleasant ones. If the patient finds it unpleasant to be spoken to in a harsh tone, he will be asked to visualize this and, when he signals that the image is clear, to replace it by an image of the response to be increased. Great care is taken to insure that the patient can immediately withdraw from the aversive stimulus upon request and replace it with the response to be increased. If, after a number of trials, there is still an overlap, a new aversive stimulus is chosen. This technique has not been widely used, but Cautela (1970a) reported success in 90% of his cases.

EXTINCTION

Extinction is the progressive weakening or diminishing frequency of a response when it is repeatedly evoked without being followed by a reinforcer. Its mechanism has been discussed in chapter 2.

A case of Ayllon and Michael (1959) is probably the earliest clinical example of a type of extinction program that is finding increasing use. The patient was a woman who for a period of 2 years had been entering the nurses' office on an average of 16 times a day. The nurses had resigned themselves to this activity on the ground that such efforts as pushing her back onto the ward bodily had failed in the past and because the patient had been classified as mentally defective and therefore "too dumb" to understand. In order to extinguish this particular problem behavior, the nurses were instructed not to give the patient any reinforcement (attention) for entering their office. What followed was a gradual and continuing diminution of entries to the nurses' office. The average frequency was down to two entries per day by the seventh week of extinction, at which time the program was terminated.

Behavior that is in the process of being extinguished diminishes at varying rates. As Thomas (1968) points out, resistance to extinction is often high in clinical cases because the responses have been sustained for long periods by intermittent reinforcement. For this reason, it is important that the cessation of reinforcement be abrupt and complete.

A massed-practice type of extinction program was introduced by Dunlap (1932) who termed it *negative practice*. He described overcoming such habits as the repeated typing of errors, tics, and stuttering by persuading the subject to repeat the undesired act a great many times. The method came to be used mainly in the treatment of tics (e.g., Jones, 1960; Rafi, 1962; Walton, 1964; Yates, 1958). With this method, it is imperative that the undesirable response be evoked to the point of exhaustion so that a high degree of reactive inhibition is produced. Otherwise, the tic may actually be reinforced, especially if it is not asymptotic to begin with. In any event, this is a tedious, time-consuming method. Kondas (1965) reported that much more rapid change can be obtained if negative practice is combined with anxiety-relief conditioning (p. 203). While the patient repeats the tic, an unpleasant electric current is continuously applied. Switching it off simultaneously with cessation of the tic sequence provides negative reinforcement nonperformance of the tic.

In recent years, Azrin has been the author of numerous programs for eliminating undesirable habits based on the concept of habit reversal. A forerunner of these programs was Taylor's (1963) treatment of a case of compulsive eyebrow plucking. Another was Wolpe's (1958, p. 188) treatment of compulsive mimicry. The habits so far treated include enuresis (Azrin & Fox, 1974), tics (Azrin & Nunn, 1973), stuttering (Azrin & Nunn, 1974; Waterloo & Gotestam, 1989), trichotillomania (Azrin, Nunn, & Frantz, 1980), and self-destructive oral habits (Azrin, Nunn, & Frantz-Renshaw, 1980). The core of habit reversal is the elicitation of an incompatible response whenever the impulse to perform the undesirable behavior arises. For example, in a case of trichotillomania, the subject learns the inconspicuous competing response of grasping or clenching the hands for 3 minutes whenever hair pulling is likely to occur or even after it has been initiated. The habit-reversal programs have been widely adopted and are stated to have achieved a high measure of success.

Habit reversal exemplifies the process of reciprocal inhibition as applied to motor responses (Wolpe, 1958, pp. 186–188; 1976, pp. 13–16), but Azrin and his colleagues have not explicitly recognized this.

13
Aversion Therapy

It is necessary to state that aversion treatment is a last resort in behavior therapy and its use is infrequent. Its essence is the administration of an aversive (unpleasant) stimulus simultaneously with an unwanted emotional response, with the object of inhibiting the latter and consequently diminishing its habit strength. For example, a painful stimulus may be employed to inhibit sexual arousal by a fetishistic object in order to weaken that arousal. Thus, aversion therapy operates by reciprocal inhibition. The chief aversive agents are strong but nondamaging electrical stimulation, nauseating drugs, and nauseating or disgusting evoked imagery. Aversion therapy must be clearly distinguished from punishment, in which the aversive stimulus follows the response of concern instead of coinciding with it. Whereas punishment is intended to discourage a response—that is, to make it less probable by reason of aversive consequences—the intent of aversion therapy is to diminish the habit strength of a response through inhibiting it by the competition of the aversive agent. In general, punishment is employed to weaken motor habits, aversion therapy to weaken autonomic habits.

We must examine what happens when, in the presence of the stimulus to an undesired response, a strong aversive stimulus, such as strong electrical stimulation of a limb, is administered. Besides eliciting an avoidance response, the shock inhibits the undesired emotional response. Whenever it does so, a measure of conditioned inhibition of the undesired response will be established—a weakening of its habit, of the bond between the response and its stimulus. At the same time, the stimulus may be to some extent conditioned to the response constellation which the shock evoked. The amount of such conditioning is generally small or else transient (e.g., Raymond, 1964). Pearce (1963) found that transvestites who had been treated by apomorphine later reported loss of interest rather than nausea at transvestite fantasies. Similarly, Bancroft (1969) and Rachman and Teasdale (1969) noted a lack of evidence that conditioned fear develops after employing shock as the aversive stimulus.

Figure 13.1 exemplifies the experimental paradigm on which all aversive therapeutic procedures are based. An animal is placed in a cage that has an electrifiable grid on its floor. Food has been dropped audibly into a food box within easy reach, and the animal has eaten it. With repetition he has acquired the habit of approaching the food box when he hears the sound of the food dropping into it. Appropriate autonomic responses accompany the approach — salivation, increased gastric motility, etc. Now, suppose that we decide to use aversion to eliminate that food-approach habit. One day, as the animal is approaching the food that he has heard drop, we pass a strong shock into his feet through the grid on the floor of the cage. The shock inhibits the conditioned approach. It produces pain, anxiety, and motor withdrawal. With each repetition, some weakening occurs of the food-approach habit, and at the same time, some conditioning of avoidance takes place. After several repetitions, the sound of food dropping into the food box evokes an avoidance response in place of the approach response to food.

The first therapeutic use of aversion seems to have been Kantorovich's (1929) treatment of alcoholic patients by painful electric shocks in contiguity with the sight, smell, and taste of alcohol. In 1935, L. W. Max reported overcoming a homosexual fetish by administering very strong shocks to the patient in the presence of the fetishistic object. Unfortunately, his promised detailed account of this historic case never found its way into

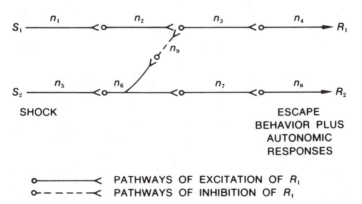

Fig. 13.1. S_1 is the stimulus to an undesired response (R_1), and S_2 a stimulus to an aversive response. When S_1 and S_2 are presented simultaneously, if S_2 is relatively strong, R_2 will be elicited, and R_1 inhibited by impulses from the inhibitory neurone, n_9. At the same time, S_1 will be conditioned to R_2 (pathway not shown).

print. Nevertheless, Max's report served to encourage others to repeat his procedure, and instigated my own first attempt, in South Africa, to treat a patient with it (Wolpe, 1954). The following is a summary of that case.

Case 46: Aversion Therapy of Food Craving

The patient was a 32-year-old woman who, among other neurotic problems, was preoccupied with warding off impulses to indulge in "eating sprees," impulses which invariably in a day or two proved irresistible. Her cravings involved two kinds of "forbidden" food—doughnuts and similar sweets, and salty foods. The former were disallowed because they made her fat (and she had a particular horror of obesity), and the latter because rheumatic heart disease had several times sent her into cardiac failure, so that a salt-limited diet had been prescribed. She would try to avoid these foods by various stratagems, such as not keeping them in her apartment, and getting her African servant to lock her in the apartment when he went off at night. But at times her impulse was so powerful that she would go out, buy food, and eat. As she went on gorging, she would have a rising feeling of disgust and despair that would culminate in a state of prostration.

I had her list all items of food that figured in her obsession, and selected an item from the list. I then attached electrodes to her forearm, told her to close her eyes and to signal by a hand movement each time she clearly formed the mental image of the selected food. At the signal, I passed a strong, brief shock into her forearm. Ten shocks were used at a session, employing a growing number of foods. After two sessions, she found that thinking of these foods at any time conjured up an image of the shock equipment, which produced anxiety. With further treatment, thoughts of the foods progressively decreased. After five sessions, she felt free of their burden for the first time in 16 years. She began to enjoy company and to buy clothes, which she had not done for years.

Aversion therapy has been applied to a considerable number of behavioral problems, including fetishism (Raymond, 1956), homosexuality (Freund, 1960; James, 1962; Feldman & MacCulloch, 1965), transvestism (Glynn & Harper, 1961; Blakemore, 1965), and the addictions—alcoholism, drug addiction, and smoking (McGuire & Vallance, 1964). A large number of clinical reports have been critically surveyed by Rachman and Teasdale (1968).

It is important to note that what is common to these problems is pleasurable experience with inappropriate objects, and that the approach behavior is motivated by this. Simultaneous aversive stimulation inhibits the pleasurable emotion and leads to the elimination of its habit. It is this that provides the answer to what Rachman and Teasdale (1968, p. xii) termed "a major puzzle" about aversion therapy—why patients refrain from their deviant behavior after they leave the hospital. If the object of deviation no longer arouses pleasure, there is no impulse to approach it.

Only occasionally is aversion the behavioral treatment of first choice. In many instances, the fetishistic or other undesirable behavior for which aversion therapy might be considered has a basis in neurotic anxiety, which should always be treated first. If the anxiety is eliminated, the behavior which is secondary to it may be expected to cease without requiring any special attention. On the other hand, if aversion therapy is mistakenly administered as the primary treatment of such a case, the "deviant" behavior will usually persist with little change; and even in those in which it is brought to a halt, the continued existence of the underlying anxiety provides a basis for relapse or symptom substitution. For example, I was once consulted about a woman whose compulsive eating had been overcome by aversion therapy but who had thereafter become severely depressed. It was soon apparent that her central problem was neurotic anxiety, and that the depression was the result of her having been deprived of what was for her the anxiety-reducing activity of eating.

DESCRIPTION OF TECHNIQUES

Electrical Stimulation

Because electrical stimulation has an unfavorable public image, it has in recent years been employed with great circumspection. It lends itself, however, to being easily quantified and precisely timed in relation to the behavior to be modified. Depending upon the circumstances of the case, one may administer the stimulus either in the presence of relevant objects or situations, or else in relation to evoked imagery or pictorial representations. Either faradic or alternating current should be used because these can, if necessary, be kept at steady levels for prolonged periods. The electrodes are usually attached to the patient's forearm. The baseline level of current is determined by gradually increasing it until the patient reports it to be distinctly unpleasant. The starting point for treatment is then usually a level that is about 25% stronger. A very satisfactory electrode is the concentric electrode (Tursky et al., 1965) which greatly minimizes the risk of burning the skin. Wet electrodes of saline-soaked gauze are also quite satisfactory. Ordinary electrocardiographic silver electrodes may be used if necessary. The aversive use of electrical stimulation varies in its details but always follows the general lines of the obsessional eating case described above.

Real stimuli have figured in the treatment of transvestism (Blakemore et al., 1963) and of compulsive gambling (Barker & Miller, 1968). One of the latters' patients had been gambling steadily on "fruit machines" for 12 years.

A machine borrowed from an inn was installed in the hospital. Shocks at about 70 volts were administered to the patient's forearm. While standing gambling continuously for 3 hours (his usual practice), he withstood a minimum of 150 shocks delivered by a third party at random to all stages of the gambling procedure from insertion of the discs to payout. He received 672 shocks altogether, designed to produce a tolerable degree of discomfort during 12 hours' gambling treatment, although he lost all desire to gamble after 6 hours. He did not resume gambling for 18 months, when, following a period of stress, he relapsed. Six hours' booster treatment, using the same technique, prevented further gambling for at least 6 months.

Feldman and MacCulloch (1965, p. 238) made extensive use of pictorial representations in their program for treating homosexuality. Rachman (1961) used both photographs and imagination in the treatment of a man who was sexually aroused by women's buttocks and underpants. His five aversive-conditioning sessions incorporated photographs of women in underpants and imagined scenes of underpants and of women with attractive buttocks. Electric stimuli were applied to the fingers 10 to 15 times for each stimulus at each session. After the final session, the patient said that he no longer felt attracted by buttocks, and disposed of his collection of pornographic photographs.

Abel, Levis, and Clancy (1970) reported an elaborate *goal-gradient in reverse* technique in which tape-recorded descriptions of behavior were used in the treatment of sexual deviations. In three cases of exhibitionism, two of transvestism, and one of masochism, tapes were made involving descriptions of each subject's individual deviant behavior divided into three sequential segments. Five of the six subjects were placed on a schedule on which, at first, the final segment of the tape was followed by shock, and at later sessions the second, and ultimately the first segment. At each session, the shocked tape runs were followed by runs in which the patient avoided shock by verbalizing normal sexual behavior in place of the deviant segment. The sixth subject was given shocks out of relation to taped material, as a control. Treatment was evaluated by measuring penile responses to sexually deviant and nondeviant tapes, clinical interviews, and behavior reports. In the experimental subjects there was reduction of erectile responses to deviant tapes, but sustained responses to nondeviant tapes. Deviant responses became weaker and less frequent, and the improvement was maintained at follow-up 18 weeks later.

A technique in which aversion apparently works through the juxtaposition of unconditioned and conditioned aversive responses with both exteroceptive and imaginally evoked cognitions was introduced by Feingold, (personal communication, 1966). His patient was a girl of 11 who persistently kept her mouth open and thus made it unfeasible for her dentist to perform certain necessary procedures. The girl and her parents were instructed to bring the therapist a record of each occasion on which her mouth was noticed to be open. Then, when she came to see him, she was given as many uncomfortable shocks to the leg as there were recorded occasions of open mouth. The number of shocks needed decreased from 48 to zero in the course of 12 sessions after which the mouth remained closed in a normal way, and the delighted dentist was able to proceed with his work. The following is my own solitary experience with this technique.

Case 47

Ron was a high-school junior who, despite high intelligence, was receiving low grades because he could not sit down to study in the evening. He felt he ought to be working between 7 and 11 p.m. He was asked to keep a record of his work each evening and was told that he would receive an unpleasant shock for each half-hour between 7 and 11 p.m. during which, in the course of the week, he did not work. At the end of the first week, he received four shocks; at the end of the second, three; after that no more were necessary. His report of improved work habits was supported by his mother's report of a rise in grades from C to A minus. It is presumed that the technique owned its efficacy to anxiety having become conditioned to the idea of not working.

With small portable shock equipment it is possible to plan aversive events in the life situation of the patient. There is no alternative to this when the target behavior cannot be evoked to order in the consulting room. For example, particular situations elicit rituals that cannot be conjured up by imagining the situations. The patient may inhibit a ritual by self-stimulation at the appropriate time. I had one case in which such self-stimulation was an effective interim measure in the treatment of kleptomania.

Use in Narcotic Addiction

The repetitive desire for narcotic drugs like morphine and meperidine (Demerol) depends on learned habits of autonomic response (Himmelsbach, 1941). Although the drug habit always includes motor acts, treatment that concentrates on motor acts without paying attention to autonomic events misses the essence of the problem. Once a narcotic habit has been established, the individual autonomic evocations that underlie the abstinence syndrome (or craving) must be in response to some antecedent stimulus. Antecedent stimuli to craving may be in the external environment (exteroceptive), or in a specific internal state (interoceptive), or both (e.g., Wikler, 1968). It is reasonable to suppose that the stimuli might be detached from the craving response by repeatedly inhibiting evocations of the latter — for example, by simultaneous electrical stimulation.

I had the opportunity to make a preliminary test of this supposition (Wolpe, 1965) in the treatment of a physician with a meperidine addiction of 5 years' standing. He had an apparently endogenously based craving for the drug, that arose about once a week and required 1,000 to 1,500 mg of the drug to allay it. By using a portable shocker, he was able to overcome three successive cravings separated by days, after which he remained abstinent for 12 weeks. Similar treatments, often more lastingly successful, were subsequently reported by Lesser (1967), Liberman (1968), and O'Brien, Raynes, and Patch (1972).

An experimental test (Wolpe, Groves, & Fischer, 1980) was made possible by the appearance on the scene of the narcotic antagonists (Jasinski et al., 1967). Intravenous injections of naloxone that were given to methadone-maintenance subjects induced craving reactions 30 to 45 minutes in duration. Continuous electric current was "titrated" against the craving in such a way as to diminish it, and was found with repetition to eliminate it. This happened with respect to increasing dosages of naloxone. As shown in figure 13.2, several subjects were eventually more or less symptom-free with doses of intravenous naloxone of the order of .65 mg—more than four times the initial dose. In no case, however, did we reach a point where a further increase of naloxone was totally unable to induce withdrawal reactions, but we went on to withdrawing methadone itself after learning from D. R. Jasinski (personal communication, 1976) that naloxone produces more powerful withdrawal effects than methadone withdrawal. Two out of three subjects experienced "painless" withdrawal from methadone. These were the only ones who had continued the treatment far enough for withdrawal to be feasible. We were at first puzzled by the general reluctance to continue treatment since it was not very uncomfortable and the subjects were reasonably well paid. We realized later that addicts really cherish their addictions and are not enthusiastic about overcoming them. The true key to the problem of narcotic addiction is to motivate participation in treatment.

Aversion Therapy by Drugs

The treatment of alcoholism by an aversion method based on the nauseating effects of drugs was introduced many years ago by Voegtlin and Lemere (1942) and has been the subject of many subsequent reports (e.g., Lemere & Voegtlin, 1950). It consists of giving the patient a nausea-producing drug, such as tartar emetic, emetine, apomorphine, or gold chloride, and then having him drink a favored alcoholic beverage. The combination of alcohol and emetic is given daily for a week to 10 days, after which the effectiveness of the procedure is tested by giving the patient alcohol alone. If there is sufficient conditioning, the very sight of alcohol will produce nausea. Booster treatments are given two or three times during the following year.

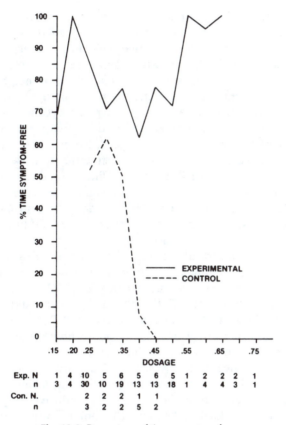

Exp. N	1	4	10	5	6	5	6	5	1	2	2	2	1
n	3	4	30	10	19	13	13	18	1	4	4	3	1
Con. N.			2	2	2	1	1						
n			3	2	2	5	2						

Fig. 13.2. Percentage of time symptom-free.

Lemere and Voegtlin (1950) found that 38% of 4,096 patients had remained abstinent for five years or longer and 23% for 10 years or longer after a course of treatment. The method is, however, extremely time consuming, tedious, and messy, and requires long-term accessibility of the patients. Applying it in private practice to about 12 patients in 1949, I found it so difficult and unrewarding that I gave it up in a few months.

Drug-induced aversion for a behavior problem was first reported by Raymond (1956). The patient was a 33-year-old man who had been arrested for acting out destructive fetishes toward perambulators (baby carriages) and handbags. The fetishistic acts gave him a pleasurable erotic sensation. For purposes of treatment, "a collection of handbags, perambulators, and colored illustrations was obtained and these were shown to the patient after he had received an injection of apomorphine and just before nausea was produced." Treatment was given every 2 hours, day and night. At the end of the first week, treatment was temporarily suspended and the patient was allowed to go home to attend to his affairs. Returning 8 days later to continue the treatment, he reported jubilantly that he had for the first time been able to have intercourse with his wife without the use of the old fantasies. His wife said that she had noticed a change in his attitude to her, but was unable to define it. Treatment was resumed, save that emetine hydrochloride was used whenever the emetic effect of apomorphine became less pronounced than its sedative effect. After several more days' treatment the patient said that the sight of the objects made him sick. Six months later, it was suggested that he have a booster course of treatment, to which he agreed although he did not consider it necessary. Nineteen months after the beginning of therapy, he stated that he had not again required the old fantasies to enable him to have sexual intercourse, nor had he masturbated with these fantasies. His wife said that she no longer worried about him and that their sexual relations had greatly improved.

Raymond carried out the above treatment under deprivation of food and rest, a condition that is almost certainly unnecessary, as Raymond himself later seemed to recognize (Raymond & O'Keefe, 1965). Its omission has not apparently marred the efforts of other therapists. Glynn and Harper (1961), Lavin et al. (1961), and Morganstern, Pearce, and Rees (1965) all successfully treated cases of transvestism with apomorphine, the last-named authors having entirely overcome the habit in seven of 13 cases.

Another physiologically acting group of aversive agents are curarelike drugs, such as succinylcholine (Scoline) (Sanderson, Campbell, & Laverty, 1963). These drugs, given in sufficient dosage, produce a temporary respiratory paralysis which, added to the patient's inability to speak or move in any way, is "a most terrifying experience." If alcohol is presented to the patient just at the height of his terror, a conditioned response of fear and aversion to the drug may be established. The initial effects of this heroic treatment were good but did not endure (Laverty, 1966). Of 12 cases treated in this way by Farrar, Powell, and Martin (1968), only two were abstinent at a one-year follow-up.

Covert Sensitization

Covert sensitization is the label Cautela (1966, 1967) has applied to the technique of pairing a verbally suggested aversive response with an imagined stimulus. It has been successful in a variety of conditions, notably obesity, homosexuality, and alcoholism. In the last-named condition, Ashem and Donner (1968) have recently noted that 6 out of 15 alcoholics were abstinent 6 months after this treatment in contrast to none in an untreated control group.

Cautela (1967) gives the following example of his instructions in relation to an obese patient in whom he wished to inhibit the eating of apple pie. The patient is relaxed and his eyes are shut:

> I want you to imagine you've just had your main meal and you are about to eat your dessert, which is apple pie. As you are about to reach for the fork, you get a funny feeling in the pit of your stomach. You start to feel queasy, nauseous, and sick all over. As you touch the fork, you can feel food particles inching up your throat. You're just about to vomit. As you put the fork into the pie, the food comes up into your mouth. You try to keep your mouth closed because you are afraid that you'll spit the food out all over the place. You bring the piece of pie to your mouth. As you're about to open your mouth, you puke; you vomit all over your hands, the fork, over the pie. It goes all over the table, over the other peoples' food. Your eyes are watering. Snot and mucous are all over your mouth and nose. Your hands feel sticky. There is an awful smell. As you look at this mess you just can't help but vomit again and again until just watery stuff is coming out. Everybody is looking at you with shocked expressions. You turn away from the food and immediately start to feel better. You run out of the room and, as you run out, you feel better and better. You wash and clean yourself up, and it feels wonderful.

It seems that the first report of the systematic use of aversion-evoking imagery was by Gold and Neufeld (1965), who used repulsive male images to overcome a 16-year-old boy's habit of soliciting men in public toilets. Davison (1967) used covert sensitization as part of a program to eliminate a sadistic fantasy. Kolvin (1967) used it to treat a fetish and an addiction to the sniffing of gasoline.

Other Aversive Agents

Anything that is unpleasant is a potential source of aversive conditioning. Philpott (personal communication, 1967) claimed to overcome obsessional thinking by getting a patient to hold her breath as long as possible each time an obsessional thought obtruded itself. Lublin (1968) has described two aversive inhalation techniques for the smoking habit. One consists of puffing stale warm cigarette smoke from a machine into the face of the subject who is smoking a cigarette. In the other, the subject has to puff regularly at a cigarette, in time to the ticking of a metronome, inhaling every 6 seconds on the first cigarette and then puffing without inhaling every 3 seconds on a second cigarette. (This strikes a familiar chord. Parents have for generations done something like this to make their children desist from smoking.) They state that both methods are very aversive; hardly any subject ever finished a whole cigarette. Of 36 patients who had an average of six 1/2 hour sessions, 16 stopped smoking completely; and all of these are reported to have stayed off cigarettes, some for as long as a year. However, none of the proffered antismoking treatments is really satisfactory. For a comprehensive review and bibliography see Orleans et al. (1981a, 1981b).

In 1956, I treated two cases of obesity by approximating a vile-smelling solution of asafetida to their nostrils while they were handling, smelling, and tasting attractive items of food. (Both of these patients also received reciprocal inhibition therapy for interpersonal anxieties to which they responded well.) Temporary control of overeating was achieved in one, and lasting control in the other who in 1965 still had a sylphlike figure. Kennedy and Foreyt (1968) described a very similar procedure using more sophisticated equipment to deliver noxious butyric acid gas.

Other physical stimuli that have been used for purposes of aversive conditioning are intense illumination and white noise. White noise was successfully employed in an unusual and interesting fashion by Philpott (personal communication, 1964) in a case that I referred to him. The patient was a 30-year-old woman who for 15 years had an extreme sensitivity to a variety of sharp sounds, such as bells, the jangling of keys, and a hammer on metal. Apart from the set of reactions, no unadaptive responses whatever were revealed in the analysis of her behavior. What Philpott did was feed white noise at high intensity to her ears through earphones while he jangled a bunch of keys before her eyes. Thus, while she saw the moving keys, their sound was completely masked by the white noise. The subject's hyperacusis was entirely overcome by this treatment. A follow-up inquiry in 1967 revealed that she had remained well and experienced no recurrence of this affliction.

Serber (1970) reported the use of shame as an aversive agent for cases of transvestism, voyeurism, pedophilia, and exhibitionism. The subject necessarily had to be embarrassed at performing his deviant act in front of witnesses. He was made to perform it for 15 to 35 minutes in the presence of increasing numbers of observers. A voyeur, for example, would be placed on the observer side of a one-way mirror to look at someone undressing behind a mirror, while observers in an adjoining room would openly observe the patient observing. Though five of the seven patients whom Serber treated were free of the deviant behavior at a 6-month follow-up, most of them later relapsed.

The reader who wishes to inquire more fully into theoretical and experimental studies of avoidance behavior should consult the work of Church (1963), Solomon (1964), Azrin and Holz (1966), Rachman and Teasdale (1968, 1969), and Campbell and Church (1969). However, it should be noted that all these authors' discussions relate to the punishment paradigm whereas, as we have noted, aversion therapy depends on reciprocal inhibition of a target response by the aversive agent.

The following practical guidelines for aversion therapy in emotionally based habits are derived and adapted from those provided by Azrin and Holz (1966) for the different purpose of eliminating motor habits by punishment:

1. The stimulus should be as intense as necessary in order to block the pleasurable response totally.
2. The aversive stimulus should be delivered contemporaneously with the response.
3. The aversive stimulus should not be increased gradually, but introduced at a previously determined high intensity.
4. The frequency of administration should be as high as possible; ideally, the stimulus should be given with every evocation of the response to be eliminated.

PART IV

COMPLEX NEUROSES

14
Complex Syndromes
With Overt Anxiety

A central argument of this book is that since neuroses are individual problems and many are complex, rational treatment depends on analysis of the dynamics of the individual case. Certain categories of complexity require special consideration. They can be logically divided into cases with prominent overt anxiety and those in which responses secondary to anxiety dominate the clinical picture.

We will consider four complex syndromes characterized by overt anxiety—agoraphobia, panic disorder, free-floating anxiety (the neurotic category of generalized anxiety disorder), and post-traumatic stress disorder.

AGORAPHOBIA

What defines a case of agoraphobia is that the patient responds with anxiety to physical distance from a place of safety or to the relative inaccessibility of a "safe" person—in some instances to both. But cases vary markedly in their stimulus-response structure and therefore so must treatments. The diversity is almost universally ignored in present-day discussions. For example, even though Barlow (1979) deplored the practice of offering package treatments for neuroses, his recent (1988) standpoint assumes homogeneity in syndromes such as agoraphobia, and this leads naturally to packages. The general adoption of the uniformity assumption has generated a consensus that the treatment of choice for agoraphobia is exposure therapy, which consists of systematically exposing the patient to increasing distances from a zone of safety. While this is suitable for many cases that consist of classically conditioned fear of separation, in many others it is not appropriate. For example, the patient's fear may be cognitively based; he may be afraid of going afield because he interprets symptoms such as light-headedness as indicative of incipient insanity. It is the misconception that must then be treated (see case 48). Or the patient may infer a heart attack whenever he feels a certain pain in the chest, and the more the patient feels removed from possible help, the more anxious he becomes. The agoraphobia is thus secondary to a hypochondriacal neurosis on which treatment should focus. Somewhat related are cases based on a fear of panic attacks (discussed in the second part of this chapter). In yet other cases, the fear is of what might be encountered in the outside world—crazy people or physical assault (one patient was afraid of roughly dressed people). This is parallel to the school phobic who fears something at school (in contrast to one who fears leaving home).

Of great interest is a group of agoraphobics whose fear of geographic separation is a function of fear of isolation, in the sense of being left to fend on their own. Most often, these are unhappily married women who are low in self-sufficiency (chapter 5). If a woman with normal self-sufficiency is dissatisfied with her husband and her endeavors to change him or to find an accommodation have failed, she is able to consider divorce or separation. The woman with low self-sufficiency does not do so because the idea of being on her own is too threatening. Even with a strong desire to leave her husband, the projected consequences of leaving make it too frightening to translate into action. In some cases, fear of being physically alone appears to be a simple generalization from the fear of the aloneness implied in the wished-for separation.

Occasionally, these cases give a history of separation fantasies in which despite aspects of satisfaction, there is a fearfulness that grows with repetition. In all cases, there is anxiety generated by avoidance-avoidance conflict: aversion to the marriage, and simultaneous aversion to the projected consequences of leaving it. Despite their complex social causation, some agoraphobias of this group respond quite well to flooding treatment. But treatment cannot be regarded as complete until the social and other related anxieties are overcome. Sometimes, as in case 49, the agoraphobia is entirely a function of marital conflict, whose successful treatment resolves the agoraphobia without any other action being needed.

It is necessary to distinguish certain cases that might be labeled *pseudoagoraphobia*. The patient is fearful of excursions because of a physical illness that puts him or her into real danger from time to time, more or less unpredictably. Such fear, clearly, is adaptive and not neurotic. For example, a 48-year-old man had been labeled agoraphobic by a number of therapists over 11 years, though his attacks had no relation to separation from home or to any other known environmental factor. Investigation revealed that he was subject to epileptic seizures, and was afraid to go out because he appropriately felt endangered by losing consciousness. Case 50 is a case of agoraphobia based on Meniére's disease.

The variety of agoraphobic structures in the foregoing paragraphs makes nonsense of the uniformity theory, and of the claim that such and such is "the best" treatment for agoraphobia. The following cases illustrate common variants of agoraphobia. The use of flooding seems clearly out of keeping for any of them. (See also case 37, p. 207).

Case 48: Agoraphobia Due Primarily to Cognitively Based Fear of Insanity

In the case to be described a classically conditioned fear of separation had developed secondarily to a cognitively based fear of insanity. It was not possible to overcome the agoraphobia as long as the primary fear existed. Miss G., age 23, had had that fear for 6 years, following two attacks of anxiety within a fortnight, each set off by a feeling of desperation at the thought that she was so fat that nobody would ever marry her. Because each time she had trembled uncontrollably and had had a feeling of numbness in her head and a sense of unreality, she had decided that she must be losing her mind. She became preoccupied with this idea, which fed upon itself by eliciting the trembling and other symptoms, especially when she was alone.

She had obtained some relief from tranquilizers, but psychiatric treatment of several kinds had been almost useless. A behaviorally oriented therapist had attempted desensitization and given her "walking assignments," without effect. Since it seemed to me that the physiological symptoms might well be due to hyperventilation, I had her hyperventilate, which produced the symptoms within a minute. This enabled me to convince her that the dreaded symptoms were caused by overbreathing, for example, by sighing, and thus we were able to overcome her fear of losing her sanity. I also showed her how to check these symptoms by shutting her mouth. It was thereafter possible to begin a program of progressively longer journeys on her own to overcome the conditioned fear of separation. It is very unlikely that that program alone would have overcome the agoraphobia, as the previous therapist had attempted to do.

Case 49: Agoraphobia Based on Marital Conflict

In this kind of agoraphobia, one must first work on the marriage, to try to make it satisfactory if possible, and, if not possible, to end it. Whatever happens to the marriage, the treatment of the case cannot be regarded as complete until the patient has also overcome her fear of being alone, which can usually be accomplished by a combination of assertiveness training and systematic desensitization. Frequently, it is the success of such measures that enables the patient to leave her husband.

Mrs. R. was a 26-year-old housewife who had suffered from agoraphobia for 8 years. At the age 14, she had married a man who treated her with scorn and indifference and whom she hated. She wanted to leave him, but could not. Not only was her self-sufficiency extremely low (Bernreuter Self-Sufficiency 13), but she was a Catholic and had five children. She was fearful of going out alone, even for a few blocks. The history provided unusually clear evidence of the relevance of the marriage to the agoraphobia. About 3 years before I first saw her, Mrs. R. had seen a man to whom she felt strongly attracted. She had gone to live with him for a month in another city and during this time had been able to go out on her own for any distance without the least discomfort. When she returned to her husband, the agoraphobia reappeared in full force.

After a variety of efforts made it obvious that there was no chance of improving the marriage, my foremost objective became to enable her to make a break from her husband. I trained her in self-assertion while desensitizing her in other areas of social anxiety. After 8 months, during which I saw her (in front of a professional group) once every 2 weeks, she felt ready for a temporary separation. She went to stay with a friend for 2 weeks. In the first week, the agoraphobia gradually faded, and she was completely free of it in the second week. When she returned home in order to satisfy the legal requirements for a separation, there was no recurrence of the agoraphobia because she now felt detached and free from her husband; and the thought of being alone was no longer threatening. She continued to put up with him for several more months until legal separation, and later divorced him. Three years later she was still free from agoraphobia.

Case 50: Pseudoagoraphobia Due to a Medical Illness

Mrs. B., a 31-year-old married woman, was referred for treatment by a psychiatrist in Connecticut for agoraphobia after a year of unsuccessful psychodynamic therapy. She had asked him if there was any alternative.

When I saw her, she complained, in addition to agoraphobia, of numerous interpersonal anxieties, reflected in a Willoughby score of 66. She said that the agoraphobia was characterized by shortness of breath and dizziness. These attacks had begun 7 years previously and were becoming worse. Mrs. B. stated that the only benefit of her previous psychiatric therapy was that she recognized her fears and was able to tell people about them. For various practical reasons, I decided to treat her as an inpatient, which facilitated our having one or more interviews each day. After the usual preliminaries, I began a program of systematic desensitization on the theme of separation from home while also deconditioning her to social fears, such as of others displaying anger. She made a considerable amount of progress, and after the 14th session, remarked that she was finding it so pleasant to walk down the long passage to my office that she was finding herself singing. The agoraphobia progressed to the extent that she was able to walk a distance of 20 blocks comfortably.

One day she arrived at my office reporting a severe "agoraphobic" attack that morning in the ward where she had been feeling perfectly calm and unworried. I decided that this warranted sending her to the Department of Internal Medicine for a full investigation. As nothing significant emerged, I next sent her to a neurologist who diagnosed Meniere's disease. She responded to medication, and in the course of the next 2 months her agoraphobia faded out completely without any further behavioral treatment. Treatment of social anxieties was continued in her home town.

Outcome Research on Agoraphobia

Outcome research on agoraphobia affords an illustration of the confusion that has resulted from the assumption of structural uniformity of cases, which pervades both therapy and research: this assumption is the reality, despite statements to the effect that there should be individually tailored treatment programs for unique problems in different clients (O'Leary & Wilson, 1975, p. 22). The general incognizance of individual dynamics is revealed in the presently accepted approach to agoraphobia (e.g., O'Brien & Barlow, 1984; Michelson, 1987). Even the recent conscientious assessment prescribed by Barlow (1988, p. 372) presupposes a basic uniformity of cases. Comparative outcome studies require of subjects only that they have agoraphobia of a certain duration and severity and conform to certain demographic criteria. The subjects are then randomly assigned to Treatment A and Treatment B, without attention to individual differences, because, the therapist is oblivious of the existence of differences. With vision thus restricted, he subscribed to the consensus that exposure therapy is the best treatment for agoraphobia.

It is not surprising in view of the agoraphobic diversity outlined above that the treatment results are not impressive. Wilson (1984, p. 94) states that behavior therapists are "well aware of the limitations" of these methods reflected in the Barlow, O'Brien, Last, and Holden (1983) estimate that "roughly 25% of agoraphobics fail to benefit from exposure treatment." Of the remaining 75%, many make only limited improvements, and few ever reach the stage where they are completely free of at least periodic anxiety symptoms. These estimates are in line with observations of Agras (1985), Barlow (1988, p. 409), and Jacobson, Wilson, and Tupper (1988).

Wilson is appropriately distressed by these unsatisfactory results. The solution that occurs to him is to have more techniques, to "broaden the treatment base." He notes Goldstein's (1982) considerably greater success in a program that included daily travel groups, group psychotherapy sessions, "significant other" groups, couples group sessions, and individual sessions. The addition of the treatment of social anxieties evidently made the difference. Goldstein applied these social measures across the board. If he had had the benefit of behavior analyses, he could have tailored his treatment to the needs of individuals and obtained still better results.

That better results can be expected from matching treatment to case dynamics is indicated by the outcome of 20 cases of agoraphobia that I treated between 1981 and 1989. Eight were apparently cured, eight were at least 80% improved, and four moderately improved — in respect not only of the agoraphobia, but also of the total spectrum of neurotic anxieties indicated by the Fear Survey Schedule. Two of the four moderately improved patients would probably have done substantially better if the recently developed schedule for treating panic disorder described below had been available.

PANIC DISORDER

The currently accepted definition of panic disorder is in the DSM-III-R whose essence can be stated in two sentences. "Panic disorder is characterized by recurrent, sometimes unpredictable, panic attacks. A panic attack consists of intense apprehension, fear and discomfort of sudden onset, and with no immediately determinable cause." Panic attacks contrast on the one hand with focal anxiety reactions, and on the other hand with generalized anxiety (DSM-III-R, 1987), discussed later in this chapter.

The most widely pervasive view of panic attacks rests on the assumption that they all have a single etiology. An influential version of this view is that the attacks result from adrenergic discharges that are somehow linked to an abnormality of lactate metabolism that affects the central nervous system (Sheehan, 1982; Sheehan & Sheehan, 1983). This theory rests heavily on the belief that panic disorder can be fundamentally overcome by tricyclic antidepressants, especially imipramine (Garakani, Zitrin, & Klein, 1984; Mavissakalian, Michelson, & Dealy, 1983; Zitrin, Klein, & Woerner, 1978, 1980; Zitrin, Klein, Woerner, & Ross, 1983). However, the causal relevance of this treatment is greatly diminished by the fact that clinical improvement is maintained only as long as the drug remains in the patient's body; relapse is usual upon cessation of its use — 86% of patients relapse within 3 months of discontinuing the drug (Sheehan, 1982). Thus, the relief is only symptomatic.

Panic attacks are broadly divisible into initial attacks and the recurrent attacks that make up "panic disorder." The initial attack may be either biologically or psychologically based, but its very occurrence usually changes the person so as to make him susceptible to recurrent attacks. The nature of the change is explained below.

The Causes of First Panic Attacks

A variety of causes, biological or psychological, may precipitate first panic attacks.

Organic Causes of the First Panic

Organic causes of panic, though various and quite common, are rarely mentioned, partly, it seems, because of the preoccupation with a single causation. Drugs, such as amphetamines, cannabis, cocaine, and LSD, can generate anxiety; and can occasionally precipitate panic (e.g., Hofmann, 1963; Hollister, 1969). A considerable number of cases are initiated during the induction of general anesthesia. Anxiety amounting to panic can also follow the withdrawal of certain drugs, such as alcohol, antidepressants, barbiturates, and benzodiazepines. (For an extensive list of drugs that can elicit anxiety and possible panic, see Slaby, 1983.)

Highly toxic solvents are reported to have caused panic attacks in three individuals (Dager, Holland, Cowley, & Dunner, 1987). Within a few weeks of the initial attack, the subjects had secondary panics provoked by olfactory cues that were present in the original situation. They also had some attacks without any extraneous precipitants. These were presumably due to endogenous stimuli.

Some medical conditions that can cause panic attacks are hyperthyroidism, hypoglycemia, pheochromocytoma (a catecholamine-producing tumor), and temporal lobe epilepsy (partial complex seizures) (see Harrison, 1987). On the other hand, there is no good evidence of a causal link between panic attacks and mitral valve prolapse (Crowe, Pauls, Kerber, & Noyes, 1980; Matuzas, Al-Sadir, Uhlenhuth, & Glass, 1987).

Psychological Causes of the First Panic

In the great majority of cases of panic, the first attack is initiated by psychological events. The attack is a climactic consequence of anxiety that is unusually high or prolonged. Even when the attack seems to come "out of the blue," careful investigation, with the help of the Willoughby Personality Schedule and the Fear Survey Schedule (Wolpe, 1982), will usually reveal undercurrents of specific anxieties. A frequent history in the first attack is of a habitually anxious and hypersensitive person who has been going through severe personal stress and who is subjected to an additional stress — which may even be from a source to which stress is appropriate, such as driving a car alone at night on an expressway.

In actuality, the first attack can develop out of a variety of stressful circumstances, as the following case illustrates. A 36-year-old married nurse gave a 3-year history of panic attacks. She had been anxious since childhood in groups and in the presence of strangers. During the 6 months before her first panic she was in a continuous state of anxiety because of complications of a miscarriage. The panic attack occurred when, against this background of anxiety, she was exposed to severe stress one evening when entertaining some of her husband's business associates. She had always been very apprehensive about this kind of event because of the "danger" that she might fail to be the "the perfect hostess." On this occasion she felt that she was performing particularly poorly. The anxiety this occasioned summated with that already present to produce a severe panic reaction. Thereafter, she suffered recurrent panic attacks and was diagnosed as having panic disorder. There was also an increase in her sensitivity to inferred social disapproval.

In general, the likelihood of a panic attack is greater in a person with a large reservoir of anxieties. The population among whom spontaneous panic attacks occur is notable for a high incidence of stressful life circumstances, such as marital or family problems, or the death or illness of a significant other (Chambless & Goldstein, 1981; Finlay-Jones & Brown, 1981). Kleiner and Marshall (1987) found that 84% of agoraphobics with panic attacks had experienced severe marital and relationship conflicts in the year preceding the onset of the panic attacks. From interviews with 404 agoraphobics, Doctor (1982) concluded that the most common events associated with panic attacks were separation and loss (30%), relationship problems (30%), and new responsibility (20%). A similar analysis by Last, Barlow, and O'Brien (1984) of 58 agoraphobics revealed that interpersonal conflict, death or illness of a significant other, and drug reactions were relevant to over 60% of initiations of panic anxiety.

The Causal Role of Hyperventilation

It was long believed that panic was simply a burgeoning of anxiety to a very high level of intensity. But Craske and Barlow (1989) and Ley (1987) found that high levels of anxiety may not lead to panic. Something more than linear anxiety is implicated. Ley (1985b, 1987) and Clark (1986) have persuasively argued that the "something more" resides in the physiological effects of hyperventilation. Many people hyperventilate when they have anxiety. In some, relatively small degrees of hyperventilation elicit such symptoms as dizziness, shortness of breath, and tingling of the extremities. If the symptoms are weak, the individual may ignore or discount them. If the symptoms intensify to include palpitations, dyspnea, dizziness, and trembling, a panic attack may be triggered. The question is, how does this happen?

A prior question concerns the temporal relation between the sensations produced by hyperventilation and the onset of panic. The evidence points clearly to panic *following* the onset of bodily sensations (Craske & Barlow, 1989; Ley, 1985a). Of 10 cases in whom Ley (1985b) investigated the sequential events leading to panic, eight reported experiencing dyspnea and palpitations *in advance* of the full-blown panic attack. This accords with the finding that in a great majority of cases, the symptoms produced by voluntary hyperventilation are perceived by the subject as similar to those that precede spontaneous panic attacks (Garssen, van Veenendaal, & Bloemink, 1983). When panic subjects are instructed to hyperventilate and to observe their bodily sensations, they often stop or protest fairly early in the procedure because they are either unable or unwilling to tolerate the growing intensity of aversive sensations.

Misattribution Theory—A Blind Alley

Ley (1985a) and Clark (1986) proposed that the symptoms due to hyperventilation elicit panic in individuals who are predisposed to give catastrophic misattributions to them, seeing them as premonitory of death, loss of consciousness, or insanity.

The misattribution hypothesis has an outward plausibility and has been widely accepted. It is, however, superimposed on the facts and not derived from the reports of patients. The literature reveals that patients are almost never questioned about the details of their experiences in the moments preceding panic attacks. There is thus no testamentary basis for the assertion that a "catastrophic thought" is the trigger to panic. The evidence of a preliminary exploration of those moments by Wolpe and Rowan (1988) is clearly to the contrary (see below). To the same effect is the observation, in a searching study by Rachman, Levitt, and Lopatka (1987), that some panic attacks are unaccompanied by fearful cognitions.

There are also other facts that conflict with misattribution theory. First, if that theory were true, panic and panic disorder would also result from other circumstances of dire threat. Panic disorder would be found in people who have been saved from firing squads or inevitable air crashes, or who have had massive coronary thromboses. But this does not seem to happen. Second, panic attacks do not yield to corrective information, as do fears that are indisputably based on mistaken beliefs. For example, a person with an insistent pain in his chest is terrified because he attributes it to heart disease. When his physician, having properly investigated the case, informs him that his heart is normal, there is usually an end to the anxiety. By contrast, the most authoritative *verbal* assurances that panic will not culminate in death or insanity are incomparably less effective in diminishing the liability to panic disorder. In the face of this array of disconfirmations, misattribution theory cannot be maintained.

A Pilot Study of the Antecedents of Panic

The failure of investigators to pay attention to the sequences of people's experiences at the time of the first panic prompted Wolpe and Rowan (1988) to do a pilot study on as many subjects as could be found for questioning. The details were easy to elicit even when there had been a lapse of a good many years — precisely because the first panic is an unforgettably vivid experience.

In each of 10 subjects, the age at the initial panic attack was determined and the sequence of experiences at the time carefully traced. The reports of the subjects were different in detail, but similar in essence (see Table 14.1). In each one there was a clear-cut prepanic experience, whose various components included dizziness, palpitations, sweating, and total helplessness. It was followed by panic, which usually lasted from one to several minutes. There was usually, *secondarily*, a feeling of threat to life or mind. Later attacks were dreaded, not because of implications of death or insanity, but first and foremost because they were "a terrible experience," and only secondarily (and not in all cases) because they cued thoughts of impending death or loss of sanity.

Unconditioned Panic Response to Physiological Disturbance and the Conditioning of Panic Disorder

The following account by Wolpe and Rowan (1988) of the basis of the initial panic, and of the subsequent development of panic disorder, is in keeping with the facts considered above. It is proposed that the first panic is an unconditioned response to a disturbing set of physiological events caused by hyperventilation, and that panic disorder is due to the conditioning of the evoked anxiety to contiguous stimuli.

The first panic, whether due to hyperventilation or to a biochemical cause, is an unprecedented, excruciating experience that no person would ever want to have repeated. In most cases, the train of events begins with a combination of strange and unpleasant sensations for which hyperventilation is responsible and which precipitate unexampled levels of anxiety. The full-blown panic syndrome is experienced as an amalgam of hyperventilation symptoms and panic. There are usually also fears of insanity or death, but these arise afterward — perhaps as attempts by the subject to rationalize what has happened to him.

Table 14.1. First Panic Experience

PATIENT	AGE AT FIRST PANIC	SEX	SUBJECTIVE SEQUENCE AT FIRST PANIC
1. B. E.	21	F	1. Nausea, feeling unreal, palpitations 2. Extreme panic 3. Felt like going crazy
2. Y. L.	35	F	1. Dizziness, unsteadiness shortness of breath, incipient blackout 2. Extreme panic 3. Fear of dying; fear of going crazy
3. P. D.	28	F	1. Palpitations, faintness, dyspnea 2. Extreme panic 3. Going crazy
4. J. D.	12	F	1. Shortness of breath, nausea, desire to flee 2. Marked panic 3. Confusion and puzzlement
5. L. L.	24	F	1. Strange sensations, feeling of unreality 2. Extreme panic 3. "I must be going insane"
6. N. G.	22	F	1. Palpitations, helplessness 2. Extreme panic 3. "I think I'm dying"
7. A. W.	39	F	1. Faintness, dizziness and weakness 2. Extreme panic 3. Ideas of disintegrating— "cracking up"
8. S. E.	35	F	1. Dizziness, tachycardia 2. Marked panic 3. Losing control, losing consciousness
9. E. G.	36	M	1. Rapid pulse, marked sweating, difficulty in breathing 2. Extreme panic 3. Fear of going crazy
10. B. G.	22	F	1. Trembling, palpitations, hot flashes 2. Marked panic 3. Losing control

Note: The numbers in the right column indicate the order of appearance of the symptoms named. The first symptoms were often swiftly merged with the panic, but "catastrophic cognitions" were always decisively third.

Hyperventilation, if severe, produces an unusual and sometimes bizarre combination of physiological responses; it is apparently to these that high anxiety (panic) is an unconditioned response. This is not without experimental precedents. For example, high anxiety is an unconditioned response to strong electrical stimulation (Masserman, 1943; Pavlov, 1941; Wolpe, 1952) and just as anxiety thus elicited becomes conditioned to contiguous stimuli to produce the manifestations of experimental neurosis (Wolpe, 1952), so may panic anxiety become conditioned to contiguous stimuli to produce panic disorder. In the latter case, however, the most potent of the conditionings are to endogenous stimuli.

The sequence of events that generate panic disorder is depicted in figure 14.1. The vulnerability to further panic attacks is a function of the range of stimuli to which anxiety has been conditioned. The conditioning can involve exogenous as well as endogenous stimuli. Conditioning to low intensity consequences of hyperventilation is a possible basis for the occurrence of so-called unprovoked panics, that is, panics that seem to occur without preliminary symptoms.

The success of the deconditioning measures outlined below is in accord with the conditioning theory of panic disorder. The anxiety responses to the endogenous stimuli that are the main antecedents of recurrent panics can be diminished either by a gradual desensitizing procedure or by a flooding procedure. In either case, inhalations of carbon dioxide can be used to reproduce the relevant endogenous stimuli (for background details, see Wolpe, 1987).

The Treatment of Panic

Our outline of treatments is limited to those known to control or eliminate panic attacks. The first aim of treatment is to abort the attack, the eventual aim is to prevent recurrences. As with all other syndromes having diverse etiologies, the therapist must in each case be guided by knowledge of its causation. In those instances in which the panic is associated with an organic state of affairs such as hyperthyroidism or temporal lobe epilepsy, the indicated course is the treatment of the underlying pathology.

Panic disorder begins with a panic attack that may be due to a biological state, a toxic substance (Dager et al., 1987), or, most often, the physiological disturbance produced by extreme hyperventilation. The recurrent attacks are elicited by endogenous conditioned stimuli, but exogenous precipitation is not infrequent. To treat recurrent panics, a number of behavioral techniques are available: (a) methods that prevent hyperventilation; (b) the elimination of the maladaptive anxieties that are the cause of hyperventilation, and (c) in some cases the deconditioning of anxiety as a response to hyperventilation-induced stimuli.

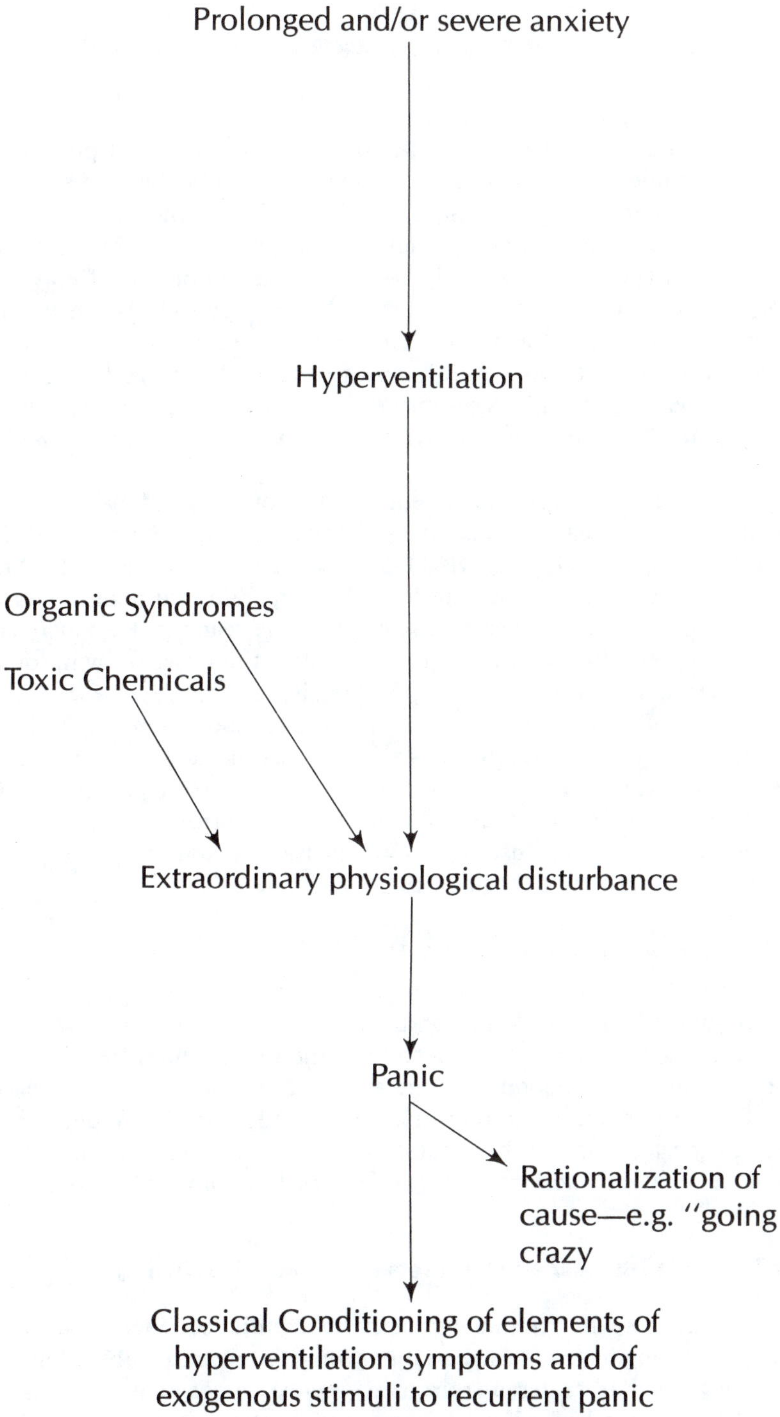

Prolonged and/or severe anxiety

↓

Hyperventilation

Organic Syndromes

Toxic Chemicals

Extraordinary physiological disturbance

↓

Panic

Rationalization of
cause—e.g. "going
crazy

Classical Conditioning of elements of
hyperventilation symptoms and of
exogenous stimuli to recurrent panic

Fig. 14.1. Flowchart of development of panic disorders.

Prevention of Hyperventilation

This procedure, which we use in almost every case, has been prescribed for recurrent panic attacks by Clark, Salkovskis, and Chalkley (1985), Ley (1985a), and Rapee (1985). It comprises two steps. The first is to demonstrate to the patient that hyperventilation produces symptoms like those that precede panic attacks. This is done by having the patient breathe deeply and rapidly, about once per second, being timed with a stopwatch. Whenever the patient becomes aware of the onset or increase of a sensation he or she is to interrupt the hyperventilation briefly and report it — "I am getting dizzy," "My heart is beating faster," "My dizziness is increasing." Hyperventilation continues until the patient reports symptoms that he or she recognizes as precursors of panic.

The second step is to show the patient how to stop hyperventilating at the first awareness of the earliest anxiety symptoms. We have mainly used the simple method described by Lewis (1959), based on the observation that most people are unable to hyperventilate when breathing through the nose. Patients are enormously relieved to discover that they can block an incipient panic attack by keeping the mouth firmly shut at the onset of symptoms. Breathing retraining methods (Clark, Salkovkis, & Chalkley, 1985; Lum, 1981) are probably equally effective. Clark et al. found among 19 patients that for most, breathing retraining was all that was necessary to put a stop to recurrent panic attacks. However, the treatment of a person suffering from maladaptive anxieties is incomplete if it stops at the control of panic attacks. Comprehensive treatment must also overcome the maladaptive anxiety that provided the foundation of the panic in the first place.

The Elimination of Maladaptive Anxiety-response Habits

Panic-inducing hyperventilation probably never occurs in the absence of maladaptive anxiety. An essential element in the fundamental treatment of panic is therefore the overcoming of the anxiety-response habits that are the source of the hyperventilation (Guttmacher & Nelles, 1984; Wolpe, 1982). As is to be expected some of these habits are classically conditioned, others are cognitively based. Their treatment is described in chapters 7 to 10.

Case 51: Panic Disorder and Its Roots in Maladaptive Anxiety

The following case illustrates a common therapeutic sequence. A 40-year-old man gave a long history of maladaptive anxiety-response habits. During the last 7 years he had suffered from panic attacks at irregular intervals. A variety of treatments had effected improvements that were always short-lived. At the end of his second interview he was asked to hyperventilate, and in the course of 90 seconds, reported tachycardia, dizziness, jumpiness, and anxiety, which he recognized as the feelings that preceded spontaneous panic attacks. He was shown how to prevent hyperventilation by keeping his mouth shut. At his third interview, 9 days later, he said that the mouth-shutting technique had greatly decreased his panic attacks. He was, however, subject to numerous maladaptive anxiety responses — notably to lightning, insects, any suggestion of personal illness, and news of the death of other people, especially those close to him in age. Exposure to any of these led to incipient hyperventilation — which happened several times a day. Accordingly, his fears were treated by systematic desensitization and, in some contexts, cognitive correction. After 5 months of weekly sessions, maladaptive anxiety was greatly diminished and there was correspondingly less hyperventilation, so that he hardly ever needed to make use of control of breathing. At follow-up, 6 months later, he felt well and had extended his gains. He had had no further panic attacks.

Extinguishing the Anxiety Response to the Physiological Effects of Hyperventilation

Learning to prevent hyperventilation by breathing control is basically an avoidance strategy — like treating a fear of harmless snakes by having the patient confine himself to a large city. The strategy may work well enough but it leaves the conditioned sensitivity unchanged, and it may need to be practiced indefinitely. It also leaves the subject vulnerable to the effects of hyperventilation that may result from a nonemotional activity such as heavy physical exercise.

To overcome this vulnerability, inhalations of carbon dioxide mixed with oxygen can be used to elicit responses that are similar to those of hyperventilation. The preferred method amounts to an in vivo desensitization (Wolpe, 1987). The patient inhales, from an open mask held about 1 inch from his face, a mixture of carbon dioxide and oxygen, which gradually induces hyperventilation. When the first disturbing symptoms appear, the administration is stopped. With repetition, these initial symptoms cease to be frightening. Then, progressively stronger evocations of symptoms are similarly treated until the patient eventually tolerates maximal symptoms without fear.

An alternative, described by Griez and van den Hout (1983), is to treat panic reactions on a flooding paradigm. The patient takes full inhalations of a mixture of 35% carbon dioxide and 65% oxygen several times during each of 10 daily sessions. In the first few trials he has severe panic attacks. With repetition, the reactions progressively decline. Griez and van den Hout (1986) compared this treatment with propranolol in 13 patients with panic attacks and found that the frequency of spontaneous attacks decreased by 50% with the carbon dioxide mixture and by 38% with propranolol. It is likely that the more gradual use of carbon dioxide described above is less prone to failure as well as being less stressful.

Discussion

The centerpoint of the theory of panic disorder presented here is the realization that the first panic attack is a high intensity unconditioned response to certain physiological events—most commonly the consequences of excessive hyperventilation. The strongest support for this view lies in the finding that panic follows the awareness of sensations attributable to hyperventilation. Most of the 10 subjects reported by Wolpe and Rowan (1988) had thoughts of dying, fainting, or going insane, but these thoughts always came *after* the onset of panic and therefore could not have caused it. The fear of later attacks was mainly a fear of recurrences of the terrible panic experience. Presumed catastrophic consequences were in mind secondarily if at all.

The learning of susceptibility to panic attacks (panic disorder) is parallel to early fear learning in children, which consists of first-order conditioning of stimuli to the autonomic responses to pain, as first shown by Ribot (1903). Other stimuli that also elicit unconditioned autonomic responses of the fear pattern are sudden loss of support (Watson, 1970, p. 153), strong auditory stimulation (Watson, 1970, p. 152), and conflict (Fonberg, 1956).

GENERALIZED ANXIETY DISORDER

This label, in the characteristic DSM mode, is supposedly an empirically defined syndrome, but is formulated with so much flexibility as to become virtually meaningless. For example, paragraph D starts with the words, "At least 6 of the following 18 symptoms are often present . . . " The distinctive feature is a negative one—the absence of another focus of anxiety as in panic attacks or social anxiety. No etiological basis is proposed.

Despite the vagueness of the definition, generalized anxiety disorder is widely accepted as an entity, not only by general psychiatrists (e.g., Hamilton, 1959; Hoehn-Saric, McLeod, & Zimmerli, 1989), but also by behavior therapists, including such well-known figures as Barlow (1988) and O'Leary and Wilson (1975). For a behavior therapist to accept the DSM-III view of generalized anxiety is to ignore the substance of the discipline. Behavior therapy is relevant only to disorders that are based on learning. In many patients who fit the DSM-III-R definition of generalized anxiety disorder, the anxiety is not learned but has an organic basis—for example, drugs or biochemical disorders (Slaby, 1983).

In a clinical setting, the behavior therapist's first task is to distinguish between learned and organically caused generalized anxiety cases. Learned cases comprise what has traditionally been called *free-floating anxiety* (I once proposed the term *pervasive anxiety* in its place [Wolpe, 1958], but it only led to confusion.)

The following is the apparent basis of free-floating anxiety. Under certain circumstances, anxiety is conditioned to more or less omnipresent properties of the environment, of which examples are light, light and shade contrasts, amorphous noise, spatiality, and the passage of time. Since these stimulus features enter into most, if not all, possible experience, it is to be expected that if any of them becomes connected to anxiety responses, the patient will be persistently and apparently causelessly anxious.

Three decades ago, I found that when carbon dioxide was inhaled in high concentrations (mixed with oxygen), it was often dramatically effective in reducing free-floating anxiety (Wolpe, 1954, 1958, p. 166). The essence of the technique is for patients to empty their lungs and then inhale as deeply as possible a mixture of more or less equal parts of carbon dioxide and oxygen. Before and after each inhalation, the patients are asked to state their subjective level of anxiety (p. 91). Usually in the course of two to five inhalations, the baseline anxiety level that may initially have been 60, goes down to zero or close to it, and remains at that level for periods ranging from hours to weeks or months. In 16 of 20 cases, lasting diminution of baseline anxiety consistently followed the procedure (Wolpe, 1958, p. 169). Recurrence of free-floating anxiety, sooner or later, is usual, however, and is associated with the elicitation of specific maladaptive anxiety responses.

How Does Carbon Dioxide Diminish Free-floating Anxiety?

Gellhorn (1967, p. 140ff) summarized the neurophysiological evidence for the inhibitory effect of carbon dioxide on anxiety. The initial lowering of anxiety by carbon dioxide is undoubtedly a pharmacological activity, but this does not explain the fact that anxiety reduction endures, for the gas is dissipated in a matter of minutes (Gellhorn, 1953, p. 450). Conditioning, on the other hand, does explain the durability of the effect. The inhibitory effect of carbon dioxide on anxiety could be the basis of conditioned inhibition. An experiment by Leukel and Quinton (1964) provides indirect support. They found that avoidance conditioning in rats was impaired by the administration of carbon dioxide; the sooner it was given after the conditioning trials, the more the conditioning was impaired.

There have been attempts to explain carbon dioxide's weakening of anxiety in other ways. One contention has been that the effects are due to nothing more than suggestion. But Slater and Leavy (1966) observed that neither inhaling air from anesthetic equipment nor mimicking the deep respiratory movements that carbon dioxide induces decreased free-floating anxiety—in contrast to using the gas itself. To test the possibility that a suggestive effect might require *strong* stimulation (such as characterizes the carbon dioxide procedure), Weinreb (personal communication 1966) had patients inhale aromatic spirits of ammonia, but this had no effect at all on the level of free-floating anxiety. Mack (personal communication 1970), by contrast, found amyl nitrite inhalations to be almost as effective as carbon dioxide. The powerful autonomic effects of amyl nitrite are a point of general similarity to carbon dioxide, and of contrast to the purely local stimulation of aromatic spirits of ammonia.

If carbon dioxide has anxiety-inhibiting effects, these should be psychophysiologically demonstrable. In a pilot study by Shmavonian and Wolpe (1972), inhalations of the gas slowed the pulse and raised skin conductance. Ley and Walker (1973) gave 10 adult neurotic subjects single, full-capacity inhalations of a mixture of 65% carbon dioxide and 35% oxygen, and gave compressed air to a similar group of 10 subjects. The carbon dioxide group showed significantly greater decreases in diastolic blood pressure and subjective anxiety than did the compressed air group. The whole topic is presented in greater detail by Wolpe (1987).

In the light of the recent findings on panic attacks described above, an observation by Haslam (1974) is of interest. He found that carbon dioxide reduced free-floating anxiety only in subjects in whom sodium lactate produced anxiety.

POST-TRAUMATIC STRESS DISORDER

The discussion of the etiology of maladaptive fears in chapter 3, indicated that many of them start from a single overwhelming experience of anxiety. The model of such onset is the war neuroses, for which the label *traumatic neuroses* was among several used during World War I.

Only recently was it recognized that while most traumatic neuroses are characterized by anxiety responses conditioned to features of the causal situation, in a certain number of cases other distressful symptoms are manifest even in the absence of the specific conditioned stimuli. To such cases the term *post-traumatic stress disorder* (PTSD) has been applied. Among the additional symptoms noted in DSM-III-R (1987), some of the most common are the following:

1. Recurrent unbidden recollections of the traumatic event
2. A sense of the event recurring
3. Recurrent distressing dreams related to the event
4. Insomnia
5. Chronic irritability
6. Exaggerated startle response
7. Feeling of detachment from others

The situations in which PTSD originates are identical with those associated with traumatic neuroses. However, relevant causal situations go beyond battle experiences to include many kinds of violence — being tortured, raped, mugged, or robbed; witnessing assaults on others; being in automobile accidents or floods; subjection to extremely frightening medical or surgical procedures.

In the field of psychiatry in general, the emergence of PTSD has raised much interest and concern, a vast amount of theoretical speculation and a good number of therapeutic proposals with psychotherapy to the forefront; but very little in the way of procedures that are effective (e.g., Foa & Kozak, 1986; Horowitz, 1989; Pitman, 1988; Goldish, 1988). Some individual successes with the use of imaginal flooding have been reported by behavior therapists (Fairbank, Gross, & Keane, 1983; Keane & Kaloupek, 1982). A controlled study by Cooper & Clum (1989) compared the effectiveness of imaginal flooding with psychotherapeutic and pharmacological methods that are standard at Veteran's Administration hospitals in the treatment of combat-related PTSD. There were seven subjects in each group. Sessions took place once or twice weekly. For subjects in the flooding group, the most personally relevant scenes were used, presenting the least distressing first. Scenes were given in as much detail as possible. All flooding subjects experienced an elimination or marked improvement of nightmares, which were unchanged in the control group. There were also notable improvements in sleep disturbance, hypersensitivity to sound, fear of loss of control, and the feeling of being scrutinized by others. But other symptoms, such as trait anxiety and depression, were not improved.

It is noteworthy that the behavioral schedule figuring in the foregoing treatment is unidimensional, reflecting the trend, repeatedly noted in this volume, in behavior therapy practice toward package treatments. Much better results are obtainable from treatments that are decided by the dynamic analysis of the individual case, as described by Scrignar (1984). Recovery is frequent and often complete, but also usually time consuming. Scrignar (1984) gives a detailed account of the highly successful treatment of four cases on the basis of excellent individual analyses. Treatment took 4 to 14 months and consisted in the main of appropriate integrations of cognitive retraining and systematic desensitization.

However, there are even then many failures. For example, many years ago I treated a war neurosis that featured unremitting free-floating anxiety (unresponsive to carbon-dioxide inhalation [p. 269]), nightmares, and flashbacks. All efforts at behavioral treatment failed. The best I could do was provide intermittent reduction of anxiety by intravenous pentothal. I also failed more recently with a welder who worked on oil tanks, and who on two occasions, separated by a year, had the horrifying experience of seeing water filling the tank on the inside of which he was working — being saved each time at the last moment. I was able only partially to diminish his anxiety to the sound of water (e.g., from a faucet) and his fear of crowded places, by in vivo desensitization. Return to work was out of the question.

A method of treatment has been described by Shapiro (1989) whose results, if confirmed, would make it a major contribution to the treatment of this difficult condition. The procedure involves eliciting from clients sequences of large-magnitude, rhythmic saccadic eye movements while holding in mind the most salient aspect of a traumatic memory. The effect of these movements was discovered accidentally by Shapiro upon noticing in herself that recurring disturbing thoughts were mysteriously disappearing and not returning. Careful self-examination ascertained that her eyes were involuntarily moving in a multisaccadic manner when the disturbing thoughts arose. The thoughts disappeared completely and, if deliberately retrieved, were no longer upsetting. The author then made deliberate use of her observation in a variety of patients.

Patients are first asked to focus on the disturbing memory and then to isolate a single traumatic picture. It is unnecessary for them to describe or discuss the memory in detail. They are then directed to assign a *suds* level to their anxiety and to identify the physical distribution of the sensations. Thereafter they visualize the traumatic scene while visually tracking the therapist's index finger 12 to 14 inches in front of their faces. The finger is moved rhythmically back and forth across the line of vision from extreme right to extreme left—two back-and-forth movements per second. The distance traveled by the hand on each sweep is at least 12 inches. The back-and-forth movement of the finger is repeated 12 to 24 times. After each set of saccades, patients are asked to bring up the picture again and to give a *sud* rating. If the *sud* level does not decrease after two sets of saccades, clients are asked, "Did the picture change?" If a different image has intruded, it is desensitized before returning to the original picture.

Shapiro states that the procedure is extremely effective in desensitizing traumatic memory contents and in eliminating attendant complaints. At follow-ups up to 12 months later, the memories are said to remain anxiety-free. The basis for the method's effectiveness is unclear. Shapiro suggests that rhythmic, multisaccadic eye movements activate a mechanism by which anxiety is reciprocally inhibited.

Shapiro states that her method has been used with equal success by a number of other therapists to whom she has taught it. I have used it with notable success in two patients. One was an accident-induced post-traumatic stress disorder that had already improved greatly with standard behavioral methods. She was, however, inordinately disturbed in certain contexts involving the litigation she had begun against the company responsible for the accident. For example, she had been on one occasion greatly upset by an official of the insurance company, Mrs. K. The patient was constantly ruminating about Mrs. K., with great distress. I had her fix her mind on Mrs. K.

while following the rapid movement of my finger from side to side. After 50 such movements she was able to think of Mrs. K. with comfort — a state of affairs that persisted 6 months later. The second patient was an obsessive-compulsive with extravagant guilt reactions in certain interrelated contexts, all of which were overcome by the eye movement procedure, but in some instances only after several repetitions over a week to a month.

John N. Marquis (personal communication, 1990) attended a workshop given by Shapiro in 1989. Following that he has used saccadic eye movement treatment in about 60 subjects with various anxiety syndromes including four with PTSD. Marked improvements were usually rapidly achieved, and the results were altogether gratifying. Among the cases, there were eight with disabling perseveration of anxiety following the San Francisco earthquake. A single series of saccadic movements sufficed to overcome the anxiety in each case. One woman reinstated the anxiety by insistent catastrophic imaging, but it was lastingly removed by one more saccadic series.

The process by which saccadic eye movements inhibit and decondition persistent anxiety with remarkable rapidity is at present a mystery. A straw in the wind may be Jacobson's (1939) observation that relaxation of the extrinsic eye muscles has extraordinary emotional potency. It suggests the existence of unforeshadowed neural processes.

15
Complex Syndromes With Background Anxiety

The syndromes of this chapter present themselves with complaints other than anxiety, but analysis shows anxiety to be at their root; its dissolution is the key to recovery. The syndromes to be considered are neurotic depression, psychosomatic syndromes including stuttering, obsessive-compulsive neuroses, sexual inadequacy, and sexual deviations.

NEUROTIC DEPRESSION

Depression is a term that is applied to constellations of behavior among whose most characteristic elements are motor and verbal retardation, crying, sadness, loss of mirth response, loss of interest, self-devaluation, sleeplessness, and anorexia (Beck, 1967). Bleuler (1911) condensed these into the "melancholic triad" of depressive affect, inhibition of action, and inhibition of thinking.

The Endogenous-Psychogenic
Dichotomy—A Brief History

The common cause of endogenous depression is a biological abnormality called *cyclothymia*. Psychogenic depression first emerged as a separate category when Kraepelin (1913) noted that certain cases of depression displayed greater emotional reactivity than others. The dichotomy thus initiated came to be generally accepted and was given various labels, of which *endogenous-neurotic* (Kendell & Gourlay, 1970) has been the most widely used. The DSM-III-R (1987) version of the dichotomy is *major depression-dysthymic disorder.*

Clinicians, however, often found it difficult to decide on which side of the dichotomy to assign a particular case. They could often positively diagnose endogenous depression but they increasingly realized that the diagnosis of neurotic depression was usually based on exclusion and was applied to cases simply because they lacked the features pathognomic of endogenous depression (Foulds, 1975; Kiloh et al., 1972; Mendels & Cochrane, 1968).

A number of efforts were made to identify salient features of neurotic depression. Some were based on psychoanalytic formulations, such as introjection; but these, as Ascher (1952) noted, were "too inconsistent and speculative to serve as diagnostic criteria." Other investigators made factor analyses of depressed clinical populations. The main result of their work was the generation of artifactual groupings. For example, Kay et al. (1969) subdivided two-thirds of their depressed patients into endogenous or neurotic groups, leaving the other third undetermined. Roth et al. (1972) concluded that anxiety and depression were separate entities, not causally interrelated. From a demographic study, Brown et al. (1977) agreed with them, in spite of having noted that the relationship between anxiety and depression "is often a close one." None of these investigators entertained the possibility that *some* depressions might be secondary to anxiety, despite West and Dally's (1959) finding that depressions with prominent anxiety and phobic symptoms were distinctively responsive to iproniazid.

Unequivocal evidence of heterogeneity came to light only relatively recently when Akiskal et al. (1979) reported a 3 to 4-year follow-up study of 100 patients who had been diagnosed as suffering from "neurotic depression." A depressed patient was given a neurotic diagnosis if reality testing was preserved, if there was insight into the psychological nature of the illness, and if hallucinations and delusions were absent. At the follow-up, all the major psychiatric diagnoses were found to be represented. Thirty-six percent of the patients had had melancholic episodes, and half of these (18% of the total) had also had changes of polarity. Ten cases were attributable to medical-surgical illnesses, and three were schizophrenic or schizoaffective. Most of the remainder were labeled *chronic secondary dysphorias* in which depression was superimposed either on longstanding *nonaffective psychiatric disorders* or on *characterological depressions.* Akiskal (1983) saw the chronic secondary dysphorias as the "clinical common pathway" of many conditions, including neurotic and characterological disorders. He thus allowed for true neurotic depressions but was not aware that there were at that time already both physiological and clinical grounds for their existence, as outlined below.

Neurotic Anxiety as a Cause of Depression

Anxiety is very often the sole neurotic manifestation, but it is also the wellspring of such others as asthma and other psychosomatic states, stuttering, sexual inadequacy, and obsessions and compulsions. In these, the causal role of anxiety is usually clear. It is less obvious that neurotic anxiety is the antecedent of some depressions, though logically only such depressions can appropriately be called neurotic. Occasionally, over the years, there were psychiatrists who made the connection between anxiety and certain cases of depression on clinical grounds. Most explicitly, Rogerson (1940) suggested that the term *affective psychosis* be used for biological depressions, and *affective neurosis* for anxiety states, which he divided into depressive neuroses and anxiety neuroses.

Physiological Demonstration of Anxiety as a Variable of Depression

Three decades ago, Shagass et al. (1956), using the sedation threshold (Shagass, 1954, 1956) as a measure of anxiety, impressively demonstrated that neurotic depressions are characterized by high levels of anxiety, in contrast to low levels in endogenous depression. The sedation threshold is the amount of sodium amobarbital (amytal) injected at a steady rate that is needed to produce certain electroencephalographic effects and such behavioral effects as cessation of conversational responding. The underlying hypothesis is that there is a direct relation between the level of ongoing anxiety and the amount of amytal required to combat it. The endogenous depressions were diagnosed on such features as psychomotor retardation, agitation, delusions, hallucinations, mutism, and negativism. The neurotic group had none of these features, but, instead, depression combined with neurotic symptoms, among which anxiety was prominent. In a comparison of 25 matched pairs, 23 of the endogenous cases and only one of the neurotic patients had a sedation threshold less than 4 mg/kg. Significantly, the mean sedation threshold in the neurotic depressions (mean 5.05) was only slightly lower than in people diagnosed as having anxiety states (mean 5.32).

Other workers, (e.g., Gilberti & Rossi, 1962; Nymgaard, 1959; Perez-Reyes, 1972a, 1972b) corroborated these observations in a variety of ways. Perez-Reyes observed that the thresholds of neurotic depressives were significantly higher, and those of psychotic depressives significantly lower, than those of normal controls. He persuasively argued that endogenous depression and neurotic depression must be separate syndromes if their thresholds are on opposite sides of the normal. These studies have been more circumstantially reviewed by Shagass (1981) and Wolpe (1986).

Noteworthy as the above observations are, they made astonishingly little impact on psychiatric thought. Typically, Roth et al. (1972) stated, in a paper dealing with the relationship between anxiety states and depression, that the problems "include the continuity or discontinuity between neurotic and endogenous depression," and did not mention the work of Shagass.

Clinical Observations on Anxiety-based Depression

Independently of the foregoing physiological research, I became aware in the early 1950s of cases in which depression appeared to be related to neurotic anxiety. Most frequently, the patient would have presented as a case of neurosis, and history taking would have revealed depression to be a prominent component of the total syndrome. It was often apparent that the depression was secondary to anxiety in the same way as relates to stuttering or other secondary neurotic responses. The relationship was usually confirmed by resolution of depression following the deconditioning of anxiety.

If human neurotic depression is a function of anxiety, there should also be other clinical evidence of this, as indeed there is. Clancy et al. (1978) documented a high incidence of depression secondary to anxiety neurosis, as did Pachman and Foy (1978). The ubiquity of anxiety in reactive depression has been directly shown by psychophysiological measurements (McCarron, 1973); and Suarez, Crowe, and Adams (1978) found that reactive depressives have raised electrodermal responsiveness to stress in the direction of anxiety.

Relatively recently I provided formal data relative to my above mentioned experiences on the basis of a randomly sampled group of 25 patients (Wolpe, 1979). Detailed study of these patients indicated that depression was dynamically related to anxiety in four different contexts, of which more than one was often found in a single case. The cases were divided according to the predominating context.

Context I.   As a consequence of severe and prolonged anxiety that is directly conditioned (11 cases)

Context II.   As a consequence of anxiety based on erroneous, self-devaluative cognitions (6 cases)

Context III. In the context of anxiety-based inability to control interpersonal situations (8 cases)

Context IV.   In the context of excessively prolonged and severe responses to bereavement (0 cases) There was, however, one case in whose depression bereavement was a factor.

The basic data are given in Table 15.1. The following is an outline of the contexts in which anxiety may generate depression.

Table 15.1. Summary of Data

PREDOMINANT BASIS OF CAUSATIVE ANXIETY	NUMBER OF CASES	MEAN TIME SINCE ONSET OF DEPRESSIVE SYMPTOMS	MEAN NUMBER OF TREATMENT SESSIONS	NUMBER RECOVERED OR MUCH IMPROVED
Classically conditioned	11	9.6 years	35.2	11
Cognitively based	6	7.3 years	24.5	5
Interpersonal inadequacy	8	4.9 years	27.5	6
Bereavement	–	–	–	–
TOTAL	25	7.4 years	30.2	22

Number of cases followed up 6 months or more: 19
Mean follow-up: 5.2 years

Source: Wolpe, 1979.

Neurotic Depression as a Consequence of Severe Classically Conditioned Anxiety

Patients with high measures of neurotic anxiety may also report depression, whose fluctuations are often correlated with the intensity of the anxiety. In some cases, depression becomes the dominant emotional tone. Where there has been free-floating anxiety (Wolpe, 1958), continuous depression may take its place. This change of affect may conceivably be due to certain overstressed neural pathways becoming inhibited and the excitation rechanneled on the basis of what Pavlov (1941, p. 176) called protective (transmarginal) inhibition. Nevertheless, it is clear from Shagass's studies that the autonomic pattern characteristic of anxiety goes on, apparently unaffected by whatever underlies the change of affect. Depression diminishes in concert with the successful deconditioning of anxiety, often ceasing completely long before the anxiety has been fully overcome.

Case 52

An example is a case of 20 years' duration, whose analysis revealed fear of disapproval and a related fear of making her demands known or resisting those of others. Her treatment consisted of assertiveness training and systematic desensitization to inappropriate fears of rejection and ridicule. After 31 sessions, she felt calmer than she could ever remember. She was able to control situations with people, was no longer upset by a neurotic range of "disapprovals," and was free from depression. At a 9-month follow-up, she had maintained her gains.

Neurotic Depression as a Consequence of Anxiety Based on Erroneous Cognitions

This context of neurotic depression differs from the previous one only in that the anxiety is not classically conditioned but based on self-devaluative misconceptions. There were six cases of this kind in our series, and these were treated by cognitive correction. Five of them did well. Case 22 (p. 105) affords an excellent example.

Neurotic Depression Due to Anxiety-based Interpersonal Inadequacy

Many neuroses are characterized by interpersonal anxiety that leads to submissiveness and inadequate handling of other people. Not infrequently depression follows interpersonal failures. The anxiety may be evoked by the prospect of self-assertion or the thought of its implications — such as hurting other people's feelings or incurring disapproval. The resulting inhibition of self-expression produces a feeling of ineffectuality that seems in turn to generate depression. Assertiveness training has a central role in the treatment of such cases. It inhibits, and with repetition weakens, the maladaptive interpersonal anxiety, employing the expression of anger or other emotions in particular circumstances. Six of the eight patients in this group did well.

Neurotic Depression Based on Overreaction to Bereavement

When the distress occasioned by a major loss or failure is unusually severe or prolonged, one must always entertain the possibility that major depression has been precipitated (e.g., Hirschfeld, Klerman, & Andreasen, 1985; Thompson & Hendrie, 1972). But in some cases it is previous conditioning of anxiety responses to loss that lies behind the persistence of the grief. The anxiety inhibits the ruminating on distressing images that would enable the grief to be extinguished ("absorbed"). Ramsay (1977) obtained striking results in intractable mourning by emotional flooding through insistent focusing on the reality of the death and on poignant images from the dead person's life. (For other relevant programs, see Lieberman, 1978; Phillips, 1978; Wanderer & Cabot, 1978.)

The Results of Treatment

The treatment of depression in the 25 cases presented in Table 15.1 aimed at overcoming the maladaptive anxiety response habits that were revealed in the assessment of the case. Although the main anxiety context is indicated by the predominant basis, other contexts usually contributed. As Table 15.1 indicates, the neurotic depression was overcome or markedly improved in 22 of the 25 cases. Two cases were unimproved, and one had repeated recurrences of depression, though at much lower levels than before. These three cases were also variously failures in terms of overcoming neurotic anxiety. It is common for depression to cease long before the complete resolution of the underlying anxiety-response habits. Nineteen of the 22 successful cases were followed up six months or more after treatment. None had relapsed.

The foregoing study calls for formal replication, but it does provide prima facie support for the proposition that neurotic depression, like other manifestations of neurosis, is a function of anxiety, and that the treatment indicated is the deconditioning of neurotic anxiety. It is relevant to note that the literature contains frequent intimations that some depressions respond to psychotherapy (e.g., Copeland, 1983; Kiloh & Garside, 1963).

Much more systematic work is needed, but for all of it a prerequisite is the confident diagnosis of neurotic depression. This topic is covered next.

The Diagnosis of Neurotic Depression

The possibility of a neurotic basis should be considered in any depression in which the criteria for major depression are absent. As demonstrated by Akiskal et al. (1979), a large number of those lacking these criteria are found in time to be endogenous; another substantial group are neurotic; and there are probably depressions with other etiologies, as suggested by Akiskal (1983) and Winokur (1985). Only the identification of the neurotic cases is considered here.

For a depression to be eligible for consideration as neurotic, there must at the same time be evidence of maladaptive anxiety. This entails the investigative procedures described in chapters 5 and 6 of this book.

Confidence in a diagnosis of neurotic depression is, naturally, enhanced if the magnitudes of anxiety and depression vary concurrently. But even if this is not clearly demonstrable, it is appropriate to embark on a program of deconditioning of anxiety, both because it is desirable in its own right and because experience has shown that alleviation of the depression is a usual consequence. Of course, this will not always happen—notably in the occasional case in which the depression is actually endogenous and exists side by side with neurotic anxiety. I have had a handful of cases in which deconditioning of anxiety has been facilitated after a concomitant endogenous depression has been recognized and effectively controlled by lithium.

Incidental features of some diagnostic value in neurotic depression are the absence of early morning wakening and the fact, reflected in our series, that they have a relatively long history, which is in keeping with the long duration of untreated neuroses. It should be noted that, contrary to what was once believed, precipitation by stress is not at all a feature of neurotic depression but much more suggestive of those that are endogenous (Hirschfeld, Klerman, & Andreasen, 1985; Leff, Roatch, & Bunney, 1970; Paykel, Meyers, et al., 1969; Thompson & Hendrie, 1972).

The Implications of Diagnostic Differentiation for Outcome Research

In recent years, nonpsychotic depression has been the subject of outcome studies involving various modes of psychotherapy—interpersonal therapy (Klerman et al., 1974; Weissman et al., 1981), cognitive therapy (Beck et al., 1985; Rush & Watkins, 1981; Shaw, 1977), social skills training (Bellack et al., 1983; Hersen et al., 1980, 1984), and reinforcement therapy (Azrin & Besalel, 1981; Lewinsohn, 1974). The results have invariably been positive, and comparisons with the use of tricyclic antidepressants and with untreated controls have favored the psychotherapies.

These findings have been the impetus for the National Institutes of Mental Health-sponsored multimillion dollar Collaborative Research Program now being conducted at George Washington University, the University of Pittsburgh, and the University of Oklahoma. It compares two of the above modes of psychotherapy—interpersonal psychotherapy and cognitive behavior therapy—with treatment by imipramine and with controls who receive a placebo and a $1/2$ hour a week of supportive discussion (not psychotherapy) with a psychiatrist.

The Collaborative Research Program, like its predecessors, assumes the uniformity of its case material, although this assumption was rendered untenable by the demonstration of Akiskal et al. (1979) which showed the heterogeneity of nonpsychotic depression. To compare the effects of different agents on psychopathologically mixed groups of depression is as futile as to compare the curative effects of medications on infections without differentiating between protozoal, fungal, and bacterial cases.

Why Psychotherapies Have Succeeded With Mixed Populations of Nonpsychotic Depression

It remains necessary to explain why the use of the various psychotherapies has been followed by the alleviation of many depressions. We must first observe that none of the authors considered the matter of diagnostic differentiation; therefore, the actual distribution of subdiagnoses in their studies is unknown. For purposes of exposition we will postulate that in each of the studies there were 100 cases with the same diagnostic distribution as the 100 followed-up patients of Akiskal et al. (1979) (p. 275). Subtracting the 36 cases whom they found to be endogenous, the 10 whose depressions were secondary to physical illness, and the two that turned out to be schizophrenic, we are left with 52 subjects whom Akiskal (1983) called *chronic secondary dysphorias*, which he divided into those in which anxiety dominated (and that were therefore presumably neurotic) and *characterological depression*. Examination of the case descriptions that Akiskal provides to illustrate the latter suggests that many of them were probably also neurotic depressions. Therefore, without denying the possibility of characterological depressions, we will, for the sake of simplicity, assume that the residual 52 depressions were neurotic. Since about half of the cases of Akiskal et al. were inpatients, who are on the whole less likely to be neurotic, it is reasonable to suggest that 60 out of 100 outpatient nonpsychotic depressions would be neurotic. (A somewhat higher proportion of neurotic cases was actually found by Kiloh & Garside, 1963.)

Among 60 cases of neurotic depression, psychotherapeutic interviewing of any kind may be expected to benefit 30, because up to 50% of neurotic patients improve markedly on the basis of any sympathetic interpersonal interaction (Coleman, Greenblatt, & Solomon, 1956; Kellner & Sheffield, 1971; Wilder, 1945). Then, of the remaining 40 cases, which we have posited as endogenous, 11 may be expected to improve substantially in the course of a few weeks, based on Klerman and Cole's (1965) placebo response rate of 27%. Adding these to the 30 recovered neurotic cases provides a baseline recovery rate of 41% to be expected when a heterogeneous group of nonpsychotic depression has had psychotherapy of any kind.

Among the four types of psychotherapeutic intervention noted above, acceptable quantitative data are available only for two — cognitive therapy and social skills training. In respect to each of these, there is evidence of efficacy over and above that attributable to the nonspecific effects. We may assume, on the findings of Ost and Hugdahl (1981) and Wolpe (1981b), that 20 of Beck's 60 neurotic cases would be predominantly cognitive. If the cognitive methods positively benefited all of these, his projected success rate would rise from 41% to 61%. If a similar number of the neurotic cases of Bellack et al. profited from social skills training, their total success rate would also rise to about 60%.

These projections are fairly similar to the actual results obtained. In the report by Beck et al. (1985), of 37 cases treated by cognitive therapy, 25 (67%) were rated as "recovered" or "much improved." Out of a total of 42 cases treated by social skills training plus placebo (Bellack et al., 1983; Hersen et al., 1984), the number "substantially" or "significantly" improved was 28 (67%). Even though the above calculations are based on hypothetical projections, they suffice to show how the advocates of particular psychotherapeutic methods may have been misled into exaggerating the efficacy of their methods in nonpsychotic depression.

Suggestions for the Future Conduct of Outcome Research on Nonpsychotic Depression

Outcome studies on mixed pathologies have very little value, except when the explicit object is symptom control — in the way that an analgesic may control pain, no matter how caused. In populations of nonpsychotic depression, it is possible with considerable assurance to distinguish neurotic cases as well as a considerable number of those that are endogenous. In due time it will no doubt become possible to diagnose others differently caused. Outcome studies should be confined to particular causal categories. In respect of neurotic cases, in addition to the categorical diagnosis, it is also necessary for comparisons to take into account different ways in which anxiety is related to depression. Cognitively based cases must, for example, be isolated if different treatments of them are to be compared. Of course, the results of a total behaviorally based treatment package could appropriately be compared with those of other packages. When other etiological categories of cases within the rubric of nonpsychotic depression are identifiable (e.g., Akiskal, 1983; Winokur, 1985) these, too, will be appropriate subject-matter for comparative outcome studies.

Investigators who study the effects of treatments of anxiety-based disorders must never forget that at least 40% of the recoveries associated with any such treatment are attributable to nonspecific effects (see p. 333). To overlook this is to run the risk of overrating the efficacy of a method.

To conclude this discussion, Beck's cognitive program calls for special comment. Both within the field of behavior therapy (e.g., Rachman, 1990, p. 220) and beyond, in psychiatry (e.g., Klerman, 1989, p. 1732), Beck's program is regarded as a notable success story. Yet it is clear from our discussion that the degree of its success has been greatly overstated. Furthermore, though Beck ascribes the benefits of his program to cognitive intervention, most of his patients have also been given such behavioral procedures as assertiveness training and systematic desensitization. It is relevant to add that Lewinsohn et al. (1981) found no evidence that depression-related cognitions are causally related to depression.

PSYCHOSOMATIC DISORDERS

Physical illness that results from excessive excitation of the autonomic nervous system is called psychosomatic illness. The relevant excitation usually occurs in autonomic response elements involved in the elicitation of anxiety, but there are exceptions (see the discussion of asthma). Unusually strong autonomic responding in a particular organ may result in overactivity that may adversely affect physiological function, sometimes to the extent of producing a lesion. Biological makeup decides which of an individual's organs may be susceptible. According to Wolf and Wolff's (1947) classic statement, there are "stomach reactors, nose reactors, pulse reactors, and blood pressure reactors." It is to be expected that if anxiety is a factor in the maintenance of a physical illness, that illness will diminish as the anxiety-response habit is overcome.

Among the illnesses called psychosomatic because they are commonly associated with emotional disturbance are asthma, peptic ulcer, irritable colon, migraine, hypertension, and neurodermatitis. A psychological factor, however, is not present in every case so diagnosed. For example, midbrain lesions also can cause the autonomic activity in the stomach that leads to the hyperchlorhydria that is the basis of peptic ulceration (Cushing, 1932), and many cases of asthma have nothing to do with emotional disturbance. It is thus imperative in the individual case to establish a positive connection between emotional arousal and the somatic illness before proceeding to psychological treatment. (Of course, if maladaptive anxiety is present, it may call for treatment in its own right even if it has no relation to the somatic illness.)

Asthma

Asthma has a variable, multifactorial etiology that includes allergic, infective, emotional, and mechanical processes of which any or all may be causally implicated in a particular case (Rees, 1956, 1964). A general subdivision has been proposed on medical criteria into cases in whom somatic predisposition to asthma is high and those in whom it is low — psychological factors playing a greater role in the latter (Block et al., 1964; Purcell, 1963). Resh (1970) found that psychosomatic asthmatics could be fairly clearly differentiated from those whose illness was physiologically based.

Several studies of the successful behavioral treatment of asthma have been reported, the first being a controlled study by Moore (1965). She used a balanced incomplete block design to compare the effects of three modes of treatment: (a) systematic desensitization, (b) relaxation therapy, and (c) relaxation combined with suggestion. For the desensitization treatment, three hierarchies were prepared: one based on an asthmatic attack, a second on any relevant situation that was productive of an allergic or infective reaction, and a third on a situation producing a key psychological stress. The dependent variables were changes in the daily number of asthmatic attacks and maximum peak flow of inspired air. During the first 4 weeks of treatment, maximum peak flow improved for all three groups, but most for desensitization. After this time, while the desensitization group continued to improve, the other two began to regress. Eight weeks after the beginning of treatment, the superiority of maximum peak flow in the desensitization group was significant at the .001 level. It was the only method to have produced a systematic weakening of the anxiety-response habits causally connected with the asthma. It is unfortunate, in the light of this study, that almost all recent behavioral treatment of asthmatic adults has been "straight" relaxation or biofeedback, with very unimpressive results (Grossman & Wientjes, 1989).

A question that has long puzzled researchers is why anxiety should be a trigger to the parasympathetically mediated response of bronchial constriction. Studies by Hahn (1966) and by Mathe and Knapp (1971) have suggested that asthmatics have an unusual profile of autonomic response to stress; unlike heart rate and blood pressure, the airway conductance and respiratory rate of asthmatics are opposite in direction to those of control subjects.

Besides the common cases of asthma whose attacks are mediated by anxiety, there are others in whom bronchial constriction has been directly conditioned to previously neutral stimuli. In an experiment on two patients, Dekker, Pelser, and Groen (1957) found that the isolated mouthpiece of the equipment through which the patients had inhaled allergenic aerosols had acquired, through its association with the attacks elicited by the aerosols, an independent and obstinately persistent power to provoke asthmatic attacks. Khan, Staerk, and Bonk (1973) showed, in a controlled study of 20 asthmatic children, that it is possible to overcome such conditioned reactions by the opposition of conditioned bronchodilation. They conditioned bronchial constriction in much the same way as had Dekker et al., and then instituted training in bronchial dilation through biofeedback reinforcement. They observed the bronchial relaxations on an electronic pulmonary function analyzer and reinforced the child by turning on a bright red light and expressing praise. Those who acquired this bronchodilatory skill were significantly improved in comparison with a control group—in frequency of asthmatic attacks and in amount of medication required—a superiority that persisted at a 12-month follow-up. Similar success in a single case was reported by Sirota and Mahoney (1974).

The behavioral approach to any case of asthma is thus first to determine whether anxiety is a causal factor. If it is, it should be treated as dictated by the behavior analysis. If not, it may still be worthwhile to attempt the conditioning of bronchodilation on the basis of biofeedback.

Essential Hypertension

Essential hypertension (high blood pressure) is a serious condition of adult life. Its usual feature is elevation of diastolic pressure accompanied by raised systolic pressures of varying magnitude. The etiology of essential hypertension is not fully understood, but it is apparent that conditioned vasoconstriction to environmental stimuli is a component of many cases, and these are the ones that may be expected to respond to behavioral methods. Jacobson (1939) demonstrated that progressive relaxation of skeletal muscles may markedly diminish both systolic and diastolic pressure, and shortly before his death he reported (1978) significant lasting diminution of blood pressure in over two-thirds of 90 patients. Benson et al. (1971) obtained reductions in systolic pressure ranging from 16 to 34 millimeters in hypertensives treated by a form of transcendental meditation. A large number of studies have been reviewed by Jacob, Kraemer, and Agras (1977), by Blanchard et al. (1979), and by Linden (1984). In some of these, biofeedback either replaced or was combined with relaxation training. The effects, however, were often trivial. Jorgensen, Houston, and Zurawski (1981) reported encouraging results from Suinn's anxiety-management training method (Suinn, 1977; Suinn & Richardson, 1971) in which the patient was required, while relaxed, to visualize actual past stress situations, this constituting a mode of counterconditioning.

A criticism that applies to most studies is that they assume that intermittent lower readings by the therapist reflect continuous diminution of blood pressure. Day-to-day and hour-to-hour blood pressure readings in the normal environment are needed to establish lasting change. A strategy suggested by Graham, Beiman, and Ciminero (1977, 1978) is to have daily blood pressure readings taken at home. In one of their patients, who was treated by relaxation training, such readings revealed a drop in blood pressure at home from 155/95 to 130/80, a change that was found to have persisted 40 weeks later. Patel et al. (1985) found that behaviorally trained hypertensives maintained reduced pressures up to 4 years, in contrast to an untreated control group.

On general grounds, one would expect relaxation training to achieve enduring diminution of blood pressure in two possible ways. One is to have the patient develop a habit of constantly relaxing all muscles not in active use — Jacobson's (1938) "differential relaxation." The other is through the identification and deconditioning of unadaptive anxiety-response habits. One version of this was adapted by Suinn and Richardson (1971) and Suinn (1977), quoted above. Two successes by Lynch et al. (1982) are probably attributable to nonspecific effects, the general importance of which has been demonstrated by Chesney and Black (1986). A case of my own (Wolpe, 1976c, p. 233), in whom apparent recovery was due to deconditioning of anxiety, was a 41-year-old mathematics professor who had presented with a variety of psychosomatic symptoms. Hypertension of at least 2 years' duration dropped from 180/110 to 120/80 after assertiveness training and desensitization of several hierarchies.

Migraine and Tension Headaches

Emotional tension is a common precipitant of attacks of migraine, and also of nonmigrainous headaches. Over the years I have repeatedly obtained recovery or marked amelioration in both categories by the use of emotional deconditioning programs. In a controlled study of migraine, Mitchell (1969) noted a 66.8% reduction of attacks in subjects treated with desensitization and assertiveness therapy, but no change in no-treatment controls. In a second study, Mitchell and Mitchell (1971) confirmed their previous results and also found that relaxation alone did not differ from no treatment. Success requires overcoming the patient's emotional reactions to relevant environmental stimuli.

Biofeedback, too, has been widely used to diminish tension headaches and migraine. Budzynski, Stoyva, and Adler (1970) treated tension headaches by having subjects relax frontalis and sometimes neck muscles by placing electrodes over these muscles and providing electromyographic (EMG) feedback. Good results were obtained, but the fact that the subjects were asked to practice relaxation at home means that emotional deconditioning may have been the basis of change. The same comment applies to Chesney and Shelton's (1976) study in which relaxation either alone or in combination with biofeedback was more effective than biofeedback alone in the treatment of tension headaches.

Gastrointestinal Disorders

Seeing that the gastrointestinal tract is innervated by the autonomic nervous system, it is not surprising that anxiety has been implicated in disturbances of the tract at all levels, from esophagus to rectum.

The first investigation of relationships between emotional states and the vascular and secretory response of the stomach was that of Wolf and Wolff (1942), who found that fear depressed gastric secretion and mobility, and hostility increased both. They also noted that the gastric mucosa became fragile and sensitive during engorgement. Despite these suggestive observations, an epidemiological survey by Pfeiffer et al. (1973) concluded that the causes of peptic ulceration remain obscure. Nevertheless, anxiety appears to be associated with exacerbation in some cases, and recovery from peptic ulcer has been known to follow deconditioning of anxiety-response habits (see, for example, Wolpe, 1958, p. 148ff).

Reports of the use of behavior therapy in conditions of the lower gastrointestinal tract are more frequent. Hedberg (1973) reported the case of a woman with a 22-year history of chronic diarrhea that was successfully overcome by 12 sessions of systematic desensitization, without recurrence at a 2-year follow-up. Furman (1973) obtained uniformly positive results in five patients suffering from functional diarrhea by a biofeedback technique involving verbal reinforcement. Furman, however, notes that his success was probably attributable to desensitizing effects based on the relaxation training that was included in his procedures. In one of his cases, systematic desensitization was explicitly added.

The prominence of anxiety in patients with irritable bowel syndrome was brought to the fore by Latimer et al. (1981), who found that the subjects' gastrointestinal reactions were no different from those of neurotic subjects who were similar in terms of anxiety and depression but without bowel symptoms (see also Latimer, 1981, 1983). The treatment of irritable bowel syndrome might thus be the treatment of the associated anxiety-response habits. However, as Hölzl (1989) concludes from a review of the field, controlled outcome studies are still lacking.

Stuttering

Stuttering is not usually grouped with the psychosomatic disorders, but it clearly conforms to the definition given above. The higher prevalence among males, the high familial incidence even without significant family contact, and the usual onset early in life, all indicate a physiological predisposition (see Shoemaker & Brutten, 1969). The speech disturbance is in most cases activated by anxiety. The anxiety is usually social, as demonstrated by the observation that almost all stutterers speak fluently when they are alone or in the presence of people with whom they are comfortable. The greater the anxiety evoked by the social situation, the worse the stutter is likely to be. A behavior analysis will identify the stimulus elements in the social contexts that trigger the anxiety; upon these will depend the therapeutic strategy. Most often, assertiveness training or some form of desensitization will be indicated, or both. Cases 53 and 54 provide illustrations.

In cases in which anxiety plays a part, the antecedent stimuli need to be identified. In some instances, typified by case 53, the dominating anxiety sources are in interpersonal contents that call for assertiveness training. In others, such as case 54, some form of systematic desensitization is indicated. The antecedent stimuli are not always obvious and insistent exploration may be needed. For example, in one case, it became clear that some social situations produced the stutter and others did not, yet the patient denied experiencing anxiety in the former. But when details unfolded, it emerged that he was trying to convey that he was not anxious at stuttering but at being scrutinized; the greater the number of people of certain categories who observed him, the greater was the anxiety and the more pronounced the stutter. In such cases, when social anxiety has been deconditioned, anxiety about the stutter ceases to be a problem.

Case 53: Stuttering Related to Timidity

Mr. M. had a severe stutter that had begun at age 5. Almost every sentence was repeatedly interrupted by the stutter, and each interruption was marked by violent facial contortions. A great many interpersonal situations could arouse anxiety in him and so worsen the stutter. It was evident that anxiety associated with direct dealings with people needed attention first. Because of it, he frequently endured aggression from others for long periods without protest, until, sometimes, his bottled-up emotions exploded in ill-directed rage. I told him that he had rights as well as duties. I drew attention to the helplessness embodied in his delayed rage reactions and emphasized the need for protest to be expressed as soon as possible if real mastery of situations was to be gained. Three days later he reported that he had been less permissive to his assistants at work and had insisted on their getting things done. He had also for the first time asked his wife to help him with work he brought home from the office. In correlation with increasingly consistent exteriorizing of feelings in relevant contexts, he developed a growing feeling of inner freedom and his speech lost its stutter except on occasions with his boss, and in conditions of unusual stress. The facial contortions ceased entirely. When seen 2 years later, he spoke without any suggestion of stutter. (For details of this case see Wolpe, 1958, p. 128.)

Case 54: Stuttering as a Function of Humiliation

Mr. B. was a man of 25 who had stuttered quite severely since he was 5 years old. He said that his stutter had always been worse with strangers. It is interesting to note that his score on the Willoughby Neuroticism Schedule was 13, which is within normal limits, indicating that he was free from neurotic anxiety in many interpersonal contexts.

Mr. B. was taught relaxation, and arising from the case analysis, hierarchies dealing with humiliation were drawn up. After desensitization to situations involving less threatening individuals had been accomplished, scenes that featured his father began to be introduced. One of the weaker scenes was sitting with his father in a restaurant and knocking over the salt. More disturbing scenes were knocking the salt off the table; knocking over the water; making an erroneous statement. After nine desensitization sessions in the course of 4 months, his fear of these humiliations steadily declined and his speech was judged to have improved 90% to 95%. About a year later his improvement was maintained both as judged by me and as reported by his wife. (For further details of this case, see Wolpe, 1969, p. 23.)

The deconditioning of anxiety is often all that is needed to overcome a stutter more or less completely and with lasting results. However, in some cases motor operants will keep the stutter going to some extent after the anxiety has been removed, and their separate extinction will be needed. Since the modifiability of dysfluency by punishment was first convincingly demonstrated (Flanagan, Goldiamond, & Azrin, 1958; Goldiamond, 1965; Siegel & Martin, 1967), a variety of applications of operant principles have been described—for example, Leach (1969) used cash rewards for fluent speech and Shames (1969) used verbal reinforcement. A very convenient method was suggested by B. Migler (personal communication, 1967) and yielded promising results in the few cases in which it was tried. It consisted of forbidding the subject to complete any word that began with dysfluency, so that only fluent behavior was rewarded, by being completed and by the social results thereof.

Meyer and Mair (1963) and Andrews et al. (1964) reexamined from a behavioral viewpoint the therapeutic potentialities of the previously disdained observation (Barber, 1940) that dysfluencies are decreased when speech becomes rhythmic. Meyer and Mair used a metronome, and Andrews and Harris used verselike scanning. They obtained lasting improvement in many cases and complete fluency in some. Building on these observations and on experiments of his own, Brady (1971) elaborated a very practical treatment of stuttering. His procedure involved the use of a miniature electronic metronome worn behind the ear like a hearing aid, which it resembles. (This metronome, called the Pacemaster, is obtained from Associated Hearing Instruments, Inc., 6796 Market St., Upper Darby, Pennsylvania, 19082. Both its frequency and its volume can be adjusted.) The first step was to find conditions under which the patient could become highly fluent with the aid of a desk metronome. For a severe chronic stutter this might require his being alone with the therapist and pacing one syllable of his speech to each beat of a loud metronome set as slow as 40 beats per minute. Almost always, conditions were found under which the patient could speak in an easy, relaxed, and fluent manner.

Once fluent verbalizations appeared, albeit at a low rate, the task was to approximate gradually the rate and cadence of normal speech and to help the patient extend his fluency to other situations to which anticipatory anxiety and tension had been conditioned. The series of small steps corresponds to a hierarchy of speaking situations, progressing from those associated with minimal stuttering to those associated with severe stuttering. For example, the first situation on the hierarchy might be "speaking with wife" and the last "giving an impromptu after-dinner speech."

During this phase of treatment it was not uncommon for the patient to experience unexpected difficulty in some situations from time to time. It was found essential for him then to regain fluency in the situation as soon as possible by the same means as before, that is, by reverting to a slower rate of speech and, if necessary, to more strict pacing (one syllable or one word per beat). On becoming more fluent and regaining the feeling of control of his speech, he gradually returned to more rapid speech and less strict pacing on a trial basis. This sometimes required much coaching by the therapist. Often it was helpful for the patient to rehearse this procedure in the therapist's office by simulating outside speaking situations.

Discontinuation of the metronome was done gradually, starting with the speaking situations that gave the least amount of difficulty. During this phase, many patients found it helpful to pace their speech to the beats of an imaginary metronome. If in any situation the patient found himself having appreciable speaking difficulty, he had to return to stricter pacing of his speech even though the metronome was not present. A few sentences might restore his control. Otherwise, he might need to return to the actual metronome.

Of 23 patients who completed Brady's treatment program, 21 (or over 90%) showed a marked increase in fluency and an improvement in their general adjustment as well. These clinical results persisted for follow-up periods that ranged from 6 months to over 3 years. Although the immediate focus of Brady's method was modifying the character of speech, he was constantly aware of the implications of his procedures for the deconditioning of anxiety.

As expected, the metronome procedure was most relevant to stuttering elicited by anxiety produced either by speech itself or by social situations that imposed speech demand. However, in certain patients there was difficulty in extending metronome-aided fluency into a particular situation or class of situations, and it was then helpful to employ systematic desensitization or assertiveness training adjunctively.

In recent years, a high degree of success has been claimed for the regulated breathing methods of Azrin & Nunn (1974) and Schwartz (1976), although their procedures are worlds apart. Azrin and Nunn found in preliminary trials, that to influence stuttering it was necessary to employ such activities as "changing the breathing pattern, self-induced relaxation and the formulation of one's thoughts." The only personal interview was a first session of about 2 hours' duration. The therapist emphasized the inconveniences and annoyances that the stuttering caused in order to heighten the patient's motivation "to engage in the necessary training effort." The patient was asked to stutter deliberately, and then to describe in detail the kinds of words on which he stuttered and the accompanying unpleasantness. He was also taught to alert himself to the likelihood of stuttering and to indicate when he felt that a stutter was imminent. Next he was shown a number of ways in which to relax: by slouching slightly; by learning to breathe deeply, slowly, and regularly; and by telling himself to relax "by letting abdominal and throat muscles go as limp as possible" while continuing to carry out the breathing instructions.

Against this background a speaking routine was instituted. The patient was instructed to formulate in advance the words he was going to use. Then, after exhaling, he was slowly to take a deep breath, inhaling while constantly relaxing the chest and throat muscles, and told to start speaking as soon as the inhalation was complete. In speaking, he was to emphasize the initial part of the statement and at first settle for short durations, gradually to be increased as he became more fluent. If he were to start stuttering, he was to recommence the routine.

Several types of structured practice were given during the session. The patient first had to practice the relaxation exercises without speaking. Then he used the breathing drill to increase progressively the number of words he could speak fluently, while reading out of a book or speaking to the counselor. At first he breathed after each word and later after an increasing number of words until he could read long passages before pausing for breath. He was instructed to telephone friends each day for the first few weeks for further practice of breathing and speaking. The counselor telephoned the patient about three times during the first week to give encouragement and to answer questions, and intermittently thereafter. These conversations also enabled the counselor to evaluate the quality of speech.

Azrin and Nunn reported that in their 14 subjects, stuttering was reduced by an average of 85% on the first day after treatment. The improvement reached 97% after 1 month and was maintained at this level for 4 months in the eight subjects who were followed up for that length of time.

Until recently, the only attempt at replication was by Andrews and Tanner (1982) in whose six subjects the results were positive but disappointing, including two failures. Waterloo and Gotestam (1988) recently furnished an experimental evaluation of Azrin and Nunn's method. They noted in advance that the original study had serious shortcomings—in particular, that it lacked an operational definition of stuttering and relied entirely on self-report. Their subjects were 32 adult stutterers with a long history of severe stuttering and who stuttered 5% or more during evaluation. They assigned 16 subjects to the regulated breathing treatment and 16 to a waiting-list control group. The experimental group received a single initial 2 to 3 hour session as described by Azrin and Nunn (1974), using information that Olausen (1978) had obtained personally from Azrin to fill in gaps in the original description. Subjects carried data sheets on which to record stuttering episodes that they totaled at the end of each day. The treated group achieved significant reductions in stuttering and significantly increased rates of speech. Treatment failed in 4 of the 16. The control group were uniformly unchanged. At an 8-month follow-up, stuttering in the treated group was significantly less than in the control group, and also significantly less than before treatment. In sum, the results were impressive, though less spectacular than Azrin and Nunn's.

As clinicians, we naturally embrace the regulated breathing treatment as a new resource for our patients. But in certain ways it is less than satisfactory. To begin with, it is not really a single treatment, but a battery of treatments—a blunderbuss that effectively diminishes a variety of stuttering-related emotional and motor habits. The therapist has little notion of the controlling factors in the individual. In a series of cases such as Waterloo and Gotestam's there is little doubt that behavior analyses would have pointed to solutions in the four failures as well as enhancing the quality and degree of change in many other cases. As Ladouceur et al. (1989) concluded from an in-depth study of nine cases, an extensive functional analysis is necessary in each case if the clinician is to maximize his power to effect change.

OBSESSIONS AND COMPULSIONS

Obsessions are recurrent, persistent ideas or impulses. The word *compulsion* is applied to those cases in which motor manifestations predominate. Some obsessional behavior has the effect of reducing anxiety, and some the effect of elevating it (Wolpe, 1958, pp. 90–91). Anxiety underlies both varieties but there are cases in which obsessional behavior persists after the deconditioning of antecedent anxiety because it has become secondarily conditioned to other stimuli. Such cases are uncommon.

The first order of business in dealing with an obsessional neurosis—as with neuroses of other kinds—is the identification of the stimuli to the antecedent anxiety, followed by a program of deconditioning. Originally, the only method available for deconditioning was systematic desensitization, which usually required a great amount of effort (Walton, 1964; Walton & Mather, 1964). This is exemplified by case 65. Sometimes, however, the method is remarkably economical. For example, for a physics professor with an obsession for tidiness that was destroying his marriage, I used desensitization, starting with a 1-inch square piece of paper lying on the floor of his living room. In the course of five sessions he was enabled to imagine all reasonable degrees of domestic disarray without disturbance. His consequent acceptance of actual untidiness at home gratifyingly transformed the marital relationship.

Usually, a heavy investment of time is required for systematic desensitization in cases characterized by fear of contamination, with frequent lack of progress. This fits in with the early finding that tactile stimuli are usually not amenable to desensitization. This circumstance stimulated a search for more effective methods. Meyer (1966) was the first to treat such cases by prolonged exposure to the "contamination," by interdicting washing, and, when necessary, rituals. In two cases, he reported that precluding the customary washing rituals resulted in their improving markedly and lastingly. Subsequently, the method was widely adopted and applied to a wide range of cases—for example, Marks (1972), Rainey (1972), and Hodgson et al. (1972). Cases 55 and 56 are personal examples. Hodgson et al. (1972), when comparing desensitization, flooding, and flooding preceded by modeling, found indications of marked superiority of the last. For a detailed modern description and discussion of flooding procedures, see Foa, Steketee, and Ozarow (1985).

Case 55: Rapidly Effective Imaginal Flooding

Flooding by the use of imagery was applied to a history professor who was incapacitated by an obsessive fear. He dreaded a negative response from a committee he was to meet several months later as they considered him for a position he greatly coveted. I had him continuously imagine that he was actually meeting with this committee and receiving negative reactions all round. The scene raised his anxiety level to 100 *suds* in the first 15 minutes; this level gradually subsided to about 60 *suds* after an hour, when the flooding was terminated. At a second flooding with the same scene a week later, it was impossible to raise his anxiety above 40 *suds*, and in a few minutes it came down to zero and stayed there. He stated that his thoughts were now switching to alternatives; this possible defeat was no longer the end of the world. He remained markedly relieved, and withstood his eventual actual rejection by the committee very well.

Case 56: Graduated Flooding in vivo

This case was described in detail by Wolpe and Ascher (1976). Celia, an unmarried woman of 20, had for 2 years been preoccupied with avoiding and removing "contamination" by people or things associated with the college she had attended and which she had regarded as beneath her intellectual potential. Her obsession had begun after a horrifying experience. One evening she had returned to her room to find her roommate conversing with another woman student who was lying on Celia's bed describing a drunken sexual experience. Suddenly, Celia noticed lice crawling in that woman's hair. This revolting sight was to Celia an emotional confirmation of her negative feelings about the school. She began to avoid touching the students or any objects they might have touched. If anyone did enter her room, she would throw out any small objects they had handled and would wash the floor, the furniture, and any clothing the visitor might have touched.

Before we saw her, Celia had had a succession of conventional treatments, including lengthy hospitalizations. After the behavior analysis, we tried systematic desensitization and imaginal flooding without success, and then decided to make our first essay into flooding with preliminary modeling.

We obtained from Celia's parents various articles she had used at college and an assortment of clothing. At her next visit, Celia was conducted into an unfamiliar office with a desk on which her articles were arranged. She was asked to list these in order of the increasing discomfort she would expect to have on contact. The therapist then picked up a pencil, which she had listed as the least anxiety evoking, and then tried unsuccessfully to get her to do the same thing. He then placed his hand on the desk some distance from the pencil and moved it slowly closer until he touched the pencil with the tips of his fingers. Next he gingerly lifted it from the table, and wrote with it. Then he asked Celia if she would copy what he had just done. She was too fearful to comply for two sessions, but at the third she was able to touch and handle the pencil. The contact made her feel contaminated and therefore anxious. In order to maintain the exposure, she was asked to refrain from washing for 2 hours, during which period her distress progressively diminished to a low level. In the course of the next few sessions, Celia came to be able to touch and use all the objects, and to wear all the clothing for increasing periods and eventually for the rest of the day without washing.

Under further guidance, she exposed herself to many other things, touching people, walls, doorknobs, and books. After several weeks she returned to her parental home and in the fall was admitted to a prestigious college. Followed up at intervals during the next 3 years, she eventually reported no vestige of her obsession.

This type of obsessive-compulsive neurosis, based on fear and avoidance of contamination, has been the main area of recent research in this field. The most important result of this research has been to establish that the majority of such patients are markedly and lastingly benefited by programs of flooding and prevention of washing, carried out several times a week for several weeks (Foa, Steketee, & Ozarow, 1985; Meyer, Levy, & Schnurer, 1974; Rabavilas, Boulougouris, & Stefanis, 1976; Rachman, Hodgson, & Marks, 1971; Rachman et al., 1979.) However, the results are frequently overrated. Zohar, Foa, and Insel (1989) make the chastening comment: "Patients who enter a course rarely find themselves symptom-free at completion. . . . Maintenance of gains is problematic for about 20%."

Often forgotten is the necessity in obsessive-compulsive cases, as in other neuroses, to have as complete a picture as possible of the patient's range of maladaptive responses. All too frequently, if a flooding program has eliminated or markedly reduced an obsessive constellation, such as compulsive hand washing, treatment is abandoned even though there are other anxieties, most often social anxieties, that require treatment in their own right. The therapist may not even be aware of their existence because he or she has focused too narrowly on the obsession.

There are also cases in which flooding succeeds only partially because several anxieties are intertwined with the obsessional behavior and stand in the way of a satisfactory resolution. This is illustrated in the following case.

Case 57: Rituals Based on Insomnia Fear and Social Fears

Laura was a 34-year-old married woman whose daily life, from the age of 17, had been marred by a variety of obsessional patterns of behavior. These had begun when, in the context of academic demands during her first year at college, she started to have difficulty in sleeping. She then became obsessed with the need to sleep. Certain things *had* to be done as a condition for sleep: she had to clean meticulously, and to limit severely her favorite activity — riding horses. It appeared to her that these compulsive and ritualistic behaviors could somehow overcome the obstacles to sleep.

Before long she had to "pay" in more and more ways. Certain numbers became "lucky" — for example, eight, because that is the standard number of hours for sleeping — and others were "unlucky" for various reasons. Sometimes she would have to touch things eight times. She often had to memorize numbers that she observed on passing motor vehicles. In horse-riding, she could not allow herself to make free use of the track but had to follow a routine of several circuits in one direction, followed by an equal number in the opposite direction. There were also attractive foods that she had to resist eating to avoid punishment by insomnia. She had had prolonged periods of *insight therapy* with four different psychiatrists without any improvement.

In treating Laura, I started with the standard program described above, of having her attempt as far as possible to oppose the ritualistic impulses. For example, she was to try to ignore the numbers on automobiles and to thwart their retention by mentally reciting other numbers. She was also to ride her horse in any way she pleased. She assiduously obeyed instructions, and within a month was able to report that the average amount of time occupied by obsessional behavior had been reduced by about 30%.

Despite some further success in the second month, Laura felt that the decrease in rituals had been at the cost of a great deal of insistent and highly fatiguing effort, so that it was almost not worthwhile. This called for a revision of strategy. I had already ascertained during the early interviews that she had a great deal of social anxiety that was reflected in a Willoughby score of 68 and in numerous heavily weighted items in the Fear Survey Schedule. These would have been treated in their own right had the routine flooding treatment been fully successful. But it now seemed likely that the less-than-satisfactory effects of that treatment were due to anxieties that were causally related to her obsessional behavior.

On this analysis, I first turned my attention to the fear of not sleeping and instituted a series of desensitizations that focused on it. In one series, since she considered 7 hours of sleep a necessary minimum, I had her imagine in a state of relaxation that she woke in the morning to realize that she had slept only 6 hours. When, with repetition, this became emotionally acceptable, the number of hours slept was reduced to 5½ hours, and so on until we reached 4 hours. During this phase, there was a substantial diminution in ritualistic behavior — this time without the rise in tension that had occurred earlier.

She had meanwhile become increasingly aware of a strong relationship between the level of anxiety she felt and the likelihood of emission of ritualistic behavior. That the anxiety had social sources was becoming more and more evident; these were in line with her responses to the questionnaires. Accordingly, programs of assertiveness training and systematic desensitization were developed. A hierarchy of disapproving statements from others was employed against which she was encouraged to make appropriate assertive statements in my office, which she did with decreasing anxiety. Systematic desensitization was carried out in other areas. This program, though quite time consuming, was gratifyingly successful. After 6 months she reached a point at which her anxiety level was usually less than five *suds* and the carrying out of rituals had been reduced by 90%, though with occasional exacerbations that always occurred under circumstances of raised anxiety. Despite the drop in rituals, she was sleeping well.

Further work on social anxiety in succeeding months brought about further improvements in spite of reversals from time to time. On the average, anxiety levels continued to drop and social competence rose. After 10 months of weekly sessions, sleep was no longer a problem. Toward the end of this period, she took steps to terminate her unsatisfactory marriage and shortly afterwards began a serious new relationship that brought many stresses. All of this produced only brief and mild resurgences of the obsessional patterns. Her Willoughby score, after 11 months of treatment, was 39. After 13 months, she estimated her obsession as 95% improved overall.

In obsessions that have antecedents other than anxiety, and in those where anxiety is an appropriate response (for example, preoccupations about death), it is necessary to try to break the thinking habit directly. The method used most often is thought stopping (see pp. 129–130). Yamagami (1971) obtained complete recovery from an 8-year-old color-naming obsession by the exclusive use of thought stopping (see p. 130). For further examples see Likierman and Rachman (1982).

Covert sensitization (Cautela, 1966) and covert reinforcement (Cautela, 1970a & b; Cautela & Wall, 1980) are additional resources for the treatment of obsessions. The procedures are illustrated in the case reported by Wisocki (1970), summarized on page 234.

SEXUAL INADEQUACY

Although much has been written on this topic during the past decade, outcome studies lack analysis of cases (e.g., Everaerd & Dekker, 1985). This section therefore remains substantially unchanged from its presentation in the third edition. Uninhibited sexual responding is correlated with intense pleasurable arousal, especially during sexual intercourse. In the great majority of cases, sexual inhibition is due to interfering responses. The commonest interference is the presence of anxiety responses in the sexual situation. An inhibitory effect may also result from other emotions, such as shame or disgust. Temporary inhibition may be caused by intercurrent stresses or interfering stimuli of many kinds, such as loud voices in the next room.

Anxiety directly inhibits the particular autonomic response elements active in the sexual response. Preorgasmic sexual arousal is predominantly parasympathetic in character (Langley & Anderson, 1895; Masters & Johnson, 1966), while anxiety is predominantly a sympathetic function. Therefore, the more intensely anxiety is aroused, the more inhibition of the early sexual response there will be (Wolpe, 1958). Reciprocally, sexual responses may be used for overcoming the anxiety habits that inhibit them. As always, such utilization depends on arranging for the sexual response to be strong enough to dominate the anxiety response, so that by inhibiting it, the sexual response will diminish the anxiety-response habit. Napalkov and Karas (1957) showed that experimental neuroses in dogs could be overcome by counterposing sexual excitation to neurotic anxiety. Of course, other inhibitors of anxiety can be used to treat the anxiety that affects sexual responding.

Although it is usually in connection with anxieties related to sexual stimuli that sexual arousal has therapeutic use, its potential is not confined to these stimuli. The neurotic reactions of the dogs treated by Napalkov and Karas were conditioned to nonsexual stimuli. Similarly, sexual emotions can be instrumental in overcoming nonsexual human neuroses. Such therapeutic effects sometimes occur fortuitously in life. A fortunate twist in a person's life may provide him with a loving or erotic relationship that has therapeutic effects.

Male Sexual Inadequacy: The Therapeutic Use of Sexual Excitation

The most common deliberate use of the anxiety-inhibiting effects of erotic arousal is in the treatment of inhibited sexual responding in the male, which is generally manifested as inadequacy of penile erection or, more often, premature ejaculation. Penile erection is a parasympathetic function. The sympathetic discharges that characterize anxiety tend both to inhibit erection and to facilitate ejaculation (Langley & Anderson, 1895). Thus, the key to the problem of impaired sexual performance is the subtraction of anxiety from the sexual encounter. Sometimes the anxiety has nonsexual antecedents, for example, a fear of traumatization of human flesh (Wolpe, 1958, p. 152), but in the great majority of cases its stimuli are to be found within the sexual situation.

To use the sexual response as an anxiety inhibitor, one must first ascertain at what point in the approach anxiety begins and what factors control it. Perhaps the man begins to feel anxiety the moment he enters the bedroom, or perhaps it is when he is lying in bed in the nude with his wife. The basic idea of the treatment is explained to him—that the sexual response, being antagonistic to anxiety, can weaken his habitual anxiety if it can be consistently counterposed to anxiety that is relatively weak. He can arrange for this by limiting his sexual approaches always to the point where anxiety begins. He obviously has to obtain his wife's cooperation. The essence of her role is to avoid making him tense and anxious. She must not mock him or goad or press him to achieve any particular level of performance. Though she may have to endure a good deal of frustration, she may expect eventually to reap the reward of her helpfulness. Actually, many women obtain a reasonable degree of relief from digitally induced orgasms during the treatment period. If the man begins to feel anxiety when merely lying next to his wife in bed, he must do nothing more active until the anxiety has subsided. Usually, before long he will say, "I feel perfectly comfortable now — only sexually excited." Then, he can go on to the next stage — perhaps to turn toward her and lie facing her on his side and fondle her breasts while she remains on her back. When this can be done without anxiety, he again advances — this time perhaps to lying on top of her, but not attempting intromission. At the next step, the penis may be approximated to the clitoris or other parts of the vulva, but still without intromission. After this he is permitted a small degree of entry, and later greater degrees, followed by small amounts of movement and then greater movement. The precondition for advancing beyond a stage is the disappearance from it of all anxiety.

The details of the treatment, naturally, must be decided individually. An adjuvant that is frequently of great value was suggested by Semans (1956). The wife manipulates her husband's penis to a point just short of ejaculation and then stops. After an interval, she does the same again. The procedure may be repeated several times during a session. Over several sessions, its effect is to increase the latency to ejaculation — sometimes from a few seconds to half an hour or more. It is easy to see how this may generalize to prolongation of intercourse when the time comes. Semans describes his technique as follows.

If fatigue is present in either partner, he or she should sleep for a brief period of time. After this, love play begins and progresses to mutual stimulation of the penis and clitoris. They must keep each other informed of the stage of sexual excitement being experienced. When the husband feels a sensation which is, for him, premonitory to ejaculation, he informs his wife and removes her hand until the sensation disappears. Stimulation soon begins again and is interrupted by the husband when the premonitory sensation returns. By continuing as described above, ejaculation can eventually be postponed indefinitely. Both husband and wife are advised that if erection subsides more than temporarily, a brief sleep or postponement of further stimulation is to be preferred to continuing their efforts at that time. Next, each is told separately, and later together, that ejaculation occurs more rapidly when the penis is wet rather than dry. It is necessary, therefore, to use a bland cream or soluble jelly to lubricate the penis in order to simulate the moist surface of the vagina.

Masters and Johnson (1970) described a maneuver that may facilitate this technique. They found that when ejaculation seems inevitable it can be inhibited if the woman applies gentle digital pressure on the penis at the coronal sulcus between the urethra and the dorsum.

In occasional cases of premature ejaculation, recovery may be obtained in a much more simple way. The couple are told to have coitus as frequently as possible. The husband is instructed to try to enjoy himself as much as possible, just letting himself go and not caring how soon he ejaculates. The wife is asked to endure the situation if she can, and, of course, some cannot. It is quite helpful in cases like this to encourage the procural of orgasm in the wife by noncoital means — by manual and oral manipulations. A method that J. H. Semans (personal communication, 1962) reported as effective is for the woman to move her clitoris rhythmically against the husband's thigh.

Case 58: A Controlled Sexual Excitation Program

Ever since the beginning of his coital life at the age of 16, Mr. I., a 36-year-old realtor, had suffered from premature ejaculation, which generally occurred within 15 seconds of intromission. He had married at age 24. His wife, though deriving some satisfaction from digital orgasms, had become increasingly conscious of incomplete fulfillment, and had in the past two years been showing interest in other men. About 18 months previously, Mr. I. had had about 25 consultations with a psychoanalytically oriented psychiatrist. His general confidence had been improved by the treatment, but sexual performance had remained unchanged. In three short-lived extramarital affairs, his performance had been no better than with his wife. He felt that he was doing the "chasing," and was being accepted on sufferance.

Mr. I.'s Willoughby score was 30, with highest loadings for humiliation, stage fright, and being hurt. He lacked assertiveness in relation to people close to him, but not at all in business affairs. A program of assertiveness training was seen as a secondary but very relevant therapeutic requirement.

Mrs. I., briefly interviewed, expressed great willingness to take part in a behavior therapy program. She stated that digital orgasms satisfied her physically, but not emotionally. She felt that even a relatively small degree of prolongation of intromission would enable her to have coital orgasms. She regarded her marriage as very satisfactory in all other aspects.

Therapy of the sexual inadequacy based upon use of sexual responses made combined use of two lines of approach: (1) graded penile stimulation by the technique of Semans (see above), and (2) gradual advances toward coitus. Mr. I. kept a detailed record of his performances, which he timed as accurately as possible with a bedside clock.

In the course of five occasions of manual stimulation by his wife, Mr. I.'s latency to preejaculation rose from 6 minutes to 33 minutes. Then there were six occasions of stimulation with Mr. I. sitting astride her. At the last of these, he felt confident enough to insert the glans penis into her vagina, maintaining it there for 5 minutes, after which they both had orgasms digitally. Subsequent occasions focused on increasing intromission, and then increasing duration of full intercourse.

Further occasions enabled gradually increasing excursions of coital movement, and finally a major breakthrough occurred on the 25th occasion. While Mr. I. retained his erection, Mrs. I. had four orgasms, and he ejaculated during the last of them. From this time onward there was mutually satisfactory sexual performance. There were 14 therapeutic interviews over 5 weeks (because they had come for treatment from overseas). Mr. I.'s Willoughby score at the last interview was 13.

Although the most frequent source of male sexual failure is anxiety about sexual performance, nonsexual sources of anxiety have the same effect. Eysenck (1960) recorded a case of impotence that was attributable to conditioned anxiety evoked by the wallpaper design in the bedroom. A case based on fear of traumatization was referred to above (p. 299). The following case was based on nonsexual social anxiety and treated by its removal.

Case 59: Impotence Overcome Mainly by Cognitive Correction

Mr. D., a prominent lawyer of 44, came for treatment with a 2-year history of difficulty in obtaining and maintaining an erection. For 12 years before this he had enjoyed a highly satisfying sex life with his wife. His problem had started with poor performances on occasions of unusual fatigue. This history led me to adopt the kind of sexual reconditioning program described above. He seemed at first to progress, but then it became evident that there was little real improvement.

I then examined his relationship with his wife more closely. Originally, she had behaved like an appendage to him. Then, about 4 years previously, she had consulted a therapist who had encouraged her to stand up for herself and assert her own personality. She had begun to rebel in diverse ways. He commented, "My feeling is that she has abandoned me." I perceived this feeling of rejection as the basis of his impaired sexual function. Having convinced him of this chain of causes, I encouraged him to discuss the relationship with his wife and to procure mutual agreement on what the rights and obligations of each should be. After a few weeks the communication between them had so greatly improved as to assure him that she had not abandoned him and still loved him. From her it removed the resentment that had caused her rebellion. I also needed to desensitize him to some of her acts of independence. These measures resulted in the restoration of his sexual abilities, in the setting of a much improved general relationship.

Biological Causes & Treatments
of Male Sexual Inadequacy

In general, patients who complain of erectile failure or insufficiency are more difficult to treat than those with premature ejaculation, for theirs is a more profound inhibition of response. In some of them, there is clearly a biological factor involved. Their number is probably much greater than has generally been assumed. Spark, White, and Connolly (1980) found that more than one-third of 105 consecutive patients with impotence had endocrine disorders. Appropriate medication restored sexual function in the great majority of them. Schumacher and Lloyd (1981) noted a surprisingly high and varied incidence of organic disease in a sample of 83 men complaining of impotence. The conclusion is obvious that medical investigation should be routinely undertaken in all cases of male sexual dysfunction, except perhaps those in whom a purely psychological basis is unequivocally clear from the start.

The onset of biologically based impotence is insidious, with erectile power diminishing over a period of months or years. The history often reveals a lifelong low level of sexual function. If there is no evidence of anxiety or other reactive source of sexual inhibition, a biological causation is highly probable. The diagnosis may be settled by laboratory estimation of urinary testosterone (Cooper et al., 1970). Less directly relevant, but more easily available, is the estimation of urinary 17-ketosteroid excretion. A distinctly low testosterone assay is a strong indication for hormone therapy; but even with a moderately high reading, the patient need not be denied the possible benefits of testosterone treatment, although most of those who are so treated fail to respond (Cooper et al., 1970). Other investigations proposed by Schumacher and Lloyd (1981) are measurement of plasma levels of cortisol, progesterone, luteinizing hormone, follicle-stimulating hormone, thyroxine, triiodothyronine, thyroid binding globulin, free thyroxine, and where indicated, thyrotropin.

The first account of the beneficial use of male sex hormones in the treatment of impotence was by Miller, Hubert, and Hamilton (1938). In the course of about 30 years, I twice succeeded in augmenting a low sex drive by daily injections of testosterone so as to enable successful sexual performance which subsequently continued without further use of the hormone. Presumably, the sexual responses that the testosterone had facilitated came to be conditioned to contiguous stimuli. More extensive reviews of the use of this substance have been provided by Cooper (1971), Jakobovitz (1970), and Miller (1968).

Drugs have also at times been used to curb anxiety and delay ejaculation (Drooby, personal communication, 1964; Singh, 1963). Repeated successful sexual performance thus achieved may enable the patient later to perform satisfactorily without their use.

It was mentioned at the beginning of this chapter that various intercurrent stresses may cause temporary inhibition of sexual responding. Chronic stress that has nothing to do with the sexual relationship as such may in parallel fashion cause chronic sexual inhibition. Prolonged stress may come from an enduring real misery, such as an incurable illness in a child. More often it is bound up with disharmonies in the relationship. A program for mutual readjustment should then be undertaken. Sometimes a few joint sessions with the couple on a "common-sense" basis are all that is needed. Other cases require more formal arrangements involving "contracts," score cards, and a token economy, as described by Stuart (1969). Case 60 affords an instructive example of the disruptive effects of nonsexual anxiety on sexual behavior.

Problems of Female Collaboration

A cooperative sexual partner is almost always an asset and usually indispensable to the success of most of the techniques described above. Many patients have a partner readily available. Others may wait months to find somebody sufficiently interested to be willing to make the effort and bear the discomforts involved in treatment. Sometimes, although the patient has a wife or consort, she is unable to participate as needed, either because she is contemptuous of her mate's disability or more often, because a long history of disappointment and frustration has quenched her amorous responses. If the woman is unmoved by her husband's prefiguration of the behavior therapy program, the therapist should arrange to speak to her himself. If she can be persuaded to take the first steps, and if she is encouraged by early progress, the rest can be plain sailing.

When all reasonable efforts have failed to extract from the wife the affectional behavior needed for the therapeutic program, it is usually appropriate to encourage the enlistment of some kind of surrogate. If moral justification is required, it may be said that if the man's sexual potency should be reinstated through this, it may lead to reconstruction of his marriage; and even if it does not, it is better both physiologically and psychologically to have outside satisfactions than to accept enforced chastity forever.

Results of Treatment

Among 18 cases I surveyed retrospectively in 1966, 14 (78%) recovered to the extent of achieving entirely satisfactory sexual performance. Another three cases (17%) attained a level that was acceptable to their partners. The

Table 15.2. Results of Behavior Therapy in 18 Cases of Impotence

PATIENT NUMBER	AGE	THERAPEUTIC TIME SPAN	OUTCOME AND REMARKS
1	31	1 week	Recovered
2	40	8 weeks	Recovered
3	46	10 weeks	Recovered
4	46	20 weeks	Recovered
5	40	4 weeks	Recovered
6	41	12 weeks (intermittent and furtive)	Much Improved
7	50	6 weeks	Recovered but no transfer to wife.
8	49	2 weeks	Recovered (major factor was removal of anxiety through wife taking contraceptive pills).
9	20	6 weeks	Recovered (major factor was resolution of doubts of masculinity raised by psychoanalytic reading).
10	49	10 weeks	Improved from almost complete erectile failure to functionally sufficient erections to make marriage possible and to satisfy and impregnate wife.
11	35	6 weeks	Marked improvement by time therapist left country. Appropriate assertion toward wife major factor.
12	36	5 weeks	Recovered.
13	44	16 weeks (infrequent opportunities)	Unimproved. No apparent sexual anxiety. Hypersensitivity of glans penis.
14	40	9 weeks	Recovered.
15	35	8 weeks (preceded by 12 weeks of overcoming interpersonal fears)	Improved from no erection to strong ones. Coitus improving at time when therapist left country.
16	18	66 weeks (very irregular opportunities at first)	Recovered.
17	53	3 weeks	Recovered with new consort. Previously no benefit in 12 weeks with uncooperative consort.
18	39	12 weeks	Recovered. At first erections occurred only after testosterone injections.

mean span of time required was 11.3 weeks and the median 8.0 weeks. Table 15.2 gives some details of these cases.

Female Sexual Inadequacy

Female sexual inadequacy is usually referred to a frigidity, which is an undesirable term inasmuch as it implies emotional coldness or a total lack of sexual response. The important thing to recognize is that there are all grades of inhibition of sexual response in women, from no response whatever to the inability to achieve coital orgasm in spite of high arousal.

Two kinds of cases must be distinguished: those in whom lack of response is in relation to males in general, and those in whom it is relative to a particular male who is in many cases the husband. The solutions required are very different.

General Inhibition of Arousal

Inhibition of female sexual arousal may be general, that is, found to occur with any partner. Some cases have an organic basis. A gynecological examination should therefore be arranged whenever there is the slightest possibility of physical pathology. I once saw a woman who had been psychoanalyzed for the 4 years of her marriage for "frigidity." Gynecological examination showed the condition to be due to vaginal spasm caused by a painful ulcer.

In the great majority of cases, general inhibition of arousal is due to negative, usually anxious, feelings having been connected to sexual stimuli. The causal basis may be informational, religious indoctrination, or negative statements from a mother or other authority. Attitudes thus learned may persist to inhibit sexual arousal in adult life. In other cases, conditioned inhibition may have developed through being punished or frightened in the act of masturbation or sex play. Inhibitory classical conditioning may also occur in the context of attempted rape or other sexual abuse, or in consequence of repeated frustration of sexual arousal. Sexual inhibition also sometimes develops, as in case 60, out of negative experiences resulting from misguided self-abnegation in a loving relationship.

The treatment of general sexual inhibition depends upon the stimulus-response analysis of the case. When there has been faulty indoctrination, it is necessary to remove misconceptions about sex and to reeducate the patient. This done, there will often still be a negative emotional attitude bound up with anxiety that has been conditioned to certain aspects of the sexual situation. The usual treatment is then systematic desensitization whose details are determined by the analysis. In yet other cases, the inhibition is a by-product of long-continued unexpressed resentment at a spouse's "failings." Sometimes the problem would be solved if the woman could make her wishes known; here the cure may lie in assertiveness training.

In each of the following four cases, frigidity was overcome by desensitization. In cases 61 and 62, typical sexual stimuli made up the hierarchical content; in case 60 it was objects of increasing size in the vagina, and in case 63 it was being seen at orgasm.

Case 60: Treatment by Imaginal and in vivo Desensitization

A 38-year-old woman, Mrs. Y., whose relationship with her husband had for years been enviable in all respects, developed a vaginitis which made intercourse painful. But her great affection for her husband had led her to go on permitting intercourse which had resulted in marked vaginismus. Subsequently, the vaginitis was successfully treated and intercourse ceased to be painful but the vaginismus had persisted so extremely that it was impossible for Mr. Y. to gain entry. When I first saw her, this state of affairs had lasted for 3 years.

Analysis revealed that the vaginismus was part of an anxiety reaction to the entry of any object into the vagina. Treatment consisted of a combination of standard and in vivo desensitization. I instructed the patient to relax and to imagine, at first, a very thin rod (1/8 inch in diameter) being inserted to a depth of 1/2 inch into her vagina. This produced a small amount of anxiety. I repeated the scene until the anxiety disappeared. I gradually increased the extent of the rod's insertion up to four inches, and subsequently repeated the whole sequence with progressively wider rods. When the width of the imaginary rod had reached 1/2 inch, I arranged for the construction of a set of wax rods that varied in diameter from 1/8 inch to 1 1/2 inches, that the patient was instructed to use at home while relaxed, starting with the insertion of the 1/8 inch rod into her vagina, slowly, inch by inch. Thereafter, in vivo "shadowing" a few widths behind the imaginary diameter became the rule. When we reached about 3/4 inch diameter in imagination, movement such as would occur during coitus was introduced. This was a new source of anxiety that required many scene presentations for desensitization. Then, in-and-out movement of the wax rod was started. Increasingly rapid movement came to be comfortably tolerated. At this point, I began to encourage careful experimentation with actual coitus, which became possible soon afterward without vaginismus or any other manifestation of anxiety.

Case 61: Treatment by Imaginal Desensitization Starting With Remote Items

This is a case of a much more common kind. Since an attempt at seduction by an uncle when she was about 15, Mrs. H., a woman of 32, had always felt a revulsion against sex. Nevertheless, she had married. She had borne four children in 6 years, because being pregnant was a defense against intercourse. Mrs. H. had been treated by conventional psychotherapy, drugs, and electroconvulsive therapy, all without benefit. Her psychiatrist, not a behavior therapist, had then decided to try systematic desensitization of which he had a reading acquaintance. The attempt had been a fiasco. The weakest item on the hierarchy was the sight of naked female breasts. When the psychiatrist presented this image to the patient, it had produced such a severe anxiety reaction that he could not continue, and in desperation referred Mrs. H. to me. I added to the weak end of the hierarchy several items that were quite remote from the bedroom. The first scene was being at a swimming pool where there was only one male present, 50 yards away, with his bare chest exposed. This man was later "brought" progressively closer. Next, we utilized, first at a distance of 50 yards and then closer, a completely nude male statue in a park. A later item in the hierarchy was seeing a little nude boy of four gamboling in a paddling pool. Eventually, after many steps, the patient was successfully desensitized to such images as dogs fornicating, pictures of nude males, four-letter words, and, finally, personal coital contingencies. It became possible eventually for Mrs. H. to indulge in and enjoy sexual intercourse with her husband.

Case 62: Treatment by Assertiveness Training and Imaginal Desensitization

A somewhat similar case was the subject of a week-to-week demonstration to a group of psychiatric residents. The patient, Mrs. D., was a 27-year-old woman with several interpersonal neurotic anxiety systems in addition to sexual inhibition. One requirement was to teach her to assert herself. She caught on to the idea quickly and soon began to act on it. After the fifth session, the main focus of therapy became the sexual problem. Though she had worked as an actress, she was extremely standoffish. She had often been darkly warned by her mother about the evils of sex. These warnings had been borne out by an attempted sexual assault by a much older man about the time of puberty. After her marriage, she had found sex unpleasant and tried to avoid it as much as possible. Central to her problem was a tense abhorrence of the male sex organ. In treating this by desensitization, I started by having her imagine looking at a nude male statue in a park, from a distance of 30 feet. After "moving" progressively closer to the statue, she eventually imagined herself handling the stone penis with equanimity. The next series of scenes began with her imagining herself at one end of her bedroom and seeing her nude husband's penis 15 feet away. As desensitization proceeded, he was brought closer and closer. Then she imagined that she quickly touched the penis. With repetition, this aroused less and less anxiety. The duration of contact was increased step by step. In vivo assignments followed close behind the imagining. By about the 20th therapeutic session, Mrs. D. was enjoying sexual relations and having coital orgasms on about 50% of occasions.

Case 63: Treatment by in vivo Desensitization

The precise details of treatment depend on behavior analysis in the treatment of frigidity just as with any other presenting complaint. This is well brought out in the case of Mrs. L., a 39-year-old mother of three children who had for many years been happily married and had enjoyed a thoroughly satisfying sex life. About 7 years earlier, her husband had begun drinking increasingly until he was eventually almost constantly under the influence.

Mrs. L. was greatly distressed by this change, but when her husband paid no attention to her entreaties, she began to find sexual contact increasingly repugnant. After a few months, she moved out of the house and filed for divorce. Both before the divorce and after it, Mrs. L. had a number of sexual affairs but was surprised and disconcerted to note that she was quite unable to have coital orgasms. She came for treatment when she found this disability affecting a new relationship in which she felt more deeply in love than ever before in her life. Careful investigation of the details of her responses revealed that the essence of the problem was a fear of being seen in the state of abandonment implicit in an orgasm. By contrast, she was easily able to induce masturbatory orgasms in private. In accordance with these facts, she was given a schedule of masturbating to orgasm at decreasing physical distance from her lover. First she did so in the dark, separated from him by the closed bathroom door, then with the door open. Then illumination was gradually increased, and thereafter he moved closer and closer, until eventually she was able to masturbate to orgasm in his full view. This, as expected, proved to be the necessary precondition to enable her to have orgasms during intercourse.

There are certain women who are sexually arousable to a considerable and often marked degree, but who have never experienced full orgasm. Many of these are easily able to have frictional clitoral orgasms — some of them, even during coitus, if special efforts are made to continue clitoral stimulation at that time. Even so, the experience is often unsatisfactory because this kind of orgasm tends to have a restricted sensory locus.

An effective solution to such problems may lie in the induction of "clinical orgasm" by suggestion (MacVaugh, 1972, 1974; Rubin, 1972). Rubin's schedule is quite simple and straightforward. MacVaugh's is very elaborate but has been more extensively studied and more fully described by its author, to whose work the interested reader is referred. After obtaining evidence of responsiveness to suggestion, MacVaugh goes on to apply a hypnotic procedure and to suggest the successive steps of imaginary lovemaking with an exciting, stimulating partner who has been previously chosen. He gives much attention to pelvic sensations, and later, when appropriate, suggests pelvic movements. He builds upon these, finally to elicit a full orgasm. His tape recordings are utterly convincing. The climax-inducing procedure takes up to about 3 hours. MacVaugh states that once a clinical orgasm has been induced, orgasmic behavior has entered the women's repertoire and is available for elicitation in real life. The whole of this schedule is unlikely to be always necessary, and a behavioral analysis beforehand should indicate what parts might be omitted.

A program that is less elaborate has been described by Lobitz and Lopiccolo (1972). It consists of nine steps, emphasizing extension of self-awareness, genital self-exploration, concentration on pleasure areas, and masturbation (with use of a vibrator if necessary). Lobitz and Lopiccolo use hetero-sexual erotic pictures or literature to supplement the above program. Three women in their program reported masturbating to their first orgasm shortly after having viewed a sexually explicit film.

Another method that has produced encouraging results and that has the advantage of being usable in groups, consists of relaxation training followed by the viewing of a long series of videotaped vignettes depicting graduated sexual behaviors (Nemetz, Craig, & Reith, 1978).

Situationally Based Sexual Inhibition

Behavior analysis may reveal that a woman who complains of frigidity is not negatively conditioned to sexual stimuli in general, but unresponsive to her particular partner. The question then is why she does not respond to him. In many cases, one finds that she simply does not care for him as a person. Perhaps she did once, but does no longer. One patient had fallen in love with her husband for his wisdom and erudition, only to discover after marriage that she had been misled. When his image slumped, so did her ability to respond to him erotically. But sometimes the deficiencies are not easy to define. When there is a general lack of attraction to the spouse, I know of nothing that can be done about it. Sometimes, though, in the course of years, a pleasant, amicable association does build up feelings of affection and love.

Certainly, one should always make every effort to identify sources of inhibition and to see whether change is possible. There may be something changeable in the husband's behavior. Perhaps he comes home from work at irregular hours without ever telling his wife in advance or phoning her. Perhaps he gets lost in reading or in televised movies or in card playing, so that there is a lack of communion. Such behavior, if persistent, may trans-form affection to dislike and passion to frigidity. One patient to whom this happened had a husband who was an "empire builder," busy establishing branches of his business all over the United States. All efforts to change his behavior failed.

Fortunately, some husbands are less immovable than this one was. Quite often, if the wife learns to behave with well-tempered assertiveness, the husband's behavior will also change favorably. In one case of situational frigidity, the husband, deeply involved in international affairs, treated his spouse essentially as a servant and caterer. He would often bring home many visitors, usually without notice. She was extremely passive and compliant. In the context of assertiveness training I had her start following the princi-ple, "If you will do things for me I will do things for you." This almost at once made his attitude toward her more pleasant. She next made a stand regarding their way of life: "I cannot have people here every night. I need some personal life." He acceded to this, a much closer relationship progressively developed, and a sex life that was gratifying to both resulted.

This unilateral approach to readjustment of marriages is not always appropriate. Discord is often a matter of spiraling bilateral resentments. One partner's feelings are hurt, and he withdraws affection or retaliates against his spouse in some other way, provoking further negative behavior from her. The solution to the vicious circle may be found in a contractual arrangement between the partners. Stuart (1969, 1975) devised a program that includes a "marital contract," a written undertaking by each person to do things that the other desires, and score cards. In effect, each partner is given the opportunity to learn that positive reinforcement of the other is compensated in kind. A key procedural point is to translate general complaints into particular instances (e.g., "You criticized my cooking in front of your parents," rather than "You're always trying to hurt me"). The process of mutual reinforcement is, however, often quite difficult to institute and has generated considerable debate (Jacobson & Martin, 1976; Jacobson & Weiss, 1978; Knudson, Gurman & Kniskern, 1980).

SEXUAL DEVIATIONS

A sexual deviation may be defined as the habitual quest for sensual satisfaction in a mode other than heterosexual intercourse between consenting adults. Examples of deviations are exhibitionism, pedophilia, frotteurism, sadomasochism, and fetishism. Homosexuality obviously conforms to this definition, but to a large number of men and women it is a satisfactory way of life. But there are some male homosexuals who find their orientation unacceptable — "ego-dystonic" homosexuality (Lief & Kaplan, 1986) — and who request treatment, as is their right. It was found in the Temple Behavior Therapy Unit that in men who requested treatment, the homosexuality was generally based on one or more of three kinds of learned habits: (a) conditioned anxiety reactions evoked by women in contexts of emotional closeness or physical proximity; (b) conditioned interpersonal anxiety of the kind that calls for assertiveness training: in these cases, this anxiety had its greatest strength at the female end of the social spectrum; (c) positive erotic conditioning to males.

The rule of giving therapeutic priority to anxiety habits clearly applies to the first two of the foregoing bases of homosexuality. Stevenson and Wolpe (1960) overcame two cases of homosexuality and one of pedophilia by assertiveness training. Aversion therapy is to be considered only when the homosexuality rests on positive erotic conditioning to males. The treatment by desensitization of exhibitionism was first reported by Bond and Hutchinson

(1960). Its treatment by the deconditioning of social anxiety, mainly through assertiveness training and systematic desensitization, was frequently successful in the Temple Behavior Therapy Unit.

For a review of many facets of sexual deviations and their treatment, the reader is referred to Brownell and Barlow (1980).

16
Four Instructive Complex Cases

The cases described in this chapter were merely labeled *complex* in previous editions of this book. Neither the adjective nor the descriptions given conveyed the real reason for their inclusion. Complexity is so common that it does not in itself call for attention. What gives these cases special interest is that each of them illustrates unusual ramifications of behavior analysis or unusual therapeutic procedures, and in respect to the two cases with sexual problems, the achievement of therapeutic effects that are not usually associated with the particular methods that were used, though these were directly indicated by the standard dynamic analysis. The four cases are given *in extenso* so that the strategies adopted may be seen in the broad perspective of the patient's history and life situation.

SOCIAL ANXIETY

Case 64: Social Anxiety and Obsession About Wife's Sexual Past

Mr. B. was a 31-year-old advertising salesman who 4 years previously had begun to notice increasing anxiety in situations from which it was difficult to get away. Within a few months, even 5 minutes in the office of a client would produce considerable anxiety accompanied by a strong desire to urinate. If he went out and relieved himself, the urge would return after a further 5 minutes, and so on. The only circumstances that could be associated with the onset of Mr. B.'s neurosis were the unsettlement of having moved to a new house in town, and his concern at the unexpected break-up of the marriage of close friends whom he had regarded as ideally mated. His only previous experience of undue anxiety was a brief one that had occurred upon moving to a new school at the age of 16. This could conceivably have conditioned anxiety to new places. The Fear Survey revealed very high anxiety to strange places, failure, strangers, bats, journeys especially by train, being criticized, surgical operations, rejection, planes, being disapproved of, losing control, looking foolish, and fainting.

Mr. B.'s early history was quite conventional. A feature of interest was strong religious training with marked emphasis on "the good and the bad." Church-going had played a prominent part in his childhood and adolescence. In his middle teens he had come to resent it, but had never outwardly rebelled. He had done well in school and got on well with both classmates and teachers. He had been trained in journal advertising, but was now engaged in advertising salesmanship, which he greatly liked.

As regards his sexual history, Mr. B. had been stimulated by erotic pictures at the age of 10. At 13, he had begun to masturbate, without fear or guilt. Dating and petting began at 14, and at 18 he had met his wife who attracted him by her intelligence, good looks, and responsiveness to his jokes. The courtship was broken by Mr. B. when she revealed that she had had an affair 2 years earlier. On reflection, he condoned the episode, and at the age of 20 married her. The relationship turned out to be a very congenial one, and sexually very satisfying to both, but Mr. B. was never really able to divest himself of the painful idea that he had been "dealt a dirty card."

At the second session, Mr. B. described how embarrassing and incapacitating he found his neurotic anxiety and the associated urge to urinate. Anxiety was greater in the presence of unfamiliar people and if there was no easy access to a toilet. Other factors that increased it were the importance of the occasion and the importance of the other person. On the whole, there was more anxiety in anticipation of a meeting than at the meeting itself. Since a desensitization program seemed to be indicated, relaxation training was started at this interview.

At his next session, 5 days later, Mr. B. reported that he had practiced relaxing, and that by means of it had been able to desist from urinating while at home for a period of 6½ hours despite quite a strong urge. Relaxation training was now extended and the general desensitization strategy worked out. It was apparent from careful questioning that the duration of interviews with clients was the most important factor determining the strength of Mr. B.'s anxiety. It was therefore decided to construct an interview hierarchy, using a time dimension for its easy quantifiability. I started the desensitization by having him imagine himself scheduled to a very brief meeting (of 2 minutes' duration) with the manager of an important firm. In spite of the fact that relaxation training had at this point involved only a limited part of his musculature, I went ahead with desensitization at this session because he seemed so calm. The first scene was presented to him as follows: "Imagine that you have just entered the office of a manager who has a rule that no representative is permitted to spend more than 2 minutes in his office." By the third presentation this scene produced no anxiety, and scenes of meetings of 4 minutes and 6 minutes were then presented in succession, to zero anxiety.

In subsequent interviews, the duration of these meetings was progressively extended, until by the ninth he could imagine being with an executive for 60 minutes without anxiety. He then found himself much better at real meetings and social situations. While visiting relatives, he urinated only three times in 5 hours. However, his anticipatory anxiety was almost as bad as ever. There was some measure of it several hours before a prospective meeting, but it became much more noticeable 30 minutes to 1 hour beforehand, and then increased rather steeply. At the ninth interview, then, desensitization of anticipatory anxiety was started. Anxiety decreased to zero in two to three presentations of each of the following scenes:

1. In his office, 60 minutes before visiting a client
2. In his office, 30 minutes before visiting a client and preparing to leave
3. Twenty minutes before visiting a client, entering his car to allow ample time
4. In his car on the way to a client 10 minutes before the appointed time
5. Emerging from his car at the premises of the client's office, with 8 minutes in hand
6. Entering the waiting room of the client's office 6 minutes before the appointed time.
7. Announcing himself to the client's secretary 5 minutes before the appointed time

At his 10th interview, a week later, Mr. B. reported considerably less anxiety about anticipated business meetings. He had for the first time in many months taken his wife to a downtown restaurant. During the 25-minute ride to that restaurant he had not, as in the past, had to stop to relieve himself in a rest room. At first slightly anxious in the restaurant, he had become almost entirely calm after the first 10 minutes. Desensitization to the anticipation of interviews was continued to the point that he could calmly imagine himself in the client's waiting room 2 minutes before he was to be called in. This hierarchy was finally disposed of at the next session. Now Mr. B. spontaneously reported that he felt far greater confidence in all respects. He had been going out to get new business — at first feeling some strain, but later increasingly comfortably. He had spent 1½ hours with a new and imposing manager of an important new client firm, with hardly any anxiety before or during the interview. He was no longer bothered at going into strange places because it no longer mattered whether he knew where the toilet was. For the same reason, he had ceased to fear using trains, airplanes, or buses.

Attention now turned to Mr. B.'s difficulty in asserting himself with strangers. Assertive behavior was instigated. To facilitate it, he was desensitized to one relevant situation — telling a waiter "This food is bad." Anxiety disappeared at the second presentation of this. Two weeks later, at his 14th interview, Mr. B. stated that he was expressing himself when required with increasing ease. For example, he had immediately and effectively spoken up at a drugstore when another customer was taken ahead of him out of turn. He had become more and more comfortable making business calls, citing as an example a 1 3/4 hour interview with a particular executive. He commented that 3 months earlier he would in the course of so long a period have had to go out to urinate about 20 times. However, he still had to push himself to do some of the things he had become accustomed to avoiding.

From this point onward, the main focus of therapy was his distress about his wife's premarital affair. First, it was mutually agreed, after reference to Kinsey and others, that Mr. B.'s reactions were irrational. Then, an attempt was made to employ imagery in a way that was suggested by Ahsen's (1965) "eidetic psychotherapy," which is behaviorally reasonable though based upon an extremely fanciful theory. The central practical idea is to ask the patient to imagine himself behaving in a new way in a past real situation that has been emotionally distressful, in order to change the associated emotion. The idea was employed in the present case by having Mr. B. project himself back to the time of his wife's affair and imagine that he was beating up the lover in a hotel. Mr. B. was enjoined, following Ahsen's routine, to practice this imaginary sequence 50 to 100 times a day. He felt himself improving for about 2 weeks, his obsession becoming about 20% less in incidence and 40% less in emotional intensity. But continuing for a further 4 weeks yielded no further benefit.

I decided, therefore, to tackle the problem by systematic desensitization. In order to desensitize Mr. B. to this long-past situation, I employed images from a fictitious film supposed to have been taken of his wife's premarital amorous activities by a hidden camera. Relaxed and with his eyes closed, Mr. B. was asked to imagine that his wife was sitting on a couch with her lover who kissed her and then put his hand on one of her breasts over her dress for exactly 5 seconds. He felt no anxiety at this. A fair amount of anxiety was evoked by the next scene in which the duration of contact was made 8 seconds, but at the third presentation of this scene anxiety disappeared. Two presentations were required to remove anxiety from him imagining the hand over the breast for 10 seconds, and five for 20 seconds.

At the following session, 6 weeks later, Mr. B. again felt anxiety to the 20-second hand contact, but it disappeared at the third presentation. Two weeks later, he reported that his feelings toward his wife were more detached and that he was thinking of her less. In general, his thoughts were turning away from the past and toward the present and future. Further scenes were presented, increasing the duration of the lover's hand upon his wife's clothed breast successively to 25 seconds, 30 seconds, 40 seconds, 1 minute, 1½ minutes, 2 minutes, and 3 minutes, and her snuggling up to him. None of these scenes produced any disturbance. On opening his eyes, Mr. B. stated that "having got over the hump last time," he no longer cared what his wife had done in the past. Recovery from the obsession (as well as the other problems) had endured at last contact 3 years later.

The successful treatment of Mr. B.'s two neurotic constellations depended on noting a quantitative relationship relevant to the controlling dynamics of each problem. Concerning the fear of urination, the key observation was that the anxiety experienced during business interviews was a function of the projected duration of the interview. In respect of the obsession about his wife's premarital affair, the key finding was that his distress about it was a function of degree of intimacy. This could be progressively increased by reference to the fictitious film, and thus provide a basis for desensitization.

MULTIDIMENSIONAL AUTOMOBILE PHOBIA

Case 65 is excerpted and adapted from an experimental study (Wolpe, 1962). The case is of interest because it shows the absolute necessity of finding a way to present accurately graded, clearly defined fear stimuli if systematic desensitization is to succeed. It also shows the feasibility (and, indeed, sometimes the indispensability) of an artificial setting to attain this end (where it parallels the sexual problem of case 64). The steps of the desensitization were influenced by several factors, the relevance of some of which became apparent only as treatment proceeded.

Case 65: Desensitization of a Multidimensional Automobile Phobia

Mrs. C. was a 39-year-old woman who complained of fear reactions to traffic situations, and whom I first saw on April 6, 1960. Her story was that in February, 1958, while her husband was taking her to work by car, they entered an intersection on the green light. She suddenly became aware of a large truck that, disregarding the red signal, was bearing down upon them from the left. She remembered the moment of impact, being flung out of the car, flying through the air, and then losing consciousness. Her next recollection was of waking in the ambulance on the way to the hospital. She was found to have injuries to her knee and neck, for which she spent a week in hospital.

On the way home from the hospital by car, she felt unaccountably frightened. She stayed at home for 2 weeks, quite happily, and then, resuming normal activities, noticed that, though relatively comfortable on the open road, she was always disturbed at seeing a car approach from either side, but not from straight ahead. Along city streets she had continuous anxiety, which, at the sight of a laterally approaching car less than half a block away, would rise to panic. She could, however, avoid a strong reaction by closing her eyes before reaching an intersection. She was also distressed in other driving situations that involved lateral approaches of cars. Reactions were extraordinarily severe in making a left turn in the face of approaching traffic on the highway. Execution of the turn momentarily placed the approaching vehicle to the right of her car, raising tension even when the vehicle was a mile or more ahead. Left turns in the city disturbed her less because of slower speeds. The entry of other cars from side streets even as far as two blocks ahead into the road in which she was traveling also constituted a lateral threat. In addition, she was anxious walking across streets, even at intersections with the traffic light in her favor and even if the nearest approaching car was more than a block away.

Questioned about previous traumatic experiences, she recalled that 10 years previously a tractor had crashed into the side of a car in which she was a passenger. Nobody had been hurt; the car had continued its journey, and she had been aware of no emotional sequel. No one close to her had ever been involved in a serous accident. Though she had worked in the Workmen's Compensation Claims office, dealing with cases of injury had not been disturbing to her. She found it incomprehensible that she should have developed the car phobia; in London during World War II, she had accepted the dangers of the blitz calmly, without ever needing to use sedatives.

Her early history revealed nothing of significance. In England during the war, she had been engaged to a pilot who was killed. After his death, she had for a time not desired other associations. Her next serious relationship was with her husband, whom she had met in 1955. They had married in 1957, about 9 months before the accident. Until the accident, the marital relationship had been good. Since then however, because of adverse comments that her husband made about her disability, her sexual interest had diminished.

At the second interview, training in relaxation and the construction of hierarchies were initiated. Mrs. C. was taught relaxation of the arms and the forehead. A hierarchy was constructed relating to traffic situations in open country. The first glimmer of anxiety reportedly occurred if her car was 200 yards from a crossing and if, 400 yards from the crossing, at right angles, another car was approaching. This information was the focus of an introductory desensitization session. Having relaxed Mrs. C., I presented to her imagination a presumably neutral scene and then the supposedly weak phobic situation described above. She reported no disturbance to the latter.

At the third interview, instruction in relaxation of muscles of the shoulder was succeeded by a desensitization session in which the following scenes were presented: (a) Mr. C.'s car, driven by her husband, had stopped at an intersection, and another car was approaching at right angles two blocks away; and (b) the highway scene of the previous session was repeated, except that now the distances were somewhat reduced. To each of these conditions Mrs. C. unexpectedly showed considered muscle tension. This made me question her further, leading to the revelation that she was *always* continuously tense in cars but had not thought this worth reporting. All the car scenes she had imagined during the sessions had aroused anxiety, but too little, she felt, to deserve mention. Mrs. C. was now asked to report *any* anxiety, and to imagine that she was about to ride two blocks on a lonely country road. This evoked considerable anxiety.

At the fifth interview, based on this observation, I elicited that even the thought of a journey raised Mrs. C.'s tension, so that if, at 9 a.m. her husband were to say, "We are going out driving at 2 p.m." she would be continuously apprehensive, and more so when actually in the car. During the desensitization session, I asked her to imagine that she was at home expecting to go for a short drive in the country 4 hours later. This scene, presented five times, evoked anxiety that did not decrease on repetition, an observation with a very important implication—that from her viewpoint any journey by car implied unpredictable, open-ended danger of exposure to laterally approaching cars.

A new strategy therefore had to be devised, by which the exposures to traffic would be completely under control. On a sheet of paper I drew an altogether imaginary, completely enclosed square field, which was represented as being two blocks (200 yards) long (see figure 16.1). At the southwest corner (lower left) I drew her car, facing north (upward), in which she sat with her husband, and at the lower right corner another car, supposed to be that of Dr. Richard W. Garnett, a senior staff psychiatrist, which faced them at right angles. Dr. Garnett (hereafter Dr. G.) was used because Mrs. C. regarded him as a trustworthy person.

This imaginary situation became the locus of the scenes in the sessions that followed. At the fifth desensitization session, Mrs. C. was asked to imagine Dr. G. announcing to her that he was going to drive his car a half-block toward her and then proceeding to do so while she sat in her parked car. As this elicited no reaction, she was next made to imagine him driving one block toward her, and then, as there was again no reaction, one and a quarter blocks. On perceiving a reaction to this scene, I repeated it three times, but without effecting any decrement in the reaction. I then "retreated," asking her to imagine Dr. G. stopping after traveling one block and two paces toward her. This produced a slighter reaction, which decreased on repeating the scene, disappearing at the fourth presentation. (The reader will note that *sud* values do not appear in this account, because the *sud* scale came into use only about 1965.) *This was the first evidence of change*, affording grounds for a confident prediction of successful desensitization.

At the sixth session, the imagined distance between Dr. G.'s stopping

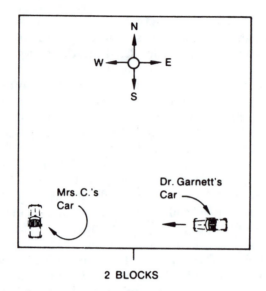

Fig. 16.1. Imaginary enclosed square where Dr. Garnett makes progressively closer advances to Mrs. C.'s car.

point and Mrs. C.'s car was decreased by two or three paces at a time, and at the end of the session he was able to stop seven-eighths of a block short of her (a total gain of about ten paces). At the seventh session, Mrs. C. could tolerate Dr. G.'s car reaching a point a half-block short of her car without disturbance; at the eighth session, three-eighths of a block (about 37 yards). At the tenth session, she was able to imagine him approaching within 2 yards of her without any reaction whatsoever.

The day after this, Mrs. C. reported that for the first time since her accident she had been able to walk across a street while an approaching car was in sight. The car was two blocks away but she was able to complete the crossing without quickening her pace. At this, the eleventh session, I began a new series of scenes in which Dr. G. drove in front of Mrs. C.'s car instead of toward it, passing at first 30 yards ahead and then gradually closer, cutting the distance eventually to about 3 yards. Desensitization to all this was rather rapidly achieved during this session. Thereupon, I drew two intersecting roads in the diagram (figure 16.2). A traffic light was indicated in the middle, and Mrs. C.'s car, as shown in the diagram, had stopped at the red signal. At first, Mrs. C. was asked to imagine Dr. G.'s car passing on the green light. As anticipated, she could at once accept this without anxiety; it was followed by Dr. G.'s car passing one way and a resident physician's car in the opposite direction. The slight anxiety this aroused was soon eliminated. In subsequent scenes, the resident's car was followed by an increasing num-

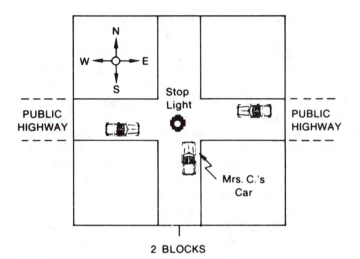

Fig. 16.2. Imaginary enclosed square with crossroads and traffic light added. Other cars pass while Mrs. C.'s car has stopped at the red light.

ber of students' cars, each scene being repeated until its emotional effect declined to zero.

At the 12th session, the roadway at right angles to Mrs. C.'s car was made continuous with the public highway system (as indicated by the dotted lines) and now, starting off again with Dr. G., we added the cars of the resident and the students, and subsequently those of strangers. Imagining two unknown cars passing the intersection produced a fair degree of anxiety, and she required five presentations at this session and five more at the next before she could accept it entirely calmly. Once this was accomplished, however, it was relatively easy gradually to introduce several cars passing from both sides.

We now began a new series of scenes in which, with the traffic light in her favor, she was stepping off the curb to cross a city street while a car was slowly approaching. At first, the car was imagined a block away, but during succeeding sessions the distance gradually decreased to 10 yards.

At this point, to check upon transfer from the imaginary to real life, I took Mrs. C. to the Charlottesville business center and observed her crossing streets at an intersection controlled by a traffic light. She went across repeatedly with apparent ease and reported no anxiety. But in the car, on the way there and back, she showed marked anxiety whenever a car from a side street threatened to enter the street in which we drove.

I now made a detailed analysis of Mrs. C.'s reaction to left turns on the highway in the face of oncoming traffic. She reported anxiety at doing a left turn if an oncoming car was in sight. Even if it was 2 miles away she could not allow her husband to turn left in front of it.

To treat this sensitive reaction, I again used Dr. G. I started by making Mrs. C. imagine (while relaxed) that Dr. G.'s car was a mile ahead when her car began to turn. But this was too disturbing and several repetitions of the scene (prolonged once for 2 minutes) brought no diminution in the magnitude of anxiety evoked. (This was one of a number of instances in the course of Mrs. C.'s therapy in which progress ceased because the anxiety was beyond the scope of her relaxation — a presumptive example of a situation in which "exposure" is not sufficient.) It seemed possible that there would be less anxiety if her husband were not the driver of the car since his presence at the time of the accident might have made him a conditioned stimulus to anxiety. Thus, I presented the scene with Mrs. C.'s brother as the driver of the car. With this altered feature, Dr. G.'s making a left turn a mile ahead evoked much less anxiety, and after four repetitions it declined to zero. We were then gradually able to decrease the distance so that she could eventually imagine making the turn with Dr. G.'s car only about 150 yards away. Meanwhile, when she was able to "do" the turn with Dr. G. three-eighths of a mile away, I introduced two new left-turn series: a strange car approaching with her brother driving and Dr. G. approaching with her husband driving — both a mile away initially. Work on all three series went on concurrently. When Mrs. C. could comfortably imagine her brother doing a left turn with the strange car five-eighths of a mile ahead, I resumed the original series in which her husband was the driver, starting with a left turn while the strange car was a mile ahead. This now evoked relatively little anxiety, and progress followed. The interrelated decrements of reaction to this group of hierarchies are summarized in figure 16.3.

Other series of related scenes were also subjected to desensitization. One comprised left turns in the city in front of oncoming cars. Since cars in the city move relatively slowly, she felt less danger at a given distance. The series in which Mrs. C. was crossing streets as a pedestrian was extended, and she was enabled in imagination to cross under all normal conditions. She reported complete transfer to the reality, which I directly verified. Altogether, 36 hierarchical series were used, all of which are detailed in the original account of this case (Wolpe, 1962). The total effect of desensitization was that Mrs. C. became completely at ease in all normal traffic situations — both as a pedestrian and as a passenger in a car. Her tension headaches ceased. In all, 57 desensitization sessions were conducted, comprising a total of 1,491 scene presentations. The last session took place on September 29, 1960.

Because Mrs. C. lived 100 miles away, treatment was episodic. At intervals of from 4 to 6 weeks she would come for about 2 weeks and be seen almost every day. Noteworthy reduction in the range of real situations that could

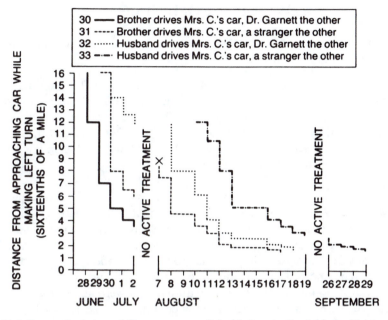

Fig. 16.3. Temporal relations of distances accomplished in imagination in desensitization series 30, 31, 32 and 33. X: indicates some relapse in hierarchy 31 following a taxi ride in which the driver insisted on exceeding the speed limit. The status of hierarchy 32 was not tested before the relapse in 31 was overcome.

disturb her occurred in the course of each period of active treatment, and practically none during the intervals.

When Mrs. C. was seen late in December 1960, she was as well as at the end of treatment. At a follow-up telephone call in February 1962, she stated that she had fully maintained her recovery and had developed no new symptoms. Her relationship with her husband was excellent. Two near-misses of accidents had had no lasting consequences. In 1969 she was still well.

The following are some noteworthy points: Mrs. C.'s sensitivity to the traumatic stimulus was of a magnitude usually associated with post-traumatic stress disorder (p. 270) but she had no other stigmata of that condition. She did not initially regard her anxiety to driving in general as enough to be worth reporting. In order to desensitize her to laterally approaching cars, it was necessary strictly to control quantities of approach. This could not be done by any program, real or imaginary, involving real driving because that always included the possibility of a major lateral threat. By using the imaginary closed-off field as illustrated, we could precisely control "degree of threat."

WASHING COMPULSION

Case 66: A Washing Compulsion Overcome by Systematic Desensitization to Urinary "Contamination"

Because of the special effectiveness noted on p. 294 of flooding treatment in compulsive neuroses based on contamination fears, it is often forgotten that other options exist. For many years, the main resource was systematic desensitization, which though laborious, was often successful, as first shown by Bevan (1960) and Walton and Mather (1964), and as in the following case adapted from Wolpe (1964a).

Mr. T., aged 18, was first seen in January 1961 with a severe washing compulsion based on a fear of contamination by urine, and most especially his own urine. His main dread was to contaminate others with it. When the treatment to be described began, he was almost completely impotentiated by his neurosis. After urinating, he would spend up to 45 minutes in an elaborate ritual of cleaning up his genitalia, followed by about 2 hours of hand washing. When he woke in the morning, his first need was to shower, which took about 4 hours. To these basic requirements were added many others occasioned by inevitable incidental daily contaminations. It is scarcely surprising that Mr. T. eventually concluded that getting up was not worth the effort, and for 2 months had spent most of his time in bed.

The neurosis originated in bizarre domestic circumstances. Until he was 15, Mr. T.'s parents had compelled him to share a bed with his sister, 2 years older, because she had a fear of being alone. The natural erotic responses aroused by this proximity to the girl had made him feel guilty and ashamed. Anger toward his parents for imposing this burden on him led to hostile and, at times, destructive thoughts about them. Horrified at these, he had come to regard himself as despicable. His urine subsequently became the prime focus of his "repulsiveness."

Treatment consisted in the first place of conventional desensitization. Analysis revealed that he was disturbed at the idea of anybody's becoming contaminated with any urine. Thus, in desensitization, the first scene he was asked to imagine was of an unknown man dipping his hand into a 40-cubic-foot trough of water into which one drop of urine had been deposited. Even this produced some disturbance in Mr. T. at first, but it waned and disappeared in the course of a few presentations. The concentration of urine was then gradually increased until, after seven sessions, the man was imagined to be inserting his hand into pure urine. Each scene was repeated until it no longer evoked any anxiety.

During the course of this treatment, which occupied about 5 months of sessions taking place about five times a week and each lasting, as a rule, about 20 minutes, there was considerable improvement in Mr. T.'s clinical condition. For example, his hand-washing time went down to about 30 minutes and his shower time to just over an hour; and he no longer found it necessary to interpose the *New York Times* between himself and his chair during interviews.

A new series of imaginary situations was then started in which Mr. T. was inserting his hand into increasingly concentrated solutions of urine. At first, he seemed to make some further progress, but then it became evident that there was diminishing transfer between what he could imagine himself doing and what he actually could do. Eventually, whereas he could without anxiety *imagine* himself immersing his hand in pure urine, to do so in actuality was out of the question. This is the only instance I have ever encountered of a developing disjunction between imaginary and real stimuli.

This impelled a switch to desensitization in vivo. Relaxation was now opposed to real stimuli evoking anxiety. Mr. T. was, to begin with, exposed to the word *urine* printed in big block letters. This evoked a little anxiety that he was soon able to relax away. The next step was to seat him at one end of a long room and present a closed bottle of urine at the other end. Again, he had to relax away the anxiety. Then, step by step, the bottle of urine was moved closer, until eventually he was handling it with only minimal anxiety which he could relax away. When the bottle of urine was no longer capable of evoking anxiety, a new series of maneuvers was started. First of all, a very dilute solution of anonymous urine (one drop to a gallon) was applied to the back of his hand, and he was made to relax until all anxiety disappeared; and then, from session to session, the concentration was gradually increased. When he was able calmly to endure pure urine, his own urine began to be used; and, finally he was enabled unflinchingly to "contaminate" all kinds of objects with his uriniferous hands — magazines, door knobs, and people's hands.

The numerous acts of desensitization achieved in the daily 15 to 20 minute sessions spanned 4 months, ending in his discharge from the hospital in June 1961. By then Mr. T. had greatly increased freedom of movement; he was dressing daily, his hand-washing time had gone down to 7 minutes, his shower time to 40 minutes, and his cleaning-up ritual was almost eliminated. In September 1961, he went back to school and was seen only occasionally until March 1962. During this time, without active treatment, he made virtually no further progress. In March 1962, he began weekly sessions as an outpatient, and then improvement resumed. When last seen in June 1962, his hand-washing time was 3 minutes and his shower time 20 minutes. He said that he was coming to think of urine as "sticky and smelly and nothing else." In February 1965, he reported that hand-washing took him 10 seconds, and he "wasn't even using soap." He was leading a normal life. In September 1967, a telephone call conveyed that his recovery had been maintained.

REVERSAL OF SEXUAL PREFERENCE

Case 67: Reversal of Homosexuality Through Overcoming General Interpersonal Anxiety

Mr. R., a 32-year-old hairdresser, was first seen in April 1954. For 7 years he had been aware of a slowly progressive diminution in his general enjoyment of life. He had emigrated to South Africa from Sweden early in 1952. Before I saw him, he had been treated for tension and depression with electroshock therapy, injections of vitamins, and some psychoanalytic psychotherapy, without effect.

Mr. R. had an only sister, 7 years younger. His father was a very good-natured religious man who never smoked, drank, or lost his temper. The father was extremely submissive in all his personal relations and much dominated by his wife, a very ambitious woman who could never be satisfied. She had been keen for Mr. R. to do her credit by becoming someone important, and was resentful when he did not turn out to be a good scholar. She would repeatedly say how disappointed she was to have borne a son, and treated him like a girl—forbidding him to play football, for example. If anything went wrong, she would invariably blame him, screaming at him and beating him. His predominant feeling toward her was fear. He felt a need to please her, and in later years condoned her harshness toward him by the thought that she knew no better.

Mr. R. disliked school and had few friends. On leaving school at 16, he was sent to work on a farm, but soon left to take up ladies' hairdressing. This angered his mother, but he persisted.

At the time of puberty, Mr. R. found himself attracted to men, although at first socially rather than sexually. He felt no sexual attraction toward women. When they occasionally made advances, he became anxious. By contrast, he found pleasure in the company of men and had a succession of attachments that led to sexual relations in which he usually took the active role. At the same time, he thought homosexuality sinful, and became increasingly anxious about it. He struggled against his inclinations and tried to fortify himself with religious reading and acts of devotion. The failure of these efforts, combined with family stresses, was almost unbearable. He sought relief by emigrating to South Africa, hoping that a drastic environmental change might effect a psychological change. Of course, this did not happen. His homosexual behavior continued in unstable relationships and contributed to the anxiety that finally brought him to treatment.

The above history required five interviews. These did not elicit any strong emotions or result in any change in his condition. Toward the end of the fifth interview, because it seemed clear that his religious beliefs were responsible for much of his stress, an effort was made to provide a different perspective through Winwood Reade's *Martyrdom of Man*. At his sixth interview a week later, he reported having read the book, and though he was at first upset by the criticisms of religion, he felt afterward that his ideas about it had been clarified. He saw that he had taken sin, particularly in relation to sexuality, too seriously. The locus of my influence up to this point was entirely cognitive.

In most social situations Mr. R. was timorous and submissive. Arguments of any kind were so unpleasant that he would avoid them at almost any cost. If a customer at the beauty shop where he worked made an unjust criticism of him he would feel hurt, tearful, and helpless, but would make no rejoinder. He was unable to ask for the repayment of considerable sums of money he had lent some friends.

The learning and unlearning of unadaptive fears was explained to him. The five interviews of the next 2 months were devoted to guiding him in the use of assertive behavior. He soon became much more firm and positive in all his relationships. In 2 months, his symptoms almost disappeared and he was almost completely at ease with his customers. In the meantime, he had formed a couple of new homosexual attachments, each of which, although satisfying while it lasted, had degenerated in less than a month. He asked whether I could help him overcome his homosexuality; I gave a negative answer, because Kallman's (1952) twin studies had then indicated that homosexuality had a genetic basis that would make it impervious to conditioning methods.

Mr. R. did not return until August 23, 2 months later. He had continued to advance in the handling of relationships and had been free of symptoms. The quality of his work had greatly improved and, in consequence, his clientele had practically doubled. He had meanwhile been offered an administrative post at a mission hospital in East Africa and had been enthusiastically studying for this.

When next seen, on October 18, he said that he had again felt considerably depressed in the past 2 weeks because of uncertainties about the mission hospital job. At the same time, he was becoming dissatisfied with hairdressing because he was finding his customers boring, and he felt that it was not a real service to humanity. He was told that any work that ministers to human needs is a service, but was advised to give up the idea of going to the mission. A week later, he reported feeling much relieved at having told the mission people that he had decided to withdraw. On November 29, he said that he was feeling fine and getting on very well, especially at his work, which was giving him such great satisfaction that he had decided to stay put. Treatment was at that point terminated, but he returned in June 1955 with the following story:

Since his treatment, Mr. R. had been finding that he could not maintain interest in a man. For a few months, he had known a girl named Jean whom he had found very likeable. She had many tastes and interests in common with his own. He had sometimes thought, "I would marry her if I were normal." When his relationships with males deteriorated, he began to take Jean out and before long wanted to see her every day. For about 3 months the relationship was purely platonic, but one night after a party when they were both slightly drunk and Jean became sentimental, he kissed her and found that it was "rather pleasant." From this time onward he began to respond to her in a sexual way, often very strongly. Even holding Jean's hand was exciting. Intercourse was not attempted because she was "not that kind of girl." The reason for Mr. R.'s visit was to ask whether he dared propose marriage. I told him that I could see no objection. The next week he reported that Jean was considering his proposal favorably. He felt wonderful. Unfortunately, inexperience with courtship caused Mr. R. to mishandle Jean, so that when next seen, he reported that she had rejected him, and that he was moving to England.

In January 1956 he wrote from London. After a party, he had taken a woman home who had suggested that he spend the night with her, but he had refused on the pretext of fatigue. Although he was strongly attracted to her, he felt afraid, and refused. But when he opened the front door to leave it was raining heavily, and he resigned himself to going to bed with her and risking the chagrin of failure. To his delight, this sexual experience was successful. At the time of writing, he had made love to her almost every night for a month and with greater enjoyment than he had ever experienced with men. He regarded this as his final vindication, convincing him that he need never again feel inferior to other men.

I saw Mr. R. in England in 1956 and again in 1957. He was emotionally well and exclusively heterosexual. In January 1959, he wrote to say that he had married a South American woman. His sex life was satisfactory and his wife was pregnant.

It is easy to follow the successive phases of Mr. R.'s sex life. His social anxieties originated with his harsh, punitive mother. Because of her he was more fearful of women than of men. This may have influenced the development during adolescence of a pleasant feeling of warmth and affection toward men, which inclined him to seek greater closeness, and later led naturally to the expression of sexual impulses. Sexual fulfillment with men reinforced this expression. The practice of assertive behavior with a wide range of individuals overcame his social fears. Once he was able to survey the world without anxiety, preference for females spontaneously emerged — a preference presumably established by social role conditioning very early in his life.

Whether the object of deviant arousal in males is other males, or male children (Edwards, 1972), or fetishistic objects, a frequent cause is the previous conditioning of anxiety to adult females. When this occurs, the logical treatment is the deconditioning of the anxiety. Success in this endeavor may be expected to restore the primacy of adult females as sex objects, as was the case with Mr. R. Although successful treatments of this kind have been known for many years (e.g., Stevenson & Wolpe, 1960), the dynamic analyses that would reveal the occasions for such treatment are not often made.

PART V

EVALUATIONS

17
Evaluation of the Effects
of Behavior Therapy

Almost all the therapeutic methods described in this book are based on experimentally tested principles or paradigms. The writing of the book is justified by the success of the methods; and this establishes behavior therapy as a distinctively effective approach to the treatment of maladaptive learned habits, and of the neuroses in particular. This chapter will consider the relevant outcome data.

Psychotherapists easily acquire a belief in the efficacy of their own methods, because, as has long been known (e.g., Eysenck, 1952; Landis, 1937; Wilder, 1945), 40% or more of neurotic patients improve markedly with nonbehavioral programs of therapy despite widely differing theories and practices. Success with this degree of frequency provides more than enough intermittent reinforcement (Skinner, 1938) to maintain a therapist's mode of practice. However, the uniform magnitude of benefit indicates that it is not attributable to the methods, which vary greatly, but to processes that are common to all of the therapies and therefore nonspecific. What is probably most relevant is the emotional impact on the patient of the therapist, a trusted and supposedly wise and competent person to whom the patient has entrusted himself. The methods that are special to a therapeutic system can be regarded as having their own potency only if, through their use, the percentage of recoveries rises substantially above the common level, or if there is evidence of greater rapidity of recovery.

Nonspecific therapeutic benefit has been recognized by psychoanalysts. They call it *transference* and attribute it to the therapist's being perceived as a parental surrogate. This does not, for behavior therapists, constitute much of an explanation, though they are equally aware of the phenomenon and make deliberate use of it at times (see chapter 10). They hypothesize that nonspecific therapy is due to the inhibition of maladaptive anxiety by positive emotions that the therapist engenders in the patient. There have, however, been remarkably few objective studies of this phenomenon. Some features of therapists favorable to change were noted by Parloff et al. (1978).

Psychophysiological studies of the impact of the therapist on the patient are indispensable to understanding nonspecific therapeutic effects. A few studies have appeared in recent years in the context of biofeedback. A study by Taub (1977) showed major effects related to emotional interaction. He found that an impersonal and skeptical experimenter succeeded in training only 2 of 22 subjects in self-regulation of tissue temperature, while a warmer and more involved one succeeded with 19 of 21 subjects. Borgeat et al. (1984) found that in tension headache subjects treated by EMG biofeedback, the effects varied with the individual therapist. On the whole, EMG activity was higher during the therapist's silent presence, but the difference between absence and presence decreased toward the end of sessions. The subjects of one therapist had significantly *lower* EMGs during his active presence, in contrast to the subjects of the other three. This accords with Taub's findings to the extent that the mere presence of the therapist had emotional effects. Much more research is clearly necessary.

THE CRITERIA OF PSYCHOTHERAPEUTIC CHANGE

The goal of psychotherapy, like that of any other branch of therapeutics, is the eradication or at least the amelioration of suffering and disability. Since in behavior therapy the therapeutic task is seen to be the elimination of persistent maladaptive habits, an informative way of measuring success would be to enumerate and assess the strength of maladaptive habits before therapy, and then after therapy to assess the extent to which each habit has been weakened. Such assessment can in principle draw upon several kinds of information: the reports of the patient, clinical observation, the observations of others, and psychophysiological studies.

The following set of indices of therapeutic change, proposed by Knight (1941), covers the ground in a practical and meaningful way:

1. Symptomatic improvement
2. Increased productiveness at work
3. Improved adjustment and pleasure in sex
4. Improved interpersonal relationships
5. Enhanced ability to handle ordinary psychological conflicts and reasonable reality stresses

Symptomatic improvement is a necessary criterion for change in every case since it is the symptoms that bring the patient to treatment. Symptomatic improvement in this context does not mean palliation but fundamental change, in that the stimuli that called forth inappropriate anxiety no longer do so, or do so in lesser measure. If there have been symptoms that are secondary to anxiety, they, too, should be seen to diminish or cease. The decline of the secondary manifestations of neurosis are also measures of improvement. Moore's (1965) study of the treatment of asthma (p. 285) is an example of this. Improvement at work, sex, and in relationships in general are mainly by-products of the diminution of anxiety although, as noted earlier, the learning of superior ways of doing things also very often contributes.

BASIC OUTCOME DATA

Beginning in the mid-1950s, there appeared a steady stream of reports of successful treatment of individual cases or small groups by behavior therapy. Many of the early studies were conveniently brought together in two volumes edited by Eysenck (1960, 1964). A feature of these studies that is unusual in the literature of psychotherapy is the display of clear temporal relationships between specific interventions and therapeutic change, as is also generally evident in the cases described in this volume.

An uncontrolled statistical comparison of outcomes was reported by Wolpe (1958), focusing on the results of behavior therapy in private practice. On Knight's criteria, 89% of 210 neurotic patients had either apparently recovered or were at least 80% improved, in a mean of about 30 therapeutic sessions. In follow-ups of 45 of these patients, 2 to 7 years later, all but one had at least maintained their gains. Table 17.1 (from Wolpe, 1964b), comparing the results of this study with those of a psychoanalytic series (Brody, 1962), shows a substantially higher percentage of recoveries for behavior therapy. It is also noteworthy that the mean number of sessions for behavior

Table 17.1. Uncontrolled Outcome Studies of Different Types of Therapy

SERIES	NUMBER OF CASES	APPARENTLY CURED OR MUCH IMPROVED	PERCENTAGE OF RECOVERIES
Behavior Therapy (Wolpe, 1958)	210	188	89.5
Psychoanalytic Therapy (Brody, 1962)	210[a]	126[a]	60
General Hospital Therapy (Hamilton & Wall, 1941)	100	53	53

[a]These figures include only the patients regarded as "completely analyzed." The total patient population in the psychoanalytic group was 595.

therapy was about 30, which contrasts with a mean of about 600 for the series reported by Brody—three or four times a week for 3 or 4 years as revealed by Masserman (1963). In the general hospital series reported by Hamilton and Wall (1941) the recovery rate was 53%.

The above comparison was augmented by Paul's (1966) landmark controlled study—which showed the superiority of systematic desensitization over insight-oriented methods and placebo treatment of subjects with severe fears of public speaking—and by Paul's (1969a) review of the treatment of 1,000 cases by 70 therapists. These positive findings stimulated great interest in behavior therapy among both psychiatrists and psychologists.

THE DEVALUATION OF BEHAVIOR THERAPY

A few years later, the seemingly impregnable fact of the superior efficacy of behavior therapy was undermined by the report of the meta-analysis of psychotherapies by Smith and Glass (1977) and Smith, Glass, and Miller (1980). Meta-analysis is a statistical technique for averaging and integrating the results of a large number of studies. Its unit is the effect size, an index of the size of the effect of a therapy. Smith, Glass, and Miller deduced from their data (incorrectly, as will be seen below) that there was no significant difference between the effectiveness of behavior therapy and that of psychoanalytically oriented brief psychotherapy.

This deduction was naturally greeted with acclaim by the psychoanalytically disposed (Garfield, 1980; Garfield & Bergin, 1978; Strupp, 1978); and members of the psychodynamically dominated establishment at large were greatly relieved at the removal of what had seemed to be a serious threat to their modus operandi: They no longer needed to take behavior therapy into account as a competitor or even as a serious addition to psychotherapy. All they now felt constrained to concede was that it probably had adjunctive value for some superficial problems, such as simple phobias and routine sexual problems (see Marmor, 1980).

A direct consequence of the lessened threat was manifest at the annual meetings of the American Psychiatric Association. For about 10 years, until 1978, behavior therapy symposia were regularly solicited by the organizers, and filled to the doors; and a considerable number of behaviorally oriented free papers were accepted for presentation. After 1978, there were no more invited symposia, and few individual papers appeared on the program.

Behavior therapists in clinical practice were incredulous at the conclusions of Smith, Glass, and Miller since they were daily observing the power of their methods, not infrequently in patients in whom prolonged psychoanalytically oriented psychotherapy had failed. The meta-analytic method was severely criticized by Eysenck (1978), Paul (1986), Wilson (1985), and Wilson and Rachman (1983). Paul's (1986) critique contained a compelling actual example. Referring to his study of the treatment of speech anxiety (1966), Paul showed that the meta-analysis would have included a considerable number of peripheral scales in calculating effect size and these would have greatly diluted the effect size contributed by the two scales that were of foremost importance in his own evaluation of outcome.

These methodological critiques were very persuasive to statisticians and to people concerned about rigor in research. They also gave many behavior therapists the feeling that the devaluation had been rebutted, but the broad population of psychiatrists and psychologists were unaware of these considerations and unmoved. As far as they were concerned, behavior therapy remained unsaddled.

THE FORMAL REINSTATEMENT
OF THERAPEUTIC SUPERIORITY

Behavior therapists, as indicated above, always disbelieved Smith and Glass's conclusions. Independent vindication came from Andrews and Harvey's (1981) reanalysis of the Smith, Glass, and Miller data. They worked from a copy of Smith, Glass, and Miller's data set of 475 controlled studies, but decided to restrict their analysis to neurotic patients, thus including only studies of persons who would normally seek psychotherapy. This reduced the data to 81 studies, comprising 2,202 patients. They integrated these data statistically, using the Smith and Glass meta-analytic technique. They divided the therapies into the original four superclasses, as shown in table 17.2: verbal, behavioral, developmental, and placebo. A total of 292 "effect sizes" were calculated from the 81 controlled trials. (It is noteworthy that almost 95% of the effect sizes of the verbal group were "dynamic.")

Table 17.2. Mean Effect Size for Each Type of Treatment

SUPERCLASS AND CLASS	NO. OF EFFECT SIZES	MEAN (SE)
Verbal	95	0.74(0.05)
Dynamic	90	0.72
Cognitive and gestalt	5	1.20
Behavioral	110	0.97(0.06)
Behavior	103	0.99
Cognitive behavior	7	0.74
Developmental	56	0.35(0.06)
Client-centered	31	0.39
Counseling	25	0.31
Placebo	28	0.55(0.06)
Unclassifiable	3	—
Total	292	0.72(0.03)

Source: Andrews & Harvey, 1981.

The benefits of the different superclasses of psychotherapy are graphically compared in figure 17.1. The graphs show the results from three different cross-sections: severity as indicated by location (i.e., college, outpatient, or inpatient); hours of therapy; and time in months after therapy. On all three graphs, behavioral psychotherapy is superior to verbal (i.e., dynamic therapy) at every measured point. The behavioral therapies' mean effects size of .97 is significantly superior to the .74 of the verbal therapies (p < .001). Andrews and Harvey can hardly be accused of bias in favor of

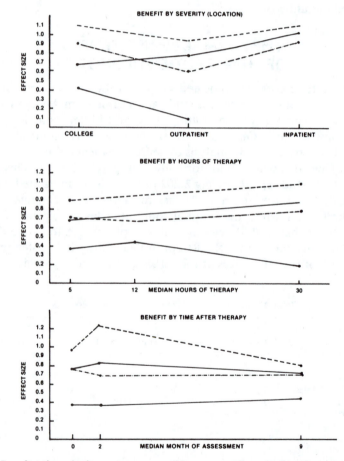

Fig. 17.1. Benefits of psychotherapy as measured by average effect size for all treatments (solid line), behavioral psychotherapy (broken line), verbal dynamic psychotherapy (dot-and-dash line), and client-centered and counseling therapy (dotted line). Results are displayed by severity as judged from location, by hours of therapy, and by time after therapy in months. From Andrews and Harvey, (November 1981) *Arch. Gen. Psychiat.*, 38:1205.

behavior therapy, for nowhere do they make the inference from their analysis that behavior therapy should receive first preference for clinical practice and therefore in the training of clinicians. They generally bracket behavior therapy and dynamic therapy together, on the rationale that because of "developments in cognitive behavior therapies . . . the conception gulf between the behavioral and verbal psychotherapies is narrowing rapidly." As it has turned out, Andrews and Harvey actually understated behavior therapy's superiority of outcomes. A reanalysis of their work by Searles (1985) showed that they had retained in their study a large amount of data that had nothing to do with neuroses, and omitted many studies that should properly have been included.

Reinstatement also occurred elsewhere. A study that had been seen as supporting the conclusions of Smith, Glass, and Miller was that of Luborsky, Singer, and Luborsky (1975). This research consisted of a survey of 19 studies comparing the outcome of behavior therapy with that of psychoanalytically oriented psychotherapy. The writers reached the conclusion that the two therapies were of "equal efficacy." However, in their original tally, behavior therapy was superior in six studies, and psychotherapy in none; and there were 13 ties. One might have thought that these figures gave behavior therapy an edge, instead of implying "equality." Giles (1983a), in a careful reexamination of the data, found that two of the ties actually favored behavior therapy (increasing its tally to 8 out of 19). In his article, aptly subtitled, "Those who have won have not received prizes," Giles wonders whether Luborsky et al. would have been as ready to see equality if the count had gone the other way.

Giles (1983b) also reassessed the data of a very well-designed study by Sloane et al. (1975) that has also been frequently represented as having demonstrated equivalent efficacy for behavior therapy and psychoanalytically oriented therapy. Of the statistically significant differences of Sloane et al. Giles noted that one favored psychodynamic therapy and eight favored behavior therapy. At 12-month follow-up, only the behaviorally treated patients were rated by the assessors as significantly more improved than the controls in terms of severity of symptoms, and only the behaviorally treated patients were significantly improved over their initial baseline in work adjustment. Analytically treated patients showing low initial pathology (mild cases) did significantly better than those with high pathology, while lows and highs did equally well with behavioral treatment. In sum, the imputation of equal effectiveness of the two kinds of therapy is not in accord with the data.

The behavioral superiority is even more noteworthy when one realizes that the Sloane study had features that biased it against behavior therapy. Two of the independent assessors were psychodynamic and the other operant/eclectic. Thus, congruence between assessor ratings and therapist ratings was probably higher for the dynamic therapists than for the behavior therapists who often formulated their targets differently. In addition, there was little effort to assess the reliability of the measurements—no mention of assessor training, of periodic feedback, or of interrater reliability (Poppen, 1976). The resulting error variance may have obscured differences between treatment effects (see Demaster, Reid, & Twentyman, 1977; Kazdin, 1977). It is also relevant that the cases in the Sloane study were generally of a mild character, which, as noted above, favored the analytic group. This feature also explains why a high proportion of the control group (50%) recovered or were much improved at 4 months without having received any formal therapy. Mild neurotic cases may be expected to benefit from almost any kind of intervention (see p. 192).

Thus, outcome evidence remains decisively on the side of behavior therapy. It remains the psychotherapy of choice and the most cost effective. As Giles (1983a) has argued, the facts are even more compelling if one takes into account the results of behavior therapy in disorders known to be refractory to other approaches. Some such areas covered in this book in which striking success has been achieved are agoraphobia, simple phobia, sexual dysfunction, obsessive-compulsive disorders, panic disorder, stuttering, tension headache, and post-traumatic stress disorder. An updated survey by Taboas (1988) reaches the same conclusion as Giles.

MUST BEHAVIOR THERAPY SOMETIMES FALL BACK ON PSYCHOANALYSIS, OR VICE VERSA?

Despite the general superiority of behavioral therapy's outcomes, it is necessary to consider the contention that there are certain neurotic problems for which behavior therapy misses the mark or is inadequate, and for which analytic methods are the solution. What are the facts? I have not encountered any published data or even a case example to support this contention. The ultimate finding of the voluminous report of the meticulously conducted Menninger Foundation Psychotherapy Research Project (Kernberg, 1972) was that out of 42 patients given psychoanalytic psychotherapy or psychoanalysis, only 10 were much improved and 11 were worse either at termination or at a 2-year follow-up—an outcome even less favorable than that of earlier studies.

Despite its unimpressive results, there is wide confidence in the basic rightness of psychodynamic theory, and a firm reliance on its methods. Sometimes the patient undergoes years of therapy without real benefit, which probably happens nowadays as often with psychoanalytically oriented therapy as with formal psychoanalysis. Schmideberg (1970), a prestigious psychoanalyst, writes of patients who "have been made to feel that analysis is the only worthwhile therapy, and that there must be something quite specially wrong with them if it cannot help them as it has helped others." She gives the example of a woman of 28 whom she saw after 12 years of ineffective psychoanalysis. The patient had embarked on the treatment without definite symptoms but in the hope of leading a fuller life and making a happy marriage. Having developed a progressively worsening agoraphobia during her first analysis, she later continued with two other analysts, steadily deteriorating.

When prolonged psychoanalytic treatment has produced no substantial benefit, it is a reason for turning to behavior therapy — and this deserves to be recognized. The literature contains numerous examples of behavior therapy succeeding, usually in a modest length of time, after prolonged psychodynamic therapy has filed. In an unpublished study, I found that 10 out of 12 patients with whom psychoanalytic therapy had failed either recovered or were much improved by behavior therapy.

The potentialities for a switch into behavior therapy are often perceptible in published accounts of psychoanalytic treatments of neurotic patients. This is apparent in each of three extremely well-presented cases that Gustafson (1984) used to illustrate brief "dynamic psychotherapy." In the case of a young man with an 8-year history of severe migraine headaches, it became clear that these were related to emotional tension "whenever others made demands for performance." The distress was easily aroused by small confrontations that would make the patient "full of the worst inclinations for revenge." The therapist states, "If he were not to have headaches, he would have to live with his own ferocity. . . . Given his new capability for recognizing his flood of anger at stupid assignments, it is unlikely that he can be the model student that he was." He continues:

> Before long, this will certainly bring on various confrontations with his teachers, which will be very emotional, since he wants them to accept him as he actually is. Whether these counterattacks can be negotiated by him, rendering something unto Caesar, keeping something for himself, remains to be seen, but it is certain that these powerful tests of his new bridging capability, these tests of "dynamic change" will come.

Everything here is left to insight and its consequences, and one can only agree with Gustafson that under these circumstances an uphill road lies ahead. The prospect could undoubtedly be lightened if at this point the interpersonal sources of stress were subjected to a behavioral analysis and appropriate treatment prescribed. From the information given, the patient would almost certainly profit from assertiveness training; and oversensitivity to devaluation and disapproval are likely targets for systematic desensitization. The problem is to get psychoanalysts to collaborate with behavior therapists to test these propositions in cases like this.

It has been proposed repeatedly (Arkowitz & Messer, 1984; Bergin & Strupp, 1972; Feather & Rhoads, 1972; Wachtel, 1978) that treatment should combine psychodynamic methods with those of behavior therapy because the different approaches may be complementary or suit different problems. The weakness of this proposal lies in the lack of evidence of the specific effectiveness of any psychoanalytic technique (as distinct from the nonspecific effects mentioned earlier in this chapter). Spending therapeutic time on nonbehavioristic measures may be expected to dilute behavior therapy efforts and to produce poor results. A possible exception (still to be tested) may be to attend in special cases to Wachtel's (1978) idea of persistent childhood behavior patterns.

Evidence from every visible angle supports the conclusion that knowledge of the factors influencing the making and breaking of habits is our most potent resource for modifying and eliminating learned maladaptive behavior. This knowledge has generated a variety of clinical methods that are vindicated by their results. This is not to deny that effective methods are occasionally stumbled on empirically. New ideas remain to be tapped (e.g., Solomon's [1980] opponent processes and Catania's [1969] behavioral contrast). And there should be renewed recourse to the experimental neuroses to which we owe so much and which have been neglected almost entirely for a quarter of a century.

Meanwhile, it is a distressing truth that the Smith and Glass (1977) report of meta-analysis of outcome studies has done lasting damage. The conclusions they reached, although manifestly misleading (pp. 338–339), seem to have erected in many minds a barrier that prevents them from dispassionately considering the therapeutic power of behavior therapy. They either insulate themselves from the outcome data or they derogate it, or both. For example, Stiles, Shapiro, and Elliott (1986) state, with complete inaccuracy, that "the overwhelming majority of investigations are laboratory analogues using brief treatments with student volunteers who present only minor difficulties." The serious consequence of this mental blindness is that needless suffering continues. A circumstantial exposé of the situation has been provided by Giles (1990), poignantly subtitled "Who Speaks for the Patients?"

18
Current Practice of Behavior Therapy: Retreat From Principles

The preface to the third edition of this book found much to deplore about behavior therapy practice and little cause to rejoice. There were inadequacies in training, widespread low standards of practice, and a general conceptual decline that had led, *inter alia*, to serious consideration being given to the view that wrong thinking is the basis of all neuroses. Also, a controversy had arisen about what behavior therapy really is. Since the definition of behavior therapy (p. 3) is a prescriptive one, it is as stated and not a matter for debate.

In the 7 years since that preface appeared, the situation has further deteriorated. Changes have been proposed and widely accepted that involve the abrogation of behavioral principles and the adoption of practices incompatible with them. These changes are not based on data but on idiosyncratic theorizing. I will relate how they came to pass and how their consequences have been uniformly negative, and will suggest what might be done to rectify matters.

INFLUENCES TOWARD MISDIRECTION

The Meta-Analytic Input

Evidence of behavior therapy's efficacy against maladaptive fears, outlined in chapter 17, gave behavior therapists confidence in their methods. It also led to increasing attention from mainstream psychotherapists in the early 1970s. As recounted in chapter 17, general interest in behavior therapy fell sharply after the appearance of Smith and Glass's (1977) meta-analysis of outcome studies, which purported to show that the benefits of behavior therapy and psychoanalytically oriented brief psychotherapy were much the same. That report also had a negative effect on many behavior therapists, causing them to question whether behavior therapy was really special after all. The endorsement of the report by some prominent behavior therapists, especially Kazdin (1979), further undermined the faith of the rank and file. Even though 4 years later Andrews and Harvey (1981) reported that when the meta-analysis was restricted to neurotic patients, behavior therapy was more effective than psychoanalytically oriented therapy at the .001 level, few people noticed. Two major symposia on the effects of psychotherapy, published in 1986 in the *American Psychologist* and the *Journal of Consulting Psychology*, respectively, quoted Smith and Glass extensively and hardly mentioned Andrews and Harvey.

The Infiltration of Nonbehavioral Concepts

The damaging effects of Smith and Glass's meta-analysis of the clinical status of behavior therapy were exacerbated through the arrival on the behavioral scene of prominent psychologists with nonbehavioral orientations. Ordinarily, when people join a discipline they have already accepted its major tenets. Atheists do not join churches, nor socialists the Republican party. It was therefore not anticipated that people who did not understand or could not absorb the experimentally-based finding that conditioning is the usual basis of neurotic behavior would join the behavior therapy movement. But this is precisely what did happen. Psychologists inimical to conditioning concepts were able to promote their own views well enough to change, in the eyes of many established members of the movement, the character of behavior therapy in a nonbehavioral direction. The agents of change were attracted to the behavioral movement for their own reasons — and no doubt were encouraged by finding welcome and acceptance. They fell into two categories — exposure therapists and cognitivists.

The Exposure Therapists

The exposure theory of therapy is essentially based on the flooding type of procedure described by Malleson (1959), and Meyer (1966). Its chief exponent has been Marks (1976, 1981), who rejects both conditioning as the basis of neurosis and counterconditioning as an agent of therapeutic change. He uses two arguments. The first is that laboratory neuroses are not analogous to human neuroses because the latter are longlasting while the former (according to him) spontaneously recover in days (Marks, 1981, p. 223). In fact, experimental neuroses persist for months and years and can last the life of the animal (Gantt, 1944; Masserman, 1943). Second, Marks asserts that "few patients give the history of traumatic or social conditioning that is demanded by conditioning theory" (Marks, 1981, p. 23). This assertion is contradicted by the reports of Symonds (1943), Lautch (1971), Ost and Hugdahl (1981), and Wolpe (1981), all of whom found that the great majority of neuroses have histories consonant with conditioning origins. (Rachman [1990, p. 168] demurs that Lautch's 34 patients with dental fear were neurotic, and 10 comparison subjects showed little sign of dental fear. Neurotic subjects would presumably have higher fear arousal, and therefore more fear conditioning, which is precisely what conditioning theory predicts — see Davey (1989), excerpted on p. 26.)

Marks (1981, p. 9) suggests that the experimental underpinnings of behavior therapy are apocryphal, originating in the "understandable struggle of clinical psychologists for identity and status." But he offers no real alternative theory. His explanation is that when anxiety is diminished by exposure to the fearful stimulus, it is because of the patient's "getting used to it," which begs the question.

Marks's clinical studies of exposure show statistically significant improvement in groups of patients, but leave the fate of the individual case obscure. A more revealing account of the effects of exposure has been provided by Agras (1985), who states that few of the patients so treated fully recover. It is instructive to contrast this finding with Wolpe's report of 88 patients (p. 335). These were treated by a variety of behavioral methods, based mainly on reciprocal inhibition; 28 of them were apparently cured and another 50 were much improved. The better outcomes are to a great extent attributable to careful study of the unique antecedents of the individual's maladaptive anxiety. The claim that exposure is all that is relevant to psychotherapeutic change is contradicted by the findings of a wide-ranging review by Thyer, Baum, and Reid (1988), and of those of Butler et al. (1984) in a controlled clinical study.

The Cognitivists

The cognitivists (Beck, 1976; Ellis, 1974; Mahoney, 1977; Meichenbaum, 1975) also reject the conditioning theory of neuroses. They claim that they have a more advanced theory, the product of a "cognitive revolution." They see themselves as the incumbents of a new paradigm a là Kuhn (1970) that has the same relation to conditioning as relativity has to Newtonian physics. They state that it is not the learning process that must be understood and invoked in dealing with the problems of neuroses but patients' misconceptions and unrealistic verbal formulations.

The technical inaccuracy of the claimed Kuhnian revolution was exposed by Scharnberg (1984). Nobody would object to a conceptual reorientation that advanced the alleviation of suffering. Behavior therapists would not oppose — indeed would applaud — therapeutic innovations that surpassed their own in effectiveness. But when we look for substantiation of superiority we find no persuasive facts but a great deal of argumentation, of which very little is convincing. The following are some specific criticisms:

1. Beck (1976) alleged that behavior therapists originally overlooked (by-passed) cognition and that a major contribution of the cognitivists was to bring it to their attention. Both allegations are untrue. Consciousness and communication are part and parcel of all human interaction and can never be by-passed. Within the special context of the operations of behavior therapy, cognition has entered ineluctably — in history taking, in giving instructions for self-assertion, in constructing hierarchies, in carrying out desensitization, and in conducting flooding (see chapter 11). Beck (1976, p. 322) states that unlike cognitive therapists, behavior therapists do not use "internal experiences as clinical data." This assertion is contradicted in every case that a skilled behavior therapist treats, as repeatedly illustrated in this book.

2. It is claimed that all maladaptive fears are cognitively based — that is, that they rest on the patient's incorrectly believing that his fears of danger are valid. This claim implies that the correction of wrong ideas is always the essential requirement of therapy. The cognitivists deny the possibility that some fears may be immediately triggered by a particular stimulus without the mediation of an idea of danger. Yet both experimental and clinical observations demonstrate that this can happen — that a stimulus may automatically and immediately elicit fear. Here are some observations in the clinical context relevant to this point (more fully treated on pp. 132–134).

a. A person who has a fear of dogs or of spiders usually also fears pictures of these animals. This is easily explicable on the basis of the generalization of conditioned fear reactions. It is not explicable on the basis of belief. A person can hardly believe that there is danger in the picture that frightens him or her.

b. When patients are questioned regarding what there is about a situation to make them afraid, they sometimes give a cognitive explanation and sometimes do not. One person sees his fear of elevators as appropriate, because he believes he might suffocate if stuck between floors. Another perceives no danger, but exposure to enclosed spaces fills the person with anxiety. The first case calls for cognitive correction of a mistaken belief; the second requires classical deconditioning.

c. In standard systematic desensitization, the patient imagines stimuli to maladaptive fear. No belief-correcting information is given. The patient who is successfully desensitized becomes aware of diminution of his fear *in consequence of* the desensitization procedure.

d. In recent years some therapists have argued strongly that panic attacks are caused by catastrophic misattributions (e.g., Clark, 1986). Misattributions are very common in panic, though not invariable (Rachman,

Levitt, & Lopatka, 1987). Wolpe and Rowan (1988) found that when there is a misattribution, it *follows* the initial panic, which is evidently an unconditioned fear response (see pp. 262–264).

e. If the "cognitive revolution" carried practical advantages for neurotic patients, this would be reflected in improved outcomes. No evidence of that has emerged. On the contrary, Latimer and Sweet (1984) reviewed five studies in which cognitive therapy was added to a behavioral treatment of known efficacy. In none of these studies did the addition confer a significant advantage. There is also nothing to show that Beck's (1976) use of "automatic thoughts" has improved results. See Last (1987) and Marshall (1988) for analyses and data to the same effect.

When cognitivists stigmatize the conditioning model as inadequate, it is partly because they do not know that conditioning has already subsumed perception and cognition (Taylor, 1962; Wolpe, 1979). To those who lived through the early years of behavior therapy, the term *cognitive behavior therapy* has redundancy (Krasner, 1987) because from the outset cognition was seen as part of behavior, communicated by verbal behavior.

The cognitive revolution that relates to general psychological theory (Baars, 1986) consists of the explicit readmission of cognitive events to the subject matter of psychology, a recognition that was never missing from behavior therapy of neuroses, even at its inception (Wolpe, 1958).

The Second Cognitive Salvo: Self-efficacy

Another rejection of conditioning came from Albert Bandura. He had started from a behavioral orientation, had written a major work on behavior modification (1969), and a laudatory survey (1967) of the conditioning approach to neuroses. He later (1974) renounced conditioning and espoused the view that thinking controls all behavior, developing this into an elaborate global theory (1986). He makes many scholarly correlations, but it is not clear what he regards as the mechanism of change. One product of Bandura's work is the self-efficacy concept (Bandura, 1986, p. 182ff). The use of self-efficacy measures and concepts to explain behavior has grown exponentially in the past decade. Questions regarding the validity of its basic propositions are however, rarely raised.

A penetrating analysis of the self-efficacy concept has been provided by Lee (1989). She shows that while the concept allows the prediction of behavior in many settings with a fair degree of accuracy, the formulations are not scientifically acceptable because they are unfalsifiable. Moreover, the process by which self-efficacy is synthesized from various inputs is not specified. Therefore, "there is no way of predicting from a knowledge of these inputs what efficacy expectation will result"; no techniques have been proposed that could reliably alter self-efficacy expectations. The theory is thus "no more than a metaphorical description of a hypothetical process" (p. 118).

These weaknesses in Bandura's position were not immediately apparent, and his general agreement with the cognitivists encouraged the alienation of behavioral practitioners from the conditioning principles on which they had been nurtured.

The growth of cognitivist-engendered disaffection is displayed in two issues, 5 years apart, of the *Annual Review of Behavior Therapy*. An overview by Franks and Wilson in the seventh edition (1979) shows the onset of a drift away from conditioning and a disposition to accept cognitive formulations even when they are arbitrary and unsupported by facts. In the tenth edition (1984), Franks, Wilson, Kendall, and Brownell claim to be spokesmen for "a maturing behavior therapy" that has "left behind the simplistic infant of the 1960s." In their preface, they write of "the attention now given to the roles of cognitive variables and therapist-client relationships" — as if this were something new (Wolpe, 1958). Franks, in an overview chapter, states that "the various conditioning-based theories of neurosis are . . . found wanting," basing this allegation mainly on five arguments from a critique by Wilson (1982), all of which have been rebutted elsewhere (Wolpe, 1986b).

Having "disposed of" conditioning theory, it might be thought that Franks et al. would offer their own theory of therapeutic change, but nothing of the sort is forthcoming. Much is said about treating anxiety from a social learning or "cognitive-behavioral" point of view, but it is nowhere explained by what process habit change occurs. In what way is the learning process different when social stimuli are implicated? Social situations and influences have always been to the forefront in traditional behavior therapy. For example, social fears of various degrees of complexity made up the content of 54 of 68 hierarchies desensitized by Wolpe (1961b; see also Table 9.2 this volume).

TRADITIONAL BEHAVIOR THERAPY PROCEDURE VERSUS NEW WAVE PROCEDURE

It is instructive to make a functional comparison between traditional behavior therapy and what we will call *new wave therapy*, alias *maturing behavior therapy*. It will emerge that it is the latter that is simplistic. A preliminary question is whether the new wave has yielded better outcomes. Neither in the 1984 Annual Review of Behavior Therapy nor elsewhere is there any evidence that it has. In fact, as noted above and below, the indications are to the contrary. And this is perhaps the reason that Franks (1984, p. 9) describes as "an aggressive success parade" the collected evidence by Giles (1983a) demonstrating the superiority of behavioral over nonbehavioral treatments. A new survey of data by Taboas (1988) supports the conclusions of Giles.

Procedure in Traditional Behavior Therapy

In the learning of a habit, specific responses are chained to specific stimulus antecedents. These antecedents must be present during the deconditioning procedure. It is easy enough to ensure this in the laboratory, but the controlling antecedents of maladaptive responses in human beings are often complex and differ among cases with the same problem. Thus, while response similarity in maladaptive habits provides a convenient basis for placing them in diagnostic pigeonholes (e.g., anorexia, claustrophobia, stuttering), common pigeonholes do not necessarily imply common treatments because the stimulus antecedents vary.

As described in chapter 5, the proper conduct of behavior therapy requires one to identify accurately the stimuli or stimulus sequences that are the actual antecedents of maladaptive behavior. The patient's initial statement of complaint frequently provides approximate information that points to heights, crowds, situations of rejection, or taking responsibility as problem areas. These are then probed in order to establish specific themes of sensitivity, in respect of each of which there will be a peak of anxiety that declines as one moves away from the peak situation. Other sources of disturbance emerge from the history and the questionnaires.

After determining the stimulus antecedents of a neurotic anxiety response, a crucial question is whether the anxiety is classically conditioned or cognitively based. The ability to make the distinction is relatively easily learned (Wolpe, Lande, McNally, & Schotte, 1985). In either case, detailed probings aim at the clearest possible specification of antecedents and their interaction with the patient's anxious sensitivities—this constituting the dynamics of the case. How different dynamics may underlie a particular presenting complaint is appropriately illustrated with reference to agoraphobia (chapter 14) whose treatment in new wave circles has routinely come to be *exposure therapy* (p. 257). This strategy is appropriate for cases who have classically conditioned fears of separation. But it is not appropriate for other cases—to begin with, in those in whom the problem is cognitively based—for example, those who are fearful of going afield because they interpret symptoms such as light-headedness as incipient insanity. The treatment indicated is cognitive correction. A second group of agoraphobics fear a physical catastrophe, such as a heart attack; and then it is the hypochondriacal fear that should be treated. In a third group, the fear is of panic attacks, for which a rational treatment battery is now available (see chapter 14). A fourth group are unhappily married women low in self-sufficiency, whose fear of geographic separation is primarily a function of fear of personal isolation. A fifth group have fears of danger in the outside world.

Having identified the thematic basis of the case, the therapist must go on to obtain the details of its dynamic structure. Good results are then the rule. Out of 20 cases of agoraphobia I have treated in the past 8 years, eight were apparently cured, eight improved at least 80%, and four moderately improved with change extending to the total spectrum of neurotic anxieties as reflected on the Fear Survey Schedule (Appendix C).

Procedure in New Wave Therapy

The proponents of new wave therapy ostensibly agree with traditional behavior therapists on the need for individual case analyses. The discussion that follows is based on O'Leary and Wilson's (1975) text because it self-consciously represents the new wave. "Individually tailored treatment programs for unique problems in different clients" are explicitly called for by O'Leary and Wilson (p. 22). They purport to be more thoroughgoing than traditional behavior therapists in consequence of having moved up to social learning theory, which "specifically dictates broader cognitive behavioral strategies" (O'Leary & Wilson, p. 11). It is not clear in what way the breadth of their investigations exceeds that of traditional behavior therapy. Nothing "broader" is discernible, either in their case examples or in their descriptions of procedure for individual syndromes. For example, their "social learning analysis" of psychophysiological disorders (p. 275) contains nothing that would not be routinely covered in the course of a traditional behavioral investigation.

The hypothetical case by which O'Leary and Wilson illustrate assessment (pp. 20–21) captures the essence of their approach to cases—the greatest attention is paid to external factors and little to the patient's conditioned emotional reactions. This kind of superficiality, omitting in-depth exploration of patients' feelings and background, is found throughout the book.

While there are undoubtedly exceptions, it is apparent that the new wave behavior therapists' "careful behavior analyses" are generally superficial. The neglect of individual dynamics is typified in their approach to agoraphobia (e.g., O'Brien & Barlow, 1984; Michelson, 1987). As noted above, they assume that their cases all embody the same problem, for which exposure therapy is the "best" treatment.

The results are predictably disappointing and are discussed at length in chapter 14. Barlow, O'Brien, and Holden (1983)) estimate that "roughly 25% of agoraphobics fail to benefit from exposure treatment" and many of the remaining 75%, make only limited improvements. Few become completely free of at least periodic anxiety symptoms. Barlow (1988, p. 409) confirms this evaluation.

Wilson (1984) expresses concern about this dismal picture. The solution he proposes is to employ more techniques—on the strength of Goldstein's (1982) considerably greater success with 34 cases in a program that included individual sessions and a variety of sessions. It is scarcely surprising that more was accomplished by a treatment schedule that brought some social anxieties into focus. What Goldstein did was to cast a wider therapeutic net but without traditional behavior analysis, and therefore without knowing the dynamics of individual cases. If Wilson's "broader treatment base" were to embrace Gestalt therapy or primal scream there might well be further successes—all unexplained, because having obliterated conditioning principles from his lexicon, Wilson has no theory of change.

Implications of the Comparative Survey

In short, traditional therapists base therapy on individualized analyses while the new wave treat patients as all the same, a simplistic and self-defeating assumption. The case of Jane illustrates the difference. Before receiving traditional behavior therapy she had had unsuccessful new wave therapy that failed because it lacked the essential dynamic analysis.

It is ironic that the new wave (e.g., Franks et al., 1984) have been calling traditional behavior therapists "simplistic." This appellation is probably a result of an inadequate acquaintance with the actual conduct of traditional behavior therapy. Another factor may be an uncritical acceptance of Lazarus's (1971) labeling of traditional behavior therapy as *narrow spectrum*—as, for example, by O'Leary and Wilson (1975, p. 15).

WHAT IS TO BE DONE?

As the example of agoraphobia illustrates, the abandonment of conditioning principles has led to stereotyped therapeutic practices that are not very successful. At the conceptual level, the new wave have thrown overboard behavior therapy's most important advantage—its roots in experimentally established paradigms. They have deprived themselves of the principles that give coherence to behavioral data and procedures. If behavior therapy were to disregard conditioning, it would have no basis for recognition as a separate discipline. An agglomeration of methods from multiple sources unconnected by a conception of underlying mechanisms or principles does not constitute a discipline.

In the past few years, at the Annual Meetings of the Association for the Advancement of Behavior Therapy, there has been a growing current of protest from both old and new members at the flouting of behavioral principles. Their sentiments have scarcely been acknowledged, much less given voice by leaders in the field.

Vigorous action is imperative, both in print and at the Annual Meetings of the Association. As an indication of the backlog to be made up, at the 1989 meeting, cognitivists gave 14 didactic presentations against 3 by traditional behavior therapists. On the initiative of Donald Levis, a group of traditional behavior therapists met informally and agreed on a number of steps to take including the development of didactic seminars and workshops, and the scheduling of plenary sessions to thrash out crucial issues. By bringing out into the open the rationality and depth of traditional behavior therapy, and contrasting it with the superficiality of the "new wave," we may look forward to a restoration of traditional behavior therapy to its rightful place as the spearhead of modern psychotherapy.

Appendix A
Willoughby Neuroticism Schedule

Instructions: The questions in this schedule are intended to indicate various emotional personality traits. It is not a test in any sense because there are no right or wrong answers to any of the questions.

After each question you will find a row of numbers whose meaning is given below. All you have to do is to draw a ring around the number that describes you best.

0 means "No," "never," "not at all," etc.
1 means "Somewhat," "sometimes," "a little," etc.
2 means "About as often as not," "an average amount," etc.
3 means "Usually," "a good deal," "rather often," etc.
4 means "Practically always," "entirely," etc.

1. Do you get stage fright? — 0 1 2 3 4
2. Do you worry over humiliating experiences? — 0 1 2 3 4
3. Are you afraid of falling when you are on a high place? — 0 1 2 3 4
4. Are your feelings easily hurt? — 0 1 2 3 4
5. Do you keep in the background on social occasions? — 0 1 2 3 4
6. Are you happy and sad by turns without knowing why? — 0 1 2 3 4
7. Are you shy? — 0 1 2 3 4
8. Do you daydream frequently? — 0 1 2 3 4
9. Do you get discouraged easily? — 0 1 2 3 4
10. Do you say things on the spur of the moment and then regret them? — 0 1 2 3 4

11. Do you like to be alone? — 0 1 2 3 4
12. Do you cry easily? — 0 1 2 3 4
13. Does it bother you to have people watch you work even when you do it well? — 0 1 2 3 4
14. Does criticism hurt you badly? — 0 1 2 3 4
15. Do you cross the street to avoid meeting someone? — 0 1 2 3 4
16. At a reception or tea do you avoid meeting the important person present? — 0 1 2 3 4
17. Do you often feel just miserable? — 0 1 2 3 4
18. Do you hesitate to volunteer in a class discussion or debate? — 0 1 2 3 4
19. Are you often lonely? — 0 1 2 3 4
20. Are you self-conscious before superiors? — 0 1 2 3 4
21. Do you lack self-confidence? — 0 1 2 3 4
22. Are you self conscious about your appearance? — 0 1 2 3 4
23. If you see an accident does something keep you from giving help? — 0 1 2 3 4
24. Do you feel inferior? — 0 1 2 3 4
25. Is it hard to make up your mind until the time for action is past? — 0 1 2 3 4

Appendix B
Revised Willoughby Questionnaire
for Self-Administration

Instructions: The questions in this schedule are intended to indicate various emotional personality traits. It is not a test in any sense because there are no right or wrong answers to any of the questions.

After each question you will find a row of numbers whose meaning is given below. All you have to do is to draw a ring around the number that describes you best.

0 means "No," "never," "not at all," etc.
1 means "Somewhat," "sometimes," "a little," etc.
2 means "About as often as not," "an average amount," etc.
3 means "Usually," "a good deal," "rather often," etc.
4 means "Practically always," "entirely," etc.

1. Do you get anxious if you have to speak or perform in any way in front of a group of strangers? — 0 1 2 3 4
2. Do you worry if you make a fool of yourself, or feel you have been made to look foolish? — 0 1 2 3 4
3. Are you afraid of falling when you are on a high place from which there is no real danger of falling — for example, looking down from a balcony on the tenth floor? — 0 1 2 3 4
4. Are you easily hurt by what other people do or say to you? — 0 1 2 3 4
5. Do you keep in the background on social occasions? — 0 1 2 3 4

6. Do you have changes of mood that you cannot explain? —0 1 2 3 4
7. Do you feel uncomfortable when you meet new people? —0 1 2 3 4
8. Do you day-dream frequently, i.e., indulge in fantasies not involving concrete situations? —0 1 2 3 4
9. Do you get discouraged easily, e.g., by failure or criticism? —0 1 2 3 4
10. Do you say things in haste and then regret them? —0 1 2 3 4
11. Are you ever disturbed by the mere presence of other people? —0 1 2 3 4
12. Do you cry easily? —0 1 2 3 4
13. Does it bother you to have people watch you work even when you do it well? —0 1 2 3 4
14. Does criticism hurt you badly? —0 1 2 3 4
15. Do you cross the street to avoid meeting someone? —0 1 2 3 4
16. At a reception or tea do you go out of your way to avoid meeting the important person present? —0 1 2 3 4
17. Do you often feel just miserable? —0 1 2 3 4
18. Do you hesitate to volunteer in a discussion or debate with a group of people whom you know more or less? —0 1 2 3 4
19. Do you have a sense of isolation, either when alone or among people? —0 1 2 3 4
20. Are you self-conscious before "superiors" (teachers, employers, authorities)? —0 1 2 3 4
21. Do you lack confidence in your general ability to do things and to cope with situations? —0 1 2 3 4
22. Are you self-conscious about your appearance even when you are well-dressed and groomed? —0 1 2 3 4
23. Are you scared at the sight of blood, injuries, and destruction even though there is no danger to you? —0 1 2 3 4
24. Do you feel that other people are better than you? —0 1 2 3 4
25. Is it hard for you to make up your mind? —0 1 2 3 4

Appendix C
Fear Survey Schedule*

The items in this questionnaire refer to things and experiences that may cause fear or other unpleasant feelings. Write the number of each item in the column that describes how much you are disturbed by it nowadays.

	Not At All	A Little	A Fair Amount	Much	Very Much
1. Noise of vacuum cleaners					
2. Open wounds					
3. Being alone					
4. Being in a strange place					
5. Loud voices					
6. Dead people					
7. Speaking in public					
8. Crossing streets					
9. People who seem insane					
10. Falling					
11. Automobiles					
12. Being teased					
13. Dentists					
14. Thunder					
15. Sirens					
16. Failure					
17. Entering a room where other people are already seated					

*A 108-item Fear Survey Schedule, by Wolpe and Lang (1969) is obtainable from Educational and Industrial Testing Service, San Diego, California 92107.

	Not At All	A Little	A Fair Amount	Much	Very Much
18. High places on land					
19. Looking down from high buildings					
20. Worms					
21. Imaginary creatures					
22. Strangers					
23. Receiving injections					
24. Bats					
25. Journeys by train					
26. Journeys by bus					
27. Journeys by car					
28. Feeling angry					
29. People in authority					
30. Flying insects					
31. Seeing other people injected					
32. Sudden noises					
33. Dull weather					
34. Crowds					
35. Large open spaces					
36. Cats					
37. One person bullying another					
38. Tough looking people					
39. Birds					
40. Sight of deep water					
41. Being watched working					
42. Dead animals					
43. Weapons					
44. Dirt					
45. Crawling insects					
46. Sight of fighting					
47. Ugly people					
48. Fire					
49. Sick people					
50. Dogs					
51. Being criticized					
52. Strange shapes					
53. Being in an elevator					
54. Witnessing surgical operations					
55. Angry people					
56. Mice					
57. Blood					
a—Human					
b—Animal					
58. Parting from friends					
59. Enclosed places					
60. Prospect of a surgical operation					
61. Feeling rejected by others					

	Not At All	A Little	A Fair Amount	Much	Very Much
62. Airplanes					
63. Medical odors					
64. Feeling disapproved of					
65. Harmless snakes					
66. Cemeteries					
67. Being ignored					
68. Darkness					
69. Premature heart beats (Missing a beat)					
70. Nude Men (a) Nude Women (b)					
71. Lightning					
72. Doctors					
73. People with deformities					
74. Making mistakes					
75. Looking foolish					
76. Losing control					
77. Fainting					
78. Becoming nauseous					
79. Spiders					
80. Being in charge or responsible for decisions					
81. Sight of knives or sharp objects					
82. Becoming mentally ill					
83. Being with a member of the opposite sex					
84. Taking written tests					
85. Being touched by others					
86. Feeling different from others					
87. A lull in conversation					

Appendix D
Bernreuter Self-Sufficiency
Inventory and Scoring Key

Instructions: Before each question, underline what applies to you — "Yes" or "No." Where you are unable to decide, underline the question mark.

1. Yes No ? Would you rather work for yourself than carry out the program of a superior whom you respect?
2. Yes No ? Do you usually enjoy spending an evening alone?
3. Yes No ? Have books been more entertaining to you than companions?
4. Yes No ? Do you feel the need for wider social contacts than you have?
5. Yes No ? Are you easily discouraged when the opinions of others differ from your own?
6. Yes No ? Does admiration gratify you more than achievement?
7. Yes No ? Do you usually prefer to keep your opinions to yourself?
8. Yes No ? Do you dislike attending the movies alone?
9. Yes No ? Would you like to have a very congenial friend with whom you could plan daily activities?
10. Yes No ? Can you calm your own fears?
11. Yes No ? Do jeers humiliate you even when you know you are right?
12. Yes No ? Do you think you could become so absorbed in creative work that you would not notice the lack of intimate friends?
13. Yes No ? Are you willing to take a chance alone in a situation of doubtful outcome?
14. Yes No ? Do you find conversation more helpful in formulating your ideas than reading?

15. Yes No ? Do you like to shop alone?
16. Yes No ? Does your ambition need occasional stimulation through contacts with successful people?
17. Yes No ? Do you have difficulty in making up your mind for yourself?
18. Yes No ? Would you prefer making your own arrangements on a trip to a foreign country to going on a prearranged trip?
19. Yes No ? Are you much affected by praise, or blame, of many people?
20. Yes No ? Do you usually avoid taking advice?
21. Yes No ? Do you consider the observance of social customs and manners an essential aspect of life?
22. Yes No ? Do you want someone with you when you receive bad news?
23. Yes No ? Does it make you uncomfortable to be "different" or unconventional?
24. Yes No ? Do you prefer to make hurried decisions alone?
25. Yes No ? If you were to start out in research work would you prefer to be an assistant in another's project rather than an independent worker on your own?
26. Yes No ? When you are low in spirits do you try to find someone to cheer you up?
27. Yes No ? Have you preferred being alone most of the time?
28. Yes No ? Do you prefer traveling with someone who will make all the necessary arrangements to the adventure of traveling alone?
29. Yes No ? Do you usually work things out rather than get someone to show you?
30. Yes No ? Do you like especially to have attention from acquaintances when you are ill?
31. Yes No ? Do you prefer to face dangerous situations alone?
32. Yes No ? Can you usually see wherein your mistakes lie without having them pointed out to you?
33. Yes No ? Do you like to make friends when you go to new places?
34. Yes No ? Can you stick to a tiresome task for long without someone prodding or encouraging you?
35. Yes No ? Do you experience periods of loneliness?
36. Yes No ? Do you like to get many views from others before making an important decision?
37. Yes No ? Would you dislike any work which might take you into isolation for a few years, such as forest ranging, etc.?
38. Yes No ? Do you prefer a play to a dance?
39. Yes No ? Do you usually try to take added responsibility upon yourself?
40. Yes No ? Do you make friends easily?
41. Yes No ? Can you be optimistic when others about you are greatly depressed?
42. Yes No ? Do you try to get your own way even if you have to fight for it?

43. Yes No ? Do you like to be with other people a great deal?
44. Yes No ? Do you get as many ideas at the time of reading as you do from a discussion of it afterwards?
45. Yes No ? In sports do you prefer to participate in individual competitions rather than in team games?
46. Yes No ? Do you usually face your troubles alone without seeking help?
47. Yes No ? Do you see more fun or humor in things when you are in a group than when you are alone?
48. Yes No ? Do you dislike finding your way about in strange places?
49. Yes No ? Can you work happily without praise or recognition?
50. Yes No ? Do you feel that marriage is essential to your happiness?
51. Yes No ? If all but a few of your friends threatened to break relations because of some habit they considered a vice in you, and in which you saw no harm, would you stop the habit to keep friends?
52. Yes No ? Do you like to have suggestions offered to you when you are working a puzzle?
53. Yes No ? Do you usually prefer to do your own planning alone rather than with others?
54. Yes No ? Do you usually find that people are more stimulating to you than anything else?
55. Yes No ? Do you prefer to be alone at times of emotional stress?
56. Yes No ? Do you like to bear responsibilities alone?
57. Yes No ? Can you usually understand a problem better by studying it out alone than by discussing it with others?
58. Yes No ? Do you find that telling others of your own personal good news is the greatest part of the enjoyment of it?
59. Yes No ? Do you generally rely on your own judgment?
60. Yes No ? Do you like playing games in which you have no spectators?

Bernreuter Key*

1. <u>Yes</u> No ?	21. Yes <u>No</u> <u>?</u>	41. <u>Yes</u> No ?
2. <u>Yes</u> No ?	22. Yes <u>No</u> ?	42. <u>Yes</u> No ?
3. <u>Yes</u> No <u>?</u>	23. Yes <u>No</u> ?	43. Yes <u>No</u> <u>?</u>
4. Yes <u>No</u> ?	24. <u>Yes</u> No ?	44. <u>Yes</u> No ?
5. Yes <u>No</u> ?	25. Yes <u>No</u> ?	45. <u>Yes</u> No <u>?</u>
6. Yes <u>No</u> ?	26. Yes <u>No</u> ?	46. <u>Yes</u> No ?
7. <u>Yes</u> No <u>?</u>	27. <u>Yes</u> No <u>?</u>	47. Yes <u>No</u> ?
8. Yes <u>No</u> ?	28. Yes <u>No</u> ?	48. Yes <u>No</u> ?
9. Yes <u>No</u> ?	29. <u>Yes</u> No ?	49. Yes <u>No</u> <u>?</u>
10. <u>Yes</u> No ?	30. Yes <u>No</u> ?	50. Yes <u>No</u> ?
11. Yes <u>No</u> ?	31. <u>Yes</u> No <u>?</u>	51. Yes <u>No</u> ?
12. <u>Yes</u> No <u>?</u>	32. <u>Yes</u> No ?	52. <u>Yes</u> No ?
13. <u>Yes</u> No ?	33. Yes <u>No</u> ?	53. Yes <u>No</u> ?
14. Yes <u>No</u> ?	34. <u>Yes</u> No ?	54. <u>Yes</u> No ?
15. <u>Yes</u> No ?	35. Yes <u>No</u> ?	55. <u>Yes</u> No ?
16. Yes <u>No</u> <u>?</u>	36. Yes <u>No</u> <u>?</u>	56. <u>Yes</u> No ?
17. Yes <u>No</u> ?	37. Yes <u>No</u> ?	57. <u>Yes</u> No ?
18. <u>Yes</u> No <u>?</u>	38. <u>Yes</u> No ?	58. Yes <u>No</u> ?
19. Yes <u>No</u> ?	39. <u>Yes</u> No ?	59. <u>Yes</u> No ?
20. <u>Yes</u> No ?	40. Yes <u>No</u> ?	60. <u>Yes</u> No ?

*Underlined answer scores one point.

References

Abel, G. G., Levis, D. J., & Clancy, J. (1970). Aversion therapy applied to taped sequences of deviant behavior in exhibitionism and other sexual deviations: A preliminary report. *J. Behav. Ther. Exp. Psychiat., 1*, 59.

Ackerman, S. H., & Sachar, E. J. (1974). The lactate theory of anxiety: A review and reevaluation. *Psychosom. Med., 36*, 69.

Agras, S. W. (1985). *Panic: Facing fears, phobias and anxiety*. New York: W H Freeman.

Ahsen, A. (1965). Eidetic psychotherapy. Lahore, India: Nai Matboat Press.

Akiskal, H. S. (1983). Dysthymic disorder: Psychopathology of proposed chronic depressive subtypes. *Am. J. Psychiatry, 140*, 11.

Akiskal, H. S., Rosenthal, R. H., Rosenthal, T. L. et al. (1979). Differentiation of primary affective illness from situational, symptomatic and secondary depression. *Arch. Gen. Psychiatry, 36*, 635.

American Psychiatric Association. (1987). *Diagnostic statistical manual of mental disorders* (4th ed.). Washington, DC: Author.

American Psychoanalytic Association. (1958). *Summary and final report of the Central Fact-Gathering Committee*. Unpublished manuscript.

Amsel, A. (1962). Frustrative nonreward in partial reinforcement and discrimination learning: Some recent history and a theoretical extension. *Psychol. Rev., 69*, 306.

Amsel, A. (1972). Inhibition and mediation in classical, Pavlovian, and instrumental conditioning. In R. A. Boakes & M. S. Halliday (Eds.), *Inhibition and learning*. London: Academic Press.

Anderson, O. D., & Parmenter, R. (1941). A long term study of the experimental neurosis in the sheep and dog. *Psychosom. Med. Monogr., 2* (3-4).

Andrews, G., Harris, M., Garside, R., & Kay, D. (1964). *Syndrome of stuttering*. London: Heinemann Medical Books.

Andrews, G., & Harvey, R. (1981). Does psychotherapy benefit neurotic patients? *Arch. Gen. Psychiat., 38*, 1203.

Andrews, G., & Tanner, S. (1982). Stuttering treatment: An attempt to replicate the regulated breathing method. *J. Speech and Hearing Disorders, 47*, 138.

Appel, J. B. (1963). Punishment and shock intensity. *Science, 141*, 528.

Arieti, S. (1974). *American Handbook of Psychiatry*. New York: Basic Books.

Arkowitz, H., & Messer, S. B. (1984). *Psychoanalytic therapy and behavior therapy: Is integration possible?* New York: Plenum Press.

Arnold, M. B. (1945). The physiological differentiation of emotional states. *Psychol. Rev., 52,* 35.

Arnold, M. B. (1960). *Emotion and personality* (Vol. 1). New York: Columbia University Press.

Ascher, E. (1952). A criticism of the concept of neurotic depression. *Am. J. Psychiatry, 108,* 901.

Ascher, L. M. (1978). Paradoxical intention: A review of preliminary research. *Internatl. Forum Logother., 1,* 18.

Ascher, L. M. (1981a). Employing paradoxical intention in the treatment of agoraphobia. *Behav. Res. Ther., 19,* 533.

Ascher, L. M. (1981b). Paradoxical intention. In A. Goldstein & E. B. Foa (Eds.), *Handbook of behavioral interventions.* New York: John Wiley & Sons.

Ascher, L. M., & Efran, J. S. (1978). The use of paradoxical intention in a behavioral program for sleep onset insomnia. *J. Consult. Clin. Psychol., 46,* 547.

Ascher, L. M., & Turner, R. M. (1979). Controlled comparison of progressive relaxation, stimulus control, and paradoxical intention therapies for insomnia. *J. Consult. Clin. Psychol., 471,* 500.

Ashem, B., & Donner, L. (1968). Covert sensitization with alcoholics: A controlled replication. *Behav. Res. Ther., 6,* 7.

Asratian, E. A. (1972). Genesis and localization of conditioned inhibition. In R. H. Brookes & M. S. Halliday (Eds.), *Inhibition and Learning.* London: Academic Press.

Ax, A. F. (1953). The physiological differentiation of anger and fear in humans. *Psychom. Med., 15,* 433.

Ayllon, T. (1963). Intensive treatment of psychotic behavior by stimulus satiation and food reinforcement. *Behav. Res. Ther., 1,* 53.

Ayllon, T., & Azrin, N. H. (1964). Reinforcement and instructions with mental patients. *J. Exp. Anal. Behav., 7,* 327.

Ayllon, T., & Azrin, N. H. (1965). The measurement and reinforcement of behavior of psychotics. *J. Exp. Anal. Behav., 8,* 357.

Ayllon, T., & Azrin, N. H. (1968). *The token economy: A motivational system for therapy and rehabilitation.* New York: Appleton-Century-Crofts.

Ayllon, T., & Michael, J. (1959). The psychiatric nurse as a behavioral engineer. *J. Exp. Anal. Behav., 2,* 323.

Ayllon, T., Smith, D., & Rogers, M. (1970). Behavioral management of school phobia. *J. Behav. Ther. Exp. Psychiat., 1,* 125.

Azrin, N. H., & Besalel, V. A. (1980). *How to use overcorrection.* Lawrence, KA: H & H Enterprises.

Azrin, N. H., & Fox, R. M. (1974). *Toilet training in less than a day.* New York: Simon & Schuster.

Azrin, N. H., & Holz, W. C. (1966). Punishment. In W. K. Honig (Ed.), *Operant behavior. Areas of research and application.* New York: Appleton-Century-Crofts.

Azrin, N. H., & Nunn, R. G. (1973). Habit reversal: A method of eliminating nervous habits and tics. *Behav. Res. Ther., 11,* 619.

Azrin, N. H., & Nunn, R. G. (1974). A rapid method of eliminating stuttering by a regulated breathing approach. *Behav. Res. Ther., 8,* 330.

Azrin, N. H., Nunn, R. G., & Frantz, S. E. (1980). Habit reversal vs. negative practice treatment of nervous tics. *Behav. Ther., 11,* 169.

Azrin, N. H., Nunn, R. G., & Frantz-Renshaw, S. E. (1980). Habit reversal treatment of thumbsucking. *Behav. Res. Ther., 18*, 395.

Baars, B. J. (1986). *The cognitive revolution in psychology.* New York: Guilford Press.

Bachrach, A. J., Erwin, W. J., & Mohr, J. P. (1965). The control of eating behavior in an anorexic by operant conditioning techniques. In L. Ullmann & L. Krasner (Eds.), *Case studies in behavior modification.* New York: Holt, Rinehart, & Winston.

Baeyens, F., Crombez, G., Van den Bergh, O., & Eelen, P. (1988). Once in contact always in contact: Evaluative conditioning is resistant to extinction. *Adv. Behav. Res. Ther., 10*, 179.

Baeyens, F., Eelen, P., & Van den Bergh, O. (1988). Contingency awareness in evaluative conditioning: A case for unaware affective-evaluative learning. *Cogn. Emot.* In press.

Baeyens, F., Eelen, P., Van den Bergh, O., & Crombez, G. (1989). Acquired affective-evaluative value: Conservative but not unchangeable. *Behav. Res. Ther., 27*, 279.

Bailey, P. (1964). Sigmund Freud: Scientific period (1873–1897). In J. Wolpe, A. Salter, & L. J. Reyna (Eds.), *The conditioning therapies.* New York: Holt, Rinehart, & Winston.

Bain, J. A. (1928). *Thought control in everyday life.* New York: Funk & Wagnalls.

Bajtelsmit, J. W., & Gershman, L. (1976). Covert positive reinforcement: Efficacy and conceptualization. *J. Behav. Ther. Exp. Psychiat., 7*, 207.

Balsam, P. D. (1988). Selection representation and equivalence of controlling stimuli. In R. C. Atkinson (Ed.), *Stevens' handbook of experimental psychology.* New York: John Wiley & Sons.

Bancroft, J. (1969). Aversion therapy of homosexuality. *Brit. J. Psychiat., 115*, 1417.

Bandura, A. (1967). Behavioristic psychotherapy. *Scient. American, 216*, 78.

Bandura, A. (1968). Modelling approaches to the modification of phobic disorders. *Ciba Foundation Symposium: The role of learning in psychotherapy.* London: Churchill.

Bandura, A. (1969). *Principles of behavior modification.* New York: Holt, Rinehart, & Winston.

Bandura, A. (1974). Behavior theory and the models of man. *Amer. Psychol., 29*, 859.

Bandura, A. (1977). Self-efficacy: Toward a unifying theory of behavioral change. *Psychol. Rev., 84*, 191.

Bandura, A. (1986). *Social foundations of thought and action: A social cognitive theory.* Englewood Cliffs, NJ: Prentice-Hall.

Bandura, A., & Adams, N. E. (1977). Analysis of self-efficacy theory of behavioral change. *Cogn. Ther. Res., 1*, 287.

Bandura, A., Blanchard, E. D., & Ritter, B. (1969). Relative efficacy of desensitization and modeling approaches for inducing behavioral, affective and attitudinal changes. *J. Pers. Soc. Psychol., 13*, 173.

Bandura, A., Grusec, J., & Menlove, F. (1967). Vicarious extinction of avoidance behavior. *J. Pers. Soc. Psychol., 5*, 16.

Barber, T. X. (1969). *Hypnosis: A scientific approach.* New York: Van Nostrand Reinhold.

Barber, V. B. (1940). Studies in the psychology of stuttering. Rhythm as a distraction. *J. of Speech Disorders, 5*, 29.

Barker, J. C., & Miller, M. B. (1968). *Recent developments and some future trends in the application of aversion therapy*. Unpublished manuscript.

Barlow, D. H. (1979). President's message. *Behav. Ther., 2*, 8.

Barlow, D. H. (1988). *Anxiety and its disorders*. New York: Guilford Press.

Barlow, D. H., O'Brien, G. T., Last, C. G., & Holden, A. E. (1983). Couples treatment of agorophobia: Initial outcome. In K. D. Craig & R. J. McMahon (Eds.), *Advances in clinical behavior therapy*. New York: Brunner/Mazel.

Barlow, J. A. (1956). Secondary motivation through classical conditioning: A reconsideration of the nature of backward conditioning. *Psychol. Rev., 63*, 406.

Baum, M. (1988). Spontaneous recovery from the effects of flooding (exposure) in animals. *Behav. Res. Ther., 26*, 185.

Beach, F. A. (1942). Comparison of copulatory behavior of male rats reared in isolation, cohabitation, and segregation. *J. Genet. Psychol., 60*, 121.

Beck, A. T. (1967). *Depression*. New York: Harper & Row.

Beck, A. T. (1976). *Cognitive therapy and the emotional disorders*. New York: International Universities Press.

Beck, A. T., Hollon, S. D., Young, I. E. et al. (1985). Treatment of depression with cognitive therapy and amitriptyline. *Arch. Gen. Psychiatry, 42*, 142.

Beck, A. T., & Mahoney, M. (1979). Schools of "thought." *Amer. Psychol., 34*, 98.

Bellack, A. S. (Ed.). (1984). *Schizophrenia: Treatment, management and rehabilitation*. Orlando, FL: Grune & Stratton.

Bellack, A. S., Hersen, M., & Himmelhoch, J. (1983). A comparison of social skills training, pharmacotherapy, and psychotherapy for depression. *Behav. Res. Ther., 21*, 101.

Benjamin, S., Marks, I. M., & Huson, J. (1972). Active muscular relaxation in desensitization of phobic patients. *Psychol. Med., 2*, 381.

Benson, H. (1975). *The relaxation response*. New York: William Morrow.

Benson, H., Shapiro, D., Tursky, B., & Schwartz, G. E. (1971). Decreased systolic blood pressure through operant conditioning techniques in patients with essential hypertension. *Science, 173*, 740.

Bergin, A. (1971). The evaluation of therapeutic outcomes. In A. E. Bergin & S. L. Garfield (Eds.), *Handbook of psychotherapy and behavior change: An empirical analysis*. New York: John Wiley & Sons.

Bergin, A. E., & Strupp, H. H. (1972). *Changing frontiers in the science of psychotherapy*. Chicago: Aldine Atherton.

Berkun, M. M. (1957). Factors in the recovery from approach-avoidance conflict. *J. Exp. Psychol., 54*, 65.

Berlyne, D. E. (1960). *Conflict, arousal, and curiosity*. New York: McGraw-Hill.

Berlyne, D. E. (1971). *Aesthetics and psychobiology*. New York: Appleton-Century-Crofts.

Bernstein, D. A. (1973). Behavioral fear assessment. In H. Adams & P. Unchil (Eds.), *Issues and trends in behavior therapy*. Springfield, IL: C C Thomas.

Bernstein, D. A., & Paul, G. L. (1971). Some comments on therapy analogue research with small animal "phobias." *J. Behav. Exp. Psychiat., 2*, 225.

Bevan, J. R. (1960). Learning theory applied to the treatment of a patient with obsessional ruminations. In H. J. Eysenck (Ed.), *Behavior therapy and the neuroses*. Oxford: Pergamon Press.

Bijou, S. W., & Ruiz, R. (1981). *Behavior modification: Contributions to education*. Hillsdale, NJ: Lawrence Erlbaum Associates.

Black, A. H. (1958). The extinction of avoidance responses under curare. *J. Comp. Physiol. Psychol., 51*, 519.

Blakemore, C. B. (1965). The application of behavior therapy to a sexual disorder. In H. J. Eysenck (Ed.), *Experiments in behavior therapy*. Oxford: Pergamon Press.

Blakemore, C. B., Thorpe, J. G., Barker, J. C., Conway, C. G., & Lavin, N. I. (1963). The application of faradic aversion conditioning in a case of transvestism. *Behav. Res. Ther., 1*, 29.

Blanchard, E. B., Miller, S. T., Abel, G. G., Haynes, M., & Wicker, R. (1979). Evaluation of biofeedback in the treatment of essential hypertension. *J. Appl. Behav. Anal., 12*, 99.

Bleuler, E. (1911). *Dementia praecox or the group of schizophrenias* (J. Zinken, Trans.). New York: International Universities Press.

Blinder, J., Freeman, D. M. A., & Stunkard, A. J. (1970). Behavior therapy of anorexia nervosa: Effectiveness of activity as a reinforcer of weight gain. *Amer. J. Psychiat., 126*, 1093.

Block, J., Jennings, P. H., Harvey, E., & Simpson, E. (1964). Interaction between allergic potential and psychopathology in childhood asthma. *Psychosom. Med., 26*, 307.

Bond, I. K., & Hutchinson, H. C. (1960). Application of reciprocal inhibition therapy to exhibitionism. *Canad. Med. Ass. J., 83*, 23.

Borgeat, F., Hade, B., Larouche, L. M., & Gauthier, B. (1984). Psychophysiological effects of therapist's active presence during biofeedback. *Psychiat. J. Univ. Ottawa, 9*, 132.

Borkovec, T. D., & O'Brien, G. T. (1976). Methodological and target behavior issues in analogue therapy outcome research. In M. Hersen, R. M. Eisler, & P. M. Miller (Eds.), *Progress in behavior modification*. New York: Academic Press.

Borkovec, T. D., & Sides, J. K. (1979). Critical procedural variables related to the physiological effects of progressive relaxations: A review. *Behav. Res. Ther., 17*, 119.

Boudewyns, P. A., & Shipley, R. H. (1983). *Flooding and implosive therapy*. New York: Plenum Press.

Boudreau, L. (1972). Transcendental meditation and yoga as reciprocal inhibitors. *J. Behav. Ther. Exp. Psychiat., 3*, 97.

Boulougouris, J. C., Marks, I. M., & Marset, P. (1971). Superiority of flooding (implosion) to desensitization for reducing pathological fear. *Behav. Res. Ther., 9*, 7.

Bower, T. G. R. (1976). Repetitive processes in child development, *Scientific American, 235*, 38.

Bower, T. G. R. (1977). *A primer of infant development*. New York: W H Freeman.

Brady, J. P. (1971). Metronome-conditioned speech retraining for stuttering. *Behav. Ther., 2*, 129.

Bregman, E. (1934). An attempt to modify the emotional attitudes of infants by the conditioned response technique. *J. Genet. Psychol., 45*, 169.

Brody, M. W. (1962). Prognosis and results of psychoanalysis. In J. H. Nodine & J. H. Moyer (Eds.), *Psychosomatic medicine*. Philadelphia: Lea & Febiger.

Brookshire, K. H., Littman, R. A., & Stewart, C. N. (1961). Residue of shock trauma in the white rat: A three-factor theory. *Psychol. Monogr., 75* (10, Whole No. 514).

Brookshire, K. H., Littman, R. A., & Stewart, C. N. (1962). The interactive effect of promazine and postweaning stress upon adult avoidance behavior. *J. Nerv. Ment. Dis., 135*, 52.

Brown, G. W., Davidson, S., Harris, U. et al. (1977). Psychiatric disorder in London and North Ulster. *Soc. Sci. & Med., 11*, 367.

Brownell, K. D., & Barlow, D. H. (1980). The behavioral treatment of sexual deviation. In A. Goldstein & E. B. Foa (Eds.), *Handbook of behavioral interventions*. New York: John Wiley & Sons.

Brownell, K. D., Heckerman, C. L., Westlake, R. J., Hayes, S. C., & Monti, P. M. (1978). The effect of couples training and partner cooperativeness in the behavioral treatment of obesity. *Behav. Res. Ther., 16*, 323.

Bruch, H. (1973). *Eating disorders: Obesity, anorexia nervosa and the person within*. New York: Basic Books.

Budzinski, T. H., & Stoyva, J. M. (1969). An instrument for producing deep muscle relaxation by means of analog information feedback. *J. App. Behav. Anal., 2*, 231.

Budzinski, T., Stoyva, J., & Adler, C. (1970). Feedback-induced muscle relaxation: Application to tension headaches. *J. Behav. Ther. Exp. Psychiat., 1*, 205.

Bunch, M. E., & Winston, M. M. (1936). The relationship between the character of the transfer and retroactive inhibition. *Amer. J. Psychol., 48*, 598.

Burchard, J., & Tyler, V. (1965). The modification of delinquent behavior through operant conditioning. *Behav. Res. Ther., 2*, 245.

Burnham, W. H. (1924). *The normal mind*. New York: Appleton-Century-Crofts.

Burns, D., & Brady, J. P. (1980). The treatment of stuttering. In A. Goldstein & E. B. Foa (Eds.), *Handbook of behavioral interventions*. New York: John Wiley & Sons.

Butler, G., Cullington, A., Munby, M., Amies, P., & Gelder, M. (1984). Exposure and anxiety management in the treatment of social phobia. *J. Consult. Clin. Psychol., 52*, 642.

Cabanac, M. (1971). Physiological role of pleasure. *Science, 173*, 1103.

Campbell, B. A., & Church, R. M. (1969). *Punishment and aversive behavior*. New York: Appleton-Century-Crofts.

Campbell, D., Sanderson, R. E., & Laverty, S. G. (1964). Characteristics of a conditioned response in human subjects during extinction trials following a single traumatic conditioning trial. *J. Abn. Soc. Psychol., 68*, 627.

Carmichael, L. (1946). *Manual of child psychology*. New York: John Wiley & Sons.

Castelucci, V. F., Carew, T. J., & Kandel, E. R. (1978). Cellular analysis of long-term habituation of the gill-withdrawal reflex of Apoysia Californica. *Science, 202*, 1306.

Catania, A. C. (1963). Concurrent performances: Reinforcement interaction and response independence. *J. Exp. Anal. Behav., 6*, 253.

Catania, A. C. (1969). Concurrent performances: Inhibition of one response by reinforcement of another. *J. Exp. Anal. Behav., 12*, 731.

Catania, A. C. (1973). Self-inhibiting effects of reinforcement. *J. Exp. Anal. Behav., 19*, 517.

Cautela, J. R. (1966). Treatment of compulsive behavior by covert sensitization. *Psychol. Rec., 16*, 33.

Cautela, J. R. (1967). Covert sensitization. *Psychol. Rep., 20*, 459.

Cautela, J. R. (1970a). Covert negative reinforcement. *J. Behav. Ther. Exp. Psychiat., 1*, 273.

Cautela, J. R. (1970b). Covert reinforcement. *Behav. Ther., 1*, 33.

Cautela, J. R. (1972). The treatment of over-eating by covert conditioning. *Psychotherapy: Theory, Research and Practice, 9*, 211.

Cautela, J. R. (1977). The use of covert conditioning in modifying pain behavior. *J. Behav. Ther. Exp. Psychiat., 8*, 45.

Cautela, J. R., & Kastenbaum, R. (1967). A reinforcement survey schedule for use in therapy, training, and research. *Psychol. Rep., 20*, 1115.

Cautela, J. R., & Wall, C. C. (1980). Covert conditioning in clinical practice. In A. Goldstein & E. B. Foa (Eds.), *Handbook of behavioral interventions.* New York: John Wiley & Sons.

Chambless, D. L., & Goldstein, A. J. (1981). Clinical treatment of agoraphobia. In M. Mavissakalian & D. H. Barlow (Eds.), *Phobia: Psychological and pharmacological treatment* (pp. 103–144). New York: Guilford Press.

Chapman, J. (1966). The early symptoms of schizophrenia. *Brit. J. Psychiat., 12,* 225.

Chesney, M. A., & Black, G. W. (1986). Behavioral treatment of borderline hypertension. *J. Cardiovascular Physiol., 8*(Suppls), 57.

Chesney, M. A., & Shelton, J. L. (1976). A comparison of muscle relaxation and electromyogram biofeedback treatments for muscle contraction headache. *J. Behav. Ther. Exp. Psychiat., 7*, 221.

Church, R. (1963). The varied effects of punishment. *Psychol. Rev., 70*, 369.

Clancy, J., Noyes, R., Hoenk, P. R., & Slyment, D. J. (1978). Secondary depression in anxiety neurosis. *J. Nerv. Ment. Dis., 166*, 846.

Clark, D. E. (1963). The treatment of monosymptomatic phobia by systematic desensitization. *Behav. Res. Ther., 1*, 63.

Clark, D. M. (1986). A cognitive approach to panic. *Behaviour Research and Therapy, 24*, 461.

Clarke, D. M., Salkoviskis, P. M., & Chalkley, A. J. (1985). Respiratory control as a treatment for panic attacks. *J. Behav. Ther. Exp. Psychiat., 16*, 23.

Clayton, P. J., & Darvish, H. S. (1979). Course of depressive symptoms following the stress of bereavement. In J. E. Barrett (Ed.), *Stress and Mental Disorders.* New York: Raven Press.

Cohen, R., & Dean, S. J. (1968). Group desensitization of test anxiety. *Proceedings of the 76th Annual Convention of the American Psychology Association, 615.*

Coleman, J. V., Greenblatt, M., & Solomon, H. S. (1956). Physiological evidence of rapport during psychotherapeutic interview. *Dis. Nerv. Syst., 17*, 71.

Compernolle, T., Hoogduin, K., & Joele, L. (1979). Diagnosis and treatment of the hyperventilation syndrome. *Psychosom., 20*, 612.

Conner, W. H. (1974). Effects of brief relaxation training on autonomic response to anxiety provoking stimuli. *Psychophysiol., 11*, 591.

Conrad, S. R., & Wincze, J. P. (1976). Orgasmic reconditioning in male homosexuals. *Behav. Ther., 7*, 155.

Cooke, G. (1966). The efficacy of two desensitization procedures: An analogue study. *Behav. Res. Ther., 4*, 17.

Cooper, A. J. (1971). Treatments of male potency disorders: The present status. *Psychosom., 12*, 235.

Cooper, A. J., Ismail, A., Smith, C. G., & Loraine, J. (1970, July 4). Androgen function in "psychogenic" and "constitutional" types of impotence. *Brit. Med. J.*

Cooper, N. A., & Clum, C. A. (1989). Imaginal flooding and supplementary treatment for PTSD: A controlled study. *J. Behav. Ther. Exp. Psychiat., 20*, 381.

Copeland, J. R. M. (1983). Psychotic and neurotic depression: Discriminant function analysis and five-year outcome. *Psychol. Med., 13*, 373.

Coppock, H. W. (1951). Secondary reinforcing effect of a stimulus repeatedly presented after electric shock. *Amer. Psychol., 6*, 277.

Crafts, L. W., Schneirla, T. C., Robinson, E. A., & Gelbart, R. W. (1938). *Recent experiments in psychology*. New York: McGraw-Hill.

Craske, M. G., & Barlow, D. H. (1989). Nocturnal panic. *J. Nerv. Ment. Dis., 177*, 160.

Craske, M. G., Sanderson, W. C., & Barlow, D. H. (1987). The relationship among panic, fear, and avoidance. *Journal of Anxiety Disorders, 1*, 153.

Crowder, J. E., & Thornton, D. W. (1970). Effects of systematic desensitization, programmed fantasy and bibliotherapy on a specific fear. *Behav. Res. Ther., 8*, 35.

Crowe, R. R., Park, D. L., Slymen, D. J., & Noyes, R. (1980). A family study of anxiety neurosis. Morbidity risk in families of patients with and without mutual valve prolapse. *Arch. Gen. Psychiat., 37*, 77.

Culler, E. (1938). Observations on direct cortical stimulation in the dog. *Psychol. Bull., 35*, 687.

Cushing, C. H. (1932). Peptic ulcers in the interbrain. *Surg. Gynecol. Obstet., 55*, 1.

Dager, S. R., Holland, J. P., Cowley, D. S., & Dunner, D. L. (1987). Panic disorder precipitated by exposure to organic solvents in the work place. *American Journal of Psychiatry, 144*, 1056.

Dale, H. (1937). Transmission of nervous effects by acetylcholine. *Harvey Lec., 32*, 229.

Daniels, L. K. (1974). *The management of childhood behavior problems in school and at home*. Springfield, IL: C C Thomas.

Darnton, R. (1968). *Mesmerism and the end of the Enlightenment in France*. Cambridge: Harvard University Press.

Darwin, P. L., & McBrearty, J. F. (1969). The subject speaks up in desensitization. In R. D. Rubin & C. M. Franks (Eds.), *Advances in behavior therapy*. New York: Academic Press.

Davey, D. C. L. (1989). Dental phobias and anxieties: Evidence for conditioning processes in the acquisition and modulation of learned fears. *Behav. Res. Ther., 27*, 51.

Davison, G. C. (1965). Systematic desensitization as a counter conditioning process. *J. Abnorm. Psycho., 73*, 91.

Davison, G. C. (1967). The elimination of a sadistic fantasy by a client-controlled counterconditioning technique. *J. Abn. Psychol., 3*, 84.

Dekker, E., Pelser, H. E., & Groen, J. (1957). Conditioning as a cause of asthmatic attacks. *J. Psychosom. Res., 2*, 97.

Delprato, D. J., & McGlynn, F. D. (1984). Behavioral theories of anxiety disorders. In S. M. Turner (Ed.), *Behavioral theories and treatment of anxiety*. New York: Plenum Press.

Deluty, M. Z. (1976). Choice and the rate of punishment in concurrent schedules. *J. Exp. Anal. Behav., 25*, 75.

Deluty, M. Z. (1977). Similarities of the matching law to other models of conditioning. *Psychol. Rec., 27*, 599.

Demaster, B., Reid, J., & Twentyman, C. (1977). Effects of different amounts of feedback on observers' reliability. *Behav. Ther., 8*, 317.

DeMoor, W. (1970). Systematic desensitization versus prolonged high intensity stimulation (flooding). *J. Behav. Ther. Exp. Psychiat., 1*, 139.

Denholtz, M. (1971). The use of tape recordings between therapy sessions. *J. Behav. Ther. Exp. Psychiat., 1*, 139.

DeRubeis, R., & Beck, A. T. (1988). Cognitive therapy. In K. S. Dobson (Ed.), *Handbook of cognitive behavior therapy*. New York: Guilford Press.

De Silva, P., & Rachman, S. (1981). Is exposure a necessary condition for fear reduction? *Behav. Res. Ther., 19*, 227–232.

De Silva, P., Rachman, S., & Seligman, M. E. P. (1977). Prepared phobias and obsessions: Therapeutic outcome. *Behav. Res. Ther., 15*, 65.

Dexter, S. L. (1982). Rebreathing aborts migraine attacks. *Brit. Med. J., 284*.

Doctor, R. M. (1982). Major results of a large scale pretreatment survey of agoraphobics. In R. L. Dupon (Ed.), *Phobia: A comprehensive survey of modern treatments*. New York: Brunner/Mazel.

Donner, L. (1970). Automated group desensitization: A follow-up report. *Behav. Res. Ther., 8*, 241.

Donner, L., & Guerny, B. G., Jr. (1969). Automated group desensitization for test anxiety. *Behav. Res. Ther., 7*, 1.

Dryden, W., & Ellis, A. (1987). *The practice of rational-emotive therapy*. New York: Springer.

Dunlap, K. (1932). *Habits: Their making and unmaking*. New York: Liveright.

Dworkin, S., Raginsky, B. B., & Bourne, W. (1937). Action of anesthetics and sedatives upon the inhibited nervous system. *Current Res. Anaesth., 16*, 283.

Ebbinghaus, H. (1913). *Memory*. New York: Teachers College.

Eccles, J. C. (1975). Under the spell of synapse. In F. G. Worden, J. P. Swazey, & G. Adelman (Eds.), *The neurosciences: Paths of discovery*. Cambridge, MA: Colonial Press.

Edelman, R. L. (1971). Operant conditioning treatment of encopresis. *J. Behav. Ther. Exp. Psychiat., 1*, 71.

Edwards, N. B. (1972). Case conference: Assertive training in a case of homosexual pedophilia. *J. Behav. Ther. Exp. Psychiat., 3*, 55.

Efran, J. S., & Marcia, J. E. (1967). The treatment of fears by expectancy manipulation: An exploratory investigation. *Proceedings of the 75th Annual Convention of the American Psychology Association*, 239.

Ellis, A. (1958). Rational psychotherapy. *J. Gen. Psychol., 59*, 35.

Ellis, A. (1962). *Reason and emotion in psychotherapy*. New York: Lyle Stuart.

Ellis, A. (1970). *Address to the 1970 meeting of the Assoc. Adv. Behav. Ther.*, Miami, FL.

Ellis, A. (1974). *Humanistic psychotherapy: The rational-emotive approach*. New York: Julian Press.

Ellis, A. (1986). *Handbook of rational-emotive therapy*. New York: Springer.

Emmelkamp, P. M. G., & Wessels, H. (1975). Flooding in imagination vs. flooding in-vivo: A comparison in agoraphobics. *Behav. Res. Ther., 13*, 7.

Engel, B. T. (1972). Response specificity. In N. S. Greenfield & R. A. Sternbeck (Eds.), *Handbook of psychophysiology*. New York: Holt, Rinehart, & Winston.

Eppinger, H., & Hess, L. (1915). Vagotonia. *Nerv. & Ment. Dis.*, Monograph 20.

Erwin, W. J. (1963). Confinement in the production of human neuroses: The barber's chair syndrome. *Behav. Ther., 1*, 175.

Erwin, W. J. (1977). A sixteen-year follow-up of a case of severe anorexia nervosa. *J. Behav. Ther. Exp. Psychiat., 8*, 157.

Evans, I. M. (1973). The logical requirements for explanations of systematic desensitization. *Behav. Ther., 4*, 506.

Everaerd, W. (1970). Reading as the counterconditioning agent in a cardiac neurosis. *J. Behav. Ther. Exp. Psychiat., 1*, 165.

Everaerd, W., & Dekker, J. (1985). Treatment of male sexual dysfunction: Exposure compared with systematic desensitization and rational emotive therapy. *Behavior Research and Therapy, 23*, 13.

Ewald, G. (1928). Psychoses in acute infections. In O. Bumkel (Ed.), *Handbook of mental diseases*. Berlin: Springer.

Eysenck, H. J. (1952). The effects of psychotherapy: An evaluation. *J. Consult. Psychol., 16*, 319.

Eysenck, H. J. (1955). Psychiatric diagnosis as a physiological statistical problem. *Psychol. Rev., 1*, 3.

Eysenck, H. J. (1957). *The dynamics of anxiety and hysteria*. London: Routledge & Kegan Paul.

Eysenck, H. J. (1960). *Behavior therapy and the neuroses*. Oxford: Pergamon Press.

Eysenck, H. J. (1962). *Maudley personality inventory*. San Diego: Educational Individual Testing Service.

Eysenck, H. J. (1963). *Experiments with drugs*. Elmsford, NY: Pergamon Press.

Eysenck, H. J. (1964). *Experiments in behavior therapy*. Oxford: Pergamon Press.

Eysenck, H. J. (1965). The effects of psychotherapy. *Internatl. J. Psychiat., 1*, 97.

Eysenck, H. J. (1970). The classification of depressive illness. *Brit. J. Psychiat., 117*, 241.

Eysenck, H. J. (1976). The learning theory model of neurosis — A new approach. *Behav. Res. Ther., 14*, 251.

Eysenck, H. J. (1978). An exercise in mega-silliness. *Amer. Psychol., 33*, 517.

Eysenck, H. J. (1979). The conditioning model of neurosis. *The Behavioral and Brain Sciences, 2*, 155.

Eysenck, H. J., & Prell, D. (1951). The inheritance of neuroticism. *J. Ment. Sci., 97*, 441.

Fairbank, J. A., Gross, R. T., & Keane, (1983). Treatment of post-traumatic stress disorder. Evaluating outcome with a behavioral code. *Behav. Mod., 7*, 557.

Farmer, R. G., & Wright, J. M. C. (1971). Muscular reactivity and systematic desensitization. *Behav. Ther., 2*, 1.

Farrar, C. H., Powell, B. J., & Martin, L. K. (1968). Punishment of alcohol consumption by apneic paralysis. *Behav. Res. Ther., 6*, 13.

Feather, B., & Rhoads, J. (1972). Psychodynamic behavior therapy: Theory and rationale. *Arch. Gen. Psychiat., 26*, 496.

Feldman, M. P., & MacCulloch, M. J. (1965). The application of anticipatory avoidance learning to the treatment of homosexuality. I. Theory, technique and preliminary results. *Behav. Res. Ther., 2*, 165.

Feldman, M. P., & MacCulloch, M. J. (1967). Aversion therapy in the management of homosexuals. *Brit. Med. J., 1*, 594.

Feldman, M. P., & MacCulloch, M. J. (1970). *Homosexual behavior: Therapy and assessment*. Oxford: Pergamon Press.

Fenz, W. D., & Epstein, S. (1967). Gradients of physiological arousal in parachutists. *Psychosom. Med., 29*, 33.

Finlay-Jones, R., & Brown, G. W. (1981). Types of stressful life events and the onset of anxiety and depressive disorders. *Psychol. Med., 11*, 801.

Flanagan, B., Goldiamond, I., & Azrin, N. (1958). Operant stuttering: The control of stuttering behavior through response-contingent consequences. *J. Exp. Anal. Behav., 1*, 173.

Foa, E. B., & Kozak, M. J. (1986). Emotional processing of fear: Exposure to corrective information. *Psychol. Bull., 99*, 20.

Foa, E. B., Steketee, G., & Milby, J. B. (1980). Differential effects of exposure and response prevention in obsessive-compulsive washers. *J. Consult. Clin. Psychol., 48*, 71.

Foa, E. B., Steketee, G., & Ozarow, B. J. (1985). Behavior therapy with obsessive-compulsive. In M. Mavissakalian (Ed.), *Obsessive-compulsive disorders*. New York: Plenum Press.

Foa, E. B., & Tillmanns, A. (1980). The treatment of obsessive-compulsive neurosis. In A. Goldstein & E. B. Foa (Eds.), *Handbook of behavioral interventions*. New York: John Wiley & Sons.

Fonberg, E. (1956). On the manifestation of conditioned defensive reactions in stress. *Bull. Soc. Sci. Lettr. Lodz. Class III. Sci. Math. Natur., 7*, 1.

Ford, J. D. (1978). Therapeutic relationship in behavior analysis. *J. Consult. Clin. Psychol., 46*, 1302.

Forrest, A. D. (1964). Comparative trial of nortriptylene and amytriptylene. *Scot. Med. J., 9*, 34.

Foulds, G. A. (1975). The relationship between the depressive illnesses. *Br. J. Psychiatry, 123*, 531.

Frankl, V. E. (1960). Paradoxical intention: A logotherapeutic technique. *Amer. J. Psychother., 14*, 520.

Frankl, V. E. (1967a). *Paradoxical intention and existentialism*. New York: Washington Square Press.

Frankl, V. E. (1967b). *Psychotherapy and existentialism*. London: Souvenir Press.

Frankl, V. E. (1975). Paradoxical intention and dereflection. *Psychother.: Theory, Res. and Prac., 12*, 226.

Franks, C. M. (1965). *Conditioning techniques in clinical practice and research*. New York: Springer.

Franks, C. M. (1984). Behavior therapy: An overview. In C. M. Franks, G. T. Wilson, P. C. Kendall, & K. P. Brownell (Eds.), *Annual review of behavior therapy: Theory and practice* (Vol. 10). New York: Guilford Press.

Franks, C. M., & Wilson, G. T. (1979). *Annual review of behavior therapy: Theory and practice* (Vol. 7). New York: Brunner/Mazel.

Franks, C. M., Wilson, G. T., Kendall, P. C., & Brownell, K. P. (Eds.). (1984). *Annual review of behavior therapy: Theory and practice* (Vol. 10). New York: Guilford Press.

Freeman, G. L., & Pathman, J. H. (1942). The relation of overt muscular discharge to physiological recovery from experimentally induced displacement. *J. Exper. Psychol., 30*, 161.

Freeman, H. L., & Kendrick, D. C. (1960). A case of cat phobia: Treatment by a method derived from experimental psychology. *Brit. Med. J., 1*, 497.

Freund, K. (1960). Some problems in the treatment of homosexuality. In H. J. Eysenck (Ed.), *Behavior therapy and the neuroses*. Oxford: Pergamon Press.

Friedman, D. E. (1966). A new technique for the systematic desensitization of phobic symptoms. *Behav. Res. Ther., 4*, 139.

Friedman, D. E., & Silverstone, J. T. (1967). Treatment of phobic patients by systematic desensitization. *Lancet, 1*, 470.

Fry, W. H. (1962). The marital content of an anxiety syndrome. *Family Process, 1*, 245.

Furman, S. (1973). Intestinal biofeedback in functional diarrhea: A preliminary report. *J. Behav. Ther. Exp. Psychiat., 4*, 317.

Gale, D. S., Sturmfels, G., & Gale, E. N. (1966). A comparison of reciprocal inhibition and experimental extinction in the psychotherapeutic process. *Behav. Res. Ther., 4*, 139.

Gambrill, E. D., & Richey, C. A. (1975). An assertive inventory for use in assessment and research. *Behav. Ther., 6,* 550–661.

Gantt, W. H. (1944). Experimental basis for neurotic behavior. *Psychosom. Med. Monogr., 3*(3 & 4).

Garakani, G., Zitrin, C. M., & Klein, D. F. (1984). Treatment of panic disorder with imipramine alone. *American Journal of Psychiatry, 141,* 446.

Garfield, S. L. (1980). *Psychotherapy: An eclectic approach.* New York: John Wiley & Sons.

Garfield, S. L. (1981). Psychotherapy: A 40-year appraisal. *Amer. Psychologist, 36,* 174.

Garfield, S. L., & Bergin, A. (1978). *Handbook of psychotherapy and behavior change.* New York: John Wiley & Sons.

Garfield, Z. H., Darwin, P. L., Singer, B. A., & McBrearty, J. F. (1967). Effect of *in vivo* training on experimental desensitization of a phobia. *Psychol. Rep., 20,* 515.

Garssen, B., van Veenendaal, W., & Bloemink, R. (1983). Agoraphobia and the hyperventilation syndrome. *Behaviour Research & Therapy, 21,* 643.

Gath, D., & Gelder, M. G. A. (1971). *Treatment of phobias — Desensitization versus flooding.* Paper delivered to Dept. of Psychiatry, Temple University Medical School, November 8.

Gaupp, L. A., Stern, R. M., & Galbraith, G. G. (1972). False heart rate feedback and reciprocal inhibition by aversion relief in the treatment of snake avoidance behavior. *Behav. Ther., 3,* 7.

Geer, J. H. (1965). The development of a scale to measure fear. *Behav. Res. Ther., 3,* 45.

Gelder, M. G., Bancroft, J. H. J., Gath, D. H., Johnston, D. W., Mathews, A. M., & Shaw, P. M. (1973). Specific and non-specific factors in behavior therapy. *Brit. J. Psychiat., 123,* 445.

Gellhorn, E. (1953). *Physiological foundations of neurology and psychiatry.* Minneapolis: University of Minnesota Press.

Gellhorn, E. (1967). *Principles of autonomic-somatic integrations.* Minneapolis: University of Minnesota Press.

Gershman, L., & Stedman, J. (1971). Oriental defense exercises as reciprocal inhibitors of anxiety. *J. Behav. Ther. Exp. Psychiat., 2,* 117.

Gerz, H. O. (1966). Experience with the logotherapeutic technique of paradoxical intention in the treatment of phobic and obsessive-compulsive patients. *Amer. J. Psychiat., 123,* 548.

Gesell, A. (1946). The untold genesis of infant behavior. In L. Carmichael (Ed.), *Manual of child psychology.* New York: John Wiley & Sons.

Gilberti, R., & Rossi, R. (1962). Proposal of a psychopharmacological test ("stimulation threshold") for differentiation of neurotic from psychotic depression. *Psychopharmacologia, 3,* 128.

Giles, T. R. (1983a). Probable superiority of behavioral interventions. 1. Traditional comparative outcome. *J. Behav. Ther. Exper. Psychiat., 14,* 29.

Giles, T. R. (1983b). Probable superiority of behavioral interventions. 2. Empirical status of the equivalence of therapies hypothesis. *J. Behav. Ther. Exper. Psychiat., 14,* 189.

Giles, T. R. (1990). Bias against behavior therapy in outcome review: Who speaks for the patient? *Behav. Therapist, 13,* 86.

Gleitman, H., Nachmias, J., & Neisser, U. (1954). The S-R reinforcement theory of extinction. *Psychol. Rev., 61,* 23.

Glynn, J. D., & Harper, P. (1961). Behavior therapy in transvestism. *Lancet, 1*, 619.

Gold, S., & Neufeld, I. (1965). A learning theory approach to the treatment of homosexuality. *Behav. Res. Ther., 2*, 201.

Goldberg, J., & D'Zurilla, T. J. (1968). A demonstration of slide projection as an alternative to imaginal stimulus presentation in systematic desensitization therapy. *Psychol. Reps., 23*, 527.

Goldfried, M. R. (1980). Toward the delineation of therapeutic change principles. *Amer. Psychol., 35*, 991.

Goldfried, M. R., & Goldfried, A. P. (1975). Cognitive change methods. In F. H. Kanfer & A. P. Goldstein (Eds.), *Helping people change*. Elmsford, NY: Pergamon Press.

Goldiamond, I. (1965). Stuttering and fluency as manipulable operant response classes. In L. Krasner & L. P. Ullmann (Eds.), *Research in behavior modification*. New York: Holt, Rinehart, & Winston.

Goldstein, A. J. (1982). Agoraphobia: Treatment successes, treatment failures, and theoretical implications. In D. Chambless & A. Goldstein (Eds.), *Agoraphobia*. New York: John Wiley & Sons.

Goldstein, A. J., Serber, M., & Piaget, J. (1970). Induced anger as a reciprocal inhibitor of fear. *J. Behav. Ther. Exp. Psychiat., 1*, 67.

Goldstein, A. P., & Krasner, L. (1987). *Modern applied psychology*. Elmsford, NY: Pergamon Press.

Goodson, F. A., & Brownstein, A. (1965). Secondary reinforcing and motivating properties of stimuli contiguous with shock onset and termination. *J. Comp. Physiol. Psychol., 48*, 381.

Gorman, J. M., Fyer, A. F., Glicklich, J., King, D. L., & Klein, D. F. (1981). Mitral valve prolapse and panic disorders: Effect of Imipramine. In D. F. Klein & J. Rabkin (Eds.), *Anxiety: New research and changing concepts*. New York: Raven Press.

Gottlieb, J. S., & Frohman, C. E. (1972). *A probable biologic mechanism in schizophrenia*. Mimeographed.

Gourevitch, M. (1968). Eloge de Frangois Leuret. *Inform. Psychiat., 44*, 843.

Graham, L. E., Beiman, I., & Ciminero, A. R. (1977). The generality of the therapeutic effects of progressive relaxation training for essential hypertension. *J. Behav. Ther. Exp. Psychiat., 8*, 161.

Graham, L. E., Beiman, I., & Ciminero, A. R. (1978). Self-control progressive relaxation training as an alternative nonpharmacological treatment for essential hypertension: Therapeutic effects in the natural environment. *Behav. Res. Ther., 16*, 371.

Granville-Grossman, K. L., & Turner, P. (1966). The effect of propranolol on anxiety. *Lancet, 1*, 788.

Gray, J. A. (1964). *Pavlov's typology*. Oxford: Pergamon Press.

Gray, J. A. (1976). The behavioural inhibition system: A possible substrate for anxiety. In M. P. Feldman & A. Broadhurst (Eds.), *Theoretical and experimental bases of the behaviour therapies*. London: John Wiley & Sons.

Greenblatt, D. J., & Shader, R. I. (1972). Digitalis toxicity. In R. I. Shader (Ed.), *Psychiatric complications of medicinal drugs*. New York: Raven Press.

Grey, S., Sartory, G., & Rachman, S. (1979). Synchronous and desynchronous changes during fear reduction. *Behav. Res. Ther., 17*, 137.

Griez, E., & Hout, M. van den. (1983). Treatment of phobophobia by exposure to CO_2 induced anxiety symptoms. *Journal of Nervous and Mental Disease, 171*, 506.

Griez, E., & Hout, M. van den. (1986). CO_2 inhalation in the treatment of panic attacks. *Behaviour Research and Therapy, 24*, 143.

Grings, W. W., & Schandler, S. L. (1977). Interaction of learned relaxation and aversion. *Psychophysiol., 14*, 275.

Grings, W. W., & Uno, T. (1968). Counterconditioning: Fear and relaxation. *Psychophysiol., 4*, 479.

Grinker, R. R., & Spiegel, J. P. (1945a). *War neuroses*. Philadelphia: Blakiston.

Grinker, R. R., & Spiegel, J. P. (1945b). *Men under stress*. London: Churchill.

Grossman, P., & Wientjes, C. J. E. (1989). Respiratory disorders. In G. Turpin (Ed.), *Handbook of clinical physiology*. New York: John Wiley & Sons.

Grosz, H. J., & Farmer, B. B. (1972). Pitts' and McClure's lactate anxiety study revisited. *Brit. J. Psychiat., 120*, 415.

Groves, P. M., & Thompson, R. F. (1970). Habituation: A dual-process theory. *Psychol. Rev., 77*, 419.

Guensberger, E. (1981). Are experimental neuroses pathological states? *J. Behav. Ther. Exp. Psychiat., 12*, 115.

Gustafson, J. P. (1984). An integration of brief dynamic psychotherapy. *Amer. J. Psychiat., 141*, 935.

Guthrie, E. R. (1935). *The psychology of human learning*. New York: Harper.

Guttmacher, L. B., & Nelles, C. (1984). In vivo desensitization alteration of lactate-induced panic: A case study. *Behavior Therapy, 15*, 369.

Haggard, E. A., & Freeman, G. L. (1941). Reactions of children to experimentally induced frustration. *Psychol. Bull., 38*, 581.

Hahn, W. (1966). Autonomic responses of asthmatic children. *Psychosom. Med., 28*, 323.

Hall, S. B. (1927). The blood pressure in psychoneurosis: An investigation of 71 cases. *Lancet, 2*, 540.

Hallam, R. S., & Rachman, S. (1976). Current status of aversion therapy. In M. Hersen, R. Eisler, & P. Miller (Eds.), *Progress in behavior modification* (Vol. 2). New York: Academic Press.

Hallsten, E. A. (1965). Adolescent anorexia nervosa treated by desensitization. *Behav. Res. Ther., 3*, 87.

Hamilton, D. M., & Wall, J. H. (1941). Hospital treatment of patients with psychosomatic disorders. *Amer. J. Psychiat., 98*, 551.

Hamilton, M. (1959). The assessment of anxiety states by rating. *Brit. J. Med. Psychol., 32*, 50.

Hampe, E., Noble, F., Miller, L. C., & Barrett, C. I. (1973). Phobic children one and two years post treatment. *J. Abnorm. Psychol., 82*(3), 446–453.

Harris, B. (1979). Whatever happened to little Albert? *Am. Psychol., 34*(2), 151–160.

Harrison's principles of internal medicine (8th ed.). (1987). New York: McGraw-Hill.

Haslam, M. E. (1974). The relationship between the effect of lactate infusion on anxiety states and their amelioration by carbon dioxide inhalation. *Brit. J. Psychiat., 125*, 88.

Hedberg, A. G. (1973). The treatment of chronic diarrhea by systematic desensitization: A case report. *J. Behav. Ther. Exp. Psychiat., 4*, 67.

Heide, F. J., & Borkovec, T. D. (1983). Relaxation-induced anxiety: Paradoxical anxiety enhancement due to relaxation training. *J. Consult. Clin. Psychol., 51*, 171.

Heide, F. J., & Borkovec, T. D. (1984). Relaxation-induced anxiety: Mechanisms and theoretical implications. *Behav. Res. Ther., 22*, 1.

mination in panic disorder and agoraphobia with panic attacks. *American
rnal of Psychiatry, 142*, 715.

R. G., & Rapport, M. (1984). Panic disorder. In S. Turner (Ed.), *Behavioral
tment of anxiety disorders.* New York: Plenum Press.

on, E. (1938). Progressive relaxation. Chicago: University of Chicago Press.

on, E. (1939). Variation of blood pressure with skeletal muscle tension and
xation. *Ann. Intern. Med., 12,* 1194.

on, E. (1940). Variation of pulse rate with skeletal muscle tension and relaxa-
. *Ann. Int. Med., 13,* 1619.

on, E. (1964). *Anxiety and tension control.* Philadelphia: J B Lippincott.

on, E. (1978). Relaxation technology applied to hypertensives. *Archiv. Fur
heitherapie,* 2:152.

n, N. S., & Martin, B. (1976). Behavioral marriage therapy: Current status.
hol. Bull., 83,* 540.

n, N. S., & Weiss, R. L. (1978). Behavioral marriage therapy: 3. The con-
of Gurman et al. may be hazardous to our health. *Family Process, 17,* 149.

, N. S., Wilson, L., & Tupper, C. (1988). The clinical significance of treatment
from exposure-based intervention for agoraphobia. *Behav. Ther., 19,* 539.

itz, T. (1970). The treatment of impotence with methyl-testosterone thyroid.
ity and Sterility, 21, 32.

. (1962). Case of homosexuality treated by aversion therapy. *Brit. Med. J.,*

. (1925). *Psychological healing, historical and clinical study.* New York:
illan.

D. R., Martin, W. R., & Haertzen, C. A. (1967). The human pharmacol-
nd abuse potential of N-allyneroxymorphone (naloxone). *J. Pharm. Exp.
157,* 420.

. W., Wing, R. R., & Stunkard, A. J. (1978). Behavioral treatment of
: The state of the art 1976. *Behav. Ther., 9,* 189.

. T., & Holmes, F. B. (1935). Methods of overcoming children's fears. *J.
l., 1,* 35.

(1941). A study of the effects of evacuation and air raids on children of
ol age. *Brit. J. of Educational Psychol., 11,* 173.

L. M. (1933). Similarity of meaning as a factor in retroactive inhibition. *J.
sychol., 9,* 377.

G. (1960). Continuation of Yates' treatment of a tiquer. In H. J. Eysenck
ehavior therapy and the neuroses.* Oxford: Pergamon Press.

C. (1924a). Elimination of children's fears. *J. Exp. Psychol., 7,* 382.

C. (1924b). A laboratory study of fear. The case of Peter. *J. Genet.
, 31,* 308.

R. S., Houston, B. K., & Zurawski, R. M. (1981). Anxiety management
in the treatment of essential hypertension. *Behav. Res. Ther., 19,* 467.

& Baker, B. L. (1968). Desensitization with minimal therapist contact. *J.
ychol., 73,* 198.

. (1981). *From behavioral science to behavior modification.* New York:
-Hill.

(1952). Comparative twin studies on the genetic aspects of male homo-
J. Nerv. Ment. Dis., 115, 283.

(1953). *Heredity in health and mental disorder.* New York: W W Norton.

. (1979). Psychotherapy and the single synapse: The impact of psychiat-
ht on neurobiological research. *N. Engl. J. Med., 19,* 1028.

Herrnstein, R. J. (1970). On the law of effect. *J. Exp. Anal*

Hersen, M. (1973). Self-assessment of fear. *Behav. Ther., 4*

Hersen, M. (1981). Complex problems require complex so
15–29.

Hersen, M., Bellack, A. S., & Himmelhoch, J. M. (198
depression with social skills training. *Behav. Modifica*

Hersen, M., Bellack, A. S., Himmelhoch, J. M. et al. (19
training, amitriptyline, and psychotherapy in unipola
Ther., 15, 21.

Herzberg, A. (1941). *Active psychotherapy.* London: Re

Himmelsbach, C. K. (1941). The morphine abstinence
treatment. *Ann. Intern. Med., 15,* 829.

Hinde, R. A. (1966). *Animal behaviour.* New York: Mc

Hirschfeld, R. M. A., Klerman, G. L., Andreasen, N.
major depressive disorder. *Arch. Gen. Psychiatry, 4*

Hoch, P. H. (1959). Drug therapy. In S. Arieti (Ed.), *A
atry.* New York: Basic Books.

Hodgson, R., Rachman, S., & Marks, I. M. (1972
obsessive-compulsive neuroses: Follow-up and f
Ther., 10, 181.

Hoehn-Saric, R., McLeod, D. R., & Zimmerli, W. D
alprazolam and imipramine in generalized anxie
World Congress of Biological Psychiatry, Philadel

Hofmann, A. (1963). Psychotomimetic substances. *I*

Hollister, L. E. (1969). *Chemical psychoses: LDS and*
C C Thomas.

Hölzl, R. (1989). Gastrointestinal disorders. In G. T
cal physiology. New York: John Wiley & Sons.

Homme, L. E. (1965). Perspectives in psychology —
operants of the mind. *Psychol. Rec., 15,* 501.

Homme, L. E., Csanyi, A. P., Gonzales, M. A., &
contingency contracting in the classroom. Chan

Horowitz, N. (1989). Posttraumatic stress disord
disorders, American Psychiatric Task Force (Vo

Horsley, J. S. (1936). Narco-analysis: A new tech
Lancet, 1, 55.

Horsley, J. S. (1946). *Narcoanalysis.* London: Ox

Hull, C. L. (1943). *Principles of behavior.* New Y

Hurwitz, H. B. M. (1956). Conditioned response
Animal Behav., 4, 31.

Huttunen, M. O. (1973). General model for the
learning. *Perspectives in Biology and Medicir*

Ihli, K. L., & Garlington, W. K. (1969). A con
desensitization of test anxiety. *Behav. Res. T*

Izard, C. E., & Blumberg, M. A. (1985). Emotic
anxiety in children and adults. In A. H. Tum
the anxiety disorders. Hillsdale, NJ: Lawren

Jacob, R. G., Kraemer, H. C., & Agras, W.
treatment of hypertension. *Arch. Gen. Psy*

Jacob, R. G., Moller, M. B., Turner, S. M., &

Kantorovich, N. V. (1929). An attempt at associative reflex therapy in alcoholism. *Psychol. Abst.*, No. 4282, 1930.

Kay, D. W. K., Garside, R. D., Roy, J. R. et al. (1969). "Endogenous" and "neurotic" symptoms of depression: A 5- to 7-year follow-up of 104 cases. *Br. J. Psychiatry, 115,* 389.

Kazdin, A. E. (1977). Artifact, bias, and complexity of assessment: The ABC's of reliability. *J. Appl. Behav. Anal., 10,* 141.

Kazdin, A. E. (1979). Fictions, factions, and functions of behavior therapy. *Behav. Ther., 10,* 629.

Kazdin, A. E., & Wilcoxon, L. A. (1976). Systematic desensitization and nonspecific treatment effects: A methodological evaluation. *Psychol. Bull., 23,* 729.

Kazdin, A. E., & Wilson, G. T. (1978). Criteria for evaluating psychotherapy. *Arch. Gen. Psychiat., 35,* 407.

Keane, T. M., & Kaloupek, D. G. (1982). Imaginal flooding in the treatment of post-traumatic stress disorder. *J. Consult. Clin. Psychol., 50,* 138.

Kellner, R., Sheffield, B. F. (1971). The relief of distress following attendance at a clinic. *Br. J. Psychiatry, 118,* 195.

Keltner, A., & Marshall, W. L. (1975). Single trial exacerbation of an anxiety habit with 2nd order conditioning and subsequent desensitization. *J. Behav. Ther. & Exp. Psychiat., 6,* 323.

Kendell, R. E., & Gourlay, J. (1970). The clinical distinction between psychotic and neurotic depressions. *Br. J. Psychiatry, 117,* 257.

Kennedy, W. A. (1971). *Child psychology.* Englewood Cliffs, NJ: Prentice-Hall.

Kennedy, W. A., & Foreyt, J. (1968). Control of eating behavior in an obese patient by avoidance conditioning. *Psychol. Rep., 22,* 571.

Kent, R. N., Wilson, G. T., & Nelson, R. (1972). Effects of false heart-rate feedback on avoidance behavior: An investigation of "cognitive desensitization." *Behav. Ther., 3,* 1.

Kernberg, O., Burnstein, E., Coyle, L. et al. (1972). Psychotherapy and psychoanalysis. Final report of the Menninger Foundation Psychotherapy Research Project. *Bull. Menninger Clinic, 36,* 89.

Khan, A. U., Staerk, M., & Bonk, C. (1973). Role of counterconditioning in the treatment of asthma. *J. Psychosom. Res., 17,* 389.

Kiloh, L. G., Andrews, G., Neilson, M., & Bianchi, G. N. (1972). The relationships of the syndromes called endogenous and neurotic depression. *Br. J. Psychiatry, 121,* 183.

Kiloh, L. G., & Garside, R. F. (1963). The independence of neurotic depression and endogenous depression. *Br. J. Psychiatry, 109,* 451.

Kimmel, H. D. (1967). Instrumental conditioning of autonomically mediated behavior. *Psychol. Bull., 67,* 337.

Kimmel, K. D., & Kimmel, E. (1970). An instrumental conditioning method for the treatment of enuresis. *J. Behav. Ther. Exp. Psychiat., 1,* 21.

Kirsch, I. (1978). The placebo effect and the cognitive behavioral revolution. *Cogn. Ther. Res., 2,* 255.

Kirsch, I., Tennen, H., Wickless, C., Saccone, A. J., & Cody, S. (1983). The role of expectancy in fear reduction. *Behav. Ther., 14,* 520.

Klein, D. F. (1964). Delineation of two drug-responsive anxiety syndromes. *Psychopharmacologia, 5,* 397.

Klein, D. F., & Rabkin, J. E. (Eds.). (1981). *Anxiety: New research and changing concepts.* New York: Raven Press.

Kleiner, L., & Marshall, W. L. (1987). The role of interpersonal problems in the development of agoraphobia with panic attacks. *Journal of Anxiety Disorders, 1*, 313.

Klerman, G. L. (1989). Mood disorders: Introduction. In *Treatments of Psychiatric disorders*. Washington, DC: American Psychiatric Association.

Klerman, G. L., & Cole, J. O. (1965). Clinical pharmacology of imipramine and related antidepressant compounds. *Pharmacol. Rev., 17*, 101.

Klerman, G. L., DeMascio, A., Weissman, M. M., Prusoff, B. A., & Paykel, E. S. (1974). Treatment of depression by drugs and psychotherapy. *Am. J. Psychiatry, 131*, 186.

Knight, R. P. (1941). Evaluation of the results of psychoanalytic therapy. *Amer. J. Psychiat., 98*, 434.

Knudson, R. M., Gurman, A. S., & Kniskern, D. P. (1980). Behavioral marriage therapy: A treatment in transition. In C. M. Franks & G. T. Wilson (Eds.), *Annual review of behavior therapy—Theory and practice* (Vol. 7). New York: Brunner/Mazel.

Kolvin, I. (1967). Aversive imagery treatment in adolescents. *Behav. Res. Ther., 5*, 245.

Kondas, O. (1965). The possibilities of applying experimentally created procedures when eliminating tics. *Studia Psychol., 7*, 221.

Kraepelin, D. (1913). *Lehrbuch der Psychiatrie* (8th ed.). Leipzig: Barth.

Krasner, L. (1988). Paradigms lost: On a historical/sociological/economic perspective. In D. B. Fishman, F. Rotgers, & C. M. Franks (Eds.), *Paradigms in behavior therapy: Present and promise*. New York: Springer.

Krasnogorski, N. I. (1925). The conditioned reflexes and children's neuroses. *Amer. J. Dis. Child., 30*, 754.

Kuhn, T. S. (1970). *The structure of scientific revolutions* (2nd ed.). Chicago: University of Chicago Press.

Lacey, J. I., Bateman, D. E., & Van Lehn, R. (1953). Autonomic response specificity: An experimental study. *Psychosom. Med., 15*, 8.

Lacey, J. I., & Lacey, B. C. (1958). Verification and extension of the principles of autonomic response specificity. *Amer. J. Psychol., 71*, 50.

Lader, M. (1975). *The psychophysiology of mental illness*. London: Routledge & Kegan Paul.

Lader, M. (1976). Physiological research in anxiety. In H. M. van Praag (Ed.), *Research in neurosis*. Utrecht: Bohn, Scheltema, & Holkema.

Lader, M. H., & Mathews, A. M. (1968). A physiological model of phobic anxiety and desensitization. *Behav. Res. Ther., 6*, 411.

Lader, M. H., & Wing, L. (1966). *Physiological measures, sedative drugs and morbid anxiety*. Maudsley Monograph No. 14. London: Oxford University Press.

Ladouceur, R. (1974). An experimental test of the learning paradigm of covert positive reinforcement in deconditioning anxiety. *J. Behav. Ther. Exp. Psychiat., 5*, 30.

Ladouceur, R., Caron, C., & Caron, G. (1989). Stuttering severity and treatment outcome. *J. Behav. Ther. Exp. Psychiat., 20*, 49.

Lande, S. (1982). Physiological and subjective measures of anxiety during flooding. *Beh. Res. Ther., 20*, 81.

Landis, C. (1937). A statistical evaluation of psychotherapeutic methods. In L. Hinsie (Ed.), *Concepts and problems of psychotherapy*. New York: Columbia University Press.

Lang, P. J. (1968). Appraisal of systematic desensitization techniques with children and adults. 2. Process and mechanisms of change, theoretical analysis and implications for treatment and clinical research. In C. M. Franks (Ed.), *Assessment and status of the behavior therapies and associated developments*. New York: McGraw-Hill.

Lang, P. J. (1970). Stimulus control, response control and the desensitization of fear. In D. J. Levis (Ed.), *Learning approach to therapeutic behavior change*. Chicago: Aldine Atherton.

Lang, P. J., & Lazovik, A. D. (1963). The experimental desensitization of a phobia. *J. Abn. Soc. Psychol., 66*, 519.

Lang, P. J., Lazovik, A. D., & Reynolds, D. (1965). Desensitization, suggestibility and pseudo therapy. *J. Abn. Psychol., 70*, 395.

Lang, P. J., Melamed, B. G., & Hart, J. (1970). A psychophysiological analysis of fear modification using an automated desensitization procedure. *J. Abn. Psychol., 76*, 221.

Langley, J. N., & Anderson, H. K. (1895). The innervation of the pelvis and adjoining viscera. *J. Physiol., 19*, 71.

Last, C. G. (1987). Simple phobias. In L. Michelson & M. Ascher (Eds.), *Anxiety and stress disorders*. New York: Guilford Press.

Last, C. G., Barlow, D. H., & O'Brien, G. T. (1984). Precipitants of agoraphobia: Role of stressful life events. *Psychological Reports, 54*, 567.

Lathrop, R. G. (1964). Measurement of analog sequential dependency. *Human Factors, 6*, 233.

Latimer, P. (1977). Carbon dioxide as a reciprocal inhibitor in the treatment of neurosis. *J. Behav. Ther. Exp. Psychiat., 8*, 83.

Latimer, P. R. (1981). Irritable bowel syndrome: A behavioral model. *Behav. Res. Ther., 19*, 475.

Latimer, P. R. (1983). *Functional gastrointestinal disorders*. New York: Springer.

Latimer, P. R., Campbell, D., & Latimer, M. (1979). Irritable bowel syndrome: A test of the colonic hyperalgesia hypothesis. *J. Behav. Med., 2*, 285.

Latimer, P. R., Sarna, S. K., Campbell, D., Latimer, M. R., Waterfall, W. E., & Daniel, E. E. (1981). Colonic motor and myoelectrical activity: A comparative study. *Gastroenterology, 80*, 893.

Latimer, P. R., & Swee, A. A. (1984). Cognitive versus behavioral procedures in cognitive behavior therapy: A critical review of the evidence. *J. Behav. Ther. Exp. Psychiat., 15*, 9.

Lautch, H. (1971). Dental phobia. *Brit. J. Psychiat., 119*, 151–8.

LaVerne, A. A. (1953). Rapid coma technique of carbon dioxide inhalation therapy. *Dis. Nerv. Syst., 14*, 141.

Laverty, S. G. (1966). Aversion therapies in the treatment of alcoholism. *Psychosom. Med., 28*, 651.

Lavin, H. I., Thorpe, J. G., Baker, J. C., Blakemore, C. B., & Conway, D. G. (1961). Behavior therapy in a case of transvestism. *J. Nerv. Ment. Dis., 133*, 346.

Lawson, R., & Brownstein, A. (1959). The effect of effort and training-test similarity on resistance to extinction. *Amer. J. Psychol., 70*, 123.

Lazarus, A. A. (1971). *Behavior therapy and beyond*. New York: McGraw-Hill.

Lazarus, A. A., & Abramovitz, A. (1962). The use of "emotive imagery" in the treatment of children's phobias. *J. Ment. Sci., 108*, 191.

Leach, E. (1969). Stuttering: Clinical application of response-contingent procedures. In B. B. Gray & G. England (Eds.), *Stuttering and the conditioning therapies*. Monterey, CA: Monterey Institute for Speech & Hearing.

Leaf, W. B., & Gaarder, K. R. (1971). A simplified electromyograph feedback apparatus for relaxation training. *J. Behav. Ther. Exp. Psychiat., 2*, 39.

Leahy, M. R., & Martin, I. C. A. (1967). Successful hypnotic abreaction after twenty years. *Brit. J. Psychiat., 113*, 383.

Lee, C. (1989). Theoretical weakness leads to practical problems: The example of self-efficacy theory. *J. Behav. Ther. Exp. Psychiat., 20*, 115.

Leff, M. J., Roatch, J. F., & Bunney, W. E. (1970). Environmental factors preceding the onset of severe depressions. *Psychiatry, 33*, 293.

Leitenberg, H., Agras, W. S., Barlow, D. H., & Oliveau, D. C. (1969). Contribution of selective positive reinforcement and therapeutic instructions to systematic desensitization therapy. *J. Abn. Psychol., 74*, 113.

Lemere, F., & Voegtlin, W. L. (1950). An evaluation of the aversion treatment of alcoholism. *Qtr. J. Stud. Alcoh., 11*, 199.

Leonhard, K. (1959). *Aufteilung der Endogenen Psychosen* (2nd ed.). Berlin: Haug.

Leschke, E. (1914). Quoted by J. G. Beebe-Center (1932) in *The psychology of pleasantness and unpleasantness*. New York: Van Nostrand Reinhold.

Lesser, E. (1967). Behavior therapy with a narcotics user: A case report. *Behav. Res. Ther., 5*, 251.

Leukel, F., & Quinton, E. (1964). Carbon dioxide effects on acquisition and extinction of avoidance behavior. *J. Comp. Physiol. Psychol., 57*, 267.

Leuret, F. (1846). De traitement moral de la folie [The mental treatment of insanity]. Quoted in M. A. Stewart (1961). Psychotherapy by reciprocal inhibition. *Amer. J. Psychiat., 188*, 175.

Levey, A. B., & Martin, I. (1987). Evaluative conditioning: A case for hedonia transfer. In H. J. Eysenck & I. Martin (Eds.), *Theoretical foundations of behavior therapy*. New York: Plenum Press.

Levis, D. J. (1980). Implementing the technique of implosive therapy. In A. Goldstein & E. B. Foa (Eds.), *Handbook of behavioral interventions*. New York: John Wiley & Sons.

Levis, D. G., & Boyd, T. L. (1979). Symptom maintenance: An infrahuman analysis and extension of the conservation of anxiety principle. *J. Abn. Psychol., 88*, 107.

Levis, D. J., & Carrera, R. N. (1967). Effects of ten hours of implosive therapy in the treatment of outpatients: A preliminary report. *J. Abn. Psychol., 72*, 504.

Levis, D. J., & Hare, N. (1977). A review of the theoretical and rational and empirical support for the extinction approach of implosive (flooding) therapy. In M. Hersen, R. M. Eisler, & P. M. Miller (Eds.), *Progress in behavior modification*. New York: Academic Press.

Levitz, L. S., & Stunkard, A. J. (1974). A therapeutic coalition for obesity: Behavior modification and patient self-help. *Amer. J. Psychiat., 131*, 423.

Lewinsohn, P. M. (1974). Clinical and theoretical aspects of depression. In K. S. Calhoun, H. E. Adams, & K. M. Mitchell (Eds.), *Innovative treatment methods in psychopathology*. New York: John Wiley & Sons.

Lewinsohn, P. M., Steinmetz, J. C., Larson, D. W., & Franklin, J. (1981). Depression-related cognitions: Antecedent or consequence? *J. Abn. Psychol., 90*, 213.

Lewis, A. J. (1938). States of depression: Their clinical and aetiological differentiation. *Br. Med. J., 2*, 875.

Lewis, B. I. (1954). Chronic hyperventilation syndrome. *J. Amer. Med. Assoc., 155*, 1204.

Lewis, B. I. (1959). Hyperventilation syndrome. A clinical and physiological evaluation. *California Medicine, 91*, 121.

Lewis, D. (1875). *Chastity: Or our secret sins*. Philadelphia: Maclean.

Ley, R. (1985a). Agoraphobia, the panic attack, and the hyperventilation syndrome. *Behaviour Research and Therapy, 23*, 79.

Ley, R. (1985b). Blood, breath, and fears: A hyperventilation theory of panic attacks and agoraphobia. *Clinical Psychology Review, 5*, 271.

Ley, R. (1987). Panic disorder and agoraphobia: Fear of fear or fear of the symptoms produced by hyperventilation? *Journal of Behavior Therapy and Experimental Psychiatry, 18*, 305.

Ley, R., & Walker, H. (1973). Effects of carbon dioxide-oxygen inhalation on heart rate, blood pressure and subjective anxiety. *J. Behav. Ther. Exp. Psychiat., 4*, 223.

Liberman, R. (1968). Aversive conditioning of a drug addict: A pilot study. *Behav. Res. Ther., 6*, 229.

Liddell, H. S. (1944). Conditioned reflex method and experimental neurosis. In J. McV. Hunt (Ed.), *Personality and disorders*. New York: Ronald Press.

Lieberman, S. (1978). Nineteen cases of morbid grief. *Brit. J. Psychiat., 132*, 159.

Lief, H. I., & Kaplan, H. S. (1986). Ego-dystonic homosexuality. *J. Sex Marital Ther., 12*, 259.

Likierman, H., & Rachman, S. (1982). Thought-stopping and habituation training for obsessions. *Behavioral Psychotherapy, 10*, 324.

Linden, W. (1984). *Psychological perspectives of essential hypertension*. New York: Karger.

Lindsley, O. R. (1956). Operant conditioning methods applied to research in chronic schizophrenia. *Psychiat. Res. Rep., 5*, 118.

Little, J. C., & James, B. (1964). Abreaction of conditioned fear after eighteen years. *Behav. Res. Ther., 2*, 59.

Lloyd, D. P. C. (1946). Facilitation and inhibition of spinal motor neurons. *J. Neurophysiol., 9*, 421.

Lobitz, W. C., & LoPiccolo, J. (1972). New methods in the behavioral treatment of sexual dysfunction. *J. Behav. Ther. Exp. Psychiat., 2*, 265.

Locke, E. A. (1971). Is "behavior therapy" behavioristic? An analysis of Wolpe's psychotherapeutic methods. *Psychol. Bull., 76*, 318.

London, P. (1964). *The modes and morals of psychotherapy*. New York: Holt, Rinehart, & Winston.

LoPiccolo, J., Stewart, R., & Watkins, B. (1972). Treatment of erectile failure and ejaculatory incompetence of homosexual etiology. *J. Behav. Ther. Exp. Psychiat., 3*, 233.

Lovaas, O. I., & Smith, T. (1989). A comprehensive behavior theory of autistic children: Paradigm for research and treatment. *J. Behav. Ther. Exp. Psychiat., 20*, 17.

Lubeskind, J. C., & Paul, L. A. (1977). Psychological and physiological mechanisms of pain. In M. R. Rosengweiz & L. W. Porter (Eds.), *Ann. Rev. Psychol., 28*.

Lublin, I. (1968). *Aversive conditioning of cigarette addiction*. Paper read at 76th Meeting of the American Psychology Association, San Francisco.

Luboni, R. E. (1973). Latent inhibition. *Psychol. Bull., 79*, 398.

Luborsky, L., Singer, B., & Luborsky, L. (1975). Comparative studies of psychotherapy: Is it true that "Everyone has won and all must have prizes?" *Arch. Gen. Psychiat., 32*, 995.

Lum, L. (1981). Hyperventilation and anxiety state. *Journal of the Royal Society of Medicine, 74*, 1.

Lynch, J. J., Tomal, S. A., Paskewitz, D. A., Malenow, D. L., & Long, J. M. (1982). Interpersonal aspects of blood pressure control. *J. Nerv. Dis., 170*, 143.

Macfarland, J. M., Allan, L., & Honz к, M. (1954). *A developmental study of the behavior problems of normal children*. Berkeley: University of California Press.

Mack, K. (1970). Unpublished data. Temple Medical School Summer Externship Program.

Mackintosh, N. J. (1974). *Psychology of animal learning*. New York: Academic Press.

MacVaugh, G. (1972). *Frigidity: Successful treatment of one hypnotic imprint session with the Oriental relaxation technique*. New York: Medcon.

MacVaugh, G. S. (1974). *Frigidity: What you should know about its cure with hypnosis*. Elmsford, NY: Pergamon Press.

Madsen, C. H. (1965). Positive reinforcement in the toilet training of a normal child: A case report. In L. P. Ullmann & L. Krasner (Eds.), *Case studies in behavior modification*. New York: Holt, Rinehart, & Winston.

Mahesh Yogi, M. (1969). *Maharishi Mahesh Yogi on the Bhagavad-Gita: A new translation and commentary*. Baltimore, MD: Penguin Books.

Mahoney, M. J. (1977). Reflections on the cognitive-learning trend in psychotherapy. *Amer. Psychol., 32*, 5.

Malleson, N. (1959). Panic and phobia. *Lancet, 1*, 225.

Malmo, R. B., & Shagass, C. (1952). Studies of blood pressure in psychiatric patients under stress. *Psychosom. Med., 14*, 82.

Mansueto, C. S. (1988). Cognitive behavioral analysis and treatment of an adolescent with severe multiform obsessive-compulsive disorder. In J. Rapoport (Ed.), *Obsessive-compulsive disorder in children and adolescents*. Washington, DC: American Psychiatric Association.

Marks, I. M. (1969). *Fears and phobias*. London: Heinemann.

Marks, I. M. (1972). Flooding (implosion) and allied treatments. In W. S. Agras (Ed.), *Learning theory application of principles and procedures to psychiatry*. New York: Little, Brown.

Marks, I. M. (1975). Behavioral treatments of phobic and obsessive-compulsive disorders: A critical appraisal. In M. Hersen, R. M. Eisler, & P. M. Miller (Eds.), *Progress in behavior modification*. New York: Academic Press.

Marks, I. M. (1976). Current status of behavioral psychotherapy: Theory and practice. *Amer. J. Psychiat., 133*, 253.

Marks, I. M. (1981). *Cure and care of the neuroses*. New York: John Wiley & Sons.

Marks, I. M., Boulougouris, J., & Marset, P. (1971). Flooding versus desensitization in the treatment of phobic patients: A crossover study. *Brit. J. Psychiat., 119*, 353.

Marks, I. M., Hodgson, R., & Rachman, S. (1975). Treatment of chronic obsessive-compulsive neurosis by in vivo exposure. *Brit. J. Psychiat., 127*, 349.

Marmor, J. (1980). Recent trends in psychotherapy. *Amer. J. Psychiat., 137*, 409.

Marquis, J. N. (1970). Orgasmic reconditioning: Changing sexual object choice through controlling masturbation fantasies. *J. Behav. Ther. Exp. Psychiat., 1*, 263.

Marshall, W. L. (1974). The classical conditioning of sexual attractiveness. *Behav. Ther., 5*, 298.

Marshall, W. L. (1988). An appraisal of expectancies, safety signals and the treatment of panic disorder patients. In S. Rachman & J. D. Maser (Eds.), *Panic: Psychological perspectives*. Hillsdale, NJ: Lawrence Erlbaum Associates.

Martin, I. (1961). Somatic reactivity. In H. J. Eysenck (Ed.), *Handbook of abnormal psychology*. New York: Basic Books.

Marzillier, I. S. (1980). Cognitive therapy and behavioural practice. *Behav. Res. Ther., 18*, 249.

Mash, E. J., & Terdal, L. G. (1976). *Behavior therapy assessment*. New York: Springer.

Masserman, J. H. (1943). *Behavior and neurosis*. Chicago: University of Chicago Press.

Masserman, J. H. (1946). *Principles of dynamic psychiatry*. Philadelphia: Saunders.

Masserman, J. H. (1963). Ethology, comparative biodynamics, and psychoanalytic research. In J. Scher (Ed.), *Theories of the mind*. New York: Free Press.

Masserman, J. H., & Yum, K. S. (1946). An analysis of the influence of alcohol on the experimental neuroses in cats. *Psychosom. Med., 3*, 36.

Masters, W. H., & Johnson, V. E. (1966). *Human sexual responses*. Boston: Little, Brown.

Masters, W. H., & Johnson, V. E. (1970). *Human sexual inadequacy*. Boston: Little, Brown.

Mathe, A. A., & Knapp, P. H. (1971). Emotional and adrenal reactions to stress in bronchial asthma. *Psychosom. Med., 33*, 323.

Mathews, A. M., Gelder, M. G., & Johnson, D. W. (1981). *Agoraphobia: Nature and environment*. New York: Guilford Press.

Mathews, A. M., Johnson, D. W., Shaw, P. M., & Gelder, M. G. (1974). Process variables and the prediction of outcome in behavior therapy. *Brit. J. Psychiat., 123*, 445.

Matuzas, W., Al-Sadir, J., Uhlenhuth, E. H., & Glass, R. M. (1987). Mitral valve prolapse and thyroid abnormalities in patients with panic attacks. *Amer. J. Psychiat., 144*, 493.

Mavissakalian, M., & Michelson, L. (1983). Self-directed *in vivo* exposure in behavioral and pharmacological treatment of agoraphobia. *Behav. Ther., 14*, 506.

Mavissakalian, M., Michelson, L., & Dealy, R. S. (1983). Pharmacological treatment of agoraphobia: Imipramine versus imipramine with programmed practice. *Brit. J. Psychiat., 143*, 348.

Mavissakalian, M., Michelson, L., Greenwald, D., Kornberts, S., & Greenwald, M. (1983). Cognitive behavior treatment of agoraphobia: Paradoxical intention vs. self-statement training. *Behav. Res. Ther., 21*, 75.

Mawson, A. B. (1970). Methohexitone-assisted desensitization in the treatment of phobias. *Lancet, 1*, 1084.

Max, L. W. (1935). Breaking up a homosexual fixation by the conditioned reaction technique: A case study. *Psychol. Bull., 32*, 734.

Maxwell, R. D. H., & Paterson, J. W. (1958). Meprobamate in the treatment of stuttering. *Brit. Med. J., 1*, 873.

McCarron, L. T. (1973). Psychophysiological discriminants of reactive depression. *Psychophysiol., 10*, 223.

McGeogh, J. A. (1932). Forgetting and the law of disuse. *Psychol. Rev., 39*, 352.

McGeogh, J. A., & McDonald, E. T. (1931). Meaningful relation and retroactive inhibition. *Amer. J. Psychol., 43*, 579.

McGeogh, J. A., McKinney, F., & Peters, H. (1937). Studies in retroactive inhibition. IX. Retroactive inhibition, reproductive inhibition and reminiscence. *J. Exp. Psychol., 20*, 131.

McGlynn, F. D., Reynolds, E. J., & Linder, L. H. (1971). Systematic desensitization with pre-treatment and intratreatment therapeutic instructions. *Behav. Res. Ther., 9*, 57.

McGlynn, F. D., & Williams, C. W. (1970). Systematic desensitization of snake-avoidance under three conditions of suggestion. *J. Behav. Ther. Exp. Psychiat., 1*, 97.

McGuire, R. J., & Vallance, M. (1964). Aversion therapy by electric shock: A simple technique. *Brit. Med. J., 1*, 151.

Mealia, W. L., & Nawas, M. M. (1971). The comparative effectiveness of systematic desensitization and implosive therapy in the treatment of snake phobia. *J. Behav. Ther. Exp. Psychiat., 2*, 85.

Meduna, L. J. (1947). *Carbon dioxide therapy*. Springfield, IL: C C Thomas.

Meichenbaum, D. H. (1975). Self-instructional methods. In F. H. Kanfer & A. P. Goldstein (Eds.), *Helping people change*. New York: Pergamon Press.

Meichenbaum, D. H. (1977). *Cognitive behavior modification*. New York: Plenum Press.

Meichenbaum, D. H., & Cameron, R. (1974). The clinical potential of modifying what clients say to themselves. *Psychotherapy: Theory, Research, and Practice, 11*, 103.

Mendel, J., & Klein, D. F. (1969). Anxiety attacks and subsequent agoraphobia. *Comprehensive Psychiatry, 10*, 190.

Mendels, J., & Cochrane, C. (1968). The nosology of depression: The endogenous-reactive concept. *Am. J. Psychiatry, 124*(Suppl), 1.

Mesmer, A. (1779). Quoted by C. L. Hull. (1933). *Hypnosis and suggestibility*. New York: Appleton-Century-Crofts.

Meyer, V. (1957). The treatment of two phobic patients on the basis of learning principles. *J. Abn. Soc. Psychol., 58*, 259.

Meyer, V. (1966). Modifications of expectations in cases with obsessional rituals. *Behav. Res. Ther., 4*, 273.

Meyer, V., Levy, R., & Schnurer, A. (1974). The behavioral treatment of obsessive-compulsive disorders. In H. R. Beech (Ed.), *Obsessional states*. London: Methuen.

Meyer, V., & Mair, J. M. (1963). A new technique to control stammering: A preliminary report. *Behav. Res. Ther., 1*, 251.

Michelson, L. (1987). Cognitive behavioral assessment and treatment of agoraphobia. In L. Michelson & L. M. Ascher (Eds.), *Anxiety and stress disorders*. New York: Guilford Press.

Michelson, L., & Ascher, L. M. (1984). Paradoxical intention in the treatment of agoraphobia. *J. Behav. Ther. Exp. Psychiat., 15*, 215.

Migler, B., & Wolpe, J. (1967). Automated desensitization: A case report. *Behav. Res. Ther., 5*, 133.

Miller, N. E., & DiCara, L. V. (1968). Instrumental learning of vasomotor responses by rats: Learning to respond differentially in the two ears. *Science, 159*, 1485.

Miller, N. E., & Dollard, J. (1941). *Social learning and imitation*. New Haven: Yale University Press.

Miller, N. E., Hubert, E., & Hamilton, J. (1938). Mental and behavioral changes following male hormone treatment of adult castration hypogonadism and psychic impotence. *Proc. Soc. Exp. Biol. Med., 38*, 538.

Miller, N., & Weiss, J. M. (1969). Effects of somatic or visceral responses to punishment. In B. A. Campbell & R. M. Church (Eds.), *Punishment and aversive behavior*. New York: Appleton-Century-Crofts.

Miller, R. E., Murphy, J. V., & Mirsky, I. A. (1957). Persistent effects of chlorpromazine on extinction of an avoidance response. *Arch. Neurol. Psychiat., 78*, 526.

Miller, W. W. (1968). Afrodex in the treatment of male impotence: A double blind crossover study. *Cur. Ther. Res., 10*, 354.

Milnor, W. R. (1968). Cardiovascular system. In V. B. Mountcastle (Ed.), *Medical Physiology* (12th ed.). St. Louis: C V Mosby.

Mineka, S. (1985). Animal models of anxiety disorders. In A. H. Tuma & J. D. Maser (Eds.), *Anxiety and the anxiety disorders*. Hillsdale, NJ: Lawrence Erlbaum Associates.

Mineka, S., Davidson, M., Cook, M., & Keir, R. (1984). Observational conditioning of snake fear in rhesus monkeys. *J. Abnorm. Psychol., 93*, 355.

Mineka, S., & Kihlstrom, J. F. (1978). Unpredictable and uncontrollable events: A new perspective on experimental neurosis. *J. Abnorm. Psychol., 87*, 256.

Mitchell, K. R. (1969). The treatment of migraine: An exploratory application of time limited behavior therapy. *Technology, 14*, 50.

Mitchell, K. R., & Mitchell, D. M. (1971). Migraine: An exploratory treatment application of programmed behavior therapy techniques. *J. Psychosom. Res., 15*, 137.

Moore, N. (1965). Behavior therapy in bronchial asthma: A controlled study. *J. Psychosom. Res., 9*, 257.

Morganstern, F. S., Pearce, J. F., & Rees, W. (1965). Predicting the outcome of behavior therapy by psychological tests. *Behav. Res. Ther., 2*, 191.

Morrison, R. L., & Bellack, A. S. (1987). Social functioning of schizophrenic patients. *Schizophrenia Bulletin, 13*, 715.

Mowrer, O. H., & Jones, H. M. (1945). Habit strength as a function of the pattern of reinforcement. *J. Exp. Psychol., 35*, 293.

Mowrer, O. H., & Viek, P. (1948). Experimental analogue of fear from a sense of helplessness. *J. Abn. Soc. Psychol., 43*, 193.

Muller, G. E., & Pilzecker, A. (1900). Experimentelle beitrage zur lehre vom gedachtniss [Experimental contributions to the process of memorizing]. *Zeitschrift fur Psychologie der sinnesorgane, Erganxungsband, 1*.

Murphy, I.C. (1964). Extinction of an incapacitating fear of earthworms. *J. Clin. Psychol., 20*, 396.

Napalkov, A. V. (1963). Information process of the brain. In N. Wiener & J. C. Sefade (Eds.), *Progress in brain research, Vol. 2: Nerve, brain and memory models*. Amsterdam: Elsevier.

Napalkov, A. V., & Karas, A. Y. (1957). Elimination of pathological conditioned reflex connections in experimental hypertensive states. *Zh. Vyssh. Nerv. Deiat., 7*, 402.

Neale, D. H. (1963). Behavior therapy and encopresis in children. *Behav. Res. Ther., 1*, 139.

Nemetz, G. H., Craig, K. D., & Reith, G. (1978). Treatment of female sexual dysfunction through symbolic modeling. *J. Consult. and Clin. Psychol., 46*, 62.

Nicassio, P., & Bootzin, R. (1974). A comparison of progressive relaxation and autogenic training as treatments for insomnia. *J. Abn. Psychol., 83*, 235.

Norton, G. R., Rhodes, L., Hauch, J., & Kaprowy, E. A. (1985). Characteristics of subjects receiving relaxation and relaxation-induced anxiety. *J. Behav. Ther. Exp. Psychiat., 16*, 211.

Nymgaard, K. (1959). Studies on the sedation threshold. *Arch. Gen. Psychiatry, 1*, 530.

O'Brien, G. T., & Barlow, D. H. (1984). In S. M. Turner (Ed.), *Behavioral treatment of anxiety disorders*. New York: Plenum Press.

O'Brien, J., Raynes, A., & Patch, V. (1972). Treatment of heroin addiction with aversion therapy, relaxation training and systematic desensitization. *Behav. Res. Ther., 10*, 77.

O'Donnell, C. R., & Worell, L. (1973). Motor and cognitive relaxation in the desensitization of anger. *Behav. Res. Ther., 11*, 473.

Ohman, A., Eriksson, A., & Olofsson, C. (1975). One-trial learning and superior resistance to extinction of autonomic responses conditioned to potentially phobic stimuli. *J. Comp. Physiol. Psychol., 88*, 619.

Ohman, A., Eriksson, G., & Lofberg, L. (1975). Phobias and preparedness: Phobic versus neutral pictures as conditioned stimuli for human autonomic responses. *J. Abn. Psychol., 84*, 41.

Olausen, S. (1978). Unpublished manuscript, Department of Psychology, University of Oslo.

Olds, J. (1962). Hypothalmic substrates of reward. *Physiol. Rev., 42*, 554.

Olds, J. (1975). Mapping the mind onto the brain. In F. G. Worden, J. P. Swazey, & G. Adelman (Eds.), *The neurosciences: Paths of discovery*. Cambridge, MA: Colonial Press.

Olds, J., Disterhoft, J. F., Segal, M., Kornblith, C. C., & Hirsh, R. (1972). Learning centers of rat brain mapped by measuring latencies of conditioned unit responses. *J. Neurophysiol., 35*, 202.

O'Leary, K. D., & O'Leary, S. G. (1977). *Classroom management*. Elmsford, NY: Pergamon Press.

O'Leary, K. D., & Wilson, G. T. (1975). *Behavior therapy*. Englewood Cliffs, NJ: Prentice-Hall.

O'Leary, K. D., & Wilson, G. T. (1988). *Behavior therapy* (2nd ed.). Englewood Cliffs, NJ: Prentice-Hall.

Oliveau, D. C., Agras, W. S., Leitenberg, H., Moore, R. C., & Wright, D. E. (1969). Systematic desensitization, therapeutically oriented instructions, selective positive reinforcement. *Behav. Res. Ther., 7*, 27.

Orleans, C. T., Shipley, R. H., Williams, C., & Haac, L. A. (1981a). Behavioral approaches to smoking cessation. 1. A decade of progress 1969–1979. *J. Behav. Ther. & Exp. Psychiat., 12*, 125.

Orleans, C. T., Shipley, R. H., Williams, C., & Haac, L. A. (1981b). Behavioral approaches to smoking cessation. 2. Topical bibliography 1969–1979. *J. Behav. Ther. & Exp. Psychiat., 12*, 131.

Orwin, A. (1971). Respiratory relief: A new and rapid method for the treatment of phobic states. *Brit. J. Psychiat., 119*, 635.

Orwin, A. (1973). The running treatment. *Brit. J. Psychiat., 122*, 175.

Osgood, C. E. (1946). Meaningful similarity and interference in learning. *J. Exp. Psychol., 38*, 132.

Osgood, C. E. (1948). An investigation into the causes of retroactive inhibition. *J. Exp. Psychol., 38*, 132.

Osgood, C. E. (1953). *Method and theory in experimental psychology*. London: Oxford University Press.

Ost, L. G. (1985). Ways of acquiring phobias and outcome of behavioral treatments. *Behav. Res. Ther., 23*, 683.

Ost, L. (1989). One session treatment for specific phobias. *Behav. Res. Ther., 27*, 1.

Ost, L., & Hugdahl, K. (1981). Acquisition of phobias and anxiety response patterns in clinical patients. *Behav. Res. & Ther., 19*, 439.

Ottaviani, R., & Beck, A. T. (1987). Cognitive aspects of panic disorders. *Journal of Anxiety Disorders, 1*, 15.

Pachman, J. S., & Foy, D. W. (1978). A correlational investigation of anxiety, self-esteem, and depression. *J. Behav. Ther. Exp. Psychiat., 9*, 97.

Padilla, A. M., Padilla, C., Ketterer, T., & Giacalone, D. (1970). Inescapable shocks and subsequent avoidance conditioning in goldfish *Carrasius Auratus. Psychonom. Sci., 20*, 295.

Palmer, H. A. (1944). Military psychiatric casualties. *Lancet, 2*, 492.

Parloff, M. G., Waskow, I. E., & Wolfe, B. I. (1978). Therapist variables in relation to process and outcome. In G. L. Garfield & A. E. Bergin (Eds.), *Handbook of psychotherapy and behavior change* (2nd ed.). New York: John Wiley & Sons.

Patel, C., Marmot, M. G., Terry, D. G., Carruthers, M., Hunt, B., & Patel, M. (1985). Trial of relaxation in reducing coronary risk: Four year follow-up. *Brit. Med. J. , 290*, 1103.

Patterson, G. R., & Gullion, M. E. (1968). *Living with children: New methods for parents and teachers*. Champaign, IL: Research Press.

Paul, G. L. (1964). *Modifications of systematic desensitization based on case study*. Paper presented at the meeting of the Western Psychological Association, Portland, Oregon.

Paul, G. L. (1966). *Insight versus desensitization in psychotherapy*. Stanford, CA: Stanford University Press.

Paul, G. L. (1968). Two-year follow-up of systematic desensitization in therapy groups. *J. Abn. Psychol., 73*, 119.

Paul, G. L. (1969a). Behavior modification research. In C. M. Franks (Ed.), *Behavior therapy: Appraisal and status*. New York: McGraw-Hill.

Paul, G. L. (1969b). Physiological effects of relaxation training and hypnotic suggestion. *J. Abn. Psychol., 74*, 425.

Paul, G. L. (1986). Can pregnancy be a placebo effect? *J. Behav. Ther. Exper. Psychiat., 17*, 61.

Paul, G. L., & Lentz, R. J. (1977). *Psychosocial treatment of chronic mental patients*. Cambridge, MA: Harvard University Press.

Paul, G. L., & Shannon, D. T. (1966). Treatment of anxiety through systematic desensitization in therapy groups. *J. Abn. Psychol., 71*, 124.

Pavlov, I. P. (1927). *Conditioned reflexes* (G. V. Anrep, Trans.). New York: Liveright.

Pavlov, I. P. (1941). Conditioned reflexes and psychiatry (W. H. Gantt, Trans.). New York: International Publishers.

Pavlov, I. P. (1955). *Selected works* (in English). Moscow: Foreign Languages Publishing House.

Paykel, E. S., Myers, J. K., Diehelt, M. N. et al. (1969). Life events and depression. *Arch. Gen. Psychiatry, 21*, 753.

Pearce, J. F. (1963). *Aspects of transvestism* (M.D. thesis, University of London).

Pecknold, J. C., Raeburn, J., & Poser, E. G. (1972). Intravenous diazepam for facilitating relaxation for desensitization. *J. Behav. Ther. Exp. Psychiat., 3*, 39.

Perez-Reyes, M. (1972a). Differences in the capacity of the sympathetic and endocrine systems of depressed patients to react to a physiological stress. In T. A. Williams, M. M. Katz, & J. A. Shield, Jr. (Eds.), *Recent advances in the psychobiology of the depressive illnesses* (DHEW Publication HSM 70-9053, pp. 131–135). Washington, DC: Government Printing Office.

Perez-Reyes, M. (1972b). Differences in sedative susceptibility between types of depression: Clinical and neurological significance. In T. A. Williams, M. M. Katz, & J. A. Shields (Eds.), *Recent advances in the psychobiology of the depressive illnesses* (DHEW Publication HSM 70-9053, pp. 119–130). Washington, DC: Government Printing Office.

Perris, C. (1966). A survey of bipolar and unipolar recurrent depressive psychoses. *Acta. Psychiat. Scand., 31*, 7.

Petit, T. L., & Markus, E. J. (1986). The cellular basis of learning and memory: The anatomical sequel to neuronal use. In N. W. Milgram, C. M. MacLeod, & T. L. Petit (Eds.), *Neuroplasticity, learning, and memory*. New York: Alan R Liss.

Pfeiffer, C. J., Fodor, J., & Geizerova, H. (1973). An epidemiologic study of the relationships of peptic ulcers in 50- to 54-year-old urban males with physical, health, and smoking factors. *J. Chronic Dis., 26*, 271.

Phillips, D. (1978). *How to fall out of love*. Boston: Houghton Mifflin.

Phillips, L. W. (1971). Training of sensory and imaginal responses in behavior therapy. In R. D. Rubin, H. Fensterheim, A. A. Lazarus, & C. M. Franks (Eds.), *Advances in behavior therapy*. New York: Academic Press.

Pichot, P. (1989). The historical roots of behavior therapy. *J. Behav. Ther. Exp. Psychiat., 20*, 107.

Pinckney, G. (1967). Avoidance learning in fish as a function of prior fear conditioning. *Psychol. Rep., 20*, 71.

Pitts, F. N., & McClure, J. (1967). Lactate metabolism in anxiety neurosis. *New Eng. J. Med., 277*, 1329.

Poppen, R. (1970). Counterconditioning of conditioned suppression in rats. *Psychol. Rep., 27*, 659.

Poppen, R. (1976). Psychotherapy versus behavior therapy. *J. Behav. Ther. Exp. Psychiat., 7*, 101.

Popper, K. R. (1959). *The logic of scientific discovery*. New York: Harper & Row.

Postman, L. (1971). Transfer, interference, and forgetting. In J. W. Kling & L. A. Riggs (Eds.), *Woodworth and Schlosberg's experimental psychology* (3rd ed., pp. 1019–1132). New York: Holt, Rinehart, & Winston.

Premack, D. (1965). Reinforcement theory. In D. Levine (Ed.), *Nebraska symposium on motivation*. Lincoln: University of Nebraska Press.

Purcell, K. (1963). Distinction between subgroups of asthmatic children: Children's perceptions of events associated with asthma. *Pediatrics, 31*, 486.

Qualls, P. J., & Sheehan, P. W. (1981). Electromyograph biofeedback as a relaxation technique: A critical appraisal and reassessment. *Psychol. Bull., 90*, 21.

Rabavilas, A. D., Boulougouris, J. C., & Stefanis, C. (1976). Duration of flooding sessions in the treatment of obsessive-compulsive patients. *Behav. Res. Ther., 14*, 349.

Rachaim, S., Lefebvre, C., & Jenkins, J. O. (1980). The effects of social skills training and behavioral and cognitive components of anger management. *J. Behav. Ther. & Exp. Psychiat., 1*(1), 3.

Rachlin, H. (1976). *Behavior and learning*. San Francisco: Freeman, Cooper.

Rachman, S. (1961). Sexual disorders and behavior therapy. *Amer. J. Psychiat., 118*, 235.

Rachman, S. (1965). Studies in desensitization. 1. The separate effects of relaxation and desensitization. *Behav. Res. Ther., 3*, 245.

Rachman, S. (1966). Studies in desensitization: 3. Speed of generalization. *Behav. Res. Ther., 4*, 7.

Rachman, S. (1971). *The effects of psychotherapy*. Oxford: Pergamon Press.

Rachman, S. (1974). *The meaning of fear*. Middlesex, England: Penguin Books.

Rachman, S. (1977). The conditioning theory of fear-acquisition: A critical examination. *Behav. Res. Ther., 15*, 375.

Rachman, S. (1978). *Fear and courage*. San Francisco: Freeman, Cooper.

Rachman, S. (1990). *Fear and courage* (2nd ed.). San Francisco: Freeman.

Rachman, S., Cobb, J., Grey, S., McDonald, B., Mawson, D., Sartory, G., & Stern, R. (1979). The behavioral treatment of obsessional-compulsive disorders, with and without clomipramine. *Behav. Res. Ther., 17*, 467.

Rachman, S., Hodgson, R., & Marks, I. M. (1971). Treatment of chronic obsessive-compulsive neurosis. *Behav. Res. Ther., 9*, 237.

Rachman, S., Levitt, K., & Lopatka, C. (1987). Panic: The link between cognitions and bodily symptoms—I. *Behav. Res. Ther., 5*, 411.

Rachman, S., & Lopatka, C. (1988). Return of fear: Underlearning and overlearning. *Behav. Res. Ther., 26*, 99.

Rachman, S., & Teasdale, J. D. (1968). Aversion therapy. In C. M. Franks (Ed.), *Assessment and status of the behavior therapies and associated developments.* New York: McGraw-Hill.

Rachman, S., & Teasdale, J. (1969). *Aversion therapy and behavior disorders.* London: Routledge & Kegan Paul.

Rafi, A. A. (1962). Learning theory and the treatment of tics. *J. Psychosom. Res., 6*, 71.

Raimy, V. (1976). Changing misconceptions as the therapeutic task. In A. Burton (Ed.), *What makes behavior change possible?* New York: Brunner/Mazel.

Rainey, C. A. (1972). An obsessive-compulsive neurosis treated by flooding in vivo. *J. Behav. Ther. Exp. Psychiat., 3*, 117.

Ramsey, R. W. (1977). Behavioral approaches to bereavement. *Behav. Res. Ther., 15*, 131.

Rapee, R. M. (1985). A case of panic disorder treated with breathing retraining. *J. Behav. Ther. Exp. Psychiat., 16*, 63.

Rathus, S. A. (1972). An experimental investigation of assertive training in a group setting. *J. Behav. Ther. Exp. Psychiat., 3*, 80.

Rauter, U., & Braud, W. (1969). Forced activity and conflict behavior. *Psychonom. Sci., 16*, 117.

Raymond, M. J. (1956). Case of fetishism treated by aversion therapy. *Brit. Med. J., 2*, 854.

Raymond, M. (1964). The treatment of addiction by aversion conditioning with apomorphine. *Behav. Res. Ther., 1*, 287.

Raymond, M., & O'Keefe, K. (1965). A case of pin-up fetishism treated by aversion conditioning. *Brit. J. Psychiat., 111*, 579.

Razran, G. (1971). *Mind in evolution.* Boston: Houghton Mifflin.

Reed, J. L. (1966). Comments on the use of methohexitone sodium as a means of inducing relaxation. *Behav. Res. Ther., 4*, 323.

Rees, L. (1956). Physical and emotional factors in bronchial asthma. *J. Psychosom. Res., 1*, 98.

Rees, L. (1964). The importance of psychological, allergic, and infective factors in childhood asthma. *J. Psychosom. Res., 7*, 253.

Reinking, R. H., & Kohl, M. L. (1975). Effects of various forms of relaxation training on physiological and self-report measures of relaxation. *J. Consult. Clin. Psychol., 43*, 5.

Reiss, S. (1980). Pavlovian conditioning and human fear. *Behav. Ther., 11*, 380.

Reiss, S., & McNally, R. J. (1985). Expectancy model of fear. In S. Reiss & R. R. Bootzin (Eds.), *Theoretical issues in behavior therapy.* New York: Academic Press.

Rescorla, R. (1969). Pavlovian conditioned inhibition. *Psychol. Bull., 72*, 77.

Rescorla, R. (1988). Pavlovian conditioning: It's not what you think it is. *Am. Psychol., 43*, 151.

Resh, M. (1970). Asthma of unknown origin as a psychological group. *J. Consult. Clin. Psychol., 35*, 424.

Ribot, T. (1903). *The psychology of the emotions.* New York: Scribner.

Rimm, D. C., & Mahoney, M. J. (1969). The application of reinforcement and participant modeling in the treatment of snake phobia behavior. *Behav. Res. Ther., 7*, 369.

Ritter, B. J. (1968). The group treatment of children's snake phobias using vicarious anticontact desensitization procedures. *Behav. Res. Ther., 6*, 1.

Robinson, C., & Suinn, R. (1969). Group desensitization of a phobia in massed sessions. *Behav. Res. Ther., 7*, 319.

Rogerson, C. H. (1940). The differentiation of neurosis and psychosis with special reference to states of depression and anxiety. *J. Ment. Sci., 86*, 632.

Rosen, G. M., & Ornstein, H. (1976). A historical note on thought stopping. *J. Consult. Clin. Psychol., 44*, 1016.

Rosen, G. M., Rosen, E., & Reid, J. R. (1972). Cognitive desensitization and avoidance behavior. *J. Abn. Psychol., 80*, 176.

Rosenthal, D., & Frank, J. D. (1958). Psychotherapy and the placebo effect. In C. F. Reed, I. E. Alexander, & S. S. Tomkins (Eds.), *Psychopathology: A sourcebook.* Cambridge, MA: Harvard University Press.

Roth, M. (1987). Some recent developments in relation to agoraphobia and related disorders and their bearing upon theories of the causation. *Psychiatry Journal of The University of Ottawa, 12*, 150.

Roth, M., Gurney, C., & Garside, R. F. et al. (1972). Studies in the classification of affective disorders. The relationship between anxiety states and depressive illnesses — 1. *Br. J. Psychiatry, 121*, 147.

Rozhdestvenskaya, V. I. (1959). Strength of nerve cells as shown in the nature of the effect of an additional stimulus on visual sensitivity. In B. M. Teplov (Ed.), *Typological features of higher nervous activity in man* (Vol. 2). Moscow: Akad. Pedagog Nauk. RSFSR.

Rubin, J., Nagler, R., Spiro, H. M., & Pilot, M. L. (1962). Measuring the effect of emotions on esophageal motility. *Psychosom. Med., 24*, 170.

Rubin, L. S. (1964). Autonomic dysfunction as a concomitant of neurotic behavior. *J. Nerv. Ment. Dis., 138*, 558.

Rubin, L. S. (1970). Pupillary reflexes as objective indices of autonomic dysfunction in the differential diagnosis of schizophrenic and neurotic behavior. *J. Behav. Ther. Exp. Psychiat., 1*, 185.

Rubin, M. (1972). Verbally suggested responses as reciprocal inhibition of anxiety. *J. Behav. Ther. Exp. Psychiat., 3*, 273.

Rush, A. J., & Watkins, J. T. (1981). Group versus individual cognitive therapy. A pilot study. *Cog. Ther. Res., 5*, 95.

Rush, A. S., Beck, A. T., Kovacs, M., & Hollon, S. (1977). Comparative efficacy of cognitive therapy and pharmacotherapy in the treatment of depressed outpatients. *Cognitive Ther., 1*, 17.

Ryle, G. (1949). *The concept of mind.* London: Hutchinson.

Salter, A. (1949). *Conditioned reflex therapy.* New York: Creative Age.

Salter, A. (1952). *The case against psychoanalysis.* New York: Holt, Rinehart, & Winston.

Salzer, H. M. (1966). Relative hypoglycemia as a cause of neuropsychiatric illness. *J. Natl. Med. Assoc., 58*, 12.

Sanderson, R. E., Campbell, D., & Laverty, S. G. (1963). Traumatically conditioned responses acquired during respiratory paralysis. *Nature, 196*, 1235.

Sandison, R. A. (1954). Psychological aspects of the LSD treatment of the neuroses. *J. Ment. Sci., 100*, 508.

Sargant, W., & Dally, P. (1962). The treatment of anxiety states by anti-depressant drugs. *Brit. Med. J., 1*, 6.

Sartory, G., Rachman, S., & Gray, S. (1977). An investigation of the relation between reported fear and heart rate. *Behav. Res. Ther., 15*, 435.

Schaefer, H. H., & Martin, P. L. (1969). *Behavioral therapy*. New York: McGraw-Hill.

Scharnberg, M. (1984). *The myth of paradigm shift*. Stockholm: Almquist & Wiksel International.

Schmideberg, M. (1970). Psychotherapy with failures of psychoanalysis. *Brit. J. Psychiat., 116*, 195.

Schultz, J. H., & Luthe, W. (1959). *Autogenic training: A psychophysiological approach in psychotherapy*. New York: Grune & Stratton.

Schumacher, S., & Lloyd, C. (1981). Physiological and psychological factors in impotence. *The Journal of Sex Research, 17*, 40.

Schwartz, M. (1976). *Stuttering solved*. New York: McGraw-Hill.

Schwitzgebel, R. R., & Kolb, D. A. (1964). Inducing behavior change in adolescent delinquents. *Behav. Res. Ther., 1*, 297.

Scrignar, C. B. (1971). Food as the reinforcer in the outpatient treatment of anorexia nervosa. *J. Behav. Ther. Exp. Psychiat., 2*, 31.

Scrignar, C. G. (1984). *Post-Traumatic stress disorder: Diagnosis, treatment, and legal issues*. New York: Praeger.

Searles, J. S. (1985). A methodological and empirical critique of psychotherapy outcome meta-analysis. *Behav. Res. Ther., 23*, 297.

Sechenov, I. M. (1965). *Autobiographical notes*. Baltimore: Caramond/Pridemark.

Seitz, P. F. D. (1953). Dynamically oriented brief psychotherapy: Psychocutaneous excoriation syndrome. *Psychosom. Med., 15*, 200.

Seligman, M. E. P. (1970). On the generality of the laws of learning. *Psychol. Rev., 77*, 406.

Seligman, M. E. P. (1971). Phobias and preparedness. *Behav. Ther., 2*, 307.

Semans, J. H. (1956). Premature ejaculation, a new approach. *South. Med. J., 49*, 353.

Serber, M. (1970). Shame aversion therapy. *J. Behav. Ther. Exp. Psychiat., 1*, 213.

Serber, M. (1972). Teaching the nonverbal components of assertive training. *J. Behav. Ther. Exp. Psychiat., 3*, 179.

Seward, J., & Humphrey, G. L. (1967). Avoidance learning as a function of pretraining in the cat. *J. Comp. Physiol. Psychol., 63*, 338.

Shagass, C. (1954). The sedation threshold: A method for estimating tension in psychiatric patients. *Electroencephalogr. Clin. Neurophysiol., 6*, 221.

Shagass, C. (1956). Sedation threshold: A neurophysiological tool for psychosomatic research. *Psychosom. Med., 18*, 410.

Shagass, C. (1981). Neurophysiological evidence for different types of depression. *J. Behav. Ther. Exp. Psychiat., 12*, 99.

Shagass, C., Mihalik, J., & Jones, A. L. (1957). Clinical psychiatric studies using the sedation threshold. *J. Psychosom. Res., 2*, 45.

Shagass, C., Naiman, J., Mihalik, J. (1956). An objective test which differentiates between neurotic and psychotic depression. *Arch. Neurol. Psychiatry, 75*, 461.

Shagass, C., Roemer, R. A., Straumanis, J. J., & Amadeo, M. (1978). Evoked potential correlates of psychosis. *Biol. Psychiat., 13*, 163.

Shagass, C., & Schwartz, M. (1963). Psychiatric correlates of evoked cerebral cortical potentials. *Amer. J. Psychiat., 119*, 1055.

Shames, G. H. (1969). Verbal reinforcement during therapy interviews with stutterers. In B. B. Gray & G. England (Eds.), *Stuttering and the conditioning therapies*. Monterey, CA: Monterey Institute for Speech & Hearing.

Shapiro, F. (1989). Eye movement desensitization: A new treatment for post-traumatic stress disorder. *J. Behav. Ther. Exper. Psychiat., 20*, 211.

Shaw, B. F. (1977). Comparison of cognitive therapy and behavior therapy in the treatment of depression. *J. Consult. Clin. Psychol., 45*, 543.

Sheehan, D. V. (1982). Current concepts in psychiatry: Panic attacks and phobias. *The New England Journal of Medicine, 307*, 156.

Sheehan, D. V., & Sheehan, D. H. (1983). The classification of phobic disorders. *International Journal of Medicine, 12*, 243.

Sheffield, F. D., & Roby, T. B. (1950). Reward value of a non-nutritive sweet taste. *J. Comp. Physiol. Psychol., 43*, 471.

Sherman, A. R. (1972). Real-life exposure as a primary therapeutic factor in the desensitization treatment of fear. *J. Abn. Psychol., 79*, 19.

Sherrington, C. S. (1906). *Integrative action of the nervous system.* New Haven: Yale University Press.

Sherry, G. S., & Levine, G. A. (1980). An evaluation of procedural variables in flooding therapy. *Behavior Therapy, 11*, 148.

Shirley, M. M. (1933). *The first two years, Vol. 3, Personality manifestations.* Institute of Child Welfare Monograph No. 8. Minneapolis: University of Minnesota Press.

Shoemaker, D. J., & Brutten, E. J. (1969). A two-factor approach to the modification of stuttering. In B. G. Gray & G. England (Eds.), *Stuttering and the conditioning therapies.* Monterey, CA: Monterey Institute for Speech & Hearing.

Shmavonian, B. M., & Wolpe, J. (1972). Unpublished data.

Shorvon, H. J., & Sargant, W. (1947). Excitatory abreaction with special reference to its mechanism and the use of ether. *J. Ment. Sci., 93*, 709.

Siegel, G. M., & Martin, R. R. (1967). Verbal punishment of dysfluencies during spontaneous speech. *Lang. and Speech, 10*, 244.

Simonov, P. V. (1967). *Studies of emotional behavior of humans and animals.* Paper read at conference on Exp Apps to the Study of Beh, NY.

Singer, E. P. (1958). The hyperventilation syndrome in clinical medicine. *New York State Journal of Medicine, 58*, 1494.

Singh, H. (1963). Therapeutic use of thioridazine in premature ejaculation. *Amer. J. Psychiat., 119*, 891.

Sirota, A., & Mahoney, M. (1974). Relaxing on cue: The self-regulation of asthma. *J. Behav. Ther. Exp. Psychiat., 5*, 65.

Skinner, B. F. (1938). *The behavior of organisms.* New York: Appleton-Century-Crofts.

Skinner, B. F. (1953). *Science and human behavior.* New York: Macmillan.

Skinner, B. F. (1988). The operant side of behavior therapy. *J. Behav. Ther. Exp. Psychiat., 19*, 171.

Skinner, B. F., & Lindsley, O. R. (1954). *Studies in behavior therapy.* Status reports 11 and 111, Office of Naval Research, Contract N5 ori-7662.

Slaby, A. E. (1983). Quality assurance and diagnostic psychiatry in the emergency setting. In W. Dublin (Ed.), *Clinics of emergency medicine: Emergency psychiatry.* New York: Churchill, Livingston.

Slater, S. L., & Leavy, A. (1966). The effects of inhaling a 35% carbon dioxide, 65% oxygen mixture upon anxiety level in neurotic patients. *Behav. Res. Ther., 4*, 309.

Sloane, R. B., Staples, F. R., Cristol, A. H., Yorkston, N. J., & Whipple, K. (1975). *Psychotherapy versus behavior therapy.* Cambridge, MA: Harvard University Press.

Smart, R. G. (1965). Conflict and conditioned aversive stimuli in the development of experimental response. *Canad. J. Psychol., 19*, 208.

Smedlund, J. (1978a). Bandura's theory of self-efficacy: A set of common sense theorems. *Scand. J. Psychol., 19*, 1.

Smedlund, J. (1978b). Some psychological theories are not empirical: Reply to Bandura. *Scand. J. Psychol., 19*, 101.

Smith, D. (1982). Trends in counselling and psychotherapy. *Amer. Psychol., 37*, 802.

Smith, M. L., & Glass, G. V. (1977). Meta-analysis of psychotherapy outcome studies. *Amer. Psychologist, 32*, 752.

Smith, M. L., Glass, G. V., & Miller, T. I. (1980). *The benefit of psychotherapy.* Baltimore, MD: Johns Hopkins University Press.

Snyder, S. H. (1978). The opiate receptor and morphine-like peptides in the brain. *Am. J. Psychiat., 135*, 645.

Sokolov, Y. N. (1963). *Perception and the conditioned reflex* (S. W. Waydenfeld, Trans.). Oxford: Pergamon Press.

Solomon, J. (1942). Reactions of children to black-outs. *Amer. J. Orthopsychiat., 12*, 361.

Solomon, R. L. (1964). Punishment. *Amer. Psychol., 19*, 239.

Solomon, R. L. (1980). The opponent-process theory of acquired motivation: The costs of pleasure and the benefits of pain. *Amer. Psychol., 35*, 691.

Solursh, L. (1988). Combat addiction post-traumatic stress disorder re-explored. *Psychiat. J. Univ. Ottawa, 13*(1).

Solyom, L. (1969). A case of obsessive neurosis treated by aversion relief. *Canad. Psychiat. Assoc. J., 14*, 623.

Solyom, L., Garza-Perez, J., Ledwidge, B. L., & Solyom, C. (1972). Paradoxical intention in the treatment of obsessive thoughts: A pilot study. *Comprehensive Psychiat., 13*, 291.

Solyom, L., & Miller, S. (1965). A differential conditioning procedure as the initial phase of the behavior therapy of homosexuality. *Behav. Res. Ther., 3*, 147.

Sommer-Smith, J. A., Galeano, C., Pineyrua, M., Roig, J. A., & Segundo, J. P. (1962). Tone cessation as conditioned signal. *Electroenceph. Clin. Neurophysiol., 14*, 869.

Southwork, S., & Kirsch, I. (1988). The role of expectancy in exposure generated fear-reduction in agoraphobia. *Behav. Res. and Ther., 26*, 112.

Spark, R. F., White, R. A., & Connolly, P. B. (1980). Impotence is not always psychogenic. *J. Amer. Med. Assoc., 243*, 750.

Stampfl, T. G. (1964). Quoted by London (1964).

Stampfl, T. G., & Levis, D. J. (1967). Essentials of implosive therapy: A learning-theory-based psychodynamic behavioral therapy. *J. Abn. Psychol., 72*, 496.

Stampfl, T. G., & Levis, D. J. (1968). Implosive therapy, a behavioral therapy. *Behav. Res. Ther., 6*, 31.

Steketee, G., & Roy, G. (1977). The anxiety inhibiting effects of carbon dioxide-oxygen mixtures. Unpublished data, Temple University School of Medicine, Philadelphia, PA.

Stetten, D. (1968). Basic sciences in medicine: The example of gout. *New Engl. J. Med., 278*, 1333.

Stevens, S. S. (1957). On the psychophysical law. *Psychol. Rev., 64*, 153.

Stevens, S. S. (1962). The surprising simplicity of sensory metrics. *Amer. Psychol., 17*, 29.

Stevenson, I., & Wolpe, J. (1960). Recovery from sexual deviation through overcoming non-sexual neurotic responses. *Amer. J. Psychiat., 116*, 737.

Stewart, M. A. (1961). Psychotherapy by reciprocal inhibition. *Amer. J. Psychiat., 118*, 175.

Stiles, W., Shapiro, D., & Elliott, R. (1986). Are all psychotherapies equivalent? *Amer. Psychol., 41*, 165.

Stoffelmayr, B. E. (1970). The treatment of a retching response to dentures by a counteractive reading aloud. *J. Behav. Ther. Exp. Psychiat., 1*, 163.

Stratton, G. M. (1897). Vision without inversion of the retinal image. *Psychol. Rev., 4*, 341.

Strupp, H. (1978). Psychotherapy research and practice: An overview. In S. Garfield & A. Bergin (Eds.), *Handbook of psychotherapy and behavior change*. New York: John Wiley & Sons.

Stuart, R. B. (1969). Operant-interpersonal treatment for marital discord. *J. Consult. Clin. Psychol., 33*, 675.

Stuart, R. B. (1975). *How to manage the blues, tension, anger or boredom*. Manhasset, NY: Weight Watchers.

Stumphauser, J. S. (1986). *Helping delinquents change*. New York: Haworth Press.

Stunkard, A. J. (1975). From explanation to action in psychosomatic medicine: The case of obesity. *Psychosom. Med., 37*, 195.

Suarez, Y., Crowe, M., & Adams, H. E. (1978). Depression: Avoidance learning and physiological correlates in clinical and analog populations. *Behav. Res. Ther., 16*, 21.

Sue, D. (1972). The role of relaxation in systematic desensitization. *Behav. Res. Ther., 10*, 153.

Suinn, R. M. (1977). *Manual—Anxiety management training*. Fort Collins, CO: Author.

Suinn, R. M., & Richardson, F. (1971). Anxiety management training: A nonspecific behavior therapy program for anxiety control. *Behav. Ther., 2*, 498.

Sushinsky, L. W., & Bootzin, R. R. (1970). Cognitive desensitization as a model of systematic desensitization. *Behav. Res. Ther., 8*, 29.

Symonds, C. P. (1943). The human response to flying stress. *Brit. Med. J., 2*, 703.

Taboas, T. B. (1988). Son todas las terapias igualmente efectivas? [Are all therapies equally effective?] *Revista Latinamericana de Psicologia, 20*, 309.

Taub, E. (1977). Self-regulation and human tissue temperature. In G. E. Schwartz & J. Beatty (Eds.), *Biofeedback: Theory and Research*. New York: Academic Press.

Taylor, F. G., & Marshall, W. L. (1977). A cognitive behavioral therapy for depression. *Cognitive Ther. and Res., 1*, 59.

Taylor, J. G. (1962). *The behavioral basis of perception*. New Haven: Yale University Press.

Taylor, J. G. (1963). A behavioral interpretation of obsessive-compulsive neurosis. *Behav. Res. Ther., 1*, 237.

Terhune, W. S. (1948). The phobic syndrome. *Arch. Neurol. Psychiat., 62*, 162.

Thomas, E. J. (1968). Selected sociobehavioral techniques and principles: An approach to interpersonal helping. *Social Work, 13*, 12.

Thompson, K. C., & Hedrie, H. C. (1972). Environmental stress in primary depressive illness. *Arch. Gen. Psychiatry, 26*, 130.

Thompson, J. K., & Williams, D. E. (1985). Behavior therapy in the 80's: Evaluation, exploitation and the existential issue. *Behav. Therapist, 8*, 47.

Thorndike, E. L. (1932). Reward and punishment in animal learning. *Comp. Psychol. Monogr. 8*, No. 39.

Thorpe, J. G., Schmidt, E., Brown, P. T., & Castell, D. (1964). Aversion relief therapy: A new method for general application. *Behav. Res. Ther., 2*, 71.

Thurstone, L. L., & Thurstone, K. G. (1930). A neurotic inventory. *J. Soc. Psych., 1*, 3.

Thyer, B. A., Baum, M., & Reid, L. D. (1988). Exposure techniques in the reduction of fear. *Advances Behav. Res. Ther., 10*, 105.

Thyer, B. A., & Himle, J. (1985). Temporal relationship between panic attack, onset and phobic avoidance in agoraphobia. *Behaviour Research and Therapy, 23*, 607.

Thyer, B. A., Papsdorf, J. D., Davis, R. & Vallecovsa, S. (1984). Autonomic correlates of the subjective anxiety scale. *J. Behav. Ther. Exp. Psychiat.*, 15, 3.

Tomlinson, J. R. (1970). The treatment of bowel retention by operant procedures: A case study. *J. Behav. Ther. Exp. Psychiat., 1*, 83.

Tsukahara, N. (1984). Classical conditioning mediated by the red nucleus: An approach beginning at the cellular level. In Lynch, McGaugh, & N. M. Wienberger (Eds.), *Neurobiology of learning and memory*. New York: Guilford Press.

Turner, R. M., DiTomasso, R. A., & Murray, M. R. (1980). Psychometric analysis of the Willoughby personality schedule. *J. Behav. Ther. Exp. Psychiat., 11*, 85.

Tursky, B,. Watson, P. D., & O'Connell, D. N. (1965). A concentric shock electrode for pain stimulation. *Psychophysiol., 1*, 296.

Ullmann, L. P., & Krasner, L. (1965). *Case studies in behavior modification*. New York: Holt, Rinehart, & Winston.

Ulrich, R., Stachnik, T., & Mabry, J. (1966). *Control of human behavior*. Glenview, IL: Scott Foresman.

Valins, S., & Ray, A. A. (1967). Effects of cognitive desensitization on avoidance behavior. *J. Pers. Soc. Psychol., 7*, 345.

Van de Venter, A. D., & Laws, D. R. (1978). Orgasmic reconditioning to redirect sexual arousal in pedophiles. *Behav. Ther., 7*, 155.

Van Egeren, L. F., Feather, B. W., & Hein, P. L. (1971). Desensitization of phobias: Some psychophysiological propositions. *Psychophysiol., 8*, 213.

Voegtlin, W., & Lemere, F. (1942). The treatment of alcohol addiction. *Qrt. J. Stud. Alcoh., 2*, 717.

Wachtel, P. L. (1978). On some complexities in the application of conflict theory to psychotherapy. *J. Nerv. Ment. Dis., 166*, 475.

Wade, T. C., Malloy, T. E., & Proctor, S. (1977). Imaginal correlates of self-reported fear and avoidance behavior. *Behav. Res. Ther., 15*, 17.

Wagner, A. R., & Rescoria, R. A. (1972). Inhibition in Pavlovian conditioning: Applications of a theory. In M. S. Halliday & R. A. Boakes (Eds.), *Inhibition and learning*. New York: Academic Press.

Wallace, R. K. (1970). Physiological effects of transcendental meditation. *Science, 167*, 1751.

Walton, D. (1960). Relevance of learning theory in the treatment of an obsessive-compulsive state. In H. J. Eysenck (Ed.), *Experiments in behavior therapy*. Oxford: Pergamon Press.

Walton, D. (1964). Experimental psychology and the treatment of a tiquer. *J. Child Psychol. Psychiat., 2*, 148.

Walton, D., & Mather, M. D. (1964). Application of learning principles to the treatment of obsessive-compulsive states. In H. J. Eysenck (Ed.), *Experiments in behavior therapy*. Oxford: Pergamon Press.

Wanderer, Z., & Cabot, T. (1978). *Letting go*. New York: Putnam.

Waterloo, K. K., & Gotestam, K. G. (1988). The regulated breathing method for stuttering: An experimental evaluation. *J. Behav. Ther. Exp. Psychiat., 19*, 11.

Watson, J. B. (1970). *Behaviorism*. New York: W W Norton.

Watson, J. B., & Rayner, P. (1920). Conditioned emotional reactions. *J. Exp. Psychol., 3*, 1.

Watts, F. M. (1979). Habituation model of systematic desensitization. *Psychol. Bull., 86*, 627.

Weinberger, N. M., Diamond, D. M., & McKenna, T. M. (1984). Initial events in conditioning: Plasticity in the pupillomotor and auditory systems. In Lynch, McGaugh & N. M. Weinberger (Eds.), *Neurobiology of learning and memory.* New York: Guilford Press.

Weinreb, S. (1966). The effects of inhaling spirit of ammonia upon anxiety level in neurotic patients. (Mimeographed)

Weissman, M. M., Klerman, G. L., Prusoff, B. A. Sholomakas, D., & Pedian, N. (1981). Depressed outpatients: Results one year after treatment with drugs and/or interpersonal psychotherapy. *Arch. Gen. Psychiatry, 38*, 51.

Weitzman, B. (1967). Behaviour therapy and psychotherapy. *Psychol. Bull., 74*, 300.

Wenger, M. A. (1966). Studies of autonomic balance: A summary. *Psychophysiology, 2*, 173.

West, E. M., & Dally, P. G. (1959). Effects of iproniazid in depressive syndromes. *Br. Med. J., 1*, 491.

Wikler, A. (1968). Interaction of physical dependence and classical and operant conditioning in the genesis of relapse. *Proceedings of the Association for Research in Nervous and Mental Disease, 46*, 280.

Wilder, J. (1945). Facts and figures on psychotherapy. *J. Clin. Psychopath., 7*, 311.

Williams, S. L., & Zane, G. (1989). Guided mastery and stimulus exposure treatment for severe performance anxiety in agoraphobics. *Behav. Res. Ther., 27*, 237.

Willis, R. W., & Edwards, J. A. (1969). A study of the comparative effectiveness of systematic desensitization and implosive therapy. *Behav. Res. Ther., 7*, 387.

Willoughby, R. R. (1932). Some properties of the Thurstone Personality Schedule and a suggested revision. *J. Soc. Psych., 3*, 401.

Willoughby, R. R. (1934). Norms for Clark-Thurstone Inventory. *J. Soc. Psych., 5*, 91.

Wilson, G. T. (1982). The relationship of learning theories to the behavior therapist. In *Learning theory approaches to psychiatry.* Chichester: John Wiley & Sons.

Wilson, G. T. (1984). Clinical issues and strategies in the practice of behavior therapy. In C. M. Franks, G. T. Wilson, P. C., Kendall, & K. D. Brownell (Eds.), *Annual review of behavior therapy* (Vol. 10). New York: Guilford Press.

Wilson, G. T. (1985). Limitations of meta-analysis in clinical psychology. *Clinical Psychology Review, 5*, 35.

Wilson, G. T., & O'Leary, K. D. (1980). *Principles of behavior therapy.* Englewood Cliffs, NJ: Prentice-Hall.

Wilson, G. T., & Rachman, S. (1983). Meta-analysis and the evaluations of psychotherapy outcome. *J. Consult. and Clin. Psychol., 51*, 54.

Winkelman, N. W. (1955). Chlorpromazine in the treatment of neuropsychiatric disorders. *J. Amer. Med. Assoc., 155*, 18.

Winokur, G. (1985). The validity of neurotic-reactive depression: New data and appraisal. *Arch. Gen. Psychiat., 42*, 1116.

Wisocki, P. A. (1970). Treatment of obsessive-compulsive behavior by covert sensitization and covert reinforcement: A case report. *J. Behav. Ther. Exp. Psychiat., 1*, 233.

Wolberg, L. (1948). *Medical hypnosis.* New York: Grune & Stratton.

Wolf, S., & Wolff, H. G. (1942). Evidence in the genesis of peptic ulcer in man. *J. Amer. Med. Assoc., 120*, 670.

Wolf, S., & Wolff, H. G. (1947). *Human gastric functions.* New York: Oxford University Press.

Wollersheim, J. P. (1970). Effectiveness of group therapy based on learning principles in the treatment of overweight women. *J. Abn. Psychol., 76*, 462.

Wolpe, J. (1948). An approach to the problem of neurosis based on the conditioned response (M.D. Thesis, University of the Witwatersrand).

Wolpe, J. (1949). An interpretation of the effects of combinations of stimuli (patterns) based on current neurophysiology. *Psychol. Rev., 56*, 277.

Wolpe, J. (1950). Need-reduction, drive-reduction, and reinforcement: A neurophysiological view. *Psychol. Rev., 57*, 19.

Wolpe, J. (1952a). Experimental neurosis as learned behavior. *Brit. J. Psychol., 43*, 243.

Wolpe, J. (1952b). The formation of negative habits: A neurophysiological view. *Psychol. Rev., 59*, 290.

Wolpe, J. (1952c). Objective psychotherapy of the neuroses. *South Afr. Med. J., 26*, 825.

Wolpe, J. (1953). Theory construction for Blodgett's latent learning. *Psychol. Rev., 60*, 340.

Wolpe, J. (1954). Reciprocal inhibition as the main basis of psychotherapeutic effects. *Arch. Neur. Psychiat., 72*, 205.

Wolpe, J. (1958). *Psychotherapy by reciprocal inhibition*. Stanford, CA: Stanford University Press.

Wolpe, J. (1961a). The prognosis in unpsychoanalyzed recovery from neurosis. *Amer. J. Psychiat., 118*, 35.

Wolpe, J. (1961b). The systematic desensitization treatment of neuroses. *J. Nerv. Ment. Dis., 112*, 189.

Wolpe, J. (1962). Isolation of a conditioning procedure as the crucial psychotherapeutic factor. *J. Nerv. Ment. Dis., 134*, 316.

Wolpe, J. (1963). Quantitative relationships in the systematic desensitization of phobias. *Amer. J. Psychiat., 119*, 1062.

Wolpe, J. (1964a). Behavior therapy in complex neurotic states. *Brit. J. Psychiat., 110*, 28.

Wolpe, J. (1964b). The comparative clinical status of conditioning therapies and psychoanalysis. In J. Wolpe, A. Salter, & L. J. Reyna (Eds.), *The conditioning therapies*. New York: Holt, Rinehart, & Winston.

Wolpe, J. (1964c). Unpublished data.

Wolpe, J. (1965). Conditioned inhibition of craving in drug addiction: A pilot experiment. *Behav. Res. Ther., 2*, 285.

Wolpe, J. (1967). Parallels between animal and human neuroses. In J. Zubin & H. F. Hunt (Eds.), *Comparative psychopathology*. New York: Grune & Stratton.

Wolpe, J. (1969). Behavior therapy of stuttering: Deconditioning the emotional factor. In B. B. Gray & G. England (Eds.), *Stuttering and the conditioning therapies*. Monterey, CA: Monterey Institute for Speech & Stuttering.

Wolpe, J. (1970). Emotional conditioning and cognitions: A rejoinder to Davison and Valins. *Behav. Res. Ther., 8*, 103.

Wolpe, J. (1971). The behavioristic conception of neurosis: A reply to two critics. *Psychol. Rev., 78*, 341.

Wolpe, J. (1973). *The practice of behavior therapy* (2nd ed.). Elmsford, NY: Pergamon Press.

Wolpe, J. (1975). Foreword. In R. B. Sloane, F. R. Staples, A. H. Cristol, N. J. Yorkston, & K. Whipple (Eds.), *Psychotherapy versus behavior therapy*. Cambridge, MA: Harvard University Press.

Wolpe, J. (1976a). Behavior therapy and its malcontents: 1. Denial of its bases and psychodynamics fusionism. *J. Behav. Ther. Exp. Psychiat., 7*, 1.

Wolpe, J. (1976b). Behavior therapy and its malcontents: 2. Multimodal eclecticism, cognitive exclusivism and exposure empiricism. *J. Behav. Ther. Exp. Psychiat., 7*, 109.

Wolpe, J. (1976c). *Theme and variations: A behavior therapy casebook*. Elmsford, NY: Pergamon Press.

Wolpe, J. (1977). Inadequate behavior analysis: The Achilles heel of outcome research behavior therapy. *J. Behav. Ther. Exp. Psychiat., 7*, 1.

Wolpe, J. (1978a). Cognition and causation in human behavior and its therapy. *Amer. Psychol., 33*, 437.

Wolpe, J. (1978b). Self-efficacy theory and psychotherapeutic change: A square peg for a round hole. *Adv. Behav. Res. Ther., 1*, 231.

Wolpe, J. (1979). The experimental model and treatment of neurotic depression. *Behav. Res. Ther., 17*, 555.

Wolpe, J. (1980). Behavior therapy for psychosomatic disorders. *Psychosom., 21*, 329.

Wolpe, J. (1981a). Behavior therapy versus psychoanalysis: Therapeutic and social implications. *Amer. Psychol., 36*, 159.

Wolpe, J. (1981b). The dichotomy between directly conditioned and cognitively learned anxiety. *J. Behav. Ther. Exp. Psychiat., 12*, 35.

Wolpe, J. (1981c). Perception as a functioning of conditioning. *Pavlovian Journal of Biological Science, 16*, 70.

Wolpe, J. (1982). *The Practice of Behavior Therapy* (3rd ed.). Elmsford, NY: Pergamon Press.

Wolpe, J. (1985a). Existential problems and the behavior therapist. *Behav. Therapist, 8*, 126.

Wolpe, J. (1985b). Panic attacks are not homogeneous. *Proceedings of the Fourth World Congress of Biological Psychiatry*. New York: Elsevier Science.

Wolpe, J. (1985c). Revised schemes for the mechanisms of stuttering: Postscript 14, p. 350. In G. H. Shames & H. Rubin (Eds.), *Stuttering: Then and now*. Columbus: Charles E Merrill.

Wolpe, J. (1986a). The positive diagnosis of neurotic depression as an etiological category. *Compr. Psychiatry, 27*, 449.

Wolpe, J. (1986b). Retreat from principles: A critical review. *J. Behav. Ther. Exp. Psychiat., 17*, 215.

Wolpe, J. (1987). Carbon dioxide inhalation treatments of neurotic anxiety. *Journal of Nervous and Mental Disease, 3*, 129.

Wolpe, J. (1988). *The effects of behavior therapy in psychoanalytic failures*. Unpublished data.

Wolpe, J., & Ascher, L. M. (1976). Outflanking "resistance" in a severe obsessional neurosis. In H. J. Eysenck (Ed.), *Case histories in behavior therapy*. London: Routledge & Kegan Paul.

Wolpe, J., & Flood, J. (1970). The effect of relaxation on the galvanic skin response to repeated phobic stimuli in ascending order. *J. Behav. Ther. Exp. Psychiat., 1*, 195.

Wolpe, J., & Fried, R. (1968). *Psychophysiological correlates of imaginal presentations of hierarchical stimuli. 1. The effect of relaxation*. Unpublished manuscript.

Wolpe, J., Groves, G. A., & Fischer, S. (1980). Treatment of narcotic addiction by inhibition of craving: Contending with a cherished habit. *Comprehensive Psychiat., 21*, 308.

Wolpe, J., Lande, S. D., McNally, R. J., & Schotte, D. (1985). Differentiation between classically conditioned and cognitively based fears: Two pilot studies. *J. Behav. Ther. Exp. Psychiatry, 16*, 287.

Wolpe, J., & Lang, P. J. (1964). A fear survey schedule for use in behavior therapy. *Behav. Res. Ther., 2*, 27.

Wolpe, J., & Lang, P. J. (1969). *Fear survey schedule.* San Diego, CA: Educational and Industrial Testing Service.

Wolpe, J., & Rowan, V. C. (1988). Panic disorder: A product of classical conditioning. *Behav. Res. Ther., 26*, 441.

Wolpe, J., & Theriault, N. (1971). Francois Leuret: A progenitor of behavior therapy. *J. Behav. Ther. Exp. Psychiat., 2*, 19.

Wolpe, J., & Wolpe, D. (1981). *Our useless fears.* Boston: Houghton Mifflin.

Wolpe, J., & Wright, R. (1988). The neglect of data-gathering instruments in behavior therapy practice. *J. Behav. Ther. Exper. Psychiat., 19*, 5.

Wolpin, M., & Pearsall, L. (1965). Rapid deconditioning of a fear of snakes. *Behav. Res. Ther., 3*, 107.

Wolpin, M., & Raines, J. (1966). Visual imagery, expected roles and extinction as possible factors in reducing fear and avoidance behavior. *Behav. Res. Ther., 4*, 25.

Woody, C. D., & Engel, J., Jr. (1972). Changes in unit activity and thresholds to electrical microstimulation at coronal-pericruciate cortex of cat with classical conditioning of different facial movements. *J. Neurophysiol., 35*, 230.

Yamagami, T. (1971). The treatment of an obsession by thought-stopping. *J. Behav. Ther. Exp. Psychiat., 2*, 133.

Yates, A. J. (1958). The application of learning theory to the treatment of tics. *J. Abn. Soc. Psychol., 56*, 175.

Yates, A. J. (1975). *Theory and practice in behavior therapy.* New York: John Wiley & Sons.

Yerkes, R. M. (1939). Sexual behavior in the chimpanzee. *Human Biol., 2*, 78.

Yeung, D. P. H. (1968). Diazepam for treatment of phobias. *Lancet, 1*, 475.

Young, J. Z. (1973). *Memory as a selective process.* Australian Academy of Science Report: Symposium on Biological Memory.

Young, J. Z. (1975). Sources of discovery in neuroscience. In E. G. Worden, J. P. Swazey, & G. Adelman (Eds.), *The neurosciences: Paths of discovery.* Cambridge, MA: Colonial Press.

Zbrozyna, A. W. (1953). Phenomenon of non-identification of a stimulus operating against different physiological backgrounds in dogs. *Lodskie Towanzystwo Naukowe, 3*(26).

Zbrozyna, A. W. (1957). The conditioned cessation of eating. *Bull. Acad. Poloniase Sci., 5*, 261.

Zitrin, C. M., Klein, D. F., & Woerner, M. G. (1978). Behaviour therapy, supportive psychotherapy, imipramine and phobias. *Arch. Gen. Psychiat., 35*, 307.

Zitrin, C. M., Klein, D. F., & Woerner, M. G. (1980). Treatment of agoraphobia with group exposure in vivo and imipramine. *Arch. Gen. Psychiat., 37*, 63.

Zitrin, C. M., Klein, D. F., Woerner, M. G., & Ross, D. C. (1983). Treatment of Phobias: 1. Comparison of imipramin hydrochloride and placebo. *Arch. Gen. Psychiat., 40*, 125.

Zohar, J., Foa, E. B., & Insel, T. R. (1989). Compulsive disorders: Behavior therapy and pharmacotherapy. In *Treatments of Psychiatric Disorders* (Vol. 3, p. 2095). American Psychiatric Association Task Force.

Author Index

Subject Index

415

About The Author

Joseph Wolpe, M.D., was born and educated in Johannesburg, South Africa. In 1933, at the age of 18 he undertook training in biology, which led on to medicine. At the same time he read extensively in the field of philosophy. His interest in psychological treatment arose during the second World War, when, having volunteered for the South African Medical Corps, he served at the base hospital that received soldiers affected with war neuroses. The failure of conventional treatments led him, after the war in 1946, to the research in animal neuroses from which behavior therapy ultimately developed. In 1956 to 1957, he was awarded a fellowship at the Center for Advanced Studies in the Behavioral Sciences at Stanford University in California, where he wrote his first book, *Psychotherapy by Reciprocal Inhibition* (1958), which described his experimental research and its clinical applications. From 1960 to 1965, he was professor of psychiatry at the University of Virginia, and from 1965 to 1982 at Temple University Medical Center. In 1979 he was awarded the American Psychiatric Association's prestigious Distinguished Scientific Award for the Applications of Psychology. In 1989 he was appointed Distinguished Professor at Pepperdine University in Culver City, California, and Visiting Professor at the University of California at Los Angeles. He has been editor of the *Journal of Behavior Therapy and Experimental Psychiatry* since its inception in 1970.

Pergamon General Psychology Series

Editors: **Arnold P. Goldstein,** Syracuse University
Leonard Krasner, Stanford University &
SUNY at Stony Brook

*Out of print in original format. Available in custom reprint edition.